MW00425245

.NET for Visual FoxPro Developers

Developers

Kevin McNeish

Hentzenwerke Publishing

Published by:
Hentzenwerke Publishing
980 East Circle Drive
Whitefish Bay WI 53217 USA

Hentzenwerke Publishing books are available through booksellers and directly from the
publisher. Contact Hentzenwerke Publishing at:
414.332.9876
414.332.9463 (fax)
www.hentzenwerke.com
books@hentzenwerke.com

.NET for Visual FoxPro Developers
    By Kevin McNeish
    Technical Editor: Cathi Gero
    Copy Editor: Nicole McNeish

Copyright © 2002 by Kevin McNeish

All other products and services identified throughout this book are trademarks or registered
trademarks of their respective companies. They are used throughout this book in editorial
fashion only and for the benefit of such companies. No such uses, or the use of any trade name,
is intended to convey endorsement or other affiliation with this book.

All rights reserved. No part of this book, or the ebook files available by download from
Hentzenwerke Publishing, may be reproduced or transmitted in any form or by any means,
electronic, mechanical photocopying, recording, or otherwise, without the prior written
permission of the publisher, except that program listings and sample code files may be entered,
stored and executed in a computer system.

The information and material contained in this book are provided "as is," without warranty of
any kind, express or implied, including without limitation any warranty concerning the
accuracy, adequacy, or completeness of such information or material or the results to be
obtained from using such information or material. Neither Hentzenwerke Publishing nor the
authors or editors shall be responsible for any claims attributable to errors, omissions, or other
inaccuracies in the information or material contained in this book. In no event shall
Hentzenwerke Publishing or the authors or editors be liable for direct, indirect, special,
incidental, or consequential damages arising out of the use of such information or material.

ISBN: 1-930919-30-1

Manufactured in the United States of America.

Our Contract with You, The Reader

In which we, the folks who make up Hentzenwerke Publishing, describe what you, the reader, can expect from this book and from us.

Hi there!

I've been writing professionally (in other words, eventually getting a paycheck for my scribbles) since 1974, and writing about software development since 1992. As an author, I've worked with a half-dozen different publishers and corresponded with thousands of readers over the years. As a software developer and all-around geek, I've also acquired a library of more than 100 computer and software-related books.

Thus, when I donned the publisher's cap five years ago to produce the *1997 Developer's Guide,* I had some pretty good ideas of what I liked (and didn't like) from publishers, what readers liked and didn't like, and what I, as a reader, liked and didn't like.

Now, with our new titles for 2002, we're entering our fifth season. (For those who are keeping track, the '97 DevGuide was our first, albeit abbreviated, season, the batch of six "Essentials" for Visual FoxPro 6.0 in 1999 was our second, and, in keeping with the sports analogy, the books we published in 2000 and 2001 comprised our third and fourth.)

John Wooden, the famed UCLA basketball coach, posited that teams aren't consistent; they're always getting better—or worse. We'd like to get better…

One of my goals for this season is to build a closer relationship with you, the reader. In order for us to do this, you've got to know what you should expect from us.

- You have the right to expect that your order will be processed quickly and correctly, and that your book will be delivered to you in new condition.

- You have the right to expect that the content of your book is technically accurate and up-to-date, that the explanations are clear, and that the layout is easy to read and follow without a lot of fluff or nonsense.

- You have the right to expect access to source code, errata, FAQs, and other information that's relevant to the book via our Web site.

- You have the right to expect an electronic version of your printed book to be available via our Web site.

- You have the right to expect that, if you report errors to us, your report will be responded to promptly, and that the appropriate notice will be included in the errata and/or FAQs for the book.

Naturally, there are some limits that we bump up against. There are humans involved, and they make mistakes. A book of 500 pages contains, on average, 150,000 words and several megabytes of source code. It's not possible to edit and re-edit multiple times to catch every last misspelling and typo, nor is it possible to test the source code on every permutation of development environment and operating system—and still price the book affordably.

Once printed, bindings break, ink gets smeared, signatures get missed during binding. On the delivery side, Web sites go down, packages get lost in the mail.

Nonetheless, we'll make our best effort to correct these problems—once you let us know about them.

In return, when you have a question or run into a problem, we ask that you first consult the errata and/or FAQs for your book on our Web site. If you don't find the answer there, please e-mail us at books@hentzenwerke.com with as much information and detail as possible, including 1) the steps to reproduce the problem, 2) what happened, and 3) what you expected to happen, together with 4) any other relevant information.

I'd like to stress that we need you to communicate questions and problems clearly. For example…

- "Your downloads don't work" isn't enough information for us to help you. "I get a 404 error when I click on the **Download Source Code** link on www.hentzenwerke.com/book/downloads.html" is something we can help you with.

- "The code in Chapter 10 caused an error" again isn't enough information. "I performed the following steps to run the source code program DisplayTest.PRG in Chapter 10, and I received an error that said 'Variable m.liCounter not found'" is something we can help you with.

We'll do our best to get back to you within a couple of days, either with an answer or at least an acknowledgment that we've received your inquiry and that we're working on it.

On behalf of the authors, technical editors, copy editors, layout artists, graphical artists, indexers, and all the other folks who have worked to put this book in your hands, I'd like to thank you for purchasing this book, and I hope that it will prove to be a valuable addition to your technical library. Please let us know what you think about this book—we're looking forward to hearing from you.

As Groucho Marx once observed, "Outside of a dog, a book is a man's best friend. Inside of a dog, it's too dark to read."

Whil Hentzen
Hentzenwerke Publishing
September 2002

List of Chapters

Table of Contents

Chapter 9: Building .NET Windows Forms Applications   251

Chapter 12: XML Web Services   379

Acknowledgements

Thanks to Whil for having me write this book, and for his guidance throughout the project. Working with Cathi was great—she provided significant feedback, which helped make this a far better book! Thanks also to Nicole, for her copy editing skills, which helped me get my points across far more clearly than I could have done myself.

A special note of thanks also goes to the many students who have come through my ".NET for Visual FoxPro Developer" classes, helping me know the kind of questions that should be answered in this book.

On a personal note, thanks to my sons, Jordan, Timothy, and Alexander, who gave up some time with Dad so I could write. Also, thanks to Nicole for her non-technical role as encourager, supporter, and sounding board!

Thanks also to Markus Egger for keeping ABBA songs alive in the 21st century!

—*Kevin*

My thanks to Kevin who was a pleasure to work with and made the experience even more enjoyable than I had hoped it would be. Whil, thanks for giving me the opportunity to be a part of this wonderful book. Thanks to my friends in the FoxPro and .NET Community for their continued source of support and assistance. Many thanks to my husband Alan, who took care of everything else in our lives so that I could have the time to concentrate on this book. And finally, thanks to my daughter Stephanie, for understanding that Mommy needed to hide away in the den to work on the book, missing out on some of the quality family time that we enjoy so much together.

—*Cathi*

About the Authors

Kevin McNeish

Kevin is President of Oak Leaf Enterprises - a company that specializes in object-oriented custom software, training, and developer tools. He uses Visual FoxPro and the new C# .NET language as his primary development tools. He is co-author of the book "What's New in Visual FoxPro 7". He has also written articles for CoDe, FoxPro Advisor, and FoxTalk magazines. Kevin is the creator of The Mere Mortals Framework for .NET and for Visual FoxPro, which won the Universal Thread's Members Choice award for "Best Framework". He has spoken at many software developer conferences and user groups throughout North America and Europe.

Kevin mentors and trains software companies in building flexible, component-based applications that scale from the desktop to the Internet. He has developed a ".NET for Visual FoxPro Developers" training class specifically designed to help developers leverage what they know about Visual FoxPro when learning about .NET. He is a Microsoft-Certified Developer and has created many enterprise-wide applications for a wide variety of vertical markets. Kevin resides in Charlottesville, VA with his wife, Nicole, and three sons.
e-mail: kevinm@oakleafsd.com, Web: www.oakleafsd.com.

Cathi Gero

Cathi Gero, C.P.A., is founder and development director of Prenia Consulting and Software Development Corporation. She is a custom software applications developer and consultant who has worked on database applications since 1986. Cathi is a Microsoft Visual FoxPro MVP and is an active member of the .NET community. Currently, she is working with the FoxPro Team at Microsoft as a contractor, working on Visual FoxPro 8. She speaks at VFP conferences and user groups and has authored whitepapers for Microsoft, including one titled 'Using ASP.NET in VS .NET with VFP 7.0'. You can frequently find Cathi's contributions on the Universal Thread site. Cathi is a contributing author to UTMag with a monthly section titled 'Cathi Gero's .NET Tips'. Cathi has extensive experience developing application solutions using VS.NET, Visual FoxPro, Crystal Reports, and SQL Server. She resides in Redmond, Washington with her family. You can reach Cathi at cgero@prenia.com.

How to Download the Files

Hentzenwerke Publishing generally provides two sets of files to accompany its books. The first is the source code referenced throughout the text. Note that some books do not have source code; in those cases, a placeholder file is provided in lieu of the source code in order to alert you of the fact. The second is the e-book version (or versions) of the book. Depending on the book, we provide e-books in either the compiled HTML Help (.CHM) format, Adobe Acrobat (.PDF) format, or both. Here's how to get them.

Both the source code and e-book file(s) are available for download from the Hentzenwerke Web site. In order to obtain them, follow these instructions:

1. Point your Web browser to www.hentzenwerke.com.

2. Look for the link that says "Download"

3. A page describing the download process will appear. This page has two sections:

- **Section 1:** If you were issued a username/password directly from Hentzenwerke Publishing, you can enter them into this page.

- **Section 2:** If you did not receive a username/password from Hentzenwerke Publishing, don't worry! Just enter your e-mail alias and look for the question about your book. Note that you'll need your physical book when you answer the question.

4. A page that lists the hyperlinks for the appropriate downloads will appear.

Note that the e-book file(s) are covered by the same copyright laws as the printed book. Reproduction and/or distribution of these files is against the law.

If you have questions or problems, the fastest way to get a response is to e-mail us at books@hentzenwerke.com.

Introduction

Why should Visual FoxPro developers be interested in .NET?

I asked myself this question when early releases of .NET first arrived on the scene. Visual FoxPro allowed me to do pretty much anything I wanted, from building single-tier applications with a VFP back end, all the way to building distributed Internet applications accessing client-server data.

Then, I started to dive into the .NET Framework to see what it had to offer, and I was amazed. First of all, I realized .NET wasn't just for building Web applications—it was also a great tool for building desktop applications. I discovered a number of things I had to spent hours writing custom code to get working in Visual FoxPro were now simple property settings! I also found Visual Studio .NET was a pleasure to work with. Although there were a few nits here and there, by and large, the VS .NET team did a great job creating tools that would save me hours of development time.

After spending a few weeks toying with Visual Studio .NET, I moved on to the .NET Framework class library. There I found over 2,000 classes providing the building blocks for creating .NET applications. Personally, I learn best by documenting, so I fired up Rational Rose and spent a few months manually documenting all the classes in the .NET Framework, building class diagrams, showing the relationships between classes in each .NET namespace. I found the .NET Framework to be well designed, extensible, and *huge*. This is where you'll find the biggest learning curve in .NET.

Next, I began studying the new C# and Visual Basic .NET languages. Both of these languages are top-notch, advanced, object-oriented languages that allow you to take full advantage of the .NET Framework base classes. Of the two languages, I personally favor C#, for its advanced language features, compact syntax, and enforcement of good programming practices. Fortunately, my technical editor helped keep me honest in providing a balanced view of both languages throughout this book.

Another benefit I've found with .NET is a single learning curve for building all different types of applications. Once you learn how to create a .NET Windows Forms application, you're about 90% up the learning curve for ASP.NET applications, Web Services, and so on. Now you don't need two teams of developers—one to create desktop applications and the other to create Web applications. You can now divide up your team in more logical units— developers who perform design and analysis, developers who create business components, developers who create user interfaces, and developers who know how to crunch data. Or, if you're a single developer on your own, you can do all of these things yourself with a much shorter learning curve.

Don't' be afraid of .NET. In all honesty, you're in a great position to learn .NET. Its object-orientation model is similar to Visual FoxPro's, and I find VFP developers are able to learn .NET quickly and begin using it to create software applications. More often than not, you may be using .NET to access your existing Visual FoxPro code. In recognition of that, Chapter 15, "Interoperability with Visual FoxPro" shows you how easy this is.

I hope this book answers many of your questions about .NET and helps you get up to speed quickly. Personally, I'm having a blast working with these technologies, and I think you will too.

Chapter 1
Introducing .NET

Every six or seven years Microsoft makes a quantum leap in technology. In February of 2002 that quantum leap was .NET. What is .NET and what does it mean for Visual FoxPro developers? This chapter provides an overview of .NET, the .NET Framework and languages, and explains why you should investigate .NET for your software development projects.

.NET burst on to the software development scene with lots of fanfare and plenty of marketing from Microsoft. In many ways .NET is a departure from previous Microsoft technologies; in other areas the change is more evolution than revolution.

Although there is a brand new .NET language, C#, a completely revamped Visual Basic .NET, and dozens of .NET ports of other languages including COBOL, Visual FoxPro is not a .NET language and Microsoft has told us that it never will be. What does this mean for you, as a Visual FoxPro developer? Why, when, and where should you use .NET technologies? This chapter aims to help you answer these questions.

What is .NET?

Originally, Microsoft pitched .NET as, "a platform for building, deploying, running, integrating, and consuming Web services". The result was most people thought you could only use .NET to build Web applications. In addition, because Web services were slow to catch on, it caused a number of developers to take a wait-and-see approach. You can compare this to marketing Visual FoxPro only for its Web services capabilities—although you *can* build Web services with VFP, it is certainly not its primary function.

After several months Microsoft recognized its marketing error and in August of 2002, Bill Gates provided an updated definition of .NET: ".NET is software to connect information, people, systems, and devices." I think this message is better, but I'm not sure it's clear or specific enough. I think a better explanation—at least from a developer's perspective—is that .NET is Microsoft's new programming model for building desktop, mobile, and Web-based applications.

What is the .NET Framework?

When most people refer to ".NET", they're usually referring to the .NET Framework. The .NET Framework is really three things:

- A library of unified core classes that provide the plumbing for applications.

- Presentation classes for developing ASP.NET and Windows Forms applications

- The Common Language Runtime (CLR), an environment in which your .NET programs are executed.

The .NET Framework class library

Before the arrival of .NET, the Windows API was the primary way you accessed services of the Windows operating system. The Windows API was developed over a number of years and can be a confusing morass of functions that are difficult to learn and use. In contrast, the .NET Framework provides a set of classes with properties, events, and methods you can use to access these same services in a far more logical, intuitive manner.

For example, the .NET Framework has an Environment class you can use to get and set information for the environment and platform on which your application is running. The following properties found in the Environment class are intuitive and self-descriptive:

- CurrentDirectory

- MachineName

- OSVersion

- SystemDirectory

- UserDomainName

You don't have to be a rocket scientist to figure out what the following methods of the Environment class do for you:

- GetCommandLineArgs

- GetEnvironmentVariables

- GetLogicalDrives

This is far easier than trying to find and learn how to use Windows API functions that give you the same information.

That said, *the* biggest learning curve for .NET is the .NET Framework classes. Here's a comparison for you—Visual FoxPro has 35 different base classes you can use in your applications, including text boxes, combo boxes, grids, containers, custom classes, sessions, and so on. In contrast, the .NET Framework has *over 2000* base classes! Figuring out what classes are available to you and which to use in a particular situation is where most of your learning curve will be.

However, to truly make a fair comparison between Visual FoxPro and the .NET Framework classes, you need to remember that there are over 500 functions, approximately 430 commands, and over 75 system variables that comprise the VFP language. In comparison, the organization of the .NET Framework classes makes it easier to find the functionality you need. For example, in Visual FoxPro, there are a few dozen commands you can use for string manipulation. When you were first learning Visual FoxPro, it probably took you a while to discover all of these commands (and maybe you haven't found them all yet!).

In contrast, .NET implements all of these string manipulation capabilities as individual methods of the String class. Once you discover the String class, you have all of this string manipulation functionality at your fingertips. You will find this holds true for all different types of functionality in the .NET Framework classes.

The Common Language Runtime

The Common Language Runtime performs a similar function as Visual FoxPro's runtime with a few key differences. Visual FoxPro is an interpreted language; executables are stored in pseudo-code (p-code) format. When it is executed, p-code is translated into machine code by the Visual FoxPro runtime (**Figure 1**).

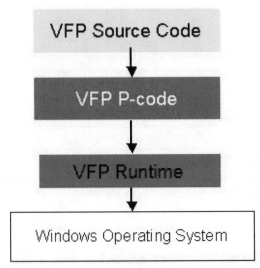

Figure 1. *The Visual FoxPro runtime translates p-code into machine code at runtime.*

In .NET, code is compiled twice—first into MS Intermediate Language (MSIL) by the compiler on your development machine and again at runtime when the code is executed by the CLR. As shown in **Figure 2**, regardless of the language in which the source code is written, whether it's C#, Visual Basic .NET or C++, it's compiled into the same intermediate language. Typically, it's this intermediate language that is distributed to your end users.

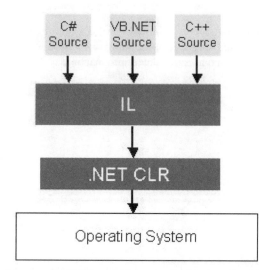

***Figure 2.** .NET code is compiled twice; first into MS Intermediate Language and again at runtime when the code is executed by the Common Language Runtime*

When MSIL is executed on the end user's machine, it is compiled again into machine code by a .NET Just-In-Time (JIT) compiler. The benefit of this approach is that CPU-specific JIT compilers can be used to compile the MSIL code into machine code that takes advantage of the specific processor on your end-user's machine. So, if the MSIL code is compiled on a machine with a newer processor and more advanced capabilities, the JIT compiler can take advantage of these.

The JIT compiler only compiles code that is to be executed. The resulting executable code is cached until the application is exited, so it does not need to be recompiled when the same code is executed again. This is different than Visual FoxPro where p-code is *interpreted* to machine code when it's run (and does not produce machine code that is cached as in .NET).

Why .NET for VFP developers?

Visual FoxPro is a great development tool for building desktop applications, Web applications, and Web services. So, why should VFP developers be interested in learning and using .NET? This section provides a number of reasons I find most compelling.

Marketability

You are probably aware that the number of new Visual FoxPro projects comprises a relatively small percentage of the total number of software systems being created. In contrast, the need for .NET developers is on the rise and will continue to increase over time. Having both a Visual FoxPro and .NET skill set can only improve your marketability as an employee or consultant.

ASP.NET

If you do nothing else with .NET, you may be interested in creating Web applications using ASP.NET. Microsoft has put a lot of energy into ASP.NET making it *much* better than its predecessor, ASP. Rather than using scripting languages to create Web applications, you can use a fully object-oriented .NET language such as C# or VB .NET.

If you learn how to create .NET Windows Forms applications using Visual Studio .NET, you can use the same set of skills and familiar IDE to create Web Forms applications and XML Web services, greatly reducing your learning curve.

Building middle-tier components

Visual FoxPro is a great tool for building middle-tier components based on its data access and string manipulation speed (which is great for XML). However, Visual FoxPro components are COM (Component Object Model) based. After several years of working with COM components, I can tell you that they are a royal pain in the neck! Here are my "three strikes" against VFP COM components:

1. They're a pain to debug. To figure out what's going on inside of a COM component, you typically have to use STRTOFILE() to output the value of variables to a text file in order to determine why a COM component isn't working. This is enough to make a grown man cry.

2. They take you to DLL hell and back again. First of all, COM DLLs must be registered in the Windows Registry, and sometimes (for reasons unknown) the registration process just doesn't work. It also means that if you have multiple versions of the same DLL on a single machine you can run into versioning problems.

3. You can't take advantage of COM+ object pooling because of Visual FoxPro's threading model—this is also true of Visual Basic 6. Object pooling allows COM+ to recycle or reuse middle-tier components. When a middle-tier object releases itself, COM+ places it in an object pool so other clients can reuse it. Note that COM+ is still the technology used to host middle tier components—even .NET components!

.NET addresses each of these issues:

1. You can easily debug .NET components with Visual Studio .NET. In fact, the debugger allows you to step through code written in any .NET language. For example, you can step through client code written in VB .NET that calls a method in a C# component.

2. .NET component DLLs are self-describing and do *not* need to be registered in the Windows Registry. Typically, all you need to do is copy a .NET DLL to a machine and it just works!

3. .NET components can be hosted in the COM+ environment and can be pooled.

Language interoperability

In many large software development shops, multiple languages are used by different teams of developers. .NET offers language interoperability at a whole new level. You can create classes in one .NET language and subclass them in another .NET language. You can also work with different languages within the same Visual Studio .NET IDE.

Interestingly, other vendors (besides Microsoft) are creating .NET versions of older programming languages such as COBOL, PERL, Eiffel, and Smalltalk among others.

Abstracting operating system services

As mentioned previously, the .NET Framework class library provides object-oriented access to services of the underlying operating system. This is far superior to making calls to the Windows API, because calls to the Windows API assume that you are running on the Window operating system!

Making calls to the .NET Framework class library adds a layer of abstraction that can eventually allow your code to be moved to non-Windows machines running on different hardware platforms such as wireless and handheld devices.

Multithreading

One of the limitations in Visual FoxPro is the inability to created multi-threaded applications. If this capability is important to you, then .NET makes it easy to create multiple threads of execution, allowing your applications to perform background tasks, such as printing, performing calculations, and sending or retrieving e-mail.

You're in a great position to learn .NET

If you've already climbed the Visual FoxPro learning curve, you're in a great position to learn .NET—much more so than Visual Basic developers. This is because the biggest learning curve for VB developers moving to .NET is object-orientation. Although VB 6 was object-based, it did not have true implementation inheritance (see Chapter 5, "Object-Orientation in C# and Visual Basic .NET" for details). In comparison, it's a much shorter learning curve for Visual FoxPro developers to learn the syntax of C# or VB .NET.

Managed Code

From the perspective of .NET there are two kinds of code in the world, *managed* and *unmanaged* code.

Managed code is executed and managed by the common language runtime. Managed code contains metadata that provides information that allows the runtime to provide services such as memory management, security, and garbage collection. All MSIL code is managed code. For more information on metadata, see the "Manifests" section later in this chapter. For more information on garbage collection, see the section "Garbage collection" in Chapter 5, "Object Orientation in C# and Visual Basic .NET".

Unmanaged code is any code that runs outside of .NET. This includes Visual FoxPro code located in COM servers (**Figure 3**).

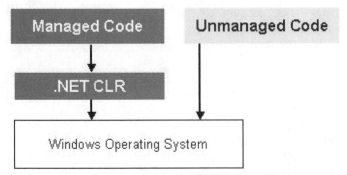

Figure 3. *Unmanaged code runs outside of the .NET common language runtime*

> *Unsafe code is different than unmanaged code. For information about unsafe code, see Chapter 3, "Introduction to C#".*

Assemblies

In Visual FoxPro, depending on the type of project you compile, the resulting code is stored in an APP, EXE, or DLL file. In .NET, Windows Forms and Console projects are compiled into EXE files that contain MSIL; Web Forms, Web Services and Class Library projects (including Windows Control libraries) are compiled into DLLs that contain MSIL. The resulting EXE and DLL files are referred to as *assemblies*.

An assembly is the primary building block of a .NET application. The term assembly is a logical rather than physical designation because, although an assembly is usually comprised of a single file, it can also be comprised of one or more files (**Figure 4**).

Multi-file assemblies allow you to break up an assembly into smaller units that are easier to maintain and are a smaller size for downloading. It also allows you to create a single assembly that is comprised of components built in multiple languages.

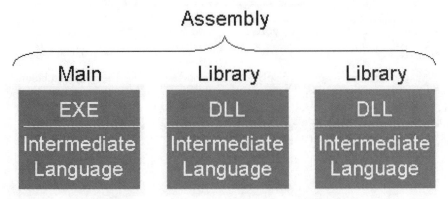

Figure 4. *A single assembly can be comprised of one or more physical files.*

An assembly is self-describing—it does not have to be registered in the Windows Registry because it possesses a manifest that contains metadata about the assembly.

Manifests

An assembly's manifest contains information such as the assembly's identity (name, version, and culture), a list of all the files in the assembly, information about all referenced assemblies, and details of all classes and their members.

A great way to examine an assembly manifest is to use the .NET IL Disassembler tool. The IL Disassembler (ildasm.exe) is found in the FrameworkSDK\Bin folder below the directory on your machine that contains the .NET Framework. To launch this program you can simply double-click on it in Windows Explorer. To open up an assembly for viewing, select File | Open from the menu, and select a .NET assembly. The Disassembler displays the assembly manifest as well as any namespaces declared within the assembly (**Figure 5**). For more information on namespaces, see the "Namespaces" section later in this chapter.

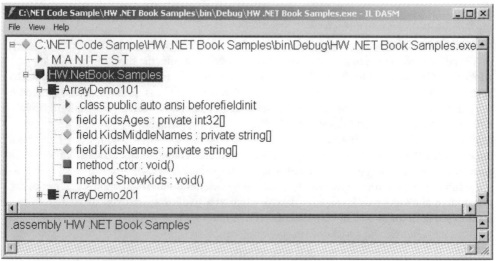

Figure 5*. The IL Disassembler allows you to examine the contents of an assembly, including any MSIL code.*

If you expand a namespace node, it displays all of the classes in the assembly that belong to the namespace. **Figure 6** shows a list of the different icons used within the disassembler and a description of how they are used. You can find this list in the help for the disassembler tool. For a detailed description of each of these elements (such as class, interface, method, static method, and so on) see Chapter 5, "Object Orientation in C# and Visual Basic .NET".

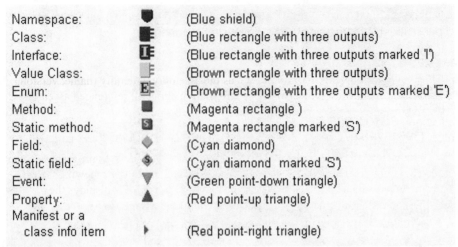

Namespace:		(Blue shield)
Class:		(Blue rectangle with three outputs)
Interface:		(Blue rectangle with three outputs marked 'I')
Value Class:		(Brown rectangle with three outputs)
Enum:		(Brown rectangle with three outputs marked 'E')
Method:		(Magenta rectangle)
Static method:		(Magenta rectangle marked 'S')
Field:		(Cyan diamond)
Static field:		(Cyan diamond marked 'S')
Event:		(Green point-down triangle)
Property:		(Red point-up triangle)
Manifest or a class info item		(Red point-right triangle)

Figure 6. *The IL Disassembler uses a variety of icons to denote different items in the assembly.*

If you double-click the Manifest node in the disassembler tree view it opens a sub-window that allows you to view the assembly's manifest. Depending on the assembly you open, at the top of the window, you may see a list of external assemblies that are referenced by the assembly (for example: "assembly extern System.Windows.Forms"). The first assembly reference you see that does not have the "extern" keyword denotes the beginning of the manifest's "identity" section. This first entry in the identity section of the manifest specifies the name of the assembly. The identity section also contains the version number of the assembly. The version number is denoted by the ".ver" directive.

Probably the coolest feature of the IL Disassembler is the ability to view MSIL code. If you double-click on a class method, it opens up a window displaying the MSIL code. If you want to see both the source code and the IL code in this window (**Figure 7**), select View | Source Lines from the IL Disassembler menu. For most developers, viewing the IL code falls under the category of "cool things you can do", versus providing any practical benefits.

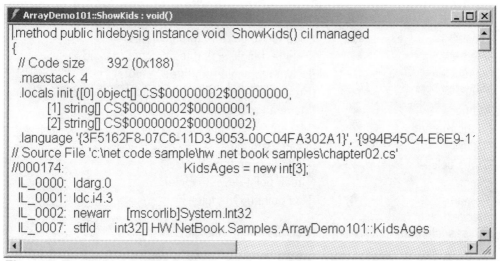

Figure 7. The IL Disassembler allows you to view the actual IL code, and optionally, the source code.

Private and shared assemblies

There are two types of .NET assemblies, *private* and *shared*. A private assembly is used by only one application. The assembly is stored in the application's folder. This makes it easy to install an application—all you have to do is copy the files to the appropriate folder. You can also store an assembly in an application subfolder, you just need to give the subfolder the same name as the assembly it contains. For example, if you have an assembly named "MyLibrary", you can place it in a subfolder named "MyLibrary" below the application folder. This allows you to segregate your external assemblies from your project files.

A shared assembly is used by more than one application. Shared assemblies are stored in a special directory known as the *Global Assembly Cache* (GAC). By default, this directory is c:\winnt\assembly or c:\windows\assembly. An example of shared assemblies is the .NET Framework. All .NET applications need access to the .NET Framework's assemblies, so these are located in the Global Assembly Cache.

Viewing assemblies in the Global Assembly Cache

When you install the .NET Platform SDK on your computer, it automatically loads a Windows shell extension called the Assembly Cache Viewer that allows you to view the Global Assembly Cache from within Windows Explorer. All you have to do is use Windows Explorer to navigate to the <windows directory>\assembly folder and you see assemblies displayed in the right pane (**Figure 8**).

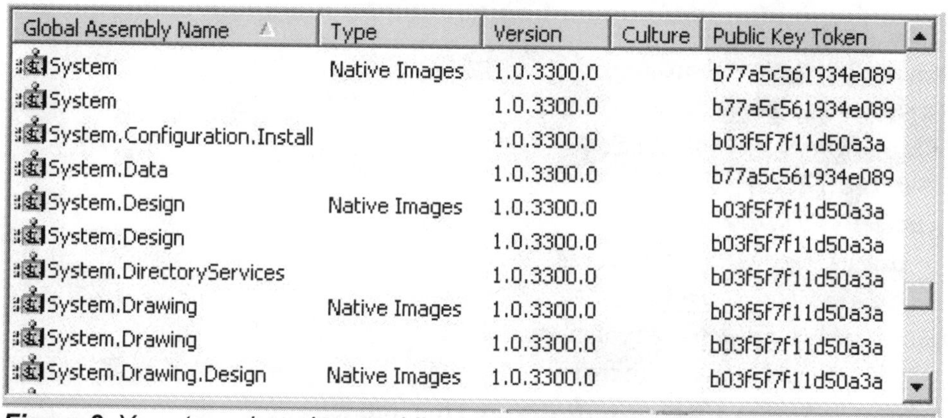

Global Assembly Name ▲	Type	Version	Culture	Public Key Token	
System	Native Images	1.0.3300.0		b77a5c561934e089	
System		1.0.3300.0		b77a5c561934e089	
System.Configuration.Install		1.0.3300.0		b03f5f7f11d50a3a	
System.Data		1.0.3300.0		b77a5c561934e089	
System.Design	Native Images	1.0.3300.0		b03f5f7f11d50a3a	
System.Design		1.0.3300.0		b03f5f7f11d50a3a	
System.DirectoryServices		1.0.3300.0		b03f5f7f11d50a3a	
System.Drawing	Native Images	1.0.3300.0		b03f5f7f11d50a3a	
System.Drawing		1.0.3300.0		b03f5f7f11d50a3a	
System.Drawing.Design	Native Images	1.0.3300.0		b03f5f7f11d50a3a	▼

Figure 8. You store shared assemblies in the Global Assembly Cache directory, which by default is c:\winnt\assembly or c:\windows\assembly.

For more information on creating and installing shared assemblies, see the section "Creating and installing shared assemblies" in Chapter 2, "Visual Studio .NET".

Namespaces

In .NET, the primary way you avoid duplicate class names is by means of *namespaces*. A namespace is a naming mechanism that allows you to declare logical categories for your classes. For example, in the .NET Framework, there are namespaces such as:

- System.Drawing
- System.Data.SqlClient
- System.Windows.Forms
- System.Web.Services.Protocols

At first, many Visual FoxPro developers equate namespaces with class libraries, but they're really quite different. A VFP class library is a physical container that holds one or more classes. A .NET namespace has nothing to do with the physical location of a class—it is purely a logical name used to categorize a class.

The parts of a namespace typically go (from left to right) general to more specific. This is similar in concept to the taxonomies of living things. For example, **Figure 9** shows the taxonomic hierarchy of the red fox. From kingdom, to phylum to subphylum to class, and so on, each level moves from general to specific. This convention allows all living things to be categorized.

Kingdom *Animalia*
  Phylum *Chordata*-- chordates
    Subphylum *Vertebrata*-- vertebrates
      Class *Mammalia*-- mammals
        Subclass *Theria*
          Infraclass *Eutheria*
            Order *Carnivora*-- carnivores
              Suborder *Caniformia*
                Family *Canidae*-- coyotes, dogs
                  Genus *Vulpes*-- kit foxes, red foxes
                    Species ***Vulpes vulpes***-- red fox, red fox

Figure 9. *Namespaces allow you to categorize your classes in a similar way as living things are categorized in taxonomies.*

Microsoft has suggested that you declare your namespaces as follows: the first part of a namespace should be your company name, the second part should be your product, the third part should specify a category of classes, and so on. For example, I have declared a namespace to which all of my company's business objects belong as "OakLeaf.MM.Business". Oak Leaf is my company name, MM is the product name (Mere Mortals Framework), and Business specifies business object classes.

For information on assigning classes to a namespace, see Chapter 3, "Introduction to C#" and Chapter 4, "Introduction to Visual Basic .NET".

.NET Programming Languages

As of this writing, there are three main .NET languages from which you can choose: Visual Basic .NET, Visual C# .NET, and Visual C++ .NET. Since the vast majority of Visual FoxPro developers using .NET will choose either Visual Basic .NET or C# as their software development language, this book concentrates on these two languages, providing examples in each and information that can help you decide which language is right for you.

Visual C# .NET

Although "Visual C# .NET" is the "official" name of the language, you almost always see it referred to as simply "C#" (pronounced C sharp), and this is the convention I use in this book.

C# is a brand new computer language written specifically for .NET and it has generated a lot of excitement. In fact, Microsoft used it to create the .NET Framework base classes. As of the writing of this book, many Visual FoxPro developers learning .NET have chosen C# as their programming language of choice.

Because C# is in the "C" family of languages, its syntax is similar to C++, but it is most similar to Java. C# can also be used to create Windows Forms applications, Web Form applications, XML Web services, console applications, class libraries, and more. C# is designed to combine the power and control of C and C++ with the ease of use often associated with Visual Basic for high productivity. For details on C#, see Chapter 3, "Introducing C#".

Visual Basic .NET

Visual Basic .NET is the newest version of Microsoft's Visual Basic programming language. The difference between VB .NET and Visual Basic 6 is as big as the difference between FoxPro 2.6 and Visual FoxPro—and then some.

Unlike its predecessor, Visual Basic 6, VB .NET is a fully object-oriented language that was completely rewritten for the .NET Framework. You can use VB .NET to create Windows Forms applications, Web Form applications, XML Web services, console applications, class libraries, and more. In its new incarnation VB .NET also continues its role as the "glue" that fills in the gaps and binds applications together. You can use Visual Basic .NET to create macros for use in the Visual Studio .NET IDE.

As you might expect, VB .NET has some nice convenience features and you will probably continue to get more of these in subsequent versions of .NET.

For details on Visual Basic .NET, see Chapter 4, "Introducing Visual Basic .NET".

Naming Guidelines

Microsoft has come up with a list of naming guidelines for .NET languages. Their hope is to have most developers jump on board with these conventions so everyone can read each other's code more easily. One guideline that has surprised many developers is the recommendation to discontinue the use of Hungarian notation.

The official naming guidelines can be found on the Web at:

`http://msdn.microsoft.com/library/en-us/cpgenref/html/cpconnamingguidelines.asp`

Overview of the development process

It's appropriate in this chapter to give you a high level overview of the development process when creating a .NET application. Seeing the big picture can hopefully place each chapter in this book in the context of the development process.

Requirements gathering

Before you write one line of code, you should gather requirements for the application. Most software development shops these days use the Unified Modeling Language (UML) and the Rational Unified Process (RUP) for this purpose. Microsoft has recognized the importance of analysis and design by adding UML diagrams to their Visio diagramming tool and integrating Visio with Visual Studio .NET.

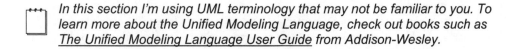

In this section I'm using UML terminology that may not be familiar to you. To learn more about the Unified Modeling Language, check out books such as The Unified Modeling Language User Guide from Addison-Wesley.

The first step in gathering requirements involves documenting how the end user will use the software system. This is primarily achieved by means of UML use case diagrams.

Building a plan for construction

After gathering your requirements, you should build a plan for construction. This includes determining how long the entire project will take to complete and choosing which parts of the application to build first, second, and so on. When using the UML, you select use cases to be further analyzed, designed, and implemented.

Designing and building business objects

During construction you further analyze your use cases and design business objects that carry out the logic of each use case. This means adding methods to business object classes that will contain the majority of your application logic. This approach is very different from the way most Visual FoxPro developers create applications today—they place the majority of application logic in the user interface. However, using business objects makes your applications far more flexible, scaleable, and maintainable.

Typically, you should create a Class Library project in either C# or VB .NET to contain your business objects. This project can be compiled into an assembly that can be referenced from a variety of applications (Windows Forms, Web Forms, Web Services, and so on).

For more information on designing and implementing business objects, see Chapter 8, ".NET Business Objects".

Data modeling

As you design your business objects, you should also start thinking about modeling your application data. Even if I'm designing an application to work with client server data, I often find creating prototype tables in Visual FoxPro is a great "proof-of-concept" technique. Because FoxPro developers tend to see the world in terms of data, placing data in tables can help work out any kinks in the object model that may otherwise go undetected.

Ultimately, before you actually create business object classes in your language of choice, you should finish modeling the associated data.

For more information on accessing data from within a .NET application, see Chapter 7, "Data Access with ADO.NET".

Building the user interface

If you're creating either a Windows Forms or Web Forms application, you need to design and build a user interface. You can create a new Windows Forms or Web Forms application using Visual Studio .NET and add a reference to your business object library to the project so these classes are accessible from your user interface.

As mentioned previously, you should not place your application logic in your user interface. Think of your user interface as the "skin" of your application, which can easily be replaced with an alternate skin.

You can place code in your user interface that instantiates business object classes and calls their methods to perform services such as retrieving data, manipulating and saving data, performing calculations, and so on.

For information on building your application's user interface, see Chapter 9, "Building .NET WinForm Applications", and Chapter 10, "Building Web Applications with ASP.NET".

Building an XML Web service

If you are creating an XML Web service, you can create a new Web services project in Visual Studio .NET. Afterwards, you can add a reference to your business object library to the Web services project so these classes are accessible from the Web service.

For more information on building an XML Web Service, see Chapter 12, "XML Web Services".

Conclusion

Microsoft is betting the farm on .NET. They've thrown a tremendous amount of resources at .NET and have come up with some very impressive technologies. It is a huge shift in technology that has evoked the full spectrum of emotions from a wide variety of people—including Visual FoxPro developers. The rest of this book will help you make informed decisions about .NET—why, when, and where you should implement it in your software development.

Chapter 2
Visual Studio .NET

Visual Studio .NET is the latest incarnation of Microsoft's suite of software development tools. The VS .NET team has done a great job of providing a top-notch experience for the developer regardless of the .NET language you use. This chapter takes you on a tour of VS .NET, familiarizing you with its features so you can get up and running quickly.

Before .NET, tools in Visual Studio were loosely related products packaged in one box—Visual Studio .NET changes all that. Teams of developers working with different languages such as C#, Visual Basic .NET, and C++ now have a common, familiar Integrated Development Environment (IDE) that's a pleasure to work in.

The Start Page

One of the biggest challenges in learning .NET is finding information. The Visual Studio .NET Start Page is all about helping you find information that can get you up and running quickly. Most developers don't take the time to explore the Start Page, so I'll take you on a quick tour.

When you launch VS. NET, the Start Page appears with the Get Started pane selected (**Figure 1**). This page is displayed in a Web browser tab (a tab refers to a tabbed document window in the VS .NET IDE), complete with a browser toolbar containing navigation buttons and a combo box, which allows you to enter any valid URL.

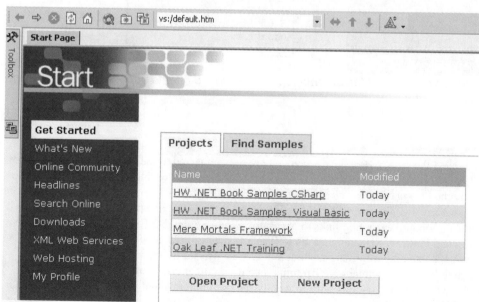

Figure 1. The VS .NET Start Page shows a list of your most recent used projects.

Get Started

The Get Started pane displays a page frame with two tabs—Projects and Find Samples. The Projects tab allows you to open or create a new project. The Find Samples tab allows you to search for online samples by language (C++, C# and Visual Basic .NET) or by Visual Studio Developer, which displays all samples. There is a wealth of examples to choose from. I highly recommend checking them out.

Setting a Filter

When you view the Online Community, Headlines, and Downloads panes, you can set a filter to limit how much information is shown (**Figure 2**). This filter is persisted between VS .NET sessions. If you set the filter on a language, I recommend that you select the language "and related" filter (for example, "Visual C# and related"). If you select a filter such as "Visual C#", you miss out on a lot of important information.

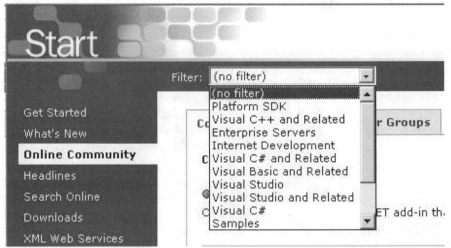

Figure 2. *You can limit the information you see in the on-line options of the Start Page by setting a filter.*

What's New

If you select the What's New pane when you are not connected to the Internet, you see a list of .NET Help topics discussing what's new with different aspects of .NET, including information on individual languages.

However, if you're connected to the Internet, you see a Technology tab containing a much fuller list of options including links to check for Visual Studio .NET service packs, Windows security and Platform SDK updates, as well as a variety of links to web pages (mostly Microsoft) containing information about .NET. You also see a Training and Events tab containing links to upcoming .NET training events. Another cool feature is the Tips and Walkthroughs tab that contains links to web-based presentations that explain both basic and more advanced .NET concepts.

Online Community

The Online Community pane allows you to locate online code samples, newsgroups, user groups, find experts on a particular .NET technology, and find third-party add-ons for .NET. **Figure 3** shows how to search for a .NET user group in your area.

Figure 3. *The* Online Community | User Groups *option on Visual Studio .NET's Start Page allows you to find a user group in your area.*

Headlines

The Headlines pane of the Start Page shows you online headlines that are also currently found on Microsoft's MSDN site at http://msdn.microsoft.com. This is a great place to keep up to date with the latest in .NET and other Microsoft technologies. I've actually had my default home page in Internet Explorer pointing to this URL for quite some time. It's a great way to keep in touch with what's new and what's coming.

Search Online

The Search Online pane allows you to search the MSDN online library. If you click the Advanced button, it opens up a new VS .NET web browser tab that allows you to search Microsoft.com, see the Top Downloads, Top Support Links, and Top Searches.

Downloads

The Downloads pane contains a wealth of download links—both free downloads and MSDN subscriber downloads.

XML Web Services

If you want to search the UDDI registry for a particular type of XML Web service, you can do so right from Visual Studio .NET. The XML Web Services pane (**Figure 4**) allows you to specify a category and additional search criteria to locate either a production environment or test environment XML Web service. For more information on UDDI, see Chapter 12, "XML Web Services".

Figure 4. You can search for both production and test Web Services from within VS .NET based on a category and additional search criteria.

Web Hosting
If you want to find an Internet service provider to host your .NET web applications, the Web Hosting pane allows you to find ISPs who are participating in the Visual Studio .NET Web Hosting Portal. These providers offer an environment in which you can upload and test your XML Web Services or ASP.NET applications.

My Profile
The My Profile pane of the Start Page allows you to set your working preferences for VS .NET. The Profile setting allows you to select a profile that sets your Keyboard Scheme, Windows Layout, and Help Filter. The Keyboard Scheme setting lists different shortcut key configurations you can choose. The Windows Layout setting specifies a default VS .NET window configuration. Help Filter specifies how (if at all) you want the VS .NET Help file filtered (**Figure 5**). The Show Help option allows you to specify whether you want to display VS .NET Help within the IDE or in a separate window outside the IDE. The At Startup option allows you to specify what appears when you first launch Visual Studio.

If you filter your Help file on a particular language, it's best to select the language "and Related" option (Figure 5). If you filter on C# or Visual Basic .NET only, many important help topics are filtered out.

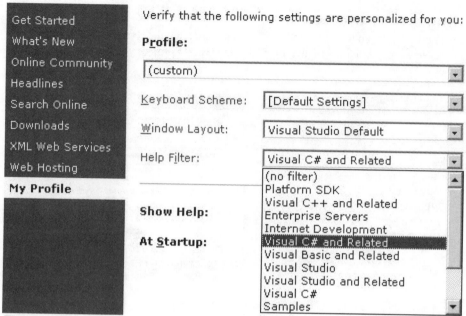

Figure 5. You can specify a default filter for the VS .NET Help file.

Showing the Start Page

When you view a help topic in VS .NET, it typically closes the Start Page. If you want to view the Start Page again, select Help | Show Start Page from the menu.

Now that you've seen where to find help in learning about .NET, I will move on to the mechanics of using Visual Studio .NET.

Solutions and Projects

One of the first concepts you should grasp is Visual Studio .NET's approach to managing and organizing your .NET applications. At its highest level of organization, VS .NET uses *solutions* and below solutions are *projects*.

A solution is a container that can hold one or more related projects. Solutions allow you to work on multiple projects in the same instance of VS .NET, as well as set options and work on items that are common to a group of projects. When you create a new project, VS .NET automatically creates a solution that contains the new project.

A project in VS .NET is very similar to a project in Visual FoxPro. It is a container that holds related files such as source code, forms, user interface controls, text files, images, and so on. You can compile a project into an EXE, DLL or a module, among other things. When you compile a solution, a separate output file is generated for each project in the solution.

Creating a new project

To create a new project, go to the VS .NET Start Page and click the New Project button. This launches the New Project dialog (**Figure 6**). Select the type of project you want in the Project Types pane.

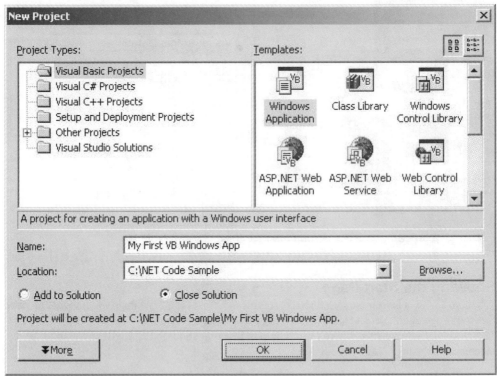

Figure 6. You can create new projects in your .NET language of choice based on a variety of project templates.

You can choose to create a Visual Basic, C#, C++, or Setup and Deployment project, or a Visual Studio Solution (an empty solution). The Other Projects node allows you to create Database projects (which include scripts and queries for accessing multiple databases), Enterprise Template projects for distributed applications, Visual Studio Analyzer projects for collecting event information and performing analysis on your projects, Extensibility projects for creating VS .NET add-ins, and Application Center Test projects.

Project Templates

In Visual FoxPro, when you create a new project, the project is empty. Although you have this option in Visual Studio .NET, there are also a wide variety of templates to choose from. If you select Visual Basic or C# Projects in the Project Types pane, it displays a list of templates in the Templates pane on the right (**Table 1**).

Table 1. *Visual Basic .NET and C# project templates*

Project Template	Description
Windows Application	Traditional Windows application (WinForms)
Class Library	Library of classes that can be reused from other projects
Windows Control Library	Library of Windows controls for use on Windows Forms
ASP.NET Web Application	Web Forms application
ASP.NET Web Service	XML Web Service
Web Control Library	Library of Web Controls that can be used on Web Forms pages
Console Application	Command-line application
Windows Service	Windows Service application that does not have a user interface
Empty Project	Empty Windows project
Empty Web Project	Empty Web project
New Project In Existing Folder	Empty project created in an existing application folder

The templates you will use most often are the Windows Application template when creating WinForms applications (see Chapter 9, "Building .NET WinForm Applications"), the ASP.NET Web Application template (see Chapter 10, "Building Web Applications with ASP.NET"), and the ASP.NET Web Service template (see Chapter 12, "XML Web Services").

Example: Building a Visual Basic Windows Application

To help you understand the mechanics of solutions and projects, I will walk you through the initial steps of building a Visual Basic Windows Application. The information in this section also applies to C# Windows Applications.

To create a new Visual Basic .NET Windows Application, follow these steps:

1. Click the New Project button on the VS .NET Start Page. This displays the Add New Project dialog.

2. Select Visual Basic Projects under the Project Types pane and Windows Application in the Templates pane.

3. In the Name text box, enter the name you want to give your new project. I'll call this one "My First VB Windows App".

4. In the Location text box, select the folder where you want to create your new project. The dialog displays the folder you specified as the default project folder when you first installed Visual Studio .NET, but you can change the folder if you wish.

    If you currently have a solution open in VS .NET, you see an additional option group that allows you to specify whether you want to add the new project to the currently open solution or close the solution (see Figure 6). If you close the solution, VS .NET automatically creates a new solution for your new project.

5. By default, the new solution is given the same name as your project. However, if you want a different solution name, click the More button. This displays a Create directory for Solution check box. If you select the check box, it enables the New Solution Name

text box, allowing you to specify a different name for your solution. In either case, at the bottom of the dialog, it displays a message "Project will be created at…" showing the name of the directory where the project will be created. Notice that VS .NET creates a new folder for your solution and project beneath the folder specified in the Location text box.

6.   To create the new project and associated solution, click the OK button. After a few moments, the new solution and project are displayed in the VS .NET IDE (**Figure** 7).

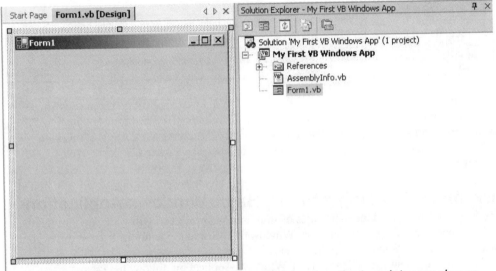

Figure 7. VS .NET creates new projects for you based on the template you choose.
The Solution Explorer presents an organized view of your projects and files.

In the left pane, VS .NET displays a new, empty form named Form1. Look at the tab above the form and you will see that you are viewing the form in Design mode and the form is stored in a file named Form1.vb.

All Visual Basic .NET source files (forms, classes, modules, components, controls) have a .vb extension. All C# source files have a .cs extension. This is different from VFP where different types of files have different extensions (.FRX for reports, .SCX for forms, .PRG for program files, and so on).

Examining the new solution with Solution Explorer

On the right side of the IDE, you should see the Solution Explorer. If the Solution Explorer is not visible, select View | Solution Explorer from the menu. The Solution Explorer provides an organized view of your projects and associated files.

The very first node in the Solution Explorer contains the name of the new solution and an indicator that shows how many projects are in the solution (Figure 7).

> By default, not all items in a solution are shown in the Solution Explorer. To see all items in a solution, click the Show All Files button at the top of the Solution Explorer (**Figure 8**)

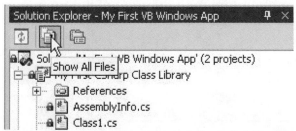

Figure 8. To see all files in a solution, click the Show All Files button

Behind the scenes, a solution definition is stored in two different files, an .sln and an .suo file. For example, the new solution you just created is comprised of a file named "my first vb windows app.sln" and "my first vb windows app.suo". The .sln file stores solution metadata detailing the projects that are associated with the solution, items that are added at the solution level (rather than belonging to a particular project), and build configurations. The .suo file stores solution-specific user options (such as document window positions) that you specify to customize the IDE. If you're the curious sort, you can open the .sln file in Visual FoxPro (it's a text file) and examine its contents.

Examining the new project

The second node of the Solution Explorer contains the name of the new project. By default, it is given the same name as the solution, which in this case is "My First VB Windows App". Directly below the project node, expand the References node and you will see a list of .NET component DLLs that have automatically been added to the project (**Figure 9**).

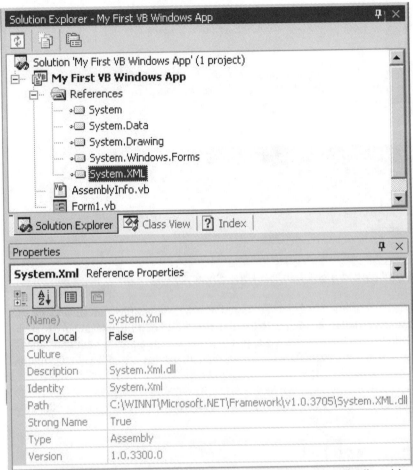

Figure 9.*When you create a new project, VS .NET automatically adds references to several .NET component DLLs to your project.*

If you click on a reference, information about the DLL displays in the Properties Window. If the Properties Window is not visible, select View | Properties Window from the menu.

Beneath the References node, there is a file named AssemblyInfo.vb. If you double-click on this file, a new tab is opened displaying the contents of the file. There are two items of note in this file. The first is the list of assembly *attributes* (**Figure 10**). Attributes allow you to add descriptive declarations that are used to annotate assemblies, classes, methods, properties, and other elements. When you compile your project, these attributes are added as extra descriptive information into the IL produced by the compiler. For more information on attributes, see Chapter 5, "Object Orientation in C# and Visual Basic .NET".

```
L' Review the values of the assembly attributes

<Assembly: AssemblyTitle("")>
<Assembly: AssemblyDescription("")>
<Assembly: AssemblyCompany("")>
<Assembly: AssemblyProduct("")>
<Assembly: AssemblyCopyright("")>
<Assembly: AssemblyTrademark("")>
<Assembly: CLSCompliant(True)>
```

Figure 10. *You can set assembly attribute values to provide additional information about your assembly to consumers.*

In addition to the attributes shown in Figure 10, there is also a Guid attribute (Globally Unique Identifier) that is automatically generated when you create a new project. This identifier is used for your assembly's type library if the project is accessed from COM. For details on interoperability with COM, see Chapter 15, "Interoperability with Visual FoxPro". At the bottom of the AssemblyInfo.vb file, there is an AssemblyVersion attribute. The comment explains that you can leave the value of this attribute "as is", with an asterisk as the minor version number, and VS .NET automatically generates the build and revision numbers for you. Otherwise, you can remove the asterisk and simply hard-code the version number.

For now, I'll save the discussion of the Windows form file, Form1.vb, for Chapter 9, "Building .NET WinForm Applications".

Adding another project to an existing solution

In this section, I'll show off .NET's language interoperability by creating a new C# project and adding it to your existing solution.

To add a project to the existing solution, first open the solution in Visual Studio .NET (if it's not already open), then follow these steps:

1. In the Solution Explorer, right-click on the solution (the very first node) and select Add | New Project from the shortcut menu or go back to the Start Page and click the New Project button. This displays the Add New Project dialog.

2. Select Visual C# Projects in the Project Types pane and select Class Library in the Templates pane.

3. In the Name text box, enter "My CSharp Class Library". Note that you have to spell out "CSharp" because project names cannot contain the pound sign (#).

4. Click OK to create the new project. After a few moments the new C# project is shown in the Solution Explorer (**Figure 11**).

Figure 11. *You can add multiple projects of the same or different languages to a single solution.*

Specifying a startup project

Notice that the "My First VB Windows App" project is shown in bold, but the new C# project is not. This indicates that the VB project is the *startup project*. The startup project specifies the project or projects that run when you start the Visual Studio debugger. If you only want one project in the solution to be the startup project, just right-click on the project in the Solution Explorer and select Set as Startup Project from the shortcut menu.

If you want to build, run, and debug more than one project in a solution when you launch the VS .NET debugger, you can specify multiple startup projects in the Solution Property Pages dialog. Launch this dialog by right-clicking the solution node in the Solution Explorer and selecting Properties from the shortcut menu. To see the startup project properties, expand the Common Properties folder in the left pane and select the Startup Project item (**Figure 12**).

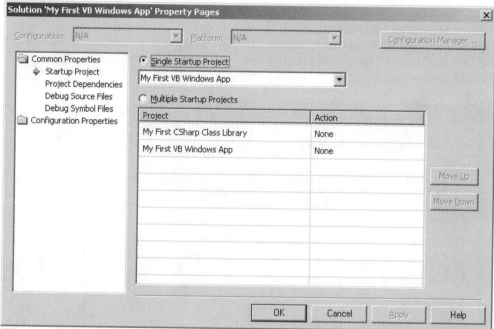

Figure 12. *The Solution Property Pages dialog allows you to specify one or more startup projects for your solution.*

By default, a solution has only one startup project. If you want to specify more than one, select the Multiple Startup Projects option. Next, click the Action combo box next to the projects you want to set as startup projects and select either Start or Start without debugging. Typically, when in production mode, you should select Start so you can debug your project. If you specify multiple startup projects, when you return to the Solution Explorer the solution is displayed in bold.

For this project, I will leave the settings "as is" and have the VB Windows project be the startup project.

Building a Solution

Although this first .NET solution is bare bones, this is a good point to learn how to compile a solution and/or project.

Build configurations

Build configurations allow you to specify how projects in a solution are to be built and eventually deployed. In Visual Studio .NET, there are two different levels of build configurations—solution build configurations and project configurations.

Solution build configurations

When you create a new solution, VS .NET automatically creates two solution build configurations for you—a "Debug" configuration and a "Release" configuration.

To see your solution's build configurations, right-click on your solution in the Solution Explorer and select Configuration Manager from the shortcut menu. This launches the Configuration Manager (**Figure 13**), which displays all projects in the solution and their configuration, their target platform, and a check box that indicates if the project should be built.

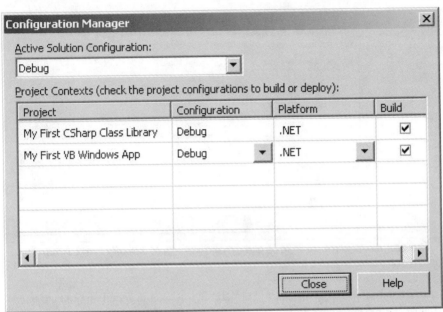

Figure 13. The Configuration Manager allows you to view, edit, and create solution build configurations.

By default, the Debug configuration is displayed in the combo box. As you design and build your application, it's typical to have the active configuration set to Debug. Once you're ready to build an application for deployment, it's typical to set the active configuration to Release. An application compiled for release does not allow you to debug your application, but as with Visual FoxPro, an application runs much faster without debugging turned on. To see the solution's default release configuration, select Release from the Active Solution Configuration combo box.

Project configurations

Project configurations allow you to specify how projects are built. They include settings that specify whether to include debug information in the build, if or how the output file should be optimized, location of the output file, and so on. This is similar to Visual FoxPro's Project Information dialog.

To view a project's build configuration, right-click on the project in the Solution Explorer and select Properties from the shortcut menu. This launches the Project Properties dialog (**Figure 14**). Under the Configuration Properties folder in the left pane there are four types of configuration settings listed: Debugging, Optimizations, Build, and Deployment.

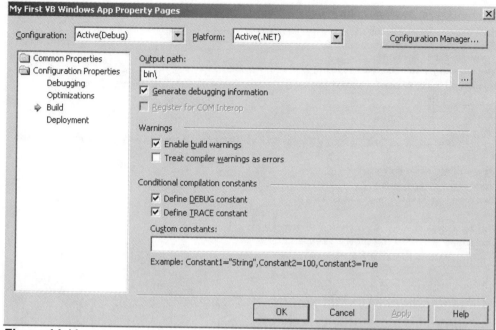

Figure 14. You can set a wide variety of build options for each project in a solution.

For additional information on these configurations, select any of these items and click the Help button.

Build options

To build a project, select Build from the menu, which shows four build options:

- Build Solution – Builds the solution, including all projects in the solution

- Rebuild Solution – Rebuilds the solution, cleaning up solution configuration files

- Build Project – Builds a particular project

- Rebuild Project – Rebuilds a particular project, cleaning up project configuration files

Building your sample solution

If you have been following the instructions for creating a sample solution, you're ready to build it now. To do this, select Build | Build Solution from the menu.

At this point, Visual Studio .NET builds the project output files for you in the directory you have specified in each of the project's configurations. When building a debug configuration, by default the output files are placed in your project's bin\Debug subfolder.

When you build your solution, if the compiler encounters any errors, it displays them in the Output window. If everything succeeds, it displays a "Done" message in the Output window indicating it found no errors (**Figure 15**).

```
------ Build started: Project: My First VB Windows App, Configuration: Debug

Preparing resources...
Updating references...
Performing main compilation...
Building satellite assemblies...



------ Build started: Project: My First CSharp Class Library, Configuration:

Preparing resources...
Updating references...
Performing main compilation...

Build complete -- 0 errors, 0 warnings
Building satellite assemblies...



-------------------- Done --------------------

    Build: 2 succeeded, 0 failed, 0 skipped
```

Figure 15. VS .NET displays the progress and result of the build process in the Output *window.*

For information on handling compiler errors, see Chapter 13, "Error Handling and Debugging in .NET".

Examining the build output files

If you look in the output directory for "My First VB Windows App", you will see two files—My First Windows App.exe and My First Windows App.pdb. The first file is obviously the Windows executable. The second file has a PDB extension. This is the "program debug database".

When you build a project, and specify that it includes debug information, VS .NET creates a program debug database for you that maps MSIL to source code. Typically, you won't use the PDB file directly—it's used by VS .NET when debugging an application.

If you look in the output directory for "My First CSharp Class Library" you'll also see two files—My First CSharp Class Library.dll and My First CSharp Class Library.pdb. Because the C# project is a class library, a DLL is generated by the compiler rather than an EXE.

Running the compiled program

To run the compiled sample application, select Debug | Start from the menu, press the F5 key or click the Start button on the Standard toolbar **(Figure 16)**.

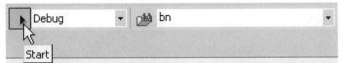

Figure 16*. Click the Start button in the Standard toolbar to run a compiled application.*

When the application is run, you see a Windows form with the caption "Form1". To close this form, just click the close button in the upper right corner of the form.

Creating and installing shared assemblies

As mentioned in Chapter 1, "Introducing .NET", you can create both private and shared assemblies. The main difference between a private and shared assembly is where they are physically located. Shared assemblies are stored in the Global Assembly Cache, which by default is your <windows directory>\assembly folder.

Creating a strong name for a shared assembly

Because a shared assembly is stored in a common Global Assembly Cache, it runs the risk of having name collisions with other assemblies. To avoid this, shared assemblies are given a unique *strong name* based on private key cryptography.

> *The details of private key cryptography are beyond the scope of this book. For details on this subject, see the .NET Help topic "Cryptography Overview".*

There are a few ways you can create a strong name for a shared assembly. The easiest method involves three steps.

First, you need to generate a new public-private key pair and store it in a strong name key file. The .NET Framework has a Strong Name command-line tool (Sn.exe) that can do this for you. To access it, run the following command at the command prompt:

```
sn -k <outfile>
```

Now, to generate the new key pair and store it in a file named keyPair.snk (the snk extension stands for "strong name key"), run the following command:

```
sn -k keyPair.snk
```

Next, you need to reference the strong name key file from the assembly. To do this, open up the solution from which the assembly is created in Visual Studio .NET. In the Solution Explorer, double-click on the AssemblyInfo.cs or AssemblyInfo.vb file to open it for editing.

If you're working with C#, you'll see the following assembly attribute:

```
[assembly: AssemblyKeyFile("")]
```

Specify the name of the strong name key file between the double quotes as follows:

```
[assembly: AssemblyKeyFile("keyPair.snk")]
```

If the file is located in a directory other than the project's output directory you need to specify a relative path so VS .NET can find the file. The path is relative to the project's output directory, so if you have the strong name key file in the project's root directory, and the project's output directory is <Project Directory>\bin\debug, you would specify the following:

```
[assembly: AssemblyKeyFile("..\\..\\keyPair.snk")]
```

In Visual Basic .NET, this assembly attribute does not already exist, so you need to add it manually. This is how it's done in VB .NET—notice that I have specified a fully qualified path. Although the .NET Help says I can specify a relative path for the key file, this doesn't seem to work in VB .NET, so for now, I have specified a fully qualified path:

```
<Assembly: AssemblyKeyFile("\MySharedAssemblyVB\bin\keyPair.snk")>
```

The final step is to compile the project. This "signs" the assembly with the strong name located in the strong name key file.

Installing an assembly into the Global Assembly Cache

Unlike private assemblies, you can't just copy assemblies into the Global Assembly Cache—you must install them. There are three main ways you can do this:

- The Microsoft Windows Installer 2.0 (recommended for production machines)

- The .NET command line utility GacUtil.exe (recommended for development machines only).

- The Assembly Cache Viewer (development machines only)

GacUtil is easy to use. You simply run the following command at the command prompt:

```
gacutil -I <assembly name>
```

For example, if you want to install an assembly named MySharedAssembly in the Global Assembly Cache, you run the following command:

```
gacutil -I MySharedAssembly.dll
```

If you have the .NET Framework SDK loaded on a development machine, the Assembly Cache Viewer (described in the section "Viewing assemblies in the Global Assembly Cache" in Chapter 1, "Introducing .NET") is the easiest way to install a shared assembly into the

Global Assembly Cache. All you have to do is drag and drop a strong-named .NET assembly into an instance of Windows Explorer where the Assembly Cache Viewer is hosted, and the assembly is automatically registered in the Global Assembly Cache for you.

Dynamic Help

Visual Studio .NET has a great little feature called *dynamic help* that "watches" what you're doing in the IDE and displays a list of help topics that it thinks will be of assistance to you.

To try out dynamic help, click on the Dynamic Help window—by default it's placed at the bottom right corner of your screen as a tab associated with the Properties window. If the window is not visible, just select Help | Dynamic Help from the main menu. Next, click on your solution in the Solution Explorer. It displays the help topics shown in **Figure 17**.

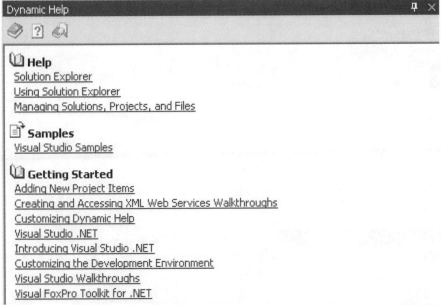

Figure 17. The Dynamic Help window displays help topics that it thinks will be of assistance to you based on what you have currently selected in the IDE.

If you have "My First VB Windows App" solution open in the Solution Explorer, right-click on Form1.vb and select View Code from the shortcut menu. Try clicking on different words in the VB .NET source file such as "Class" and "Inherits". Do the same thing with the C# Class1.cs source code file and click on "using", "namespace", "public", and "class". You can also try clicking on some of the other windows in the IDE—you'll see applicable help topics appear in the Dynamic Help window.

To customize dynamic help, launch the Options dialog by selecting Tools | Options from the main menu. The dynamic help settings are located in the Environment folder.

The Properties Window

The Visual Studio .NET Properties Window (**Figure 18**) is similar in functionality to Visual FoxPro's Properties Window, however there is one big difference. In VFP, you use the Properties Window to view/edit properties, events, and methods of an object. In Visual Basic .NET, you can only use the Properties Window to view/edit properties. In C#, you can use it to view/edit both properties and events.

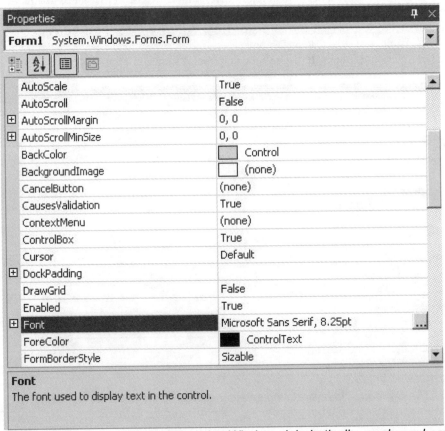

Figure 18. You can sort the Properties Window alphabetically, as shown here, or by category.

A combo box at the top of the Properties Window displays the name of the object and the fully qualified class (complete namespace and class name) on which it is based.

As with Visual FoxPro, if you change the default value of a property it is shown in bold in the Properties Window. *Unlike* Visual FoxPro, there is no way to display only the properties that have been changed.

If a property has a finite set of values, you can double-click on the property and rotate through the possible values. If you select the default value, the property is marked as "unchanged" in the Properties Window. This is different (and better) than VFP, which marks a property as "non-default" even if you enter the default value.

Sorting items in the Properties Window

There are two ways to sort the items in the Properties Window—alphabetically or by category. **Figure 18** shows the Properties Window sorted alphabetically (my personal preference).

To sort the Properties Window alphabetically, click the Alphabetic button, (the second button from the left at the top of the Properties Window)

When you sort the Properties Window by category, related properties are grouped together under several different categories. For example, when you are viewing the properties of a Windows Form the categories are: Accessibility, Appearance, Behavior, Configurations, Data, Design, Focus, Layout, Misc, and Window Style. To sort the Properties Window by category, click the Categorized button (the first button on the left at the top of the Properties Window). Properties within each category are sorted alphabetically.

Displaying events

If you edit an object in C#, the Properties Window gives you the added ability to view an object's events (**Figure 19**).

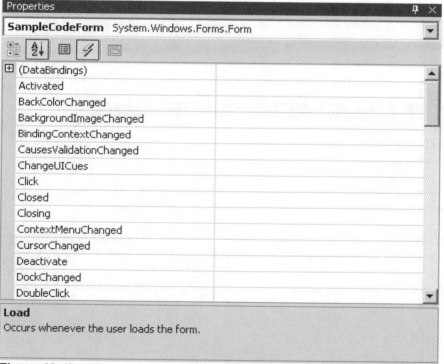

Figure 19. If you're using C#, you can also view an object's events in the Properties Window.

You can view events in the Properties Window by clicking the Events button (the fourth button from the right at the top of the Properties Window—the "lightning bolt"). To go back to viewing properties, click the Properties button (the third button from the right).

In Visual Basic .NET, although you can't view events in the Properties window, you can get to them using the combo boxes at the top of the code-editing windows. If you select (Base Class Events) from the combo box on the left (**Figure 20**), a list of corresponding events appear in the combo box on the right (**Figure 21**).

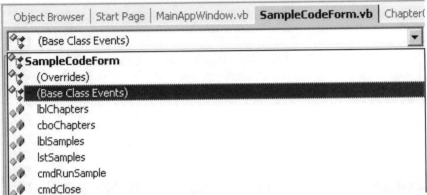

Figure 20. To view events in VB .NET, select (Base Class Events) from the combo box at the top left of the code-editing window.

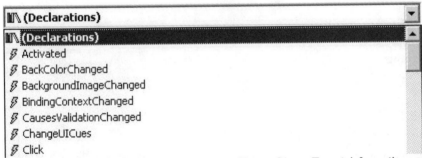

Figure 21. In VB .NET, when you select (Base Class Events) from the combo box, it displays the events in the combo box at the top right of the code-editing window.

For more information on events, see Chapter 5, "Object Orientation in C# and Visual Basic .NET".

Code editing

To demonstrate the code editing capabilities of Visual Studio .NET, in the Solution Explorer, right-click on the Class1.cs file located in the "My First CSharp Class Library" project, and select View Code from the shortcut menu. This opens up a code-editing window in the IDE (**Figure 22**).

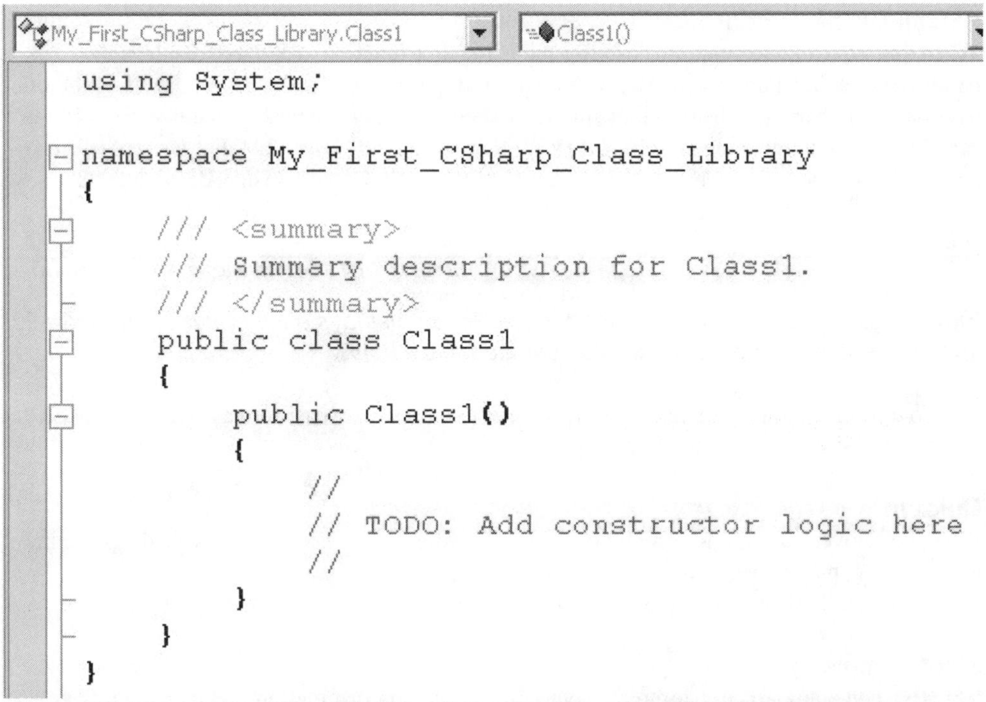

```
My_First_CSharp_Class_Library.Class1    ▼   Class1()                              ▼

    using System;

    namespace My_First_CSharp_Class_Library
    {
        /// <summary>
        /// Summary description for Class1.
        /// </summary>
        public class Class1
        {
            public Class1()
            {
                //
                // TODO: Add constructor logic here
                //
            }
        }
    }
```

Figure 22. *The code-editing window allows you to easily select the class and method to be edited, and provides color-coding like Visual FoxPro.*

At the top left of the code-editing window is a combo box listing all classes in the source file. At the top right is a combo box listing each of the currently selected class members. As you page down through the source code file, these combo boxes automatically display the current class and member where the cursor is located. If you select an item from these combo boxes, the cursor is placed in the source code of the corresponding item.

IntelliSense
If you're familiar with IntelliSense in Visual FoxPro 7 and later, you'll be comfortable using IntelliSense in Visual Studio .NET. IntelliSense comes in the form of member lists, parameter information, quick info, word completion, and brace matching.

Member lists
When you enter the name of a class or structure and then enter a period, IntelliSense displays all valid members in a scrollable list from which you can select the desired member. Once the member you want is highlighted in the list, you can insert it into your code a few different ways. First, you can type the character that follows the member, such as a comma, space, or parenthesis. Alternately, you can press TAB, Ctrl+Enter, Enter, or double-click.

To close the members list, press Escape at any time. The easiest way to redisplay the members list is to press Ctrl+J.

Parameter information

When you type an open parenthesis after the name of a function, VS .NET displays the parameters list in a popup window, with the current parameter displayed in bold. If a method is overloaded, it displays a list of all available methods and their associated parameters that you can scroll through by using the UP and DOWN arrow keys (**Figure 23**). For an explanation of overloaded methods, see Chapter 5, "Object Orientation in C# and Visual Basic .NET".

```
MessageBox.Show(|
```
▲ 1 of 12 ▼   System.Windows.Forms.DialogResult MessageBox.Show (**System.Windows.Forms.IWin32Window owner**, string text)
Displays a message box in front of the specified object and with the specified text.

Figure 23. _If a method is overloaded, IntelliSense displays a list of available methods and their associated parameters you can scroll through_

To close the parameters list, press Escape at any time. The easiest way to redisplay the parameters list is to press Ctrl+Shift+Space.

Quick Info

When you hover your mouse pointer over any identifier in your code, VS .NET displays the identifier's complete declaration in a yellow pop-up box.

To manually display the quick info pop-up, press the Ctrl+K, and then Ctrl+I.

Word completion

VS .NET can automatically complete a variable, command or function name once you have entered enough of the name to distinguish it. To invoke word completion, enter the first few letters of the variable, command, or function name, and then press Alt+RightArrow. If you have not entered enough letters to uniquely identify the word, VS .NET displays a scrollable list from which you can choose.

For example, if you type "Oper" in the Code Window and then press Alt+RightArrow, VS. NET inserts "OperatingSystem" for you.

Brace matching

When you type a closing brace, both the starting and ending brace are displayed in bold until you press another key or move the cursor. Brace matching works for parentheses ( ), brackets [], braces { },. and angle brackets < >.

If you are using C#, you can move back and forth between matching braces by placing the cursor to the left of any kind of brace and pressing Ctrl+]. This feature is not available in VB .NET.

Visual Basic .NET-specific IntelliSense

When using Visual Basic .NET, you get additional IntelliSense features, such as completion on the keywords goto, Implements, Option, and Declare. You also get completion Enum and Boolean, as well as syntax tips.

Modifying IntelliSense

By default, all of the IntelliSense options appear automatically in the IDE. However, if you prefer to turn off the automatic IntelliSense and manually invoke it only when you need it, you can do so by setting IntelliSense options.

To turn off automatic IntelliSense, select Tools | Options from the menu. Expand the Text Editor folder and select the language you want to customize. Select the General item under the language and clear the check boxes for the IntelliSense options you want to turn off.

Outlining

The Visual Studio .NET code editor allows you to hide and show your code by means of a feature called *outlining*. In some circles, VS .NET's code editor is referred to as a *folding editor*.

If you look at a code-editing window (**Figure 24**), you can see VS .NET automatically adds a minus sign (-) next to the start of code blocks, such as namespaces, class definitions, and method definitions. When you click a minus sign, the code between the minus sign you clicked and the next minus sign is hidden, and a plus sign is displayed next to the start of the code block along with a ". . ." displayed in a box at the end of the line (Figure 24). These are visual indicators that code has been hidden.

What's particularly nice about this is if you hover your mouse pointer over the box containing ". . .", it displays a Quick Info box showing the contents of the collapsed code.

To expand code that has been collapsed, either click on the minus sign or double-click on the box containing ". . .".

```
using System;

namespace My_First_CSharp_Class_Library
{
    /// <summary>
    /// Summary description for Class1.
    /// </summary>
    public class Class1
    {
        public Class1()...
    }
}
```

Figure 24. Visual Studio .NET's outlining feature allows you to hide code so you can easily see only the code you want.

In addition to VS .NET's automatic outlining, you can manually create your own outlining. To do this, simply select the text you want to outline, right-click on the selected text, and select Outlining | Hide Selection from the shortcut menu.

There are six additional options available in the Outlining shortcut menu:

- Hide Selection – Hides the currently selected text. In C#, you only see this option when auto-outlining is off or Stop Outlining is selected.

- Toggle Outlining Expansion – Reverses the current collapsed or expanded state of the selected code, or the outlining section in which the cursor is located.

- Toggle All Outlining – Sets all code outlining in the document to the same state.

- Stop Outlining – Turns off outlining for the entire document.

- Stop Hiding Current – Removes outlining information from the currently selected user-defined region. In C#, you only see this option when auto-outlining is off or Stop Outlining is selected.

- Collapse to Definitions – Creates outlining regions for all procedures in your document and then collapses them.

Bookmarks

You can bookmark your code much the same way you do in Visual FoxPro, except bookmarks in Visual Studio .NET are persisted between sessions and bookmarks in VFP are lost when you exit your Visual FoxPro session.

To create a bookmark, place your cursor on a line of code (or select one or more lines of code) and select Edit | Bookmarks | Toggle Bookmarks from the menu. You can also press Ctrl+K twice to toggle a bookmark.

To move to the next bookmark in a document, press Ctrl+K, and then Ctrl+N. To move to a previous bookmark, press Ctrl+K, and then Ctrl+P. To clear all the bookmarks in a document, press Ctrl+K, and then Ctrl+L. These hotkey functions are also available as menu items under Edit | Bookmarks.

Formatting text

The Edit | Advanced menu selection provides a number of options for formatting text. **Table 2** contains a quick rundown on these options.

Table 2. *A variety of Text formatting options are available, a few of them not found in Visual FoxPro.*

Project Template	Description	Hot Key
Format Document	Applies smart indenting rules to the entire document. Only available when editing VB .NET source code	Ctrl+K, Ctrl+D
Format Selection	Applies smart indenting rules to the selected code	Ctrl+K, Ctrl+F
Tabify Selection	Converts white space to tabs	-
Untabify Selection	Converts tabs to spaces	-
Make Uppercase	Uppercases the selected text. Use this and "Make Lowercase" with care in case-sensitive languages such as C#.	Ctrl+Shift+U
Make Lowercase	Lowercases the selected text	Ctrl+U
Delete Horizontal White Space	Deletes the horizontal white space in the selected text. This option does not delete blank lines	Ctrl+K, Ctrl+\
View White Space	Displays a visible representation of all white space in the current document. Tabs appear as arrows and spaces appear as dots.	Ctrl+R, Ctrl+W
Word Wrap	Turns on word wrap in the current document	Ctrl+R, Ctrl+R
Incremental Search	Turns on incremental search in the current document. As you type characters, the cursor moves to the first matching word.	Ctrl+I
Comment Selection	Comments out the selected text	Ctrl+K, Ctrl+C
Uncomment Selection	Uncomments the selected text	Ctrl+K, Ctrl+U
Increase Line Indent	Indents the selected text	-
Decrease Line Indent	Decreases the indent on the selected text	-

By default, the Decrease Line Indent, Increase Line Indent, Comment Selection and Uncomment Selection options can also be invoked by a button on the Text Editor toolbar (**Figure 25**).

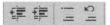

Figure 25. *There are Decrease Line Indent, Increase Line Indent, Comment Selection and Uncomment Selection buttons found on the Text Editor toolbar.*

Visual Studio .NET Windows

Visual Studio .NET gives you a lot of flexibility in customizing the IDE windows to work the way that suits you best—including auto-hiding, docking, splitting windows, tab-linking, and the ability to drag windows around the IDE. I recommend playing with these different settings to see what environment setup works best for you. This section provides a quick overview of some of these features. Check the Visual Studio .NET Help file for more information.

There are a two main window types in the Visual Studio .NET IDE—tool windows and document windows.

Tool windows

Tool windows are found in the VS .NET View menu and include the Solution Explorer, Class View, Server Explorer, Resource View, Properties Window, Toolbox, Web Browser, Macro Explorer, Object Browser, Document Outline, Task List, Command Window, Output Window, Find Results windows, and Favorites. They have the ability to auto-hide, dock, float, be tab-linked with other tool windows, and even be displayed on other monitors. To set the mode in which you want a tool window to operate, right-click on the window and select the desired setting from the shortcut menu.

Each of the tool windows mentioned here are discussed in detail later in this chapter.

Displaying tool windows on other monitors

If you have configured your computer to support multiple monitors, you can display a tool window on another monitor by simply dragging it to that monitor.

Document windows

Document windows are automatically created when you open items in your solution. You can choose to work with document windows in either Tabbed Documents mode (the default) or MDI (Multiple Document Interface) mode. You can change your document window mode by selecting Tools | Options from the menu to launch the Options dialog, and then expand the Environment folder and select General. The document window mode setting is listed at the top of the form.

Split windows

If you need to view two parts of a document at the same time, you can split the window (**Figure 26**).

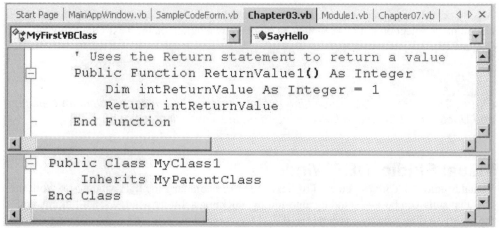

Figure 26*. If you need to view two parts of the same document simultaneously, you can split the window.*

To split a document window, choose Window | Split from the menu. To remove the split, choose Window | Remove Split from the menu.

Full Screen mode

You can view a document window in Full Screen mode by selecting View | Full Screen from the menu. This temporarily hides all tool windows and displays the currently selected document full screen.

To return to normal viewing mode, click the Full Screen floating toolbar that automatically appears when you go into Full Screen mode.

Searching and Replacing

Visual Studio .NET has powerful search and replace capabilities. If you select Edit | Find and Replace from the menu, it displays five options:

- Find
- Replace
- Find in Files
- Replace in Files
- Find Symbol

Find and Replace

Selecting either Find or Replace from the menu eventually gets you to the same place. If you are in the Find dialog, and click the Replace button the Find dialog turns into the Replace dialog (**Figure 27**). The hot key for launching the Find form is Ctrl+F and the hot key for the Replace form is Ctrl+H.

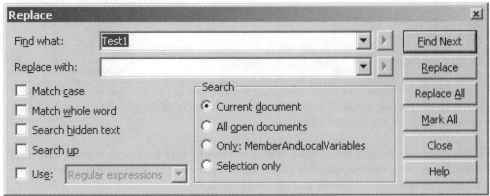

Figure 27. *The Replace dialog offers a variety of options for searching and replacing text*

There are a set of check boxes and an option group that allow you to control how the search is performed. One of the options that may not be familiar to you is Search hidden text. If you check this box, VS .NET searches concealed text, such as a design-time control's metadata or a hidden / collapsed area of an outlined document.

The Search option group allows you to narrow your search to the current document, the current block in which the cursor is located, or within the currently selected text. You can also expand your search to all open documents.

If you have one or more words in a single line selected when you launch the Find or Replace dialogs, those words are automatically inserted into the Find What box.

After you have selected and entered your search criteria, use the Find Next, Replace, Replace All, and Mark All buttons to perform the search and optionally replace. The Mark All button adds a bookmark to each line of code that contains the specified text. You can then navigate between bookmarks to see each instance that was found. See the "Bookmarks" section earlier in this chapter for details.

Find in Files and Replace in Files

Selecting Find in Files or Replace in Files also eventually gets you to the same place. If you click the Replace button in the Find in Files dialog, it turns into the Replace in Files dialog (**Figure 28**). The hot key for launching the Find in Files dialog is Ctrl+Shift+F and the hot key for launching the Replacing in Files dialog is Ctrl+Shift+H.

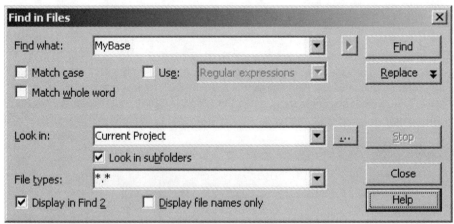

Figure 28. The Replace in Files dialog allows you to search for text in all the same places as the Replace dialog, plus you can also search all files in the current project, a specified file, or a specified directory.

There is a set of check boxes that allow you to specify how the search is performed. One interesting option is Keep modified files open after Replace All. This leaves files open so you can verify changes that were made and optionally undo them.

The Look in combo box allows you to specify where to search for the specified text. You can search in all the same places as the Replace dialog, but you can also select to search all files in the current project. In addition, you can manually type in the name of a file or a directory you want to search. The Look in subfolders check box specifies that the search should include files located in subfolders. You can also specify the types of files you want to search. The default is all files (*.*).

After executing a find, the criteria as well as the search results are displayed in a Find Results window (**Figure 29**). If you double-click on any of the search results, it automatically opens the associated file and places the cursor on the line containing the search text.

```
Find all "MyBase", Subfolders, Find Results 2, All Searchable Items, "*.*"
C:\NET Code Sample\My First VB Windows App\Form1.vb(7):         MyBase.New()
C:\NET Code Sample\My First VB Windows App\Form1.vb(23):        MyBase.Dispose(disposing)
Total found: 2    Matching files: 1    Total files searched: 6
```

Figure 29. The Find Results window displays the search criteria as well as the search results.

The Display in Find 2 check box specifies that you want search results to be displayed in the Find Results 2 window rather than the Find Results 1 window. This allows you to view multiple result sets.

Find Symbols

The Find Symbols dialog (**Figure 30**) allows you to search for symbols, which in this context are objects (classes, structures, interfaces, namespaces, and so on) and their members. This option lets you narrow your search so it doesn't include text found in comments or within methods. The hot key for launching the Find Symbols dialog is Alt+F12.

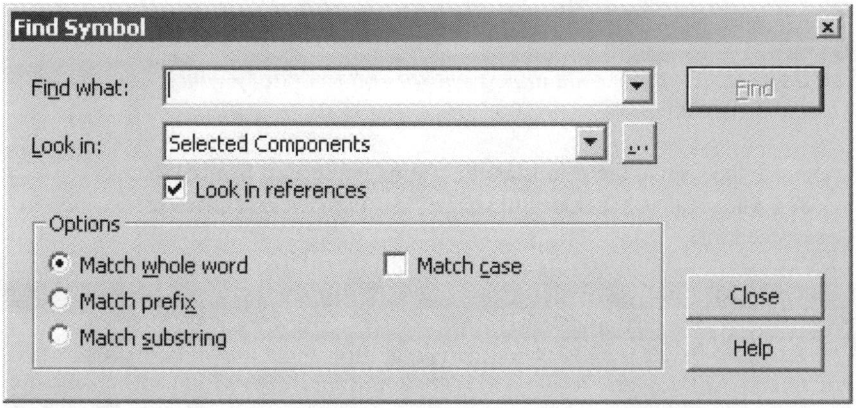

Figure 30. The Find Symbol dialog allows you to search objects and their members for the specified text.

The Look in combo box allows you to specify whether to search in the "Active Project" or "Selected Components". If you specify to search Selected Components, click the Browse button (…) to launch the Selected Components dialog (**Figure 31**), where you can specify which components to search.

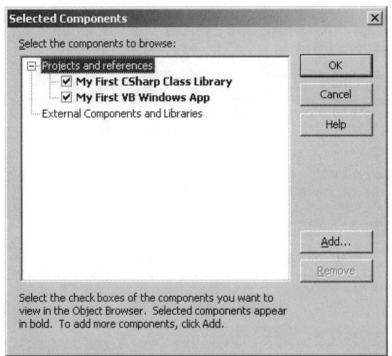

Figure 31*. The Selected Components dialog allows you to specify which components to search for the specified symbol.*

When you execute the search, the results are displayed in the Find Symbol Results window (**Figure 32**). The result list includes file name, line number, and character position of the symbol you searched for.

Figure 32*. The Find Symbol Results window displays the file name, line number, and character position of the symbols you search for.*

Another cool feature of Find Symbols is you can search for .NET classes, interfaces, and so on. In this case, search results are displayed in the VS .NET Object Browser. For more information on the Object Browser, see the "Object Browser" section later in this chapter.

Setting IDE options

The Visual Studio .NET IDE is highly customizable. The Options dialog (**Figure 33**) allows you to change the following categories of IDE behavior:

- Environment

- Source Control

- Text Editor

- Analyzer

- Database Tools

- Debugging

- HTML Designer

- Projects

- Windows Forms Designer

- XML Designer

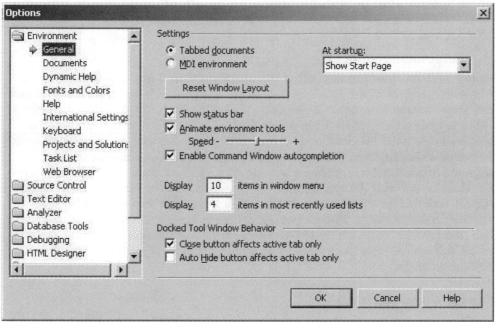

Figure 33. *Taking time to examine all of the settings in the Options dialog allows you to set up the IDE in a way that best suits the way you work.*

To launch the Options dialog, select Tools | Options from the menu. For a detailed explanation of each setting, select a category and click the Help button.

Object Browser

Visual Studio .NET's Object Browser (**Figure 34**) is similar in functionality to Visual FoxPro's Object Browser. It allows you to examine both .NET components and COM components. You can launch the Object Browser by selecting View | Other Windows | Object Browser from the menu or by pressing Ctrl+Alt+J.

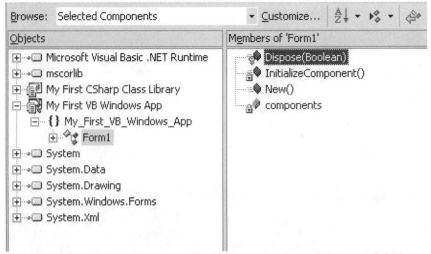

Figure 34.The Object Browser lets you examine both .NET and COM components.

When you launch the Object Browser, it lists all of the projects in your current solution as well as any components referenced in these projects. You can drill down into projects and components using the tree view in the left pane of the Object Browser. As you select objects, their members are displayed in the Members pane on the right. If you click on a member, a description of the member is displayed in the description pane at the bottom of the browser.

There are dozens of different icons used in the Object Browser. For a list describing each of these, check out the .NET Help topic "Class View and Object Browser Icons".

One particularly useful feature of the Object Browser is the ability to right-click on one of your custom classes and select Go To Definition from the shortcut menu. If the source code is available, it automatically opens the file that contains the class and positions you at the start of the class definition.

Class View window

The Class View window (**Figure 35**) is similar to the Object Browser, but it is only used to view the symbols found in your solution rather than in external components. In addition, it provides a hierarchical view (by project and namespace) of your symbols. To launch the Class View window, select View | Class View from the menu or press Ctrl+Shift+C.

If you double-click on a class or class member in the Class View window, it automatically opens the associated source code file (if it's not already open), and places your cursor on the corresponding code. This always works the other way. If you are in the code-editing window, right-click on a class or class member and select Synchronize Class View from the shortcut menu, the Class View window receives focus, highlighting the item you have selected.

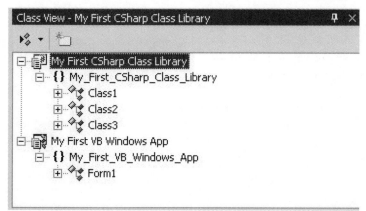

Figure 35. *The Class View window displays the symbols in your solution by project and namespace.*

C# special Class View features

If you right-click on a C# class, you see a few extra options in the shortcut menu that are not available in VB .NET. The most interesting is the Add option (**Figure 36**), which allows you to add a method, property, field, or indexer to a class directly from the Class View window.

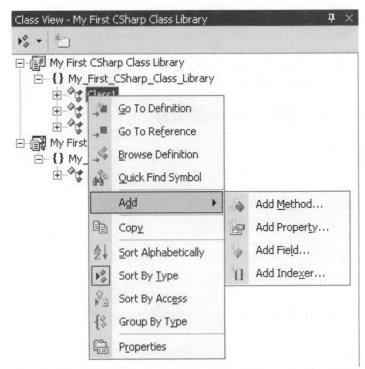

Figure 36. C# has a special feature that allows you to add a method, property, field, or indexer directly from the Class View window.

For more information on methods, properties, fields, and indexers, see Chapter 5, "Object Orientation in C# and Visual Basic .NET".

Task List

VS .NET's Task List (**Figure 37**) is very similar to Visual FoxPro's Task List. It's a tool that helps you organize your project tasks. The Task List is usually found as a tab at the bottom of the VS .NET IDE. If you don't see the Task List, you can view it by selecting View | Other Windows | Task List from the menu or by pressing Ctrl+Alt+K.

!	✔	Description	File	Line
		Click here to add a new task		
		TODO: Add constructor logic here	C:\NET Code Sample\My... Class Library\Class1.cs	13
✔	☐	public class Class3 : Class1	C:\NET Code Sample\My... Class Library\Class1.cs	18

Figure 37. The Task List contains tasks automatically added by VS .NET as well as tasks you have entered yourself.

VS .NET automatically adds items to the Task List. For example, when you add a new class to your project and VS .NET creates a constructor method (which is similar to a Visual FoxPro class Init method), it adds a TODO item to the list telling you to add code to the constructor method.

You also add items to the Task List by clicking in the top line of the window and manually typing the task description. In addition, you can add an item to the Task List by right-clicking a line of source code and selecting Add Task List Shortcut from the shortcut menu.

Command Window

If you're thinking that Visual Studio .NET's Command Window comes anywhere near Visual FoxPro's Command Window, you'll be sadly disappointed! You can launch the Command Window by selecting View | Other Windows | Command Window from the menu or by typing Ctrl+Alt+A. For more information on the Command Window, check out Chapter 13, "Error Handling and Debugging in .NET".

Favorites

The Favorites window displays your Web browser's favorites within the VS .NET IDE (**Figure 38**). You can display the Favorites window by selecting View | Other Windows | Favorites from the menu or by typing Ctrl+Alt+F. If you right-click on an item in the Favorites window, you see the same shortcut menu that is available within Internet Explorer, allowing you to delete favorites, rename favorites, create new folders, and so on.

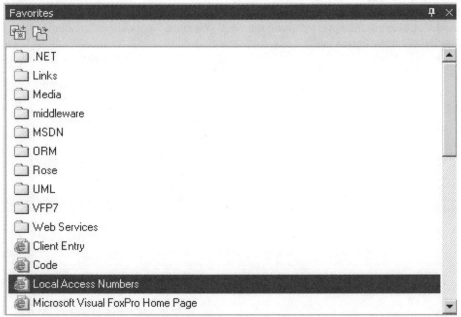

Figure 38. The Favorites window allows you to display your Web browser favorites within the VS .NET IDE.

Toolbox

By default, the VS .NET Toolbox is automatically hidden in the IDE. To display the Toolbox, simply hover your mouse pointer over the hammer and wrench icon (**Figure 39**) on the left side of the desktop.

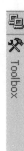

Figure 39. Hovering your mouse pointer over the Toolbox icon automatically displays the Toolbox window.

If you don't see this icon, open the Toolbox by selecting View | Toolbox from the menu.

The Toolbox contains several different tabs that display a variety of items, depending on what you currently have selected in the IDE. For example, if you have a Windows Form selected, it displays the Windows Forms tab containing dozens of different user interface controls that you can add to your form (**Figure 40**).

You will see details in various chapters throughout this book of how each one of these tabs is used. For example, Chapter 9, "Building .NET WinForm Applications" demonstrates how to use the Windows Forms tab.

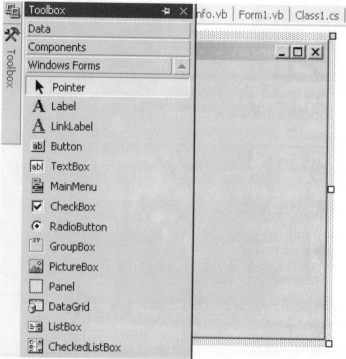

Figure 40. *The Toolbox displays a variety of items depending on what you currently have selected in the IDE.*

Server Explorer

The Server Explorer is great feature of Visual Studio .NET. It allows you to open data connections, log on to servers, and work with databases. You can work with servers such as SQL Server and Oracle—you can also use Server Explorer to work with MSDE (Microsoft Database Engine)!

By default, the Server Explorer is auto-hidden on the left side of the VS .NET IDE. You can make the Server Explorer visible if you hover your mouse pointer over the Server Explorer tab or by selecting View | Server Explorer from the menu.

The Server Explorer tree view contains two main nodes—Data Connections and Servers (**Figure 41**).

Figure 41. The Server Explorer allows you to create connections to servers, view their databases, event logs, message queues, performance counters, and system services.

Data Connections

You can add a connection to any server to which you have network access by right clicking on the Data Connections node and selecting Add Connection... from the shortcut menu. This launches the Data Link Properties tabbed dialog. You can select a provider on the Provider tab, then set properties in the Connection, Advanced and All tabs for your data connection. Click the Help button if you need assistance in setting up a connection.

Once you have created a connection to a database, you can view and manipulate its data without leaving the Visual Studio IDE. For example, if you create a connection to the SQL Server Northwind database, expand the Tables node under the connection to see a list of all tables in the database. If you right-click on a table, you see options to retrieve data from the table, design the table, create a new table, and so on.

Figure 42 shows the results of right clicking on the Northwind database's Employees table and selecting Retrieve Data from Table.

dbo.Employees...DLI.Northwind)	Object Browser	AssemblyInfo.vb	Form1.vb	C ◁ ▶ ✕

EmployeeID	LastName	FirstName	Title	TitleOfCourtesy
1	Davolio	Nancy	Sales Representati	Ms.
2	Fuller	Andrew	Vice President, Sale	Dr.
3	Leverling	Janet	Sales Representati	Ms.
4	Peacock	Margaret	Sales Representati	Mrs.
5	Buchanan	Steven	Sales Manager	Mr.
6	Suyama	Michael	Sales Representati	Mr.
7	King	Robert	Sales Representati	Mr.
8	Callahan	Laura	Inside Sales Coordi	Ms.
9	Dodsworth	Anne	Sales Representati	Ms.

Figure 42. If you use the Server Explorer to retrieve data, the result set is displayed in the VS .NET IDE.

When the results tab has focus, the Query toolbar is automatically displayed, containing buttons such as Run Query, Verify SQL Syntax, Sort Ascending, Sort Descending, Remove Filter, and so on.

Servers
The Servers node in Server Explorer displays the list of servers currently available for use. Beneath each server is a node for Crystal Services (Crystal Reporting options), Event Logs, Message Queues, Performance Counters, Services, and SQL Servers.

For more details on the Server Explorer, check out the Visual Studio .NET Help topic "Introduction to Server Explorer".

Source control
As you might expect, Microsoft integrated Visual Studio .NET with Visual SourceSafe to provide source control capabilities. Visual SourceSafe 6.0c is a "re-release", in Microsoft terms, of the 6.0 product that shipped with Visual Studio 6.0. It rolls-up all of the fixes up to and including Visual Studio 6, Service Pack 5 (the most recent). In addition, 6.0c includes some bug fixes, speed enhancements, and interface extensions that make it compatible with the VS. NET IDE.

You can add a project or an entire solution to source control. To add a project to source control:

- Select the project in the Solution Explorer
- Select File | Source Control | Add Selected Projects to Source Control...

As with Visual FoxPro, when you add a project to source control, icons are displayed next to project items indicating their source control status such as "checked in" and "checked out" (**Figure 43**).

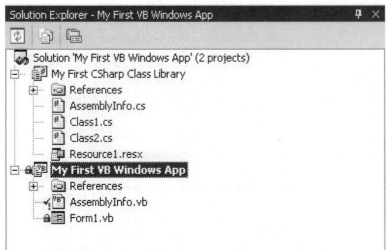

Figure 43. You can add individual projects or an entire solution to source control.

To add an entire solution to source control:

- Right-click on the solution in the Solution Explorer and select Add Solution to Source Control… from the shortcut menu.

- If prompted, log on to source control.

- When the Add to SourceSafe Project dialog appears, it displays the name of your solution. Select (or create) the folder where you want to store your project, and then click OK.

Details on working with VS .NET and Visual SourceSafe are available on the web at http://msdn.microsoft.com/library/?url=/library/en-us/dnbda/html/tdlg_rm.asp?frame=true or see the .NET Help topic "Source Control Basics", which contains links to several other source control topics. For even more information on working with Visual SourceSafe, check out "Essential SourceSafe" by Ted Roche, available from Hentzenwerke Publishing. An addendum to the book specifically for Visual Studio .NET and SourceSafe 6.0c, is scheduled to be published on the Hentzenwerke web site soon.

Macro Explorer

Macros allow you to automate repetitive actions or series of keystrokes during development. Visual Studio .NET takes creating and managing macros to a new level. The Macro Explorer tool window shows you all the macros available for a solution. In VS .NET, macros are stored in macro projects, which can be shared by multiple solutions. Macros are the area where Visual Basic .NET rules supreme—you can't create macros using any other .NET language.

To view the Macro Explorer, select View | Other Windows | Macro Explorer from the menu (**Figure 44**). The Macro Explorer allows you to create new macro projects, load existing macro projects, or unload projects.

Figure 44*. The Macro Explorer is your window to creating and managing macros in Visual Studio .NET.*

Macros IDE

VS .NET contains a separate Macros IDE that allows you to create, manage, and run your macros (**Figure 45**). This IDE comes complete with its own Project Explorer, Class View, Properties Window, Toolbox, Web Browser, Dynamic Help, Debugger, and so on.

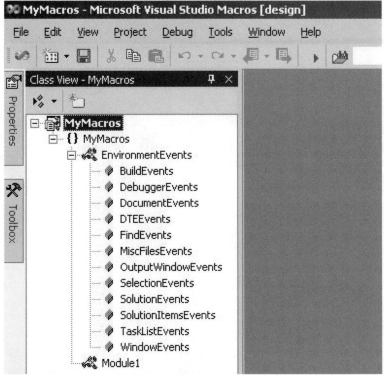

Figure 45*. VS .NET has a separate Macros IDE you can use to create and manage your macros.*

To launch the IDE, right-click the top-most Macros node in the Macro Explorer and select Macros IDE... from the shortcut menu.

For details on creating, running, and managing your macros check out the .NET Help topic "Managing Macros".

Conclusion

This chapter took a quick tour of Visual Studio .NET's many features. You can see that Microsoft has put a great deal of effort into making VS .NET a great environment for developing software. However, this chapter could have been twice its size to really cover all the features of VS .NET. I recommend you take the time to go through the VS .NET Help file to learn more about what it can do for you.

Chapter 3
Introduction to C#

Some developers are "afraid" of C# because C-based languages have a reputation for being advanced, and therefore difficult to learn and use. This chapter aims to dispel any misgivings you might have by providing a side-by-side comparison of C# and Visual FoxPro—you'll be amazed at their similarities. It will also help you leverage your knowledge of Visual FoxPro in learning the basics of C#.

There has been a lot of excitement generated about C#, Microsoft's newest programming language. It's a very clean and elegant implementation of an object-oriented .NET language. However, new doesn't mean it's untested or "wet behind the ears". Microsoft put C# to the test and used it to write the .NET Framework's base classes (For the record, the .NET Framework *could* have been written in Visual Basic .NET. C# was chosen because most developers working on the .NET Framework were C++ developers and the C# compiler was completed before the VB .NET compiler).

Of all the existing programming languages, C# is the most similar to Java. The October, 2000 issue of Java™ Report states: "C# is Java with single inheritance; automatic memory management; 41 of the same 43 operators; all the same flow of control statements, plus foreach; 38 of 50 Java keywords; and if you allow for synonyms, 46 of the same 50 keywords."

Although C# is new, it still has many features that are associated with more mature languages such as Visual FoxPro. In this chapter you will start out learning the basics—strong typing vs. weak typing, variables, constants, data types, conditional statements, flow of control loops, jump statements, and converting between different data types.

Although I will touch on basic object-oriented elements of C# in this chapter, such as declaring a simple class, the real discussion of C# and VB .NET's object-oriented features takes place in Chapter 5, "Object Orientation in C# and Visual Basic.NET".

> *For a side-by-side comparison of C#, Visual Basic.NET, and Visual FoxPro's operators and keywords, check out "Appendix A – Language Comparison Tables". For a comparison of each language's data types, see "Appendix B – Data Type Comparison".*

Weak typing vs. strong typing

One of the biggest differences between C# and Visual FoxPro is weak typing vs. strong typing. Visual FoxPro is a weakly typed language. This means that you can store a value of any type in a variable. For example, as shown in the following code, you can store a DATETIME value in a variable, save a string in the same variable, and then turn around and store an integer in the same variable without having the Visual FoxPro compiler complain:

```
LOCAL MyVariable
MyVariable = DATETIME()
MyVariable = "Hello World!"
MyVariable = 6
```

While this may be incredibly flexible, it has its downside. First of all, from a readability perspective, it's far better to create three different variables to hold each of these values, rather than reusing the same variable. Second, and more importantly, weak typing allows bugs to sneak through. For example, if you store an integer value in MyVariable, and then attempt to run the following code, you'll get an "Operator/operand mismatch" error at runtime:

```
REPLACE CustomerName WITH "Customer " + MyVariable IN Customer
```

You would probably notice this bug pretty quickly when you run the code—but that's the problem—"when you run the code". What if the code never gets run until it's in the end-user's hands?

In contrast, C# is a strongly typed language (VB .NET is also a strongly typed language, but C# is more strongly typed. See Chapter 4, "Introduction to Visual Basic .NET" for details). In the world of variables, strong typing means that you must declare the type of all variables. For example, the following code creates a date variable named MyDate, a string variable named MyString, and an integer variable named MyInteger:

```
DateTime MyDate;
string MyString;
int MyInteger;
```

If you do not declare the type of a variable, the C# compiler gives you an error and exits without finishing the compilation of your application.

Another common error in Visual FoxPro coding that causes bugs is using a variable without declaring it first. For example, the following code doesn't declare MyVariable before using it:

```
MessageBox("Hello World" + MyVariable, 0+48, "Weak Typing Demo")
```

The Visual FoxPro compiler does not catch this kind of error. However, when this code is executed at runtime, your end users see a message such as "Variable 'MyVariable' is not found".

In contrast, C# does not allow you to use variables unless they have been declared *and* initialized first. For example, if you create the following code:

```
string MyString;
MessageBox.Show(MyString, "Strong Typing Demo");
```

the compiler displays the error "Use of unassigned local variable 'MyString'".

To change these lines of code so they work properly, you need to assign an initial value to MyString:

```
string MyString = "I love strong Typing!";
MessageBox.Show(MyString, "Strong Typing Demo");
```

C#'s strong typing also applies to variables that store object references. This aspect of strong typing is covered in Chapter 5, "Object Orientation in C# and VB .NET".

The practical value I've seen in my coding boils down to this—in Visual FoxPro, when I create a page worth of code, invariably there are a few bugs. I can't find those bugs until I step through the code line by line. With .NET languages, I can write the same amount of code and the compiler will catch a majority of the syntax bugs (sorry, no compiler will catch all of the bugs in your application logic!).

A simple C# program

Although this chapter is not about object-orientation, you need to know the basics of creating a simple program and a simple class in order to understand how the basic constructs of the C# language work in context. So, you will create the obligatory "Hello World" program now. The call to Console.WriteLine displays "Hello .NET World!" in a .NET console application:

```
using System;

class MyFirstCSharpProgram
{
  public static int Main()
  {
      Console.WriteLine("Hello .NET World!");
      return 0;
  }
}
```

There are a few things to note about this code. Every C# program must have a Main method. This method is called when the program is first executed and it must return nothing (void) or an integer. Optionally, you can specify that the Main method accept a string array parameter. If any command-line parameters are sent when the program is executed, they are placed into this array:

```
using System;

class MyFirstCSharpProgram
{
  public static int Main(string[] args)
  {
      // Here is a comment
      Console.WriteLine("Hello .NET World"); //Here is another comment

      // Process any parameters
      if (args.Length > 0)
      {
          // Build a string containing all parameters
          String Parms = "";
          foreach (string parameter in args)
          {
              Parms += parameter + " ";
```

```
        }
        // Display the parameters
        Console.WriteLine("\nParameters: " + Parms);
    }

    return 0;
    }
}
```

The code I've placed in this sample for processing parameters contains some C# features I haven't covered yet, such as array handling and `foreach` loops. You will find information on these features later in this chapter.

C# syntax

In this section, I'll give you an overview of C#'s syntax compared to Visual FoxPro's. I'll start out by showing you the two things that take the most getting used to in C#.

Case sensitivity

Visual FoxPro is a case-*insensitive* language. The following code declares a variable "MyString" and assigns it a value. In the next line, I use that variable, but I refer to it as "mystring" (all lowercase). In Visual FoxPro, the two names refer to the same variable.

```
MyString = "Visual FoxPro is case-insensitive"
MESSAGEBOX(mystring, 0+48, "Case insensitive")
```

C# is a case-*sensitive* language. "MyString" and "mystring" refer to two completely different variables. In addition, all keywords are in lower case. If you enter a keyword with mixed case, the compiler flags it as an error. Some developers have a hard time getting used to C#'s case sensitivity. However, if you already write case-sensitive code in Visual FoxPro, it's not as big an issue.

Semicolons and multi-line statements

In Visual FoxPro, you don't need to put an ending character after each statement. However, if a single statement continues over multiple lines, you need to add a semi-colon, which is Visual FoxPro's continuation character:

```
MESSAGEBOX("This command continues " + ;
  "to another line", 0+48, "Continuation Character")
```

This is the opposite of how C# works. As you can see by looking at the code sample in the previous section, all C# statements must end in a semicolon. This allows a single statement to continue to the next line without a continuation character. For example:

```
MessageBox.Show("This command continues " +
  "to another line without a continuation character");
```

For Visual FoxPro developers using C#, this can be a little irritating at first, but it doesn't take long before you're typing a semi-colon without even thinking about it.

Code placement

In Visual FoxPro, you place code in classes or in standalone functions, procedures, and programs. This allows you to do a mix of both procedural and object-oriented programming.

In C#, *all* code must be contained within classes or *structures* which are similar to classes. Structures are discussed in detail in Chapter 5, "Object-Orientation in C# and Visual Basic .NET". Given a choice between the two approaches, I think C#'s approach is better. VFP's approach may be more flexible, but it can, and often does, promote poor object-oriented programming practices.

Grouping statements together

The convention in Visual FoxPro for grouping statements together is to use a beginning and ending keyword. For example, you group all the members of a class together within DEFINE CLASS and ENDDEFINE keywords. You group code contained in class methods within PROCEDURE and ENDPROC or FUNCTION and ENDFUNC keywords:

```
DEFINE CLASS MyClass AS Session

  PROCEDURE MyProcedure
  ENDPROC

  FUNCTION MyFunction
  ENDFUNC

ENDDEFINE
```

C# uses curly braces consistently to group code together. Here's a code sample that defines a class named CodeGroupingDemo and it contains two methods named MyMethod1 and MyMethod2:

```
public class CodeGroupingDemo
{

  public void MyMethod1()
  {
  }

  public void MyMethod2()
  {
  }

}
```

Although at first you may find this style of coding difficult to read, it is less verbose than Visual FoxPro (and VB .NET for that matter), it means less typing, and it's consistent throughout the language.

Comments

In Visual FoxPro, you use the familiar asterisk (*) to indicate a comment at the beginning of a line. You can also use a double ampersand (&&) to add a comment at the end of a line.

C# uses two forward slashes consistently to indicate a comment either at the beginning of a line or at the end of a line of code. For multi-line comments, it uses a forward slash and asterisk (/*) at the beginning of the first comment line and an asterisk and forward slash (*/) at the end of the last comment line:

```
public class CommentDemo
{
  /* Multi-line comment
     Here's the second line */

  // Comment
  public void MyCommentedMethod()        // Another comment
  {
  }
}
```

C# has a very cool feature that allows you to document your code using XML. See the "XML Documentation" section at the end of this chapter for details.

Namespaces

All classes in .NET belong to a namespace. Remember that namespaces are not a physical grouping of classes, such as a project or a class library in Visual FoxPro. They are simply a naming convention that logically groups classes together. For example, all of the source code associated with this book belongs to the namespace HW.NetBook.Samples. For more information on namespaces, see Chapter 1, "Introduction to .NET".

To assign a class to a namespace, all you have to do is place the class within the curly braces of a namespace declaration:

```
namespace HW.NetBook.Samples
{
  public class MyDemoClass
  {
  }

  public class MyOtherDemoClass
  {
  }
}
```

Since a namespace is not a physical designation, you can place code in different physical source files or assemblies and assign them to the same namespace. This is different from Visual FoxPro, where a class is designated by its physical location—either a class library or a PRG file.

In Visual FoxPro, before you can instantiate a class, you have to SET CLASSLIB or SET PROCEDURE to the class library or PRG file that contains your class definitions. Similarly, in C#, you must specify that you are "using" the namespace to which a class belongs. The following code specifies that it is using two different namespaces, System and System.Windows.Forms:

```
using System;
using System.Windows.Forms;

namespace HW.NetBook.Samples
{
}
```

When you declare that you are using the System namespace, it does not give you automatic access to the namespaces that are "below" the System namespace such as System.Windows.Forms. You must explicitly declare each namespace you are using. The `using` declaration tells C# where to find classes that are referenced within the code below it.

Defining a simple class

As I promised, I won't go into too much object-orientation in this chapter, but in order to understand the rest of the sample code in this chapter, you need to at least understand how to define a simple class and a simple method.

Here is the simplest class definition in C# (not much fat here):

```
class MyFirstCSharpClass
{
}
```

Below is the simple class with a single, simple method. Notice I've put it in the context of a namespace (HW.NetBook.Samples) and have referenced the System.Windows.Forms namespace. This is necessary because the MessageBox class belongs to this namespace.

```
using System.Windows.Forms;

namespace HW.NetBook.Samples
{
  public class MyFirstCSharpClass
  {
      public void SayHello()
      {
          MessageBox.Show("Hello .NET World!", "C#");
      }
  }
}
```

The default base class

In Visual FoxPro, the term "parent class" is used to specify the class from which a class is derived. In the .NET world, the term "base class" is used instead. In VFP, the term 'base class' refers to the top-level Visual FoxPro classes (such as textbox, combobox, custom, container, and so on). The reason I bring this up is because in the definition of MyFirstCSharpClass, no parent or base class was specified.

In C#, if you don't specify otherwise, a class is assumed to be derived from the Object class. The Object class is the topmost class in the .NET hierarchy (the queen mother of all base classes). Every class in the .NET Framework can trace its heritage back to the Object class.

Defining class methods

You've already seen an example of a simple class method. Here's the official syntax for a class method:

```
[modifiers] returnType MethodName([parmType parmName])
{
  // Method body
}
```

In C#, both the return value's type and the parameter's types must be explicitly specified. This is in keeping with C#'s strongly typed nature. Methods that return nothing have a return type of `void`.

Declaring variables

Variables declared within methods are local variables (there is no other kind). This means they are only visible within the method they are declared. Based on this, you don't have to specify a scope (local, private, public) when declaring a variable.

To declare a variable, specify its type, followed by its name:

```
int Count;      // Declare an integer variable named "Count"
Count = 5;      // Assign Count the value of 5
```

You can also declare a variable and assign it a value in a single command:

```
// Declare an int variable named Height and assign it a value of 6
int Height = 6;
```

If you want to declare multiple variables of the same type in a single statement, simply separate them with commas:

```
int Top = 5, Left = 39;
```

Fields

As mentioned in the previous section, variables declared at the method level are known as local variables. However, as shown in the following code, variables declared at the class level are known as *fields*:

```
public class FieldsAndLocalVars
{
  string Test1 = "Test1";      // Declares a field

  public void ShowFieldsAndVars()
  {
      string Test2 = "Test2";  // Declares a local var
      MessageBox.Show("Displaying Field " + Test1);          // Display the
field
      MessageBox.Show("Displaying Local Variable " + Test2); // Display the
field
  }
}
```

You might think at first that fields are equivalent to Visual FoxPro's properties, but they're not. In addition to fields, C# classes can also have properties which are discussed in Chapter 5, "Object-Orientation in C# and Visual Basic .NET". For now, just think of fields as variables defined at the class level that accessible to all methods in the class.

One other point to note is you can reference fields the same way you reference local variables. You don't need a `this` qualifier in C# as you do in Visual FoxPro. In the previous example, you could have referenced the Test1 field as `this.Test1`, but it's not required.

After teaching a good number of C# classes, I highly recommending using "this" to preface members. Since C# is case-sensitive, using "this" allows IntelliSense to kick in and allow you to select members from a list rather than having to type them manually, with the potential of typing them incorrectly.

If you declare a local variable with the same name as a field in the containing class, the local variable, while in scope, hides the field. In this situation, if you need to refer to the field, you must use a `this` prefix before the field name.

Field modifiers

A field modifier is a keyword used to amend a field declaration. For example, there are five accessibility modifiers you can apply to fields (**Table 1**) that specify the visibility of a field:

Table 1. Field modifiers allow you to specify the visibility of your fields

Modifier	Description
public	Access is not restricted
internal	Access is limited to the current project
protected	Access is limited to the containing class or subclasses
protected internal	Access is limited to the current project or to subclasses
private	Access is limited to the containing class

It's considered good object-oriented form to declare fields as private. To promote this practice, if you don't specify a modifier, C# considers a field private by default. If you want to allow other classes to access this field, you can create a protected or public property for this purpose (see the "Properties" section in Chapter 5, "Object-Orientation in C# and Visual Basic .NET" for details).

Value and reference types

.NET makes a strong distinction between value types and reference types. Value type variables store their data directly and reference type variables store the address where their associated data can be found. Reference variables are actually pointers dressed up in an object—but you can't access the pointer directly. To understand this concept more clearly, you need to learn how C# allocates memory behind the scenes.

Understanding the stack and the heap

There are two places where the .NET runtime allocates memory for your data types—the *stack* and the *heap*. The stack is an area of memory used to store value types that are a fixed length. This includes basic data types such as integers, boolean, long, float, double, and character. **Figure 1** provides a conceptual view of how this works. When you declare the integer variable "x", the runtime allocates space for the variable on the stack. When you assign a value to the variable, the .NET runtime stores the value into the space it already allocated on the stack.

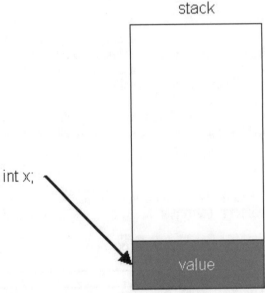

Figure 1. When you declare a value-type variable, the .NET runtime allocates space for the variable on the stack. When you assign a value to the variable, the value is stored in the space already allocated on the stack.

What happens when you copy one value variable to another value variable as shown here?

```
int x;
int x = 5;
int y = x;
```

This creates two copies of the same data on the stack. When you declare variable x it allocates space for the variable on the stack. When you assign variable x a value of 5, it stores a 5 in the allocated space for variable x on the stack. When you assign x to y, it allocates space for variable y on the stack and copies the value 5 from variable x into the space allocated for variable y. This gives you two copies of the same data on the stack.

The heap is an area of memory used to store reference type data such as classes, arrays, and strings. When you declare a reference type variable, the runtime allocates space for the reference variable on the stack—the same as it does for a value type variable. However, when you instantiate the reference type object (see **Figure 2**), rather than storing the object's data on the stack, it is stored on the heap, and a pointer to the address of the object's data is stored in the reference variable located on the stack.

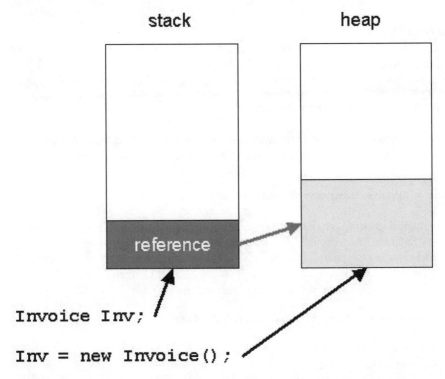

Figure 2. When you declare a reference variable, the .NET runtime allocates space for the variable itself on the stack. However, when you instantiate the object, it stores the object's data on the heap and stores a pointer to the heap data in the reference variable on the stack.

What happens when you copy one reference variable to another reference variable?

```
Invoice Inv;
Inv = new Invoice();
Invoice Inv2 = Inv;
```

This creates two references to the same data located on the heap. When you declare the variable Inv, the runtime allocates space for the reference variable on the stack. When you instantiate the Invoice object, it stores the object's data on the heap and stores a pointer to the Invoice object data in the Inv variable. When you copy the Inv variable to the Inv2 variable, it first allocates space for the Inv2 variable on the stack. Afterwards, it adds a pointer to the same Invoice data pointed to by the Inv variable.

Value and reference type performance
Primitive base types such as integers, bool, decimal, and char are value types and provide better performance because you don't have the overhead of creating an object on the stack every time you use one of these types.

The string type
The string class is a reference type; although from all outward appearances, the commands you use to manipulate strings make them seem like value types.

You can assign a value to a string variable using a string literal enclosed in double quotes:

```
string Caption = ".NET for VFP Developers";
```

Unlike Visual FoxPro, you can't use single quotes or square brackets to delimit strings. You concatenate strings in C# the same way as in VFP—by using a plus (+) sign:

```
string Title = "Sir"
string Name = Title + "Laurence Olivier";
```

The next logical question is "How do I create a string literal that contains double quotes such as Louis "Satchmo" Armstrong?" This requires the use of *character escapes*.

Table 2 shows a list of special characters called character escapes that you can add to a string. For example to add a line break to a string, you use the \n character escape. The following code adds a new line between the city/state and the zip code:

```
string CityStateZip = "Charlottesville, VA \n22903";
```

To answer the original question, you can display double quotes contained within a string by using the double quote escaped character \ ":

```
string ManlyMen = "Louis \"Satchmo\" Armstrong";
```

Table 2. *This table shows a list of common character escapes, or special characters, you can add to your strings.*

Escaped character	Description
\a	Alarm (bell)
\t	Tab
\r	Carriage return
\n	New line
\"	Double quote

You tell C# to ignore escaped characters in a string by prefixing the string with an @ sign:

```
string Folder = @"c:\temp";
```

Assigning one string to another

The .NET runtime treats strings differently than other reference types. At first, when you assign the value of one string to another string:

```
string State1 = "California";
string State2 = State1;
```

it acts as expected. This code creates two variables on the stack, State1 and State2, and it points both variables to the same "California" string located on the heap.

However, if you change the first string:

```
string State1 = "Sunny California";
```

the .NET runtime creates a new string object on the heap and stores a reference to the new data in the State1 variable located on the stack while State2 still points to the old data on the heap. Armed with this information, you can make better choices about how you manipulate strings so as not to create excess string data on the heap. For example, if you need to concatenate a number of strings together in a loop, it's best to use the .NET StringBuilder class instead of using strings. The StringBuilder class has an Append method to concatenate strings together:

```
StringBuilder StrBuilder = new StringBuilder;
StrBuilder.Append("Texas, ");
StrBuilder.Append("New Mexico, ");
StrBuilder.Append("Colorado");
MessageBox.Show(StrBuilder.ToString());
```

Enumerations

C# lets you define your own complex value types. One of these value types is *enumerations* (the other is *structures*, covered in Chapter 5, "Object Orientation in C# and VB .NET").

Enumerations are a convenience feature of C# that allow you to group related integer-based constants together. You can think of them as an array of constants. There is no Visual FoxPro equivalent to enumerations, but it's easy to see how they can be very useful.

The following code lists a group of constant definitions found in the FoxPro.h include file (located in the Visual FoxPro home directory). These constants define all the possible values for a VFP cursor's "Buffering" setting:

```
#DEFINE DB_BUFOFF              1
#DEFINE DB_BUFLOCKRECORD       2
#DEFINE DB_BUFOPTRECORD        3
#DEFINE DB_BUFLOCKTABLE        4
#DEFINE DB_BUFOPTTABLE         5
```

When you use one of these constants in a command, such as CursorSetProp(), you often have to open up the FoxPro.h file to see what the possible values are. Here's where enumerations can help.

In C#, you can define an enumeration that groups together all the possible values for the Buffering setting:

```
public enum Buffering
{
  BufOff = 1,
  BufLockRecord = 2,
  BufOptRecord = 3,
  BufLockTable = 4,
  BufOptTable = 5
}
```

You access an enumeration by referring to its name and specifying the desired member. The compiler converts it to its associated integer value:

```
Buffering.BufOptRecord
```

As shown in **Figure 3**, enumerations hook into VS .NET IntelliSense. When you type the name of the enumeration and a period, IntelliSense shows you a list of all possible values in the enumeration.

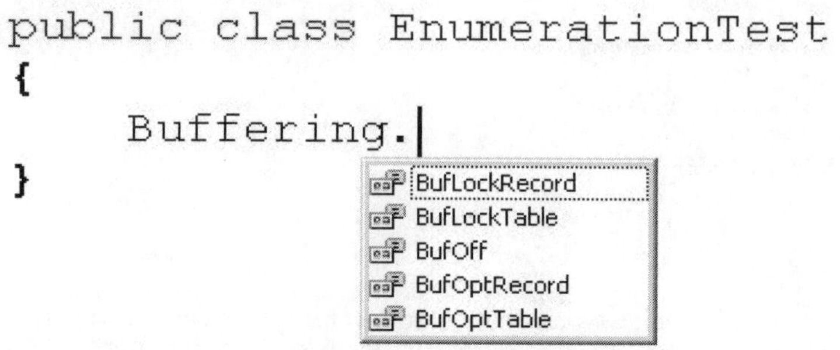

Figure 3. Enumerations hook into VS .NET IntelliSense, making it easy to select the proper value from a qualified list.

Even though enumerations are integer-based, the compiler complains if you try to store an enumeration to an integer variable as shown here:

```
int BufferMode = Buffering.BufOptRecord;
```

The compiler complains that it can't implicitly convert "Buffering" to an integer. Although you can use a cast to explicitly convert the enumeration value to an integer, (see the "Casting" section later in this chapter) you can also get around this by specifying the variable as the type "Buffering":

```
Buffering BufferMode = Buffering.BufOptRecord;
```

Although enumerations are integer types by default, you can specify them as byte, sbyte, short, ushort, int, uint, long, or ulong instead. For example:

```
public enum Buffering : long
```

In this context, : long specifies that the Buffering class is derived from the type long. For details on subclassing and inheritance, see Chapter 5, "Object Orientation in C# and Visual Basic.NET".

Arrays

There are many similarities between arrays in Visual FoxPro and in C#. One of the big differences is arrays in C# are treated as objects with methods and properties. Another difference is Visual FoxPro allows you to mix different types of data in an array (integers, strings, dates, etc), but in C# all array elements must be of the same type.

> *You can get around the limitation of array elements having to be of the same type by declaring the array contains items of the type "Object", which is the base type of all classes in the .NET Framework.*

A third difference is that C# arrays are zero-based, meaning the first array element is zero (0). In Visual FoxPro, the first array element is one (1).

Declaring arrays

In C#, arrays are declared the same way as other variables, except you add square brackets [] between the variable type and the variable name. For example, the following statement declares an integer array named "KidsAges":

```
int [] KidsAges;
```

You can also declare an array and size it in one step:

```
string [] KidsNames = new string[3];
```

Once you declare the length of an array, you can't resize it. If you want an array whose size is changable at run time, use the ArrayList object instead, found in the System.Collections namespace. See the .NET Help file for details.

You determine the length of any array dimension by calling the array's GetLength method and passing the desired array dimension:

```
MessageBox.Show("Number of kids = " + KidsNames.GetLength(0));
```

Storing values to arrays

You set initial values of array elements when you declare the array:

```
string [] KidsMiddleNames = {"Christopher","Mark","James"};
```

Or you can store values in the array elements after declaring the array:

```
string [] KidsNames = new string[3];
KidsNames[0] = "Jordan";
KidsNames[1] = "Timothy";
KidsNames[2] = "Alexander";
```

Sorting arrays

To easily sort the elements of an array, you call the Array class's Sort method:

```
Array.Sort(KidsNames);
```

You reverse the sort order by calling the Array class's Reverse method:

```
Array.Reverse(KidsNames);
```

Multidimensional arrays

All of the arrays you've seen so far have only one dimension. Visual FoxPro allows you to create both one and two-dimensional arrays. C# goes a step further and allows you to create multidimensional arrays—arrays with three or more dimensions! However, unless you have special requirements, you probably won't need more than a two-dimensional array.

Multidimensional arrays are either rectangular (every row has the same number of columns) or jagged (each row can have a different number of columns). Visual FoxPro has rectangular arrays, but does not have jagged arrays.

Defining multidimensional rectangular arrays

You declare an array as multidimensional and rectangular by adding one or more commas within the square brackets of the array declaration. Each comma you add specifies an additional array dimension. Here is the definition of a two-dimensional, rectangular array with two columns and three rows:

```
string[,] ArrayKids = { {"Jordan", "McNeish"},
                        {"Timothy", "McNeish"},
                        {"Alexander", "McNeish"} };
```

Defining jagged arrays

A jagged array is an "array of arrays". They are multidimensional, but, unlike rectangular arrays, each row can have a different number of columns. You define a jagged array by adding an extra set of square brackets for each dimension. In the following example, the jagged array has three elements in its first dimension. Its second dimension has a different size for each row. The first row has three columns, the second row has two columns, and the third row has one column:

```
string[][] Musicians = new string [3][];
Musicians[0] = new string[] {"Stevie", "Ray", "Vaughn"};
Musicians[1] = new string[] {"Jimi", "Hendrix"};
Musicians[2] = new string[] {"Bono"};
```

Type conversions

When working with strongly typed languages, converting between different data types is an important consideration. C# provides both implicit and explicit type conversion.

> For a list of C# data types, and a comparison between C#, VB. NET and VFP data types, check out "Appendix C – Data Type Comparison".

Implicit type conversions

C# implicitly converts some values from one type to another. In the following example, C# automatically converts a short value to an integer and then to a double:

```
short x = 10;
int y = x;
double z = y;
```

Table 3 lists the types that can be implicitly (automatically) converted in C#.

Table 3. *Types that can be implicitly converted in C#*

From Type	To Type
byte	ushort, short, uint, int, ulong, long, float, double, decimal
sbyte	short, int, long, float, double, decimal
short	int, long, float, double, decimal
ushort	uint, int, ulong, long, float, double, decimal
char	ushort, uint, int, ulong, long, float, double, decimal
int	long, float, double, decimal
uint	long, ulong, float, double, decimal
long	float, double, decimal
ulong	float, double, decimal
float	double

Explicit type conversion using casts

If the compiler refuses to implicitly convert a value from one type to another, you use a *cast* instead. As shown in the following example, you specify that you want to cast a value from one type to another by prefixing the value to be converted with the destination type in parentheses. This code converts an integer to a byte (which the compiler will *not* do implicitly):

```
int x = 20;
byte y = (byte)x;
```

Converting to string

If you need to convert a value to a string, the Object class has a ToString method (inherited by all classes in the .NET Framework) that returns the string representation of the object. So, to get a string representation of an integer, you do the following:

```
int i = 10;
string s = i.ToString();
```

Using Parse to convert strings

If you need to convert strings to other value types, you use the Parse method of the desired destination type. For example, if you want to convert a string to an integer, you use the Parse method of the int type:

```
string StringAmt = "100";
int IntAmt = int.Parse(StringAmt);
```

If you want to convert string value to long, you use the Parse method of the long type:

```
string StringAmt = "100";
long IntAmt = long.Parse(StringAmt);
```

You can also convert strings to boolean values using Parse. However, the string value must be either "True" or "False" (case insensitive) or you will get a runtime error stating "string was not recognized as a valid boolean".

Boxing and unboxing values

Boxing describes the process of converting a value type to a reference type. *Unboxing* describes converting the value of a reference type back to a value type.

Boxing occurs implicitly when you store an integer type into an object:

```
int i = 10;
object o = i;
```

Figure 4 demonstrates what happens when this code is executed. In the first line, space for int "i" is allocated on the stack and a value of 10 is assigned to the variable. In the second line, a reference variable for object "o" is allocated on the stack, and the value of 10 is copied from integer "i" to the space allocated on the heap for object "o"'s data.

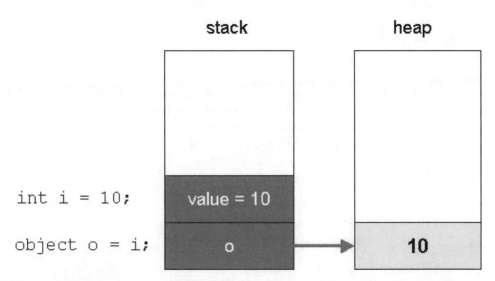

Figure 4. Value types can be implicitly boxed when you store the value of an integer (or other value type) into an object.

Unboxing only occurs explicitly. You can only unbox a variable that has been previously boxed. For example:

```
// Boxing
int MyInteger = 10;
object MyObject = MyInteger;

// Unboxing
int MyUnboxedInt = (int)MyObject;
```

The `is` operator

You determine if an object is a specific type by using the `is` operator. This is useful in situations where a method receives a parameter of a generic object type and wants to determine its specific type. For example, the following method receives a parameter of type object. It then checks to see if it is of type MyClass1:

```
public void CheckClass(object testObject)
{
  if (testObject is MyClass1)
  {
      MessageBox.Show("TestObject is MyClass1",
          "is operator");
  }
  else
  {
      MessageBox.Show("TestObject is not MyClass1",
          "is operator");
  }
}
```

`if` statement

C#'s `if` statement is similar to Visual FoxPro's IF...ENDIF statement. If the expression in the parentheses following the `if` evaluates to true, the code within curly braces is executed. Optionally, you can add an `else` statement to the `if` that gets executed if the condition expression evaluates to false. C# also allows you to nest `if` statements.

You don't need to add the curly braces if there is only one statement following the `if` or `else`, however it's considered good form to do so.

```
bool HavingFun = true;

if (HavingFun)
{
  MessageBox.Show("We are having fun!","if demo");
}
else
{
  MessageBox.Show("We are NOT having fun","if demo");
}
```

`switch` statement

The C# `switch` statement is equivalent to Visual FoxPro's DO CASE statement. Based on the value of the expression, one of the `case` statements is selected for execution. You can specify a `default` case, which is the same as VFP's OTHERWISE clause. If the `switch` expression does not match any of the cases, control is passed to the default case. If no `default` case is present, control passes to the first command after the end of the switch.

```
testValue int = 2;
switch (testValue)
```

```
{
  case 1:
       MessageBox.Show("testValue = 1","switch");
       break;
  case 2:
       MessageBox.Show("testValue = 2","switch");
       break;
  case 3:
  case 4:
       MessageBox.Show("testValue = 3 or 4","switch");
       break;
  default:
       MessageBox.Show("testvalue is not 1,2,3 or 4",
           "switch");
       break;
}
```

As shown in the previous example, you cannot fall through one case to another unless a case is empty. This means you must specify one of the following jump statements:

- `break` – indicates the end of a case and control is passed to the statement following the switch.

- `goto` – specifies control be passed to a specific case (e.g. "goto case 2") or to the default case (e.g. "goto default").

- `return` – indicates the end of a case and terminates the execution of the current method.

`for` loop

C# `for` loops are equivalent to Visual FoxPro's FOR...ENDFOR command. It iterates through a loop while a particular condition is true.

In the parentheses that follow the `for` statement, there are three different items. The first is the initializer (e.g. `i=0;`). You place any variables to be initialized in this part of the statement, although it's most common to specify a single variable to be initialized. The second part of the parenthetical statement is the expression to be evaluated (e.g. `i < 4`). This expression is evaluated before the loop is executed. The third part of the parenthetical statement is the *iterators* (e.g. `i++`). This is the expression used to increment or decrement the loop counter.

In C#, the ++ operator increments a variable and the -- operator decrements a variable. For more information on C# operators, see "Appendix A – Language Comparison Tables"

```
int i;

string Message = "";

for (i=0; i < 4; i++)
{
  Message += "Message " + i + "\n";
}
MessageBox.Show(Message, "For Loop");
```

while loop

The C# `while` loop is equivalent to Visual FoxPro's DO...WHILE loop. It is a pre-test loop, which means if the condition evaluates to false, the loop is not executed at all. `While` loops are often used to repeat a block of code for an undetermined number of times.

```
bool Condition = true;
while (Condition)
{
  // This loop only executes once
  int i = 1;
  MessageBox.Show("While loop count " + i, "while loop");
  i++;
  Condition = false;
}
```

do loop

The C# `do` loop is similar to C#'s own `while` loop, except the condition is checked at the end of the iteration rather than at the beginning. This means the loop is always executed at least once. This is different than Visual FoxPro's DO...WHILE loop, which evaluates at the top of the loop.

```
bool Condition = false;
do
{
  // This loop only executes once because the condition
  // is tested at the end of the loop
  int i = 1;
  MessageBox.Show("Do While loop count " + i,"do...while loop");
  i++;
} while(Condition);
```

You exit a do loop by using the `break`, `goto`, or `return` statements.

foreach loop

The C# `foreach` loop executes a group of statements for each element in an array or item in a collection. It is equivalent to Visual FoxPro's FOR EACH command.

```
string VersionList = "";
string[] VSNetVersions = {"Standard","Professional",
                  "Enterprise Developer", "Enterprise Architect"};

foreach (string Version in VSNetVersions)
{
  VersionList += "VS .NET " + Version + "\n";
}
MessageBox.Show(VersionList,"ForEach loop");
```

XML Documentation

C# has a very cool feature that allows you to document your code using XML.

If you type three forward slashes in a row in the line immediately preceding a user-defined type (such as a class, structure, enumeration, delegate, or interface) or preceding a member (such as a field, property or method), an XML documentation template is automatically inserted where you can add your comments. For example, suppose you have the following C# class:

```
public class CommentDemo2
{
  public string GetString(int value)
  {
      return value.ToString();
  }
}
```

If you enter three forward slashes on the line before the start of the class definition and preceding the method definition, the following XML documentation template is added to your code:

```
/// <summary>
///
/// </summary>
public class CommentDemo2
{
  public string GetString(int value)
  {
  /// <summary>
  ///
  /// </summary>
  /// <param name="value"></param>
  /// <returns></returns>
  return value.ToString();
  }
}
```

You enter a description of your class between the <summary> tag preceding the class definition and a description of your method in the <summary> tag preceding the method definition. Notice that C# is smart enough to create XML tags for parameters and return values. You can also place descriptions in the <param> and <returns> tags. For example:

```
/// <summary>
/// Comment Demo class
/// </summary>
public class CommentDemo2
{
  /// <summary>
  /// Converts an integer value to a string
  /// </summary>
  /// <param name="value">Integer value to be converted</param>
  /// <returns>Converted string value</returns>
  public string GetString(int value)
```

```
    {
          return value.ToString();
    }
}
```

So what does placing your comments in XML format do for you? The C# development environment in Visual Studio .NET can read your XML documentation and automatically convert it to "comment web pages"!

To build these web pages, open your C# solution in VS .NET and select Tools | Build Comment Web Pages from the menu. This displays the Build Comment Web Pages dialog (**Figure 5**). This dialog allows you to specify whether you want to create comment web pages for your entire solution or for selected projects. You can even add it to your "Favorites" in your Web browser.

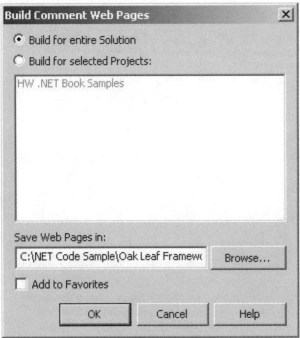

Figure 5. *You can build comment web pages for all projects in your solution or for a single project.*

When you click OK, web comment pages are generated for you. When it's done, you'll see a Code Comment Web Report displayed in a tab of Visual Studio .NET (**Figure 6**).

Figure 6. After building comment web pages, a Code Comment Web Report page is displayed that lists all of the projects for which you have generated web pages.

If you click the project hyperlink, a web page displays a list of all namespaces in your project. If you expand the namespace node, a list of classes belonging to the namespace appears. Selecting a particular class displays information about the class and all of its members, derived from the XML documentation you have inserted in your C# source code (**Figure 7**).

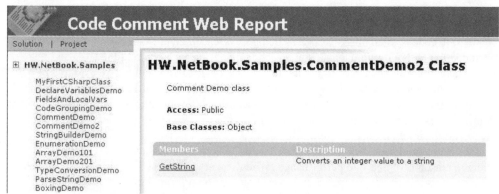

Figure 7. The comment web pages display information about classes derived from the XML documentation you have inserted in your C# source code.

If you click on a member name such as a method, it displays details regarding the method's parameters and return values (**Figure 8**).

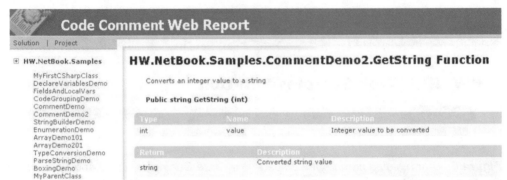

Figure 8. Comment web pages also display details regarding a method's parameters and return value.

Comment web pages are a great addition to the Visual Studio .NET environment because, not only are they cool, they encourage developers to document their code!

Unsafe Code

C# has an advanced feature that is not available in Visual Basic .NET—the ability to create *unsafe code.*

Unsafe code is often misconstrued as being *unmanaged* code. As mentioned in Chapter 1, "Introduction to .NET", unmanaged code is code that executes outside of the CLR and not able to take direct advantage of .NET services such as garbage collection. An example of running unmanaged code is calling a method on an object in a Visual FoxPro COM server.

In contrast, unsafe code is still managed code, but it allows you to access memory directly by means of pointers. The term unsafe doesn't necessarily mean your code is a danger to itself and to you. It simply means the runtime cannot *verify* that it is safe.

So, why would you want to write unsafe code? There are a few reasons. The most common reason is to improve performance. When you are able to access memory addresses using pointers rather than reference variables, you are going through one less layer, which provides a performance advantage. If you have time-critical portions of your application where you want to wring out the highest possible speed, you may consider creating unsafe code.

Another reason you may want to create unsafe code is to access a legacy DLL, such as a Windows API call or a legacy COM DLL that calls for a pointer to be passed as a parameter.

For more information on creating unsafe code in C#, check out the MSDN article *Unsafe at the Limit* by Eric Gunnerson of Microsoft:

```
http://msdn.microsoft.com/library/default.asp?url=/library/en-
us/dncscol/html/csharp10182001.asp
```

C# as an international, industry standard language

Microsoft has done something of great interest with the C# language. In October of 2000, Microsoft submitted C# for review to the European Computer Manufacturers Association (ECMA), an international standards organization, hoping to make it an industry standard language. On December 13, 2001, the ECMA ratified C# and the Common Language Infrastructure (CLI) as international standards. (The CLI is similar to Java's virtual machine—it includes libraries and components that allow C# to run on non-Windows operating systems).

What does this mean for Microsoft and the C# developer? First of all, it means that C# and the CLI are official standards administered by ECMA, although Microsoft retains the right to decide who gets to license the technology. In addition, although there are a number of theories stating that Microsoft has done this "just for show" (Sun Microsystems submitted their Java programming language to the ECMA, then pulled it back again), ultimately, it means that you may be able to write programs in C# that run on non-Windows operating systems such as Linux, Unix and the Palm—something that has been a key feature of Java since its inception. This is similar to the capabilities you have today for creating a C++ application for multiple platforms.

Conclusion

Hopefully this chapter proved useful in giving you a good overview of C#'s syntax, data types, conversions, conditional, and flow of control statements. Although the use of curly braces and semicolons may throw you at first, many developers are surprised at how easy it is to learn C# and how straightforward it is to use.

Although I've covered the basics of C# syntax in this chapter, you can learn more from books such as *Professional C# - Second Edition*, by Wrox Publishing.

Chapter 4
Introduction to
Visual Basic .NET

Many Visual FoxPro developers have an aversion to anything that bears the name "Visual Basic". This chapter aims to help you look past this prejudice and take a fresh look at the new incarnation of Visual Basic—Visual Basic .NET. As you read this side-by-side comparison of Visual FoxPro and Visual Basic .NET, you'll see that Visual Basic has grown up and is a first-class citizen alongside C# and C++.

Visual Basic has been around for many years. It was the first language offered by Microsoft that brought Windows programming to the masses. The relationship between Visual FoxPro and Visual Basic communities has often been combative and characterized by religious fervor on both sides of the fence.

One of the biggest bones of contention has been the claim by VB developers that Visual Basic 6 is object-oriented—which most VFP developers argue loudly against! But things have changed. For all intents and purposes, Visual Basic .NET is a new language. Its syntax is similar to Visual Basic, but it was completely rewritten for .NET.

In the next chapter, I'll cover detailed information on both C# and VB .NET's object-oriented features. In this chapter, I focus on the syntax of VB .NET compared to VFP. So, hopefully you can put aside any preconceived notions and take a good look at what VB .NET has to offer.

For a side-by-side comparison of Visual Basic .NET, C#, and Visual FoxPro's operators and keywords, check out "Appendix A – Language Comparison Tables". For a comparison of each language's data types, see "Appendix B – Data Type Comparison".

Changes for Visual Basic 6 backward compatibility

As you learn Visual Basic .NET, you'll come across a few things that are a little different from the .NET norm. After Visual Studio .NET Beta 1 was released, Microsoft restored some Visual Basic 6 functionality to VB .NET based on feedback from the Visual Basic community. The changes provide an easier upgrade path from Visual Basic 6 to Visual Basic .NET. These are the three main changes:

- **The value of True** – In almost every programming language, when a boolean True is coerced to an integer, its value is one (1). In Visual Basic, it's always been a minus 1 (-1). Originally, Microsoft was going to change this so VB .NET was in line with other .NET languages, but for backward compatibility reasons VB .NET's True still evaluates to -1.

- **Behavior of And/Or/Not/XOr** – Originally, Microsoft intended to change the And, Or, Not, and XOr operators from bitwise operators (as they were in Visual Basic 6) to logical operators. Based on feedback from the VB community, they left these as bitwise operators and added two new operators instead: AndAlso and OrElse.

- **Declaring Arrays** – To bring VB .NET in line with other .NET languages, Microsoft intended to change the way arrays are declared from how it was done in Visual Basic 6. Again, to maintain backward compatibility, they changed it back to the Visual Basic 6 model. Check out the "Arrays" section later in this chapter for details.

Weak Typing vs. Strong Typing

While VB .NET is a strongly typed language, C# is a more strongly typed language. The difference is in C# you must declare all variables and their types before using them. In VB .NET, this is optional.

Option Explicit and Option Strict

VB .NET has two settings that specify how the compiler treats variables—Option Explicit and Option Strict.

The Option Explicit setting specifies whether you can use undeclared variables—not just undeclared variable types, but the variable itself. By default, the Option Explicit setting is "**Off**", which allows you to use variables without declaring them. When Option Explicit is "On", VB .NET acts like C# by forcing you to declare all variables before using them.

> *Although having the flexibility of being able to turn off variable declaration checking may seem like a "plus", it's actually not. You should always turn Option Explicit "On" so the compiler will catch the use of undeclared variables. If Option Explicit is "Off", the compiler won't catch variable names with typos resulting in unpredictable behavior at runtime.*

Even when Option Strict is "On", Visual Basic .NET differs a bit from C# when it comes to using variables. In C#, you must initialize a variable's value before using it. In Visual Basic .NET, you can use a variable without first setting its value (VB .NET sets all variables to a default value when you declare them). Depending on whether you're an advocate of compiler enforcement or of flexibility you can argue whether this is a good or a bad thing!

The Option Strict setting specifies whether the compiler enforces strict typing. If Option Strict is "Off" (the default), the compiler does not require you to specify a type when you declare a variable. If Option Strict is "On", then VB .NET acts like C#, forcing you to declare the type of all variables. Option Strict also specifies how much checking the compiler performs when converting between different variable types. If Option Strict is "Off", no type conversion checking is performed. If Option Strict is "On", the compiler warns you of any type conversions that may result in a loss of data. For example, if Option Strict is "On" when you copy the value of a Long variable into an Integer variable, the compiler complains because a Long variable can hold values larger than can fit in an Integer. However, if you do the opposite (copy the value of an Integer variable into a Long), the compiler does not complain.

In general, it's best to set Option Strict "On". This allows the compiler to catch any conversions that may result in a loss of data, rather than trying to catch them at run time. In addition, explicitly specifying type conversions has speed advantages over allowing them to occur implicitly (automatically). This is because implicit conversions require extra work at runtime to determine the types involved in a conversion.

Assuming that Option Strict and Option Explicit are both "On", you declare variables by specifying their name followed by their type. For example, the following code declares a data variable named MyDate, a string variable named MyString, and an integer variable named MyInteger:

```
Dim MyDate As DateTime
Dim MyString As String
Dim MyInteger As Integer
```

You specify the setting of Option Explicit and Option Strict at the application level by means of VS .NET's Solution Explorer. Just right-click on a project, select Properties from the shortcut menu, and select the Build node under Common Properties in the tree view (**Figure 1**). You can then set Option Explicit and Option Strict and it will affect all code in your project.

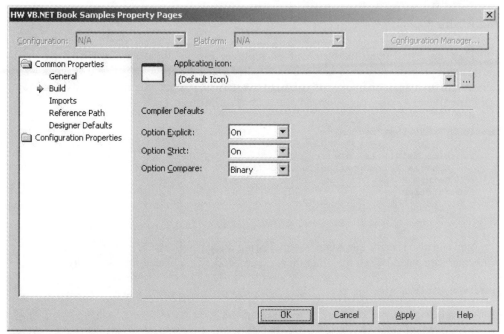

Figure 1. Typically, you should set Option Explicit and Option Strict "On", so the compiler catches undeclared variables, variable types, and type conversion errors.

It is possible to override these project-level settings by declaring a different setting for Option Explicit or Option Strict at the top of your source files. For example:

```
Option Explicit Off
Public Class MyForm
    Inherits System.Windows.Forms.Form
End Class
```

Based on the "best practice" of using strong typing and explicit variable declaration, the rest of the Visual Basic .NET sample code in this book assumes that both of these options are set to "On".

A simple Visual Basic .NET program

Although this chapter is not about Visual Basic .NET's object-oriented features, it's difficult to learn the language syntax without first learning how to create a simple program. Here is a "Hello .NET World" program in VB .NET:

```
Module MyFirstVBNetProgram

    Sub Main()
        Console.WriteLine("Hello .NET World")
    End Sub

End Module
```

There are a few things to note about this program. First of all, every VB .NET program must have a procedure named Main, which is called when the program is first executed. It must return nothing or an integer. If you want to return an integer, you must specify that Main is a Function Procedure instead of a Sub Procedure:

```
Module MyFirstVBNetProgram

    Function Main() As Integer
        Console.WriteLine("Hello .NET World")
        Return 0
    End Function

End Module
```

You can also specify that Main accept a string array parameter. If any command-line parameters are passed when the program is executed, they are placed into this array:

```
Module MyFirstVBNetProgram

  Function Main(ByVal CmdArgs() As String) As Integer
     Console.WriteLine("Hello .NET World")

     ' Process any parameters
     If CmdArgs.Length > 0 Then
     ' Build a string containing all parameters
        Dim Parms, Parameter As String
        For Each Parameter In CmdArgs
            Parms += Parameter & " "
        Next
```

```
        ' Display the parameters
        Console.WriteLine(Parms)
    End If

    Return 0
End Function

End Module
```

Notice the use of the += operator. In Visual Basic .NET this is a shortcut for:

```
Parms = Parms + Parameter
```

Although it's technically accurate for a VB .NET program to have a procedure named Main, in practice, you may not see such a method anywhere in your source code. For example, if you create a new Visual Basic .NET Windows Application using Visual Studio .NET, you won't find a Main method. What's happening is behind the scenes the compiler injects a Main method into the IL for you. You can override this behavior and manually create your own Main method.

Visual Basic .NET Syntax

This section provides an overview of VB .NET's language syntax compared to Visual FoxPro.

Case insensitivity

Visual Basic .NET is like Visual FoxPro in that it is case *insensitive*. Although the convention in VB .NET is to proper case keywords, you can make them upper case, lower case, or anything in between and the compiler treats them all the same. In C#, keywords are in lower case. If you use upper case or mixed case, the compiler flags it as an error.

To demonstrate case insensitivity, in the following code I have declared a variable, "MyString", and assigned it a value. In the next line, I reference that variable, but I refer to it as "mystring" (all lowercase). In VB .NET and Visual FoxPro, these two names refer to the same variable:

```
Dim MyString As String = "Visual Basic .NET is case-insensitive"
Console.WriteLine(mystring)
```

In contrast, as mentioned in Chapter 3, "Introduction to C#", C# is case *sensitive*. If you are the type of developer who tends to mix case freely, this can be a real factor when choosing between Visual Basic .NET and C#. If you tend to be stricter with your casing (and you let IntelliSense "fill in the blanks" for you), it's not as big of an issue.

End-of-line and line continuation characters

In the area of end-of-line and line continuation characters, Visual Basic .NET is again similar to Visual FoxPro. In VB .NET, a CR+LF indicates the end of a line. If you need to have a statement span multiple lines, you must use the continuation character. In Visual FoxPro, the continuation character is the semicolon (;), but in Visual Basic .NET, it is the underscore (_) character.

Grouping statements together

Visual Basic .NET groups statements together by matching beginning and ending keywords. For example, a class definition begins with the `Class` keyword and ends with `End Class`. A subroutine starts with the keyword `Sub` and ends with `End Sub`:

```
Class MyClass
  Public Sub MySubroutine()
  End Sub
End Class
```

The use of starting and ending keywords is similar to Visual FoxPro:

```
DEFINE CLASS MyClass AS Session

  PROCEDURE MyProcedure
  ENDPROC

  FUNCTION MyFunction
  ENDFUNC

ENDDEFINE
```

Comments

In VB .NET, you use a single quote character to indicate the start of a comment. This is consistent whether the comment is at the beginning of a line or following a statement:

```
' Here is a comment at the beginning of a line
Dim MyInteger As Integer = 100    ' Here is a comment following a statement
```

Since statements cannot automatically span lines in Visual Basic .NET without a continuation character, there is no multi-line comment indicators available as in C#.

Namespaces

In Visual Basic .NET, you use the `imports` keyword to specify where the compiler should look to find classes that are not declared in the current namespace. For example:

```
Imports System.Data.OleDb
Imports System.Data.SqlClient
Imports System.Data.SqlTypes
```

All Visual Basic .NET projects automatically import several default namespaces. Since these are imported globally at the project level, you do not need to import these namespaces elsewhere in your project. Different types of projects automatically import different namespaces. To see the default namespaces imported into your project, right-click on your project in the Solution Explorer and select Properties from the shortcut menu. Select the

Imports node located under the Common Properties node and you will see a list of default namespaces in the Project Imports list box (**Figure 2**). Visual Studio .NET allows you to add and remove namespaces from this list.

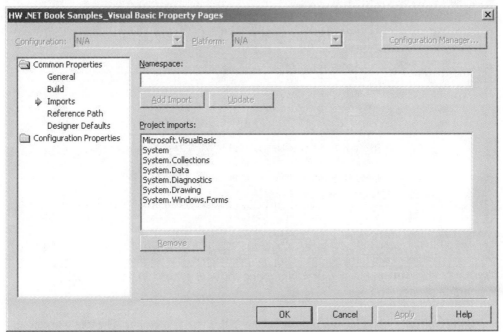

Figure 2. *Visual Basic .NET automatically adds several default namespaces to each project you create. If a namespace appears in this list, you do not need to explicitly declare that you are using the namespace elsewhere.*

Visual Basic .NET has another interesting namespace feature—a project *root namespace*. To see your project's root namespace, right-click on your project in the Solution Explorer and select Properties from the shortcut menu. Select the General node located under the Common Properties node and you will see your project's root namespace (**Figure 3**).

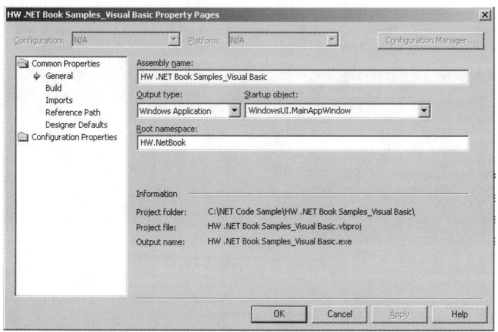

Figure 3*. You can specify a root namespace for your project in your project's Properties dialog.*

By default, all classes in your project belong to this root namespace. The root namespace acts as a prefix for all other namespaces declared in the project. For example, if a project's root namespace is "HW.NetBook", declaring the "Business" namespace in the following code sample associates the Employee class with the HW.NetBook.Business namespace.

```
Namespace Business

   Public Class Employee
   End Class

End Namespace
```

Defining a simple class

Although I am reserving most of the information about object-orientation in Visual Basic .NET for the next chapter, it's easier to understand VB .NET's syntax in the context of a class definition. Here is the simplest class definition in VB .NET:

```
Class MyFirstVBClass
End Class
```

Below is the simple class with a single, simple method. Notice I've associated the class with the namespace Samples. If the project's root namespace is HW.NetBook (as it is in this book's sample code), the fully qualified namespace of this class is HW.NetBook.Samples.

```
Namespace Samples

  Public Class MyFirstVBClass
       Public Sub SayHello()
            MessageBox.Show("Hello .NET World!", "Visual Basic .NET")
       End Sub
  End Class

End Namespace
```

Unlike the equivalent C# sample code in the previous chapter, you do not need to explicitly import the System.Windows.Forms namespace to use the MessageBox class because, by default, this namespace is imported at the project level.

The default base class

If you do not specify a parent (base) class, it is assumed that a class is derived from the Object class. As mentioned previously, the Object class is the topmost class in the .NET Framework hierarchy.

Defining class methods

Visual Basic .NET has two different types of methods—subroutines and functions. If your method does not return a value, you must declare it as a subroutine. If it *does* return a value, you must declare it as a function.

Here is the subroutine declaration syntax:

```
[Attributes][ProcedureModifier] Sub Identifier [([ FormalParameterList ])]
  ' Method body
End Sub
```

Here is the function declaration syntax:

```
[Attributes][ProcedureModifier] Function Identifier [([ FormalParameterList ])]
[ As [Attributes] TypeName]
  ' Method body
End Function
```

Notice that functions have an additional As clause that specifies the return value and its type. As discussed in the "Option Strict and Option Explicit" sections earlier in this chapter, if Option Strict is "On", you must specify the types of parameters and return values. If it is "Off" and no return type is specified for the function, an Object type is automatically returned.

Returning values from a method

There are two different ways to return a value from a function. You can use the Return statement (which is new in Visual Basic .NET):

```
Public Function ReturnValue1() As Integer
  Dim intReturnValue As Integer = 1
      Return intReturnValue
End Function
```

You can also return a value from a method by setting the name of the function to the value to be returned:

```
Public Function ReturnValue2() As Integer
  Dim intReturnValue As Integer = 2
  ReturnValue2 = intReturnValue
End Function
```

I recommend using the `Return` statement to return a value from a Visual Basic .NET method, because it is far more intuitive than setting the name of the function to the value being returned. This makes it easier for others who are perusing your code to figure out what's going on.

Details regarding the syntax of method declarations are discussed further in Chapter 5, "Object Orientation in C# and Visual Basic .NET".

Declaring variables

Variables declared within methods are known as local variables (there are no other kind). They are only visible within the method where they are declared. This is different from Visual FoxPro, which allows you to declare variables within a method that are local, private, or global.

> *Having only local variables at your disposal in both Visual Basic .NET and C# is not restrictive. Good programming practice dictates that you should always declare method variables as local. In Visual FoxPro, rather than using private "mystery" variables, if you want a sub method to see a variable, you should pass it explicitly as a parameter.*

To declare a local variable, use the `Dim` statement followed by the variable name, the `As` keyword, and the type of the variable:

```
Dim Count As Integer ' Declare an integer variable named Count
Count = 5              ' Assign Count the value of 5
```

You can also declare a variable and assign it a value in a single command:

```
Dim Height As Integer = 6 ' Declare an int variable and assign it a value of 6
```

If you want to declare multiple variables of the same type in a single statement, simply separate them with commas:

```
Dim Top, Left As Integer
```

When you declare multiple values in a single line, you can't specify default values as you can in C#. However, Visual Basic .NET does allow you to do something you can't in C#—declare multiple variables of different types in a single line.

```
Dim Bottom As Integer, FieldName As String
```

Member variables

As mentioned previously, variables declared at the method level are known as local variables. However, variables declared at the class level are known as *member variables* or *instance variables*:

```
Public Class MemberAndLocalVariables

    Private Test1 As String = "Test1" ' Declare a member variable

    Public Sub DeclareVariables()
        Dim Test2 As String = "Test2" ' Declare a local variable

        MessageBox.Show("Displaying " & Test1, 'Member Variable')
        MessageBox.Show("Displaying " & Test2, 'Local Variable')

    End Sub

End Class
```

At first, it may seem that member variables are the same as Visual FoxPro properties, but they're not. In addition to member variables, VB .NET classes can also have properties, which are discussed in Chapter 5, "Object-Orientation in C# and Visual Basic .NET". For now, just think of member variables as variables declared at the class level that are accessible to all methods in the class.

One other point to note is you can reference member variables the same way you reference local variables. You don't need a qualifier such as "this" as you do in Visual FoxPro. In the previous example, you could have referenced the Test1 field as "Me.Test1". The keyword Me in Visual Basic .NET is equivalent to "This" in Visual FoxPro.

Member variable modifiers

There are five different accessibility modifiers you can apply to member variables (**Table 1**).

Table 1. Field modifiers allow you to specify the visibility of your fields

Modifier	Description
public	Access is not restricted
friend	Access is limited to the current project
protected	Access is limited to the containing class or subclasses
protected friend	Access is limited to the current project or to subclasses
private	Access is limited to the containing class

It's usually best to specify that a member variable is private. To promote this practice, if you don't declare an accessibility modifier, Visual Basic .NET considers it private by default. If you want other classes to have access to this field, rather than changing the accessibility modifier, you should create a protected or public property (for details, see the "Properties" section in Chapter 5, "Object-Orientation in C# and Visual Basic .NET").

Value and reference types

In Chapter 3, "Introduction to C#", the "Value and reference types" section discussed the difference between value and reference types in the .NET Framework. The distinction between these two different types is the same for all .NET languages—including Visual Basic .NET. Refer to this section in chapter 3 for more details.

The string type

Although the commands used to manipulate a string make it seem like a value type, a string is actually a reference type.

You assign a value to a string variable using a string literal enclosed in double quotes:

```
Dim Caption As String = ".NET for VFP Developers"
```

Unlike Visual FoxPro, you can't use a single quote or square brackets to delimit strings (the single quote is reserved for comments in VB .NET). You concatenate strings in Visual Basic .NET by using either an ampersand (&) or a plus (+) sign (as in VFP):

```
MessageBox.Show(str1 & " " & str2, "Concatenate with &")
MessageBox.Show(str1 + " " + str2, "Concatenate with +")
```

Again, the next logical question is, "How do I create a string literal that contains double quotes such as Louis "Satchmo" Armstrong"? You can do this easily by using two double quote marks consecutively:

```
Dim ManlyMen As String = "Louis ""Satchmo"" Armstrong"
```

Visual Basic .NET does not recognize any other special character escapes within a string (such as "\n" for a new line in C#). For details, see the "The string type" section in Chapter 3, "Introduction to C#".

Rather than using character escapes, VB .NET provides enumerated values instead (**Table 2**). For details, see the "Enumerations" section later in this chapter.

Table 2. VB .NET has enumerated values you can concatenate to your strings. This table contains a partial list.

Enumeration	Description
CrLf	Carriage return / linefeed
Cr	Carriage return
Lf	Line feed
NewLine	New line character (same as carriage return / line feed)
Tab	Tab
FormFeed	Form feed

If you import the Microsoft.VisualBasic.ControlChars namespace, you can simply use the values specified in the "Enumeration" column of Table 2. For example:

```
MessageBox.Show("Line 1" + NewLine + "Line 2", "New Line Demo")
```

Strings as reference types

.NET runtime treats strings a bit differently than other reference types. From a practical perspective, this only becomes an issue when you are concatenating a number of strings together (such as in a loop), because the runtime can proliferate an excess amount of string data on the heap. In situations such as this, you should use the .NET StringBuilder class instead of using Strings.

The StringBuilder class has an Append method you use to concatenate strings together:

```
Dim StrBuilder As New StringBuilder()
StrBuilder.Append("Texas, ")
StrBuilder.Append("New Mexico, ")
StrBuilder.Append("Colorado")
MessageBox.Show(StrBuilder.ToString(), "StringBuilder")
```

Enumerations

Visual Basic .NET allows you to define your own complex value types. One of these value types is enumerations and the other is structures (covered in Chapter 5, "Object Orientation in C# and VB .NET").

Enumerations are a convenience feature of Visual Basic .NET that allows you to group related constants together. For more information on the beauty of enumerations, check out "Enumerations" in Chapter 3, "Introduction to C#".

Here is an example of declaring an enumeration in Visual Basic .NET:

```
Public Enum Months As Integer
   January = 1
   February = 2
   March = 3
   April = 4
   May = 5
   June = 6
   July = 7
```

```
August = 8
September = 9
October = 10
November = 11
December = 12
End Enum
```

You access an enumeration by referencing its name and specifying the desired member. The compiler converts it to its associated integer value:

```
Public Class EnumerationTest
    Public Function GetBookPubMonth() As Integer
        ' Access the enumeration
        Dim PubMonth As Months = Months.September
    Return PubMonth
    End Function
End Class
```

Although an incrementing integer is the most common form of an enumeration, your enumeration constant values can be any integer value, including negative numbers, and in any order. For example, the following enumeration lists three people's last names in alphabetical order, causing their windsurfing ability rating to appear in non-sequential order:

```
Public Enum WindSurfingAbility As Integer
    Egger = 9
    Fabulous_Ferguson = 8
    McNeish = -3
    Strahl = 10
End Enum
```

Although enumerations are Integer types by default, you can specify that they are Byte, Integer, Long, or Short. For example:

```
Public Enum HairLength As Long
```

As Long specifies that the HairLength class is derived from the type "Long". For details on subclassing and inheritance, see Chapter 5, "Object Orientation in C# and Visual Basic .NET.

Arrays

All arrays in VB .NET are zero-based, meaning the first element of the array is zero (0), rather than one (1) as in Visual FoxPro. In addition, all arrays must contain values of the same type. You can't mix and match integers, strings, dates, and so on in a single array.

Declaring Arrays

In Visual Basic .NET, arrays are declared the same way as other variables, except you add parentheses after the array name:

```
Dim KidsAges() As Integer
```

You can also declare an array and size it in one step:

```
Dim KidsNames(2) As String
```

If you compare this line of VB .NET code to the same C# code, you'll notice a difference in the declared size of the array. In C#, I would set the size of the array to three (3) elements. Here, it looks like I've sized the array to only contain only two—however, this is not the case. In order to maintain backward compatibility with Visual Basic 6, the way you declare arrays in Visual Basic .NET is slightly different from other .NET languages.

When you declare the size of an array in VB .NET, you declare the upper limit of the array rather than the total number of elements. For example, in the KidsNames array declared here, I want a total number of three elements. Since arrays are zero-based, the first element is zero, the second element is one, and the last element is two. In VB .NET, I use this upper element value to specify the size of the array.

Although this is non-standard, this concession was made by Microsoft's VB .NET engineers to allow backward compatibility with Visual Basic 6.

Redimensioning arrays

Unlike C#, you *can* change the size of any array dimension by using VB .NET's ReDim statement. The following code shows how to dimension and redimension an array:

```
Dim ScaryAnimals() As String = {"Lions", "Tigers"}
ReDim Preserve ScaryAnimals(2)
```

The first line of this code dimensions the array size to two implicitly, since I have specified two string elements (Lions and Tigers). The second line redimensions the array to hold three elements (remember, VB .NET's idiosyncrasy—you specify the highest element number rather than the total number of elements). Notice the use of the keyword `Preserve`. If you do not add this keyword, VB .NET clears out the other array elements when it redimensions the array. Note that `ReDim` can only be used on an existing array—you can't initialize a new array by using `ReDim`. Also, you can only change the size of an array dimension using `ReDim`; you can't change the number of dimensions.

Storing values to arrays

You set initial values of array elements when you declare an array:

```
Dim KidsMiddleNames() As String = {"Christopher", "Mark", "James"}
```

Or, you can store values in the array elements after declaring the array:

```
Dim KidsNames(2) As String
KidsNames(0) = "Jordan"
KidsNames(1) = "Timothy"
KidsNames(2) = "Alexander"
```

Sorting arrays

You easily sort the elements of an array by calling the Array class' Sort method:

```
Array.Sort(KidsNames)
```

You reverse the sort order by calling the Array class' Reverse method:

```
Array.Reverse(KidsNames)
```

Multidimensional arrays

In Visual FoxPro, you can create one and two-dimensional arrays. Visual Basic .NET allows you to create multidimensional arrays—arrays with three or more dimensions.

Multidimensional arrays are either rectangular (every row has the same number of columns) or jagged (each row can have a different number of columns).

Defining multidimensional rectangular arrays

In VB .NET, you declare a multidimensional, rectangular array by adding one or more commas within the parentheses of the array declaration. Each comma you add specifies an additional array dimension. Here is the definition of a two-dimensional, rectangular array:

```
Dim ArrayKids(,) As String = {{"Jordan", "McNeish"}, _
             {"Timothy", "McNeish"}, _
             {"Alexander", "McNeish"}}
```

Defining jagged arrays

A jagged array is an "array of arrays". They are also multidimensional arrays, but each row can have a different number of columns. You define a jagged array by adding an extra set of parentheses for each dimension. In the following example, the jagged array has three elements in its first dimension. Its second dimension has a different size for each row. The first row has three columns, the second row has two columns, and the third row has one column:

```
Dim Musicians()() As String = {New String() {"Stevie", "Ray", "Vaughn"}, _
    New String() {"Jimi", "Hendrix"}, _
    New String() {"Bono"}}

' Show all three names of the first musician
MessageBox.Show(Musicians(0)(0) + " " & _
Musicians(0)(1) & " " & _
Musicians(0)(2), "Jagged Arrays")
```

Type conversions

When working with strongly typed languages, converting between different data types is an important consideration. VB .NET provides both implicit and explicit type conversion.

> For a list of VB .NET data types and a comparison between VB .NET, C#, and VFP data types, check out "Appendix C – Data Type Comparison".

Implicit type conversions

Visual Basic .NET implicitly converts some values from one type to another. In the following example, VB .NET converts a short value to an integer and then to a double:

```
Dim x As Short = 10
Dim y As Integer = x
Dim z As Double = y
```

Table 3 lists the types that Visual Basic .NET can implicitly (automatically) convert.

Table 3. Types that Visual Basic .NET can implicitly convert.

From Type	To Type
byte	ushort, short, uint, int, ulong, long, float, double, decimal
sbyte	short, int, long, float, double, decimal
short	int, long, float, double, decimal
ushort	uint, int, ulong, long, float, double, decimal
char	ushort, uint, int, ulong, long, float, double, decimal
int	long, float, double, decimal
uint	long, ulong, float, double, decimal
long	float, double, decimal
ulong	float, double, decimal
float	double

Explicit type conversion

If the compiler refuses to implicitly convert a value from one type to another, you can explicitly convert it yourself. Visual Basic .NET provides a number of ways to do this.

The first method is to use Visual Basic .NET's conversion keywords (**Table 4**).

Table 4. Visual Basic .NET provides conversions keywords you can use to explicitly convert values from one type to another.

Keyword	Description
CBool	Converts any numeric type, String, Object to Boolean
CByte	Converts any numeric type, any enumerated type, Boolean, String, Object to Byte
CChar	Converts String, Object to Char
CDate	Converts String, Object to Date
CDbl	Converts Any numeric type, Boolean, String, Object to Double
CDec	Converts any numeric type, Boolean, String, Object to Decimal
CInt	Converts any numeric type, Boolean, String, Object to Integer
CLng	Converts any numeric type, Boolean String, Object to Long
CObj	Converts any type to Object
CShort	Converts any numeric type, Boolean, String, Object to Short
CSng	Converts any numeric type, Boolean, String, Object to Single
CStr	Converts any numeric type, Boolean, Char, Char() array, Date, Object to String

For example, to convert an Integer to Byte you use the `CByte` keyword:

```
Dim x As Integer = 20
Dim y As Byte = CByte(x)
```

You can also use the System.Convert class to perform conversions instead. The Convert class has a number of different conversion methods to use for converting values (**Table 5**). For example, to perform the same conversion in the previous example using the Convert class, you do it this way:

```
Dim x As Integer = 20
Dim y As Byte = Convert.ToByte(x)
```

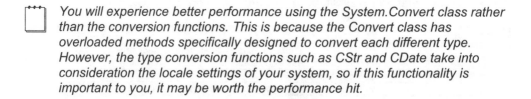

You will experience better performance using the System.Convert class rather than the conversion functions. This is because the Convert class has overloaded methods specifically designed to convert each different type. However, the type conversion functions such as CStr and CDate take into consideration the locale settings of your system, so if this functionality is important to you, it may be worth the performance hit.

Table 5. The Convert class contains a number of methods to use for converting values from one type to another. This is a partial list.

Keyword	Description
ToBoolean	Converts a value to Boolean
ToByte	Converts a value to an 8-bit unsigned integer
ToChar	Converts a value to a Unicode character
ToDateTime	Converts a value to DateTime
ToDecimal	Converts a value to Decimal
ToDouble	Converts a value to Double
ToInt16	Converts a value to a 16-bit signed Integer
ToInt32	Converts a value to a 32-bit signed Integer
ToInt64	Converts a value to a 64-bit signed integer
ToSByte	Converts a value to an 8-bit signed integer
ToSingle	Converts a value to a single-precision floating point number
ToUInt16	Converts a value to a 16-bit unsigned integer
ToUInt32	Converts a value to a 32-bit unsigned integer
ToUInt64	Converts a value to a 64-bit unsigned integer

The CType function

The conversion keywords and System.Convert class discussed in the previous section are great for converting basic value types, but you need something else if you want to convert more complex objects. That something else is the `CType` function.

`CType` is a Visual Basic .NET function that allows you to convert an expression to a data type, an object, structure, class, or interface. The `CType` function accepts two parameters. The first parameter is an expression to be converted. Often this first parameter contains an object reference. The second parameter is the destination type you want the expression converted to. For example, the following code converts an integer to decimal:

```
Dim x As Integer = 100
Dim y As Decimal = CType(x, Decimal)
```

Converting to string

If you need to convert a value to a string, the Object class has a ToString method that is inherited by all classes in the .NET Framework. This method returns the string representation of the object. So, for example, do the following to get a string representation of an integer:

```
Dim i As Integer = 10
Dim s As String = i.ToString()
```

Converting strings with `Val`

If you need to convert strings to value types, you can use one of the conversion keywords listed in the "Explicit type conversion" section earlier in this chapter. In addition, you can use the `Val` function, which is a little more forgiving when it comes to converting strings to numeric values—it lets you convert strings that contain both numeric and character values.

Val() stops converting a string when it hits a character that it can't recognize as part of a number. In the following example, the string containing the value "567 Test" is converted by the Val() function. The resulting value is 567:

```
Dim i As Double
Dim z As String = "567 Test"
i = Val(z)      ' Returns 567
```

Boxing and unboxing in Visual Basic .NET

As described previously, boxing is the process of converting a value type to a reference type. Unboxing is the process of converting the value of a reference type back to a value type.

For example, Boxing occurs implicitly when you store an integer into an object:

```
Dim x As Integer
Dim y As Object = x
```

For a diagram showing what happens in memory when a value is boxed, check out "Boxing and unboxing values" in Chapter 3, "Introduction to C#".

In Visual Basic .NET, you cannot explicitly unbox values the same way as you can in C#.

> *Because Visual Basic .NET cannot explicitly unbox values, it relies on the helper functions found in the Microsoft.VisualBasic.Helpers namespace, which are far less efficient than C#'s explicit unboxing.*

The `TypeOf` operator

You can determine if an object is of a particular type by using the `TypeOf` operator. This is useful in situations where a method receives a generic Object parameter and wants to determine its specific type. For example, the following method receives a parameter of type Object. It then checks if it is of the type MyClass1:

```
Public Class TypeOfOperatorDemo
    Public Sub CheckClass(ByVal TestObject As Object)
        If TypeOf TestObject Is MyClass1 Then
            MessageBox.Show("TestObject is MyClass1", "TypeOf operator")
        Else
            MessageBox.Show("TestObject is not MyClass1", "TypeOf operator")
        End If
    End Sub
End Class
```

`If` statement

Visual Basic .NET's `If` statement is similar to Visual FoxPro's IF..ENDIF statement. If the expression being evaluated is true, the code following `Then` is executed. Optionally, you can add an `Else` statement to the `If` that gets executed if the condition expression evaluates to False. You can also nest `If` statements.

```
Dim HavingFun As Boolean = True
If HavingFun Then
  MessageBox.Show("We are having fun!", "if demo")
Else
  MessageBox.Show("We are NOT having fun!", "if demo")
End If
```

If you want to test an additional condition in the `Else`, use `ElseIf`:

```
Dim MyInteger As Integer = 99
If MyInteger < 10 Then
  MessageBox.Show("MyInteger is less than 10", "If...End If")
ElseIf MyInteger < 100 Then
  MessageBox.Show("MyInteger is more than 9, but less than 100", "If...End If")
End If
```

Select...Case statement

The Visual Basic .NET `Select...Case` statement is equivalent to Visual FoxPro's DO CASE statement. Based on the value of the expression, one of the case statements is selected for execution. You can specify a `Case Else`, which is the same as VFP's OTHERWISE clause. If the switch expression does not match any of the cases, control is passed to the `Case Else`. If no `Case Else` is present, control passes to the first command following the `End Select`.

```
Dim TestValue As Integer = 3
Select Case TestValue
  Case 1
      MessageBox.Show("TestValue = 1", "Select...Case")
  Case 2
      MessageBox.Show("TestValue = 2", "Select...Case")
  Case 3, 4
      MessageBox.Show("TestValue = 3 or 4", "Select...Case")
  Case Else
      MessageBox.Show("TestValue is not 1, 2, 3, or 4", "Select...Case")
End Select
```

Unlike C#, you don't have to add a `break` statement at the end of each case, which is a nice feature!

For...Next loop

Visual Basic .NET's `For...Next` loops are equivalent to Visual FoxPro's FOR...ENDFOR command. It iterates through a loop while a particular condition is true.

In the `For...Next` loop, the loop executes for as long as the counter variable is between the specified values. The `Next` statement is typically used to increment or decrement the counter value.

```
Dim i As Integer
Dim Message As String

For i = 0 To 3
  Message += "Message " + i.ToString() + NewLine
Next i
```

You exit out of a `For...Next` loop at any point by using the `Exit For` statement.

While loop

The `While` loop is equivalent to Visual FoxPro's DO...WHILE loop. It is a pre-test loop meaning that if the condition evaluates to false, the loop is not executed at all. `While` loops are often used to repeat a block of code for an undetermined number of times.

```
Public Sub WhileLoopDemo()
    Dim Condition As Boolean = True
    While Condition
        Dim i As Integer = 1
```

```
            MessageBox.Show("While loop count " + i.ToString(), _
               "While loop")
            i += 1
            Condition = False
      End While
End Sub
```

You exit out of a While loop at any point by using the Exit While statement.

Do loop

The Visual Basic .NET Do loop repeats a block of statements while a condition is true or until a condition becomes true. If you use the Do While construct, the loop executes while a condition is true. If you use the Do Until construct, the loop executes until the condition becomes true.

The While and Until keywords can be used at either the top or bottom of the loop. If they are used at the top of the loop, the condition is checked before the loop is executed. If they are placed at the bottom of the loop as shown in the following example, the condition is checked after the loop executes. This means the loop always executes at least once. This is different than Visual FoxPro's DO WHILE loop, which only evaluates the condition at the top of the loop.

```
Dim Condition As Boolean = False
Do
  Dim i As Integer = 1
  MessageBox.Show("Do While loop count " + i.ToString(), _
    "Do...While loop")
  i += 1
Loop While Condition
```

You exit out of a Do loop at any point by using the Exit Do statement.

For Each loop

The Visual Basic .NET For Each loop executes a group of statements for each element in an array or item in a collection. It is equivalent to Visual FoxPro's FOR EACH command.

```
Dim VersionList, Version As String
Dim VSNetVersions() As String = {"Standard", "Professional", _
  "Enterprise Developer", _
  "Enterprise Architect"}
For Each Version In VSNetVersions
  VersionList += "VS .NET " + Version + NewLine
Next
MessageBox.Show(VersionList, "ForEach loop")
```

You exit out of a For Each loop at any point by using the Exit For statement.

With statement

Visual Basic .NET's `With` statement is equivalent to Visual FoxPro's WITH...ENDWITH command. You specify an object reference at the top of the `With` statement, then refer to properties and methods of the object within the statement by specifying the name of the object. Any expression starting with a period in the `With` statement is evaluated as if it is prefixed by the object name. For example:

```
Dim ReturnDemo As New ReturnValuesDemo()
Dim ReturnValue As Integer
With ReturnDemo
  ReturnValue = .ReturnValue1()
  ReturnValue = .ReturnValue2()
End With
```

XML Documentation Tool

Although XML documentation was not built into Visual Studio .NET for VB .NET, several months after the release of VS .NET, a stand-alone tool was released by Microsoft that allows you to create XML documentation for VB .NET projects. To get this tool, download it from the VB .NET "GotDotNet" Web site: http://www.gotdotnet.com/team/vb.

This tool works a bit differently than the Visual Studio .NET XML documentation tool for C#. With C# XML documentation, you enter your XML comments directly in your code. These comments are compiled into the assembly and can be viewed in an Object Browser and with IntelliSense. In addition VS .NET automatically builds XML Comment Web pages for you from these XML comments (see Chapter 3, "Introduction to C#" for details).

With the VB .NET XML Documentation Tool, your XML comments are not stored in the source code, but in a separate XML file. Like C#, these XML comments can also be viewed in an Object Browser and with IntelliSense. However, there is no facility to create Comment Web pages from these VB .NET XML comments. In addition, since the comments are not stored in the source code this means that:

1. Either, you don't put any comments in your source code (*not* recommended).

2. Or, you duplicate your comments—one copy in your source code and one in the XML file.

I see this as a serious limitation of this tool. You really *should* place comments in your source code for your benefit and the benefit of developers who have to examine your code.

After downloading the VB .NET XML Documentation Tool, you run it by double-clicking the "XML Documentation Tool.exe" file. This launches the XML Documentation Tool dialog (**Figure 4**).

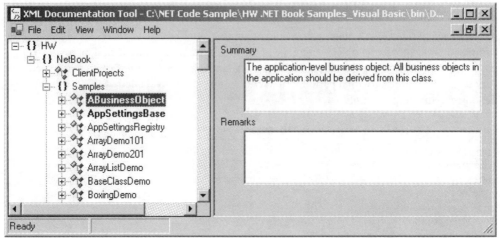

Figure 4. *The XML Documentation Tool for Visual Basic .NET allows you to create XML comments for developers who do not have access to your source code.*

Check out the associated ReadMe.htm file for information on how to use this tool to create XML comments for your VB .NET code.

Conclusion

Visual Basic .NET has come a long way from Visual Basic 6 and is now a powerful, fully object-oriented language. It's as different as FoxPro 2.6 and Visual FoxPro (and then some). Of all the .NET languages, its syntax is most similar to Visual FoxPro and, as you would expect from Visual Basic, there are a number of convenience features that make it worth looking at as your programming language of choice. Since Microsoft has always stressed Visual Basic's ease of use, you can expect this emphasis to translate into even more convenience features in the future.

Chapter 5
Object Orientation in
C# and Visual Basic .NET

With the release of Visual FoxPro 3.0, FoxPro became object-oriented. For those of you who have already made the leap to object-oriented programming, you know how difficult the transition can be. Fortunately, once you've learned OOP in VFP, it's easy to learn the basics of OOP in .NET. This chapter shows how different object-oriented features are implemented in C# and Visual Basic .NET, while providing a comparison to Visual FoxPro's object-orientation.

By its very nature, this chapter is one of the more controversial in this book. The two previous chapters were devoted to the basics of C# and Visual Basic .NET syntax, but this chapter moves into the meatier topic of object-orientation, providing a side-by-side comparison of the two languages. Many of you may use the information in these chapters to decide which .NET language to choose—and choice of language is often a religious issue!

As in the previous chapters, I'll point out the differences in C# and VB .NET and offer some editorial comments on the approach I think is better. Although both languages compile down to the same intermediate language (MSIL), they implement .NET's object-oriented features a little differently—and in some cases, one language has object-oriented features not available in the other language. Throughout this chapter, I'll draw comparisons to Visual FoxPro's object-oriented features so you can leverage your existing knowledge of OOP.

Where do you put your code?

Visual FoxPro allows you to place code in class methods, in functions or procedures stored in PRG files, or as procedural code stored in PRG files.

In contrast, all code in C# must be placed in classes. This is similar to other pure object-oriented programming languages, such as Java and SmallTalk that impose more discipline on developers.

Visual Basic .NET takes an approach more like Visual FoxPro, in allowing you to place code and variables in either classes or *modules*. Similar to a class, a module is derived from the System.Object class and used to encapsulate items contained within it. The main differences between a class and a module are a class can be instantiated and implement interfaces, but a module cannot.

Another difference is in referencing members of a class, you must specify the name of the class followed by the member (for example, Customer.GetCreditLimit). In contrast, members declared in a module are like global variables and functions accessed from anywhere within your application. By default, members of a module are *shared* (For details, see the "Instance and static (Shared) members" section later in this chapter). You can compare placing code in modules to creating global variables, functions, and procedures in a Visual FoxPro PRG.

Are modules a "good thing" or a "bad thing"? I think the answer to this is subjective. Personally, I tend to prefer a more "pure" object-oriented approach, because I believe it promotes better programming practices. However, you may prefer the convenience of being able to create standalone functions and procedures in a Visual Basic .NET module.

Classes

At the very heart of any object-oriented language are classes. I'll begin by discussing the mechanics of where and how you define classes.

In Visual FoxPro, you define classes visually in VCX files or manually in PRG files. Defining classes in C# and VB .NET takes an approach somewhere in between. In these languages, you can place class definitions in source files (either .cs or .vb files), which are similar to Visual FoxPro's PRG files. However, Visual Studio .NET lets you easily navigate to a particular class and a specific method in a source code file using the class and member combo boxes at the top of the code-editing window.

The class combo box (**Figure 1**) contains a list of all classes defined in a source code file. Selecting a class from this combo box takes you to the class definition in the source code.

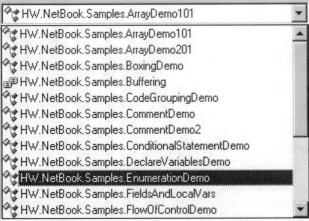

Figure 1. *The class combo box, at the top left of the code-editing window, contains a list of all classes defined in the source code file.*

The member combo box (**Figure 2**) contains a list of all members defined for the currently selected class. Selecting a member from this combo box takes you to the member in the source code file.

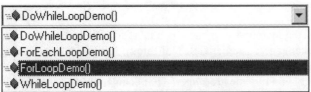

Figure 2. *The member combo box at the top right of the code-editing window contains a list of all members for the currently selected class.*

As you manually page or arrow up/down in the source code file, the selected items in these boxes change to reflect your current location in the source code—a nice feature.

Defining classes

In Chapter 3, "Introduction to C#", and Chapter 4, "Introduction to Visual Basic .NET", you learned the basics of defining classes. In this chapter I'll review some of that information and expand on it.

Here's an example of the most simple class definition in C#:

```
public class SimpleClass
{
}
```

And in VB .NET:

```
Public Class SimpleClass

End Class
```

In both cases, this code defines a class named "SimpleClass". The `public` keyword is an access modifier specifying the visibility of the class. If you don't specify an access modifier, the visibility defaults to "internal" for C# and the equivalent "friend" for VB .NET. **Table 1** lists the access modifiers that apply to classes.

Table 1. C# and VB .NET class access modifiers

C# Access modifier	VB .NET Access modifier	Description
public	public	Indicates no restrictions for accessing the class.
internal	friend	Indicates the class is only accessible from code within the same assembly where the class is defined.

Defining fields (member variables)

As discussed in Chapter 3, "Introduction to C#", variables declared at the class level are known as *fields*, and as discussed in Chapter 4, "Introduction to Visual Basic .NET", they are known as *member variables* in VB .NET. I don't want to skip mentioning this here, but check out the corresponding chapter for details on each of these.

Defining properties

C# and Visual Basic .NET properties are similar to Visual FoxPro properties with associated access and assign methods. They are implemented as `get` and `set` accessor methods containing any code you want. Here is an example of a property used to retrieve and store the value of a private field (member variable in VB .NET).

In C#:

```
private int age = 99;

public int Age
{
  get
  {
      return this.age;
  }
  set
  {
      this.age = value;
      }
  }
```

And in Visual Basic .NET:

```
Private _age As Integer = 99

Public Property Age() As Integer
    Get
        Return _age
    End Get
    Set(ByVal Value As Integer)
        _age = Value
    End Set
End Property
```

In this code, the property has a `get` method used to retrieve the value from a private field, and a `set` method that stores a value to the private field. Notice the C# code sample takes advantage of C#'s case sensitivity, by naming the private field `age` and the property `Age`. Because VB .NET isn't case sensitive, you need to give any associated member variable a different name than the property.

> It is not required for a property to have an associated field (member variable), although they often do. For example, rather than getting and setting the value of a field, code within a property might read and write data instead.

Notice in the C# sample code, the `set` method uses an intrinsic parameter named `value`. When client code saves a value to a property, it is stored in this intrinsic `value` variable. In contrast, although the `Set` method in the VB .NET sample code explicitly declares a variable named `Value`, you are allowed to change the name of this variable (although I can't think of a compelling reason to do so).

Read-only and write-only properties

In C#, if you want to create a read-only property, all you have to do is leave out the `set` accessor method. For example:

```
private int height;

public int Height
{
  get
  {
      return this.height;
  }
}
```

You do the same thing in Visual Basic .NET, but you must also add the `ReadOnly` keyword to the property definition:

```
Private _height As Integer

Public ReadOnly Property Height() As Integer
    Get
        Return Me._height
    End Get
End Property
```

If you want to create a write-only property in C#, just leave out the `get` accessor method. You do the same thing in Visual Basic .NET, but you must also add the `WriteOnly` keyword to the property definition.

Defining methods

A class doesn't do much without methods. Here's an example of a simple method declaration in C#:

```
public void SimpleMethod()
{
}
```

And in Visual Basic .NET:

```
Public Sub SimpleMethod()

End Sub
```

This code defines a method named "SimpleMethod" that returns nothing (`void`, in C#). Both C# and VB .NET require parentheses after the name of the method. As shown in the next section, these parentheses contain a list of parameters passed to the method. In this case, even though there are no parameters, you must still add the parentheses as a placeholder.

Here's an example of a C# method that returns a boolean value:

```
public bool SimpleMethodBool()
{
  return true;
}
```

This is exactly the same as the previous C# method declaration, except I specified the return value is boolean rather than void, and I added a line of code that returns a boolean value. This is extremely consistent syntax.

Now here's the same method in Visual Basic .NET:

```
Public Function SimpleMethodBool() As Boolean
   Return True
End Function
```

Notice the method is declared as a function rather than a subroutine (`Sub`) and has an additional `As` clause specifying the type of the return value. What's going on here?

In VB .NET, to specify a method return nothing, you must declare it as a subroutine (`Sub`). If a method returns a value, you must declare it as a Function and use the `As` clause to specify the return value type.

In all the methods shown above, the `public` keyword is an access modifier specifying the class visibility. **Table 2** lists all access modifiers for C# and VB .NET members.

Table 2. C# and VB .NET class member access modifiers

C# Access modifier	VB .NET Access modifier	Description
public	Public	No restrictions for accessing the member.
protected	Protected	The member is only accessible from within the class or from classes derived from the class.
internal	Friend	The member is only accessible from code within the assembly where the member is defined.
protected internal	Protected Friend	The member is only accessible from within the class or from code within the assembly where the member is defined.
private	Private	The member is only accessible within the containing class.

Specifying method parameters

There are a few different kinds of method parameters in C# and VB .NET (**Table 3**) described in the following sections.

Table 3. C# and VB .NET method parameters

C# parameter keywords	VB .NET Access modifier	Description
(no keyword needed)	ByVal	Value parameter—the default for C# and VB .NET
reference	ByRef	Reference parameter
params	ParamArray	Parameter array
out	Not required	Output parameter
n/a	Optional	Optional parameter

Value parameters

Just as in Visual FoxPro, the default parameter type in both C# and Visual Basic .NET is a *value parameter*. In practical terms, if the method you call changes the value of the parameter, the value is not changed in the calling method. Here's an example of a method with a value parameter in C#:

```
public void ValueParam(int age)
{
  age++;
}
```

And in Visual Basic .NET:

```
Public Sub ValueParam(ByVal age As Integer)
    age = age + 1
End Sub
```

In C#, if you don't specify otherwise, the parameter is passed by value. In VB .NET, if you don't specify the kind of parameter, Visual Studio .NET automatically inserts the `ByVal` keyword for you.

Reference parameters

When you pass a parameter by reference, if the method changes its value, the value is also changed in the calling method. Here's an example using a reference parameter in C#:

```
public void ReferenceParam(ref int age)
{
  age++;
}
```

And in Visual Basic .NET:

```
Public Sub ReferenceParam(ByRef age As Integer)
    age += 1
End Sub
```

In C#, if a method accepts a reference parameter, you must specify in the method call that you are passing the value by reference:

```
PtDemo.ReferenceParam(ref age);
```

In Visual Basic .NET, you don't have to specify you're passing the value by reference:

```
PtDemo.ReferenceParam(Age)
```

Array parameters

You can pass a variable number of parameters to a C# or VB .NET method by declaring an array parameter. Within the method body, you can use a `foreach` loop to access all items in the passed array.

In C#:

```
public void ArrayParam(params int[] ages)
{
  string AgeMsg = "";

  foreach (int i in ages)
  {
      AgeMsg += i + ": ";
  }

  MessageBox.Show("Ages: " + AgeMsg, "Array Parameter demo");
}
```

In Visual Basic .NET:

```
Public Sub ArrayParam(ByVal ParamArray ages() As Integer)
    Dim AgeMsg As String = ""

    Dim i As Integer
    For Each i In ages
        AgeMsg += i.ToString() & ": "
    Next i

    MessageBox.Show("Ages: " & AgeMsg, "Array Parameter demo")
End Sub 'ArrayParam
```

Output parameters

C# has output parameters—a parameter type not available in Visual Basic .NET. An output parameter is similar to a reference parameter, but it allows you to pass a variable to a method without first specifying an initial value. If you remember from Chapter 3, "Introduction to C#", in an effort to encourage good programming practices, C# requires you to specify a value for all variables before using them. Output parameters are the one exception to the rule. To demonstrate, here's a C# method that declares a single output parameter:

```
public void OutParam(out int age)
{
  age = 39;
}
```

And here's an example of code calling this method:

```
int JackBennysAge;
PtDemo.OutParam(out JackBennysAge);
```

Notice this code declares the variable JackBennysAge, but never stores an initial value. So why aren't output parameters available in VB .NET? Because VB .NET does not require you to initialize variables (although it's a good idea to specify initial values anyway!).

Optional parameters

Visual Basic .NET has a type of parameter not available in C#—optional parameters. Optional parameters provide a way to specify a particular parameter that is not mandatory. When declaring an optional parameter, you must specify a default value in case the caller doesn't pass a value for the optional parameter. For example, here's a VB .NET method that declares a single optional parameter with a default value of 50:

```
Public Sub OptionalParam(Optional ByVal age As Integer = 50)
```

At first, optional parameters might seem like a great feature. However, you should probably avoid using them! One reason is C# does not recognize optional parameters—it sees them as mandatory, just like every other parameter. This is an important consideration if you anticipate C# clients may be accessing your code. Optional parameters can also introduce problems if you ever decide to change the default value of the optional parameter. For details, see the MSDN article "Exploiting New Language Features of Visual Basic .NET, Part 2" (http://msdn.microsoft.com/msdnmag/issues/01/08/instincts/instincts0108.asp).

In reality, avoiding optional parameters is not a real loss. You can actually accomplish the same thing by means of *overloaded methods*.

Overloaded methods

In Visual FoxPro, all class methods must have unique names. You may be surprised to learn this is not true in C# or Visual Basic .NET. Both languages allow you to create multiple methods with the same name—as long as the number and type of parameters is different. For example, the following code defines a class with two methods, both named "DisplayMessage".

In C#:

```
public class OverloadedMethodsDemo
{
    public void DisplayMessage(string message, string caption)
    {
        MessageBox.Show(message, caption);
    }

    public void DisplayMessage(string message)
    {
        this.DisplayMessage(message, "Application Message");
    }
}
```

And in Visual Basic .NET:

```
Public Class OverloadedMethodsDemo

    Public Overloads Sub DisplayMessage(ByVal message As String, _
        ByVal caption As String)
```

```
    MessageBox.Show(message, caption)
End Sub 'DisplayMessage

Public Overloads Sub DisplayMessage(ByVal message As String)
    Me.DisplayMessage(message, "Application Message")
End Sub 'DisplayMessage

End Class 'OverloadedMethodsDemo
```

Although these methods have the same name, they have a different *signature*. In object-oriented terminology, the word signature refers to the type and order of a method's parameters. In this case, the first overload of the DisplayMessage method accepts two string parameters—one named "message" and the other named "caption". The second overload accepts only one string parameter named "message".

When a client calls the DisplayMessage method, the compiler examines the parameters passed to the method and determines which overloaded method should be called. For example, the following code instantiates the OverloadedMethodsDemo class. The second line of code calls the DisplayMessage method with a single string parameter, and the third line of code calls the method with two string parameters.

In C#:

```
OverloadedMethodsDemo OverloadDemo = new OverloadedMethodsDemo();
OverloadDemo.DisplayMessage("Overloaded methods are great!");
OverloadDemo.DisplayMessage("Overloaded methods are great!", "Overload demo");
```

In Visual Basic .NET:

```
Dim OverloadDemo As New OverloadedMethodsDemo()
OverloadDemo.DisplayMessage("Overloaded methods are great!")
OverloadDemo.DisplayMessage("Overloaded methods are great!", "Overload demo")
```

The compiler is satisfied with these two calls because there are overloaded methods matching each set of parameters. However, if you try to call the DisplayMessage method with an incorrect number of parameters (for example, no parameters, more than two parameters, or parameters that are not string types), the compiler displays an error message.

Visual Studio .NET's IntelliSense lets you know if a method you are calling is overloaded. For example, **Figure 3** shows the popup displayed by VS .NET when entering code that calls the DisplayMessage overloaded method.

Figure 3. When you enter code that calls an overloaded method in Visual Studio .NET's code editor, a popup displays showing details of the overloaded methods.

So, where would you use overloaded methods? When you have a method with optional parameters, you should create overloaded methods representing the different variations of parameters that can be passed to the method. This is much cleaner than having a single method checking which parameters have been passed.

Constructor methods

All Visual FoxPro classes possess an Init method that automatically executes when a class is instantiated. C# and VB .NET also have constructor methods that perform a similar function.

In C#, you declare a constructor method by adding a method with the same name as the containing class:

```
public class ConstructorDemo
{
  public ConstructorDemo()
  {
  }
}
```

In Visual Basic .NET, you declare a constructor by adding a New method to the class definition:

```
Public Class ConstructorDemo
    Public Sub New()

    End Sub
End Class
```

I actually prefer the VB .NET convention, because it's easier to quickly identify a constructor that's consistently named the same.

Notice in both code samples that neither constructor specifies a return value. This is because .NET constructors are not allowed to return values unlike Visual FoxPro where you can return a boolean False to prevent a class from instantiating.

Constructors with parameters

As in Visual FoxPro, you can specify parameters for constructor methods in .NET. This allows you to pass values to a class when it is first instantiated.

Here's an example in C#:

```
public class ConstructorDemo
{
  private string connectString;

  public ConstructorDemo(string connect)
  {
      this.connectString = connect;
  }
}
```

And in Visual Basic .NET:

```
Public Class ConstructorDemo
    Private connectString As String
```

```
Public Sub New(ByVal connect As String)
    Me.connectString = connect
End Sub

End Class
```

In this code, the value passed in the constructor is used to initialize the value of a private field. If you don't explicitly declare a constructor, a default constructor is automatically provided.

Here is an example of passing a value to the constructor of a class when it is instantiated. In C#:

```
ConstructorDemo ConstructDemo = new
  ConstructorDemo("server=(local);uid=sa;pwd=;database=Northwind;");
```

And in Visual Basic .NET

```
Dim ConstDemo As _
    New ConstructorDemo("server=(local);uid=;pwd=;database=NorthWind;")
```

As with other methods, you can also create overloaded constructor methods. Based on the parameters you pass when instantiating a class, the appropriate constructor is called.

Destructor methods

Visual FoxPro classes have a Destroy method that executes when an object is released. Typically you place code in this method to perform cleanup for the object. This works well because you have complete control over when an object is destroyed in Visual FoxPro.

In contrast, .NET has something called *non-deterministic finalization*. This means you don't have explicit control over when an object is destroyed. When the last reference to a .NET object is released, the object itself is not released from memory. The object is not released until the next time the common language runtime's garbage collector runs (see the "Garbage collection" section later in this chapter for details).

In both C# and Visual Basic .NET classes, you can add a Finalize method that executes when the object is destroyed. Just remember you can't determine when this method is executed.

Class inheritance

One key feature of object-orientation is class inheritance, also known as *implementation inheritance*. C# and Visual Basic .NET both have single inheritance, meaning a class can only have one parent class. In .NET, the term *base class* is used in place of Visual FoxPro's "parent class". Personally, I prefer the term "parent class" because it's more descriptive and more readily understood.

Specifying a base class

When you define a class in C# or VB .NET, if you don't specify otherwise, its default base class is the .NET Framework's System.Object class. Here is an example showing how to specify a base class.

In C#:

```
public class BaseClassDemo : Component
{
}
```

In Visual Basic .NET:

```
Public Class BaseClassDemo
    Inherits Component
End Class
```

This code defines a class named BaseClassDemo derived from the .NET Framework's Component class (System.ComponentModel.Component). In C#, you declare a base class by placing a colon followed by the base class name (`: Component`) at the end of the first line of the class declaration. In Visual Basic .NET, you place the keyword `Inherits` followed by the base class name on the second line of the class declaration.

Inheritance works the same way in .NET as it does in Visual FoxPro. A subclass inherits all members (properties, events, methods, and fields) from its base class, including implementation code.

Overriding inherited methods

At times, you may want a class to override an inherited method. In Visual FoxPro, the simple act of placing code in a method causes the method to be overridden. Unfortunately, in VFP all it takes is a single space character to unintentionally override a parent method.

You can "accidentally" override a method in C# and Visual Basic .NET by creating a method in a class with the same name and signature as an inherited method. For example, the following code declares a class named MyBaseClass with a single method named DisplayMessage. It also declares a subclass of MyBaseClass named "OverrideMethodDemo" that contains a duplicate DisplayMessage method.

In C#:

```
public class MyBaseClass
{
  public void DisplayMessage()
  {
      MessageBox.Show("Base class method!", "Override demo");
  }
}

public class OverrideMethodDemo : MyBaseClass
{
  public void DisplayMessage()
  {
      MessageBox.Show("Subclass method!", "Override demo");
  }
}
```

In Visual Basic .NET:

```
Public Class MyBaseClass
    Public Sub DisplayMessage()
        MessageBox.Show("Base class method!", "Override Demo")
    End Sub
End Class

Public Class OverrideMethodDemo
    Public Sub DisplayMessage()
        MessageBox.Show("Subclass method!", "Override Demo")
    End Sub
End Class
```

When you run this code, the OverrideMethodDemo.DisplayMessage method is executed, but the base class method is not. In reality, this is not a legal way to override a method in either C# or Visual Basic .NET. In both languages, the compiler catches this error and displays it as a warning (**Figure 4**).

cannot override inherited member '...DisplayMessage()' because it is not marked virtual, abstract, or override (C#)

'DisplayMessage' overrides a sub in the base class 'MyBaseClass' that is not declared 'Overridable'. (VB .NET)

Figure 4. _The C# and VB .NET compilers display a warning if you create a method in a class with the same name and signature as an inherited method._

The following code demonstrates the proper syntax for overriding methods by using the override keyword (C#) or the Overrides keyword (VB .NET) in the method declaration.
In C#:

```
public class MyBaseClass
{
    public virtual void DisplayMessage()
    {
        MessageBox.Show("Base class method!", "Override demo");
    }
}

public class OverrideMethodDemo : MyBaseClass
{
    public override void DisplayMessage()
    {
        MessageBox.Show("Subclass method!", "Override demo");
    }
}
```

And in Visual Basic .NET:

```
Public Class MyBaseClass
    Public Overridable Sub DisplayMessage()
        MessageBox.Show("Base class method!", "Override Demo")
    End Sub
End Class
```

```
Public Class OverrideMethodDemo
    Inherits MyBaseClass
    Public Overrides Sub DisplayMessage()
        MessageBox.Show("Subclass method!", "Override Demo")
    End Sub
End Class
```

When you instantiate the OverrideMethodDemo class and run its DisplayMessage method, the code in the OverrideMethodDemo subclass is executed, but the DisplayMessage method in the parent is not executed.

Virtual (Overridable) methods

Virtual methods can be overridden by a subclass. In Visual FoxPro, all methods are virtual because you can override any inherited public or protected method simply by placing code in the method of a subclass. There is no such thing as a "non-virtual" method in Visual FoxPro.

In contrast, methods are non-virtual by default in C# and VB .NET and cannot be overridden. In order to override a method, it must be specifically marked as `virtual` (C#) or `Overridable` (VB .NET) in the base class. If you look closely at the code in the previous section, you will see the DisplayMessage method in MyBaseClass was marked `virtual` (`Overridable` for VB .NET).

> If you override a virtual method, the method in the subclass marked "override" is automatically virtual too.

Extending inherited methods

More often than not, you extend rather than completely override an inherited method. In Visual FoxPro you accomplish this by placing code in a method, then issuing a DODEFAULT command. You can run DODEFAULT first, before executing your subclass code, or you can run your code first, and then issue a DODEFAULT.

To call a base class method in C#, you use the `base` keyword:

```
public class CallBaseMethodDemo : MyBaseClass
{
  public override void DisplayMessage()
  {
      MessageBox.Show("Subclass method!", "Call base method demo");
      base.DisplayMessage();
  }
}
```

To call a base class method in VB .NET, you use the `MyBase` keyword:

```
Public Class CallBaseMethodDemo
    Inherits MyBaseClass
    Public Overrides Sub DisplayMessage()
        MessageBox.Show("Subclass method!", "Call base method demo")
```

```
      MyBase.DisplayMessage()
   End Sub
End Class
```

In this example, code first executes in the subclass method and afterwards calls the base class method. You can easily reverse this order by placing the call to the base class first in the subclass method.

Polymorphism and virtual methods

Visual FoxPro is a weakly typed language, so you don't specify the types of variables. You simply declare a variable and instantiate an object. For example:

```
x = CREATEOBJECT("MyClass")
```

As you've already seen, when instantiating an object in C# and in Visual Basic .NET, you always declare the type of the variable that holds a reference to the object (assuming VB .NET's Option Strict is "On"). For example, the following code declares a variable named "ClientObj" of the type Client, and then stores a new instance of the Client class into the variable.

In C#:

```
Client ClientObj;
ClientObj = new Client();
```

And in Visual Basic .NET:

```
Dim Client As ClientObj
ClientObj = New Client()
```

In this example, the code declares a variable of a specific type, and then instantiates an object from that type—no surprises here.

However, in both C# and VB .NET, when you declare a variable of a particular type it can also hold a reference to any subclass of that type. Take for example the class hierarchy shown in **Figure 5**, which shows Client and Invoice classes derived from the ABusinessObject class.

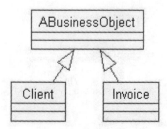

Figure 5. *When you declare a variable of a particular type it can also hold a reference to any subclass of that type.*

Given this hierarchy, you can declare a variable of type ABusinessObject and then store a reference to either the Client or Invoice object in this variable.

In C#:

```
ABusinessObject BizObj;
BizObj = new Client();
BizObj = new Invoice();
```

And in Visual Basic .NET:

```
Dim BizObj As ABusinessObject
BizObj = New Client()
BizObj = New Invoice()
```

This technique allows you to write more generic code that works with families of objects, making use of object-oriented polymorphism rather than coding to a specific class.

Hiding inherited methods

So far, you've learned about overriding and extending inherited methods. However, there are other situations where you may want to completely hide an inherited method and redeclare it.

To hide an inherited method in C#, use the `new` keyword in the method declaration:

```
public class HideMethodDemo : MyBaseClass
{
  public new void DisplayMessage()
  {
      MessageBox.Show("Subclass method!", "Hide method demo");
  }
}
```

To hide an inherited member in Visual Basic .NET, use the `shadows` keyword in the method declaration:

```
Public Class HideMethodDemo
    Inherits MyBaseClass
    Public Shadows Sub DisplayMessage()
        MessageBox.Show("Subclass method!", "Hide method demo")
        MyBase.DisplayMessage()
    End Sub
End Class
```

In what situations might you choose to completely hide an inherited method? First of all, you can use it to override a method not marked as `virtual` (or `Overridable`). Although I said earlier only virtual methods can be overridden, you can get around this rule by redeclaring a method with the `new` or `shadows` keyword.

Be judicious when deciding to hide an inherited method. If a base class method has not been marked as "virtual", the developer may have a good reason for not allowing you to override the method. Test your code well!

For example, the following code declares a class named BaseClass with a single non-virtual method named "DisplayMessage". It then declares a subclass of HideMethodBase named "HideMethodDemo" that redeclares the DisplayMessage method. This method even contains a call to the base class DisplayMessage method!

In C#:

```csharp
public class HideMethodBase
{
  public void DisplayMessage()
  {
      MessageBox.Show("Base class method!", "Override demo");
  }
}

public class HideMethodDemo : HideMethodBase
{
  public new void DisplayMessage()

  {
      MessageBox.Show("My new method", "Hide method demo");
      base.DisplayMessage();
  }
}
```

In Visual Basic .NET:

```vb
Public Class HideMethodBase
    Public Sub DisplayMessage()
        MessageBox.Show("Base class method!", "Override demo")
    End Sub
End Class

Public Class HideMethodDemo
    Inherits HideMethodBase
    ' Hide the DisplayMessage method in the base class
    Public Shadows Sub DisplayMessage()

        MessageBox.Show("My new method", "Hide method demo")
        MyBase.DisplayMessage()
    End Sub
End Class
```

There's one "gotcha" when hiding an inherited method in this way. If you use the polymorphic trick of declaring a variable of the type HideMethodBase, but you actually instantiate an instance of the HideMethodDemo subclass instead, you get unexpected behavior when calling the DisplayMessage method.

Here's this scenario in C#:

```
HideMethodBase HideBase = new HideMethodDemo();
HideBase.DisplayMessage();
```

And in Visual Basic .NET:

```
Dim HideBase As HideMethodBase = New HideMethodDemo()
HideBase.DisplayMessage()
```

When you run this code, rather than calling the DisplayMessage method belonging to the HideMethodDemo class, it calls the DisplayMessage method belonging to the HideBase base class instead! This is opposite of the behavior you might expect, so you need to write code with this in mind.

Another good example of a scenario where you can hide an inherited method involves third-party .NET components. Say you purchase a third-party component, subclass it, and add a custom method called PrintMessage. What happens if the company who created the component releases a new version and adds their own PrintMessage method? This leaves you with two choices. You can rename your custom method, but you may have countless lines of code in your applications calling the PrintMessage method and they all need to change.

Another option is to hide the newly inherited method causing the problem. You can then add a custom method to your subclass that calls it in the base class.

Here's the solution shown in C#:

```
public class MyBaseClass
{
  public virtual void PrintMessage()
  {
      MessageBox.Show("Printing message!", "Hide method demo");
  }
}

public class HideMethodDemo : MyBaseClass
{
  // Hide the PrintMessage method in the base class
  public new void PrintMessage()
  {
      MessageBox.Show("Hiding the inherited method!", "Hide method demo");
  }

  // Create a custom method that calls the base class method
  public void PrintMsg()
  {
      base.PrintMessage();
  }
}
```

And in Visual Basic .NET:

```
Public Class MyBaseClass
    Public Overridable Sub PrintMessage()
        MessageBox.Show("Printing message!", "Hide method demo")
    End Sub
End Class

Public Class HideMethodDemo
    Inherits MyBaseClass
    ' Hide the PrintMessage method in the base class
    Public Shadows Sub PrintMessage()

        MessageBox.Show("Hiding the inherited method!", "Hide method demo")
    End Sub
    ' Create a custom method that calls the base class method
    Public Sub PrintMsg()
        MyBase.PrintMessage()

    End Sub
End Class
```

In this code, the HideMethodDemo class hides the PrintMessage method in the base class. It then declares a method named PrintMsg that calls PrintMessage method in the base class.

Preventing inheritance

As mentioned in the section "Virtual (Overridable) Methods", C# and VB .NET methods are non-virtual by default, meaning they cannot be overridden in subclasses. In contrast, methods marked as "virtual" can be overridden.

There may be cases where you override a virtual method in a base class, but you don't want other subclasses to override the method in your class. You can prevent someone from overriding your method by marking it as `sealed` (C#) or `NotOverridable` (VB .NET).

For example, the following code declares a base class named "PreventInheritanceBase" containing a single virtual method named "DisplayMessage". It also declares a subclass of PreventInheritanceBase named "PreventInheritanceSubclass" that marks the DisplayMessage method as sealed. This prevents subclasses of PreventInheritanceSubclass from further overriding this method.

In C#:

```
public class PreventInheritanceBase
{
  public virtual void DisplayMessage()
  {
      MessageBox.Show("This is a virtual method!", "Prevent inheritance
demo");
  }
}
```

```
public class PreventInheritanceSubclass : PreventInheritanceBase
{
    public override sealed void DisplayMessage()

    {
        MessageBox.Show("Sealed method!", "Prevent inheritance demo");
    }
}
```

In Visual Basic .NET:

```
Public Class PreventInheritanceBase

    Public Overridable Sub DisplayMessage()
        MessageBox.Show("This is a virtual method!", _
            "Prevent inheritance demo")
    End Sub 'DisplayMessage
End Class 'PreventInheritanceBase

Public Class PreventInheritanceSubclass
    Inherits PreventInheritanceBase

    Public NotOverridable Overrides Sub DisplayMessage()
        MessageBox.Show("This overrides a virtual method, then seals it!", _
            "Prevent inheritance demo")
    End Sub 'DisplayMessage
End Class 'PreventInheritanceSubclass
```

In addition to preventing inheritance at the method level, you can also specify an entire class cannot be inherited using the `sealed` keyword (C#) or the `NotInheritable` keyword (VB .NET). For example, the following code declares the "PreventClassInheritDemo" class cannot be subclassed.

In C#:

```
public sealed class PreventClassInheritDemo
{
}
```

In Visual Basic .NET:

```
Public NotInheritable Class PreventClassInheritDemo

End Class
```

Abstract classes and methods

There are two main types of classes in object-oriented programming—*concrete* and *abstract*. All of the classes you have seen so far are concrete; they have code in their methods that implements specific functionality. For example, in the previous section, the DisplayMessage method displays a message to the user. Concrete classes are meant to be instantiated and their methods called by client code.

In contrast, an abstract class is not intended to be instantiated. Its main purpose is to define an interface for a family of classes. It is abstract in the sense that it is conceptual as opposed to concrete. For example, you may conceive the need to create a class to access application settings. This class needs a method to retrieve settings and another method to save settings.

The following code shows how to declare an abstract class named "AppSettingsBase" that represents this concept.

In C#:

```csharp
public abstract class AppSettingsBase
{
  public abstract string GetSetting(string key);
  public abstract void SetSetting(string key, string value);
}
```

And in Visual Basic .NET:

```vbnet
Public MustInherit Class AppSettingsBase

    Public MustOverride Function GetSetting(ByVal key As String) As String
    Public MustOverride Sub SetSetting(ByVal key As String, _
        ByVal value As String)
End Class 'AppSettingsBase
```

To mark a class as abstract, use the modifier `abstract` (C#) or `MustInherit` (VB .NET) in the class definition. In the AppSettingsBase class there are two abstract methods. These abstract methods represent the concept of retrieving and saving application settings. An abstract method does not contain implementation code. It simply defines a method signature including the method name, parameters and their types, and a return value and its type. To mark a method as abstract, use the modifier `abstract` (C#) or `MustOverride` (VB .NET).

You now have a class that defines an interface for retrieving and saving application settings. Now you can create concrete implementations of this abstract class to do the real work. For example, **Figure 6** shows the abstract AppSettingsBase class with two subclasses. AppSettingsRegistry accesses settings stored in the Windows Registry and AppSettingsXml accesses settings stored in an XML file.

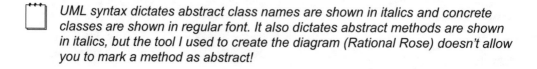

UML syntax dictates abstract class names are shown in italics and concrete classes are shown in regular font. It also dictates abstract methods are shown in italics, but the tool I used to create the diagram (Rational Rose) doesn't allow you to mark a method as abstract!

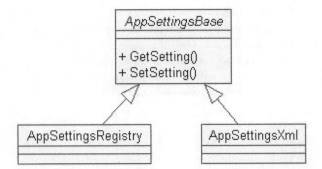

Figure 6. *You can define an abstract class that defines an interface for a family of related classes.*

The following code defines the AppSettingsRegistry class in C#:

```csharp
public class AppSettingsRegistry : AppSettingsBase
{
  public override string GetSetting(string key)
  {
      string setting = "";
      // Code that reads a setting from the Windows Registry
      return setting;
  }
  public override void SetSetting(string key, string value)
  {
      // Code that stores a setting to the Windows Registry
  }
}
```

And in Visual Basic .NET:

```vbnet
Public Class AppSettingsRegistry
    Inherits AppSettingsBase

    Public Overrides Function GetSetting(ByVal key As String) As String
        Dim setting As String = ""
        ' Code that reads a setting from the Windows Registry
        Return setting
    End Function 'GetSetting

    Public Overrides Sub SetSetting(ByVal key As String, _
        ByVal value As String)
        ' Code that stores a setting to the Windows Registry
    End Sub 'SetSetting
End Class 'AppSettingsRegistry
```

Obviously, these classes don't do much "as is" because there are comments in the methods where there should be implementation code. Notice the subclass provides an implementation for both the GetSetting and SetSetting methods. When you create a class derived from an abstract class, both C# and VB .NET require you provide an implementation for all abstract methods. If you don't, the compiler displays a warning accordingly.

Concrete methods in abstract classes

C# and VB .NET allow you to have both abstract and concrete methods in an abstract class. Why would you declare a concrete method in an abstract class? If there is common or default behavior you want all classes to inherit, you can create concrete methods containing code inherited by all subclasses. A subclass can choose to override a concrete method inherited from an abstract class if the default behavior does not suit that particular class.

When to create abstract classes

So, in what situations would you create an abstract base class? You should create an abstract class when there are multiple ways to implement application functionality. The application settings class just discussed is a good example of this. There are multiple ways you can implement an application settings class—by storing settings in the Windows Registry, an XML file, an INI file, and so on. You can create a concrete class for each of these implementations.

Instantiating concrete subclasses

To make the best use polymorphism with abstract and concrete classes, you should write generic code when working with concrete subclasses.

For example during application startup, you might instantiate a concrete AppSettingsRegistry class. For the most flexibility, you should declare a field of the type AppSettingsBase and store an instance of the concrete subclass in this field.

In C#:

```csharp
public class MyApp
{
    public AppSettingsBase AppSettingsObj;

    public MyApp()
    {
        this.CreateAppSettingsObj();
    }

    public virtual void CreateAppSettingsObj()

        this.AppSettingsObj = new AppSettingsRegistry();
    {
    }
}
```

And in Visual Basic .NET:

```vb
Public Class MyApp

    Public AppSettingsObj As AppSettingsBase

    Public Sub New()
        Me.CreateAppSettingsObj()
    End Sub 'New
```

```
  Public Sub CreateAppSettingsObj()
      Me.AppSettingsObj = New AppSettingsRegistry()
  End Sub 'CreateAppSettingsObj
End Class 'MyApp
```

This code declares a class named "MyApp" with a field named "AppSettingsObj" of the type AppSettingsBase—the abstract class defined in the previous section. This field holds a reference to the application settings object. In the constructor of this class, a call is made to the CreateAppSettingsObj method containing code that creates an instance of AppSettingsRegistry and stores it in the AppSettingsObj field. This is the only method in your application that needs to know the specific concrete class that was instantiated. All other code in your application references the application settings object as if it were of the type AppSettingsBase.

> *If you add new members to concrete subclasses, you can't access those members when referencing an object by the abstract base class type. To keep your code as generic as possible, try to add methods at the abstract level rather than the concrete level.*

The real beauty of this design is its extensibility. Imagine you later decide to save application settings to a DBF, rather than the Registry. All you have to do is create a new concrete subclass of AppSettingsBase (for example, AppSettingsDbf) to access settings stored in a DBF and change the code in the CreateAppSettingsObj to instantiate the new class.

In C#:

```
public virtual void CreateAppSettingsObj()
{
    this.AppSettingsObj = new AppSettingsDbf();
}
```

And in Visual Basic .NET:

```
Public Overridable Sub CreateAppSettingsObj()
    Me.AppSettingsObj = New AppSettingsDbf()
End Sub 'CreateAppSettingsObj
```

This makes your application far more extensible, and maintainable.

Programming to an interface rather than an implementation

What you have just seen is an example of "programming to an interface rather than an implementation". This concept is commonly discussed in object-oriented books, but I find many developers have difficulty understanding this concept.

"Programming to an implementation," is undesirable. It means writing software hard-coded to a specific concrete functionality. For example, you might hard-code reading and writing application settings to an XML file.

In contrast, "programming to an interface" is desirable. In this particular case, it means creating an abstract base class to define an interface for a family of classes and writing code to talk to the interface.

Interface inheritance

When Visual FoxPro 3 was released, it introduced *implementation inheritance* to FoxPro. With implementation inheritance, subclasses inherit the properties, events, and methods of their base class, as well as any associated code. Visual FoxPro 7 introduced *interface inheritance*, (which was unfortunately limited to COM components). In contrast, C# and Visual Basic .NET have full support for both implementation and interface inheritance.

Interfaces are similar to classes in defining properties and methods that other classes can inherit. However, an interface only defines method signatures. It does not contain any implementation code that can be inherited. For example, the following code defines an interface named IDbConnection with four properties and six methods.

> *All your interface names should be Pascal-cased and prefixed with an uppercase "I". This means the first two letters of an interface name are always in upper case (for example, IDbConnection). This is a naming convention used by Microsoft that helps easily differentiate between classes and interfaces.*

If you're familiar with ADO.NET, the IDbConnection interface should look familiar to you. It is one of the interfaces defined in the .NET Framework's System.Data namespace.

In C#:

```
public interface IDbConnection
{
  // Properties
  string ConnectionString();
  string ConnectionTimeOut();
  string Database();
  ConnectionState State();

  // Methods
  IDbTransaction BeginTransaction();
  IDbTransaction BeginTransaction(IsolationLevel level);
  void ChangeDatabase(string databaseName);
  void Close();
  IDbCommand CreateCommand();
  void Open();
}
```

In Visual Basic .NET:

```
Public Interface IDbConnection
    ' Properties
    Function ConnectionString() As String
    Function ConnectionTimeOut() As String
    Function Database() As String
    Function State() As ConnectionState
```

```
' Methods
Overloads Function BeginTransaction() As IDbTransaction
Overloads Function BeginTransaction(level As IsolationLevel) _
    As IDbTransaction
Sub ChangeDatabase(databaseName As String)
Sub Close()
Function CreateCommand() As IDbCommand
Sub Open()
End Interface 'IDbConnection
```

As you can see, defining an interface is similar to defining a class, except there is no code in the properties or methods.

Implementing interfaces

After you have defined an interface, you can specify that one or more classes *implement* the interface. When a class implements an interface, it is agreeing to a contract. This contract specifies the class will implement all the properties and methods in the interface. For example, there are a few classes in the .NET Framework class library that implement the IDbConnection interface including SqlConnection, OracleConnection, and OleDbConnection. If you look at the help file for these classes, you see each of them implement all the properties and methods in the IDbConnection interface.

What if you want to create a new .NET class that connects to Visual FoxPro data? You can declare a class and specify that it implements the IDbConnection interface.

In C#:

```
public class VfpConnection : IDbConnection
{
}
```

And in Visual Basic .NET

```
Public Class VfpConnection
    Implements IDbConnection
End Class 'VfpConnection
```

In C#, you specify a class implements an interface by placing a colon and the name of the interface at the end of the first line of the class definition (: IDbConnection). This is similar to the syntax for declaring a base class. In Visual Basic .NET, you add the Implements keyword and the name of the Interface on a line following the initial line of the class definition.

If you compile this class "as is", the compiler displays ten errors, one for each member of the IDbConnection interface. The error messages inform you that you are not living up to your contract. You have indicated you are implementing the IDbConnection interface, but you have not declared an implementation for each of these members in the VfpConnection class.

To satisfy the compiler, you must declare a property and method for each of the properties and methods in the IDbConnection interface. The following code provides a bare bones implementation of each interface member. If you were really creating this Visual FoxPro connection class, you would place implementation code in each property and method.

In C#:

```csharp
public class VfpConnection : IConnection
{
  // Properties
  public string ConnectionString()
  {
      return null;
  }
  public string ConnectionTimeOut()
  {
      return null;
  }
  public string Database()
  {
      return null;
  }
  public ConnectionState State()
  {
      return new ConnectionState();
  }

  // Methods
  public IDbTransaction BeginTransaction()
  {
      return null;
  }
  public IDbTransaction BeginTransaction(System.Data.IsolationLevel level)
  {
      return null;
  }
  public void ChangeDatabase(string databaseName)
  {
  }
  public void Close()
  {
  }
  public IDbCommand CreateCommand()
  {
      return null;
  }
  public void Open()
  {
  }
}
```

And in Visual Basic .NET:

```
Public Class VfpConnection
    Implements IConnection

    ' Properties
    Public Function ConnectionString() As String _
        Implements IConnection.ConnectionString
        Return Nothing
    End Function 'ConnectionString

    Public Function ConnectionTimeOut() As String _
        Implements IConnection.ConnectionTimeOut
        Return Nothing
    End Function 'ConnectionTimeOut

    Public Function Database() As String _
        Implements IConnection.Database
        Return Nothing
    End Function 'Database

    Public Function State() As ConnectionState _
        Implements IConnection.State
        Return New ConnectionState()
    End Function 'State


    ' Methods
    Public Overloads Function BeginTransaction() As IDbTransaction _
        Implements IConnection.BeginTransaction
        Return Nothing
    End Function 'BeginTransaction

    Public Overloads Function BeginTransaction _
        (ByVal level As System.Data.IsolationLevel) As IDbTransaction _
        Implements IConnection.BeginTransaction
        Return Nothing
    End Function 'BeginTransaction

    Public Sub ChangeDatabase(ByVal databaseName As String) _
        Implements IConnection.ChangeDatabase
    End Sub 'ChangeDatabase


    Public Sub Close() _
        Implements IConnection.Close
    End Sub 'Close


    Public Function CreateCommand() As IDbCommand _
        Implements IConnection.CreateCommand
        Return Nothing
    End Function 'CreateCommand

    Public Sub Open() _
        Implements IConnection.Open
    End Sub 'Open
End Class 'VfpConnection
```

Implementing multiple interfaces

Although C# and Visual Basic .NET have a single implementation inheritance model (a class can be derived from only one base class), a class can implement multiple interfaces. For example, the following code declares a class named "Person" derived from the Component class that implements the IEmployee and IStockHolder interfaces.

In C#:

```
public class Person : Component, IEmployee, IStockHolder
{
}
```

In Visual Basic .NET:

```
Public Class Person
    Inherits Component
    Implements IEmployee, IStockHolder
End Class 'Person
```

Implementing interfaces with the Class View window in C#

If you are implementing an interface with more than a few members, it can be quite a bit of work implementing each interface member. If you are implementing an interface found in the .NET Framework class library, this usually entails copying and pasting into your code method signatures from a .NET Help topic detailing the interface.

If you are using C#, the Class View window provides a much easier way to implement an interface (this feature is not available in Visual Basic .NET). First, enter the class definition in the code-editing window. For example:

```
public class VfpConnection : IDbConnection
{
}
```

Next, right-click on the class definition and select Synchronize Class View from the shortcut menu. This opens the Class View window with the VfpConnection class highlighted in the tree view (**Figure 7**).

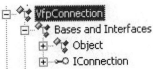

Figure 7. *The Class Viewer displays the base class a class is derived from and any interfaces it implements.*

If you expand the VfpConnection class node, you see a Bases and Interfaces node. If you expand this node, you see the base class of VfpConnection (Object) and the interfaces it implements (IConnection).

If you expand the IConnection interface node, you see a list of all properties and methods in the interface. To implement an interface member in the VfpConnection class, just right-click the member and select Add | Override from the shortcut menu (**Figure 8**).

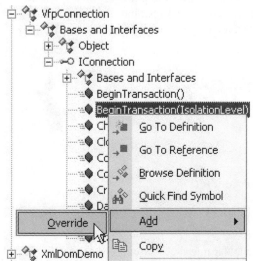

Figure 8. *In C#, you can use the Class Viewer to implement interfaces and methods from base classes.*

After selecting this menu option, a method declaration is automatically added to the VfpConnection class. For example:

```
public System.Data.IDbTransaction BeginTransaction(System.Data.IsolationLevel
  level)
{
  return null;
}
```

Notice VS .NET fully qualifies class names in the code it generates. If you have already referenced the necessary namespace, you can remove the fully qualified name:

```
public IDbTransaction BeginTransaction(IsolationLevellevel)
{
  return null;
}
```

This is nice because it's not just for interfaces. It also works for base class members. If you expand the base class node in the Class Viewer, right-click on a property or method, and select Add | Override from the shortcut menu, a declaration is added for the selected member.

Referencing classes by interface

In the section on abstract classes, you learned how to declare a variable that is the type of an abstract class, and then reference subclasses using the variable. This lets you write generic code that "programs to an interface, rather than an implementation". This same principle holds true for interfaces.

You can declare a variable of a specific interface type, and then use the variable to reference any class that implements the interface. For example, the following code declares a variable of the type IDbConnection and stores a reference to a VfpConnection object. The subsequent lines of code show you can also store a reference to the SqlConnection, OracleConnection, and OleDbConnection object.

In C#:

```
IDbConnection Command = new VfpConnection();
Command = new SqlConnection();
Command = new OracleConnection();
Command = new OleDbConnection();
```

In Visual Basic .NET:

```
Dim Command As IDbConnection = New VfpConnection()
Command = New SqlConnection()
Command = New OracleConnection()
Command = New OleDbConnection()
```

When you reference an object through a particular interface, the only members you can access are the members of the specified interface—even if the class has other members in addition to those present in the interface. For example, given the above sample code, VS .NET IntelliSense on the Command object only displays the members shown in **Figure 9**.

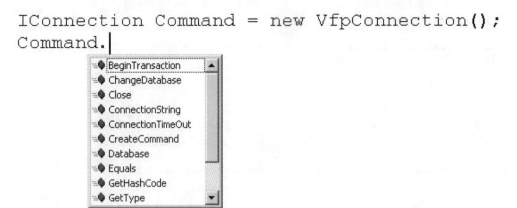

Figure 9. When you reference an object via a specific interface, you only have access to the members of that interface.

Polymorphism and interfaces

In the previous sections, I used a data access interface (IDbConnection) to demonstrate the basics of .NET interfaces, because it provides a real world example of how you can achieve generic data access in your applications. The .NET Framework class library contains a number of generic data access interfaces implemented by concrete .NET data providers, such as the SQL Server data provider and the Oracle data provider. This is an example of polymorphism, because each interface can take many concrete forms.

However, if you instantiate the concrete classes that comprise these .NET data providers and use them directly, you are effectively hard-coding your data access. In contrast, if you reference these classes through the generic interfaces they implement, you are programming to an interface, rather than an implementation. This allows you to access data generically, giving your applications flexible data access.

Deciding between abstract classes and interfaces

When you get down to it, abstract classes and interfaces provide similar benefits. They both define interfaces that concrete classes can inherit, providing the flexibility that comes with object-oriented polymorphism. So, how do you decide whether to use an abstract class or an interface in a given situation?

There are a variety of criteria you can use, but one of the more practical considerations is whether or not the classes implementing the common behavior are related. If you are defining functionality for a family of related classes (as with the application settings classes discussed earlier in this chapter), you can use an abstract class. If the common functionality needs to be implemented across unrelated classes, then use interfaces.

For more information, see the .NET Help topic "Recommendations for Abstract Classes vs. Interfaces".

Instance and static (Shared) members

There are two main types of class members—*instance* and *static* (*Shared* in VB .NET) members. Instance members are the default type of member in both C# and Visual Basic .NET. They are fields, properties, methods, and so on, which belong to each instance of a class. For example, the following code declares a class named InstanceMemberDemo with a public instance field named Counter. The class also contains an IncrementCounter method that increments the Counter field and displays its value in a MessageBox.

In C#:

```
public class InstanceMemberDemo
{
  public int Counter = 1;

  public void IncrementCounter()
  {
      this.Counter++;
      MessageBox.Show("Counter = " + Counter);
  }
}
```

And in Visual Basic .NET:

```
Public Class InstanceMemberDemo
    Public Counter As Integer = 1
```

```
Public Sub IncrementCounter()
    Me.Counter += 1
    MessageBox.Show(("Counter = " & Counter.ToString()))
End Sub 'IncrementCounter
End Class 'InstanceMemberDemo
```

Now take a look at the following code that creates and manipulates instances of this class. In C#:

```
InstanceMemberDemo InstanceDemo1 = new InstanceMemberDemo();
InstanceMemberDemo InstanceDemo2 = new InstanceMemberDemo();
InstanceDemo1.IncrementCounter();
InstanceDemo2.IncrementCounter();
```

And in Visual Basic .NET:

```
Dim InstanceDemo1 As New InstanceMemberDemo()
Dim InstanceDemo2 As New InstanceMemberDemo()
InstanceDemo1.IncrementCounter()
InstanceDemo1.IncrementCounter()
```

The first two lines of code create instances of the class named "InstanceDemo1" and "InstanceDemo2". At this point, both Counter fields are set to 1. After running the third line of code that calls the IncrementCounter method of InstanceDemo1, the Counter field in InstanceDemo1 is set to two, and the Counter field in InstanceDemo2 is still set to one. After running the fourth line of code that calls the IncrementCounter method of InstanceDemo2, both instances have their Counter field set to two (**Figure 10**). This is because each instance has its own copy of the variable. This is the way Visual FoxPro works. All members of Visual FoxPro classes are instance members.

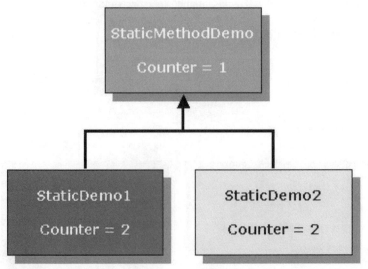

Figure 10. Each instance of a class has its own copy of all instance members

Now you're ready to look at static members. Static members belong to the class itself, rather than to each instance of the class. Only one copy of a static member exists in an application regardless of how many instances of the class are created.

To illustrate this point, I'll change the Counter field in the previous example to a static member. Notice I also changed the way I reference the Counter field. Rather than referencing it as `this.Counter` (C#) or `Me.Counter` (VB .NET), it must simply be referenced as `Counter`. When you think about it, this makes sense. The keywords `this` and `Me` refer to an instance of an object, and in this scenario, the Counter field does not belong to instances of the class, it belongs to the StaticMethodDemo class itself.

In C#:

```
public class StaticMemberDemo
{
  public int Counter = 1;

  public void IncrementCounter()
  {
      Counter++;
      MessageBox.Show("Counter = " + Counter);
  }
}
```

And in Visual Basic .NET

```
Public Class StaticMemberDemo
    Public Shared Counter As Integer = 1


    Public Sub IncrementCounter()
        Counter += 1
        MessageBox.Show(("Counter = " & Counter.ToString()))
    End Sub 'IncrementCounter
End Class 'StaticMemberDemo
```

Now, take a look at the code that instantiates and manipulates these classes.
In C#:

```
StaticMemberDemo StaticDemo1 = new StaticMemberDemo();
StaticMemberDemo StaticDemo2 = new StaticMemberDemo();
StaticDemo1.IncrementCounter();
StaticDemo2.IncrementCounter();
```

And in Visual Basic .NET:

```
Dim StaticDemo1 As New StaticMemberDemo()
Dim StaticDemo2 As New StaticMemberDemo()
StaticDemo1.IncrementCounter()
StaticDemo2.IncrementCounter()
```

When the first two lines of code are executed, the Counter field is set to its initial value of one, but remember this value is stored at the class level, rather than with each instance of the class. When the IncrementCounter method is called on the StaticDemo1 object, the Counter field is set to two. When the IncrementCounter method is called on the StaticDemo2 object, the Counter field is set to three (**Figure 11**).

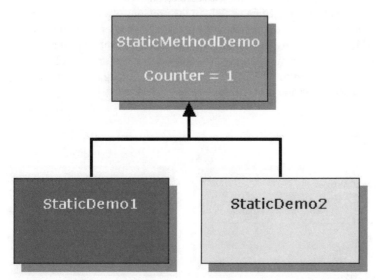

Figure 11. Static members belong to the class itself rather than to each instance of the class.

Because this is a static field, the field and its value are stored at the class level. When you reference the Counter field from within either object, it points back to the field and value stored at the class level.

Static properties and fields are similar to global variables in Visual FoxPro.

Referencing static class members

As you've already seen, when you reference a static class member from within an instance of a class, you don't use this or Me. So, how do you access static members from outside the class? You do this by using the syntax "ClassName.Member". For example, look at the following code that references the static Counter field declared in the StaticMemberDemo class.

In C#:

```
MessageBox.Show("Counter: " + StaticMemberDemo.Counter);
```

And in Visual Basic .NET:

```
MessageBox.Show(("Counter: " & StaticMemberDemo.Counter.ToString()))
```

It may take a little while to wrap your mind around static members, because they're new to Visual FoxPro developers, but in reality I've used them extensively in the sample code shown so far. For example, look at the previous code sample calling "MessageBox.Show". Notice I never instantiated an instance of the MessageBox class—I simply called its Show method directly. As you might guess, the Show method of the MessageBox class is a static member. If you look at the .NET Help topic "MessageBox Members", you'll see the Show method is marked with a yellow "S", to indicate it is static ("Shared" in VB .NET).

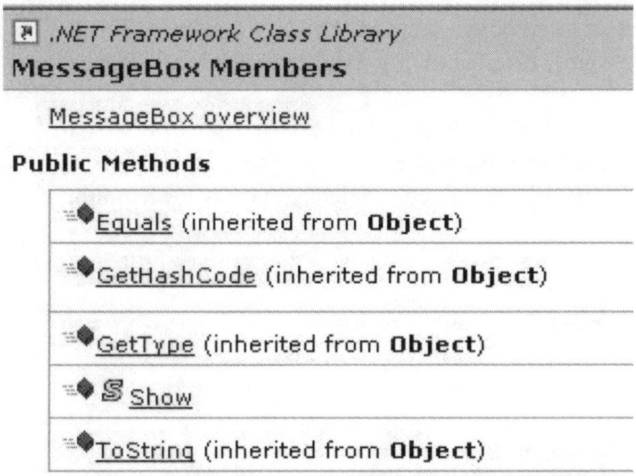

Figure 12. *The .NET Help file displays a yellow "S" next to all static class members.*

This convention is used throughout the .NET Help file, so you can easily determine whether members are instance or static.

Events and delegates

Events happen. Objects raise events and other objects respond to them. Visual FoxPro has traditionally been weak in the area of events. Although you can write code that responds to events in VFP, you can't raise your own custom events as in Visual Basic 6. Although Visual FoxPro's event model is limited, it is simple and straightforward. All you have to do is place code in an event, and it executes when the event fires.

In contrast, C# and VB .NET both have full support for raising and responding to events. The .NET event model is more robust and flexible than Visual FoxPro's, but with this flexibility comes a small learning curve in understanding and implementing events.

The .NET event model is based on the object-oriented Observer design pattern. This model involves three main entities:

- An event transmitter

- An event receiver

- A delegate

The event transmitter is responsible for raising the event, which is usually fired as a result of an action. For example, if the user clicks a button, the button raises its Click event. An event receiver, or handler, is an object that captures and responds to an event. As with the Observer design pattern, the event transmitter does not know which object or specific method on an object handles the event it raises. Due to this loose coupling, you need an object to act as an intermediary between the event transmitter and event receiver. This object is the delegate.

Delegates

A delegate is a class that holds a reference to an object method. This is something new to VFP developers. In Visual FoxPro, there are *object* references, but a delegate holds a reference to a single *method* on an object!

Each delegate class can only refer to methods matching one specific signature. When you define a delegate class, you specify the signature of the methods it references. For example, the .NET Framework class library contains a generic delegate class for handling events called "EventHandler".

Here is its definition in C#:

```
delegate void EventHandler(object sender, EventArgs e);
```

And in Visual Basic .NET:

```
Delegate Sub EventHandler(sender As Object, e As EventArgs)
```

This code is a bit different from how you declare "normal" classes. When you declare a delegate, you specify an associated method signature. The EventHandler delegate has a signature with two parameters. The first parameter is an "object" type. It holds a reference to the event transmitter. The second parameter is an "EventArgs" type. It is used to pass any information from the event transmitter to the event receiver. The EventArgs class is the base class for all classes passing data from events. It represents an event that does not pass any data.

If your event transmitter does not pass any information to the event receiver, you can use this generic EventHandler delegate class with its object and EventArgs parameters. Otherwise, you must create your own custom delegate class.

An events example

This section takes you through creating your own custom event transmitter, delegate, and event receiver demonstrating how to localize your application text by means of .NET events ("localizing" is the process of translating text to another language). To do this, you will create a LanguageMgr object that raises a Localize event. You will also create a MyLabel class, which is a Windows Forms label acting as the event receiver, or handler, responding to the Localize event. Finally, you will create a "LocalizeDelegate" class to act as an intermediary between the language manager object and the label object (**Figure 13**).

Figure 13. *In the .NET event model, there are three primary objects; the event transmitter, the delegate, and the event receiver.*

Creating a delegate

In this example, you need to create a delegate to act as an intermediary between the LanguageMgr and the MyLabel objects. When the LanguageMgr class raises its Localize event, it passes a single integer argument to any objects that handle the event. This integer represents the primary key of a record in a Language table. Because this parameter needs to be passed, you cannot use the .NET Framework's generic EventArgs class when declaring this delegate (it represents an event that does not pass any data).

So, here is the event arguments definition in C#:

```csharp
public class LocalizeEventArgs : EventArgs
{
    // The language property and associated field
    private int language;
    public int Language
    {
        get { return language; }
        set { language = value; }
    }

    // The constructor
    public LocalizeEventArgs(int language)
    {
        this.Language = language;
    }
}
```

And in Visual Basic .NET:

```vbnet
Public Class LocalizeEventArgs
    Inherits EventArgs
    ' The language property and associated field
    Private _language As Integer

    Public Property Language() As Integer
        Get
            Return _language
        End Get
        Set(ByVal Value As Integer)
            _language = Value
        End Set
    End Property
```

```
' The constructor
Public Sub New(ByVal language As Integer)
    Me.Language = language
End Sub 'New
End Class 'LocalizeEventArgs
```

Now, you're ready to declare a delegate that uses this new LocalizeEventArgs class. The following code declares a delegate named LocalizeDelegate that holds references to methods with the following signature:

- An object parameter

- A LocalizeEventArgs parameter

- No return value

Here is the delegate declaration in C#:

```
public delegate void LocalizeDelegate(object sender, LocalizeEventArgs e);
```

And in Visual Basic .NET:

```
Public Delegate Sub LocalizeDelegate(ByVal sender As Object, _
    ByVal e As LocalizeEventArgs)
```

If you try to make the delegate hold a reference to an object method that does not have this signature, you will get a compiler error.

Creating an event transmitter

Now it's time to create an event transmitter. The following code declares a class named LanguageMgr that contains a custom Localize event. This is the part you can't do in Visual FoxPro. You are allowed to hook into existing VFP events, but you can't create your own custom events.

This class also contains a method named SetNewLanguage that accepts a single integer parameter specifying the unique id of a language. This method instantiates a LocalizeEventArgs class and passes the language integer in the class constructor. It then passes the LocalizeEventArgs object to its OnLocalize method.

In C#, the OnLocalize method first checks if the Localize event is null. If no delegates are registered with the Localize event, then it *will* be null. If it's not null, the method passes the event arguments object to the Localize event. In Visual Basic .NET, you don't need to perform this check. If no delegates have been registered with the event, you can raise the event without throwing an exception.

In C#:

```
public class LanguageMgr
{
    /// Specifies a custom event member that is of the type LocalizeDelegate
    public event LocalizeDelegate Localize;

    public void SetNewLanguage(int language)
```

```
    {
        LocalizeEventArgs e = new LocalizeEventArgs(language);
        this.OnLocalize(e);
    }

    /// This method raises the event by invoking the delegates
    protected virtual void OnLocalize(LocalizeEventArgs e)
    {
        if (Localize != null)
        {
            // Invoke the delegates, specifying this class as the sender
            Localize(this, e);
        }
    }
}
```

And in Visual Basic .NET:

```
Public Class LanguageMgr
    ' Specifies a custom event member that is of the type LocalizeDelegate
    Public Event Localize As LocalizeDelegate

    ' This method raises the event by invoking the delegates
    Protected Overridable Sub OnLocalize(ByVal e As LocalizeEventArgs)
        RaiseEvent Localize(Me, e)
    End Sub 'OnLocalize

    Public Sub SetNewLanguage(ByVal language As Integer)
        Dim e As New LocalizeEventArgs(language)
        Me.OnLocalize(e)
    End Sub 'SetNewLanguage
End Class 'LanguageMgr
```

When the Localize event fires, it passes the LocalizeEventArgs object to all delegates registered with the event. In the next section, you will create an event handler object and register it with the event transmitter using the custom delegate class.

You may wonder why the LanguageMgr class has a separate method called "OnLocalize" containing the code that raises the event. Why not just put this code directly in the SetNewLanguage Method? Because placing this code in a separate method allows subclasses of LanguageMgr to handle the event by overriding this method. For details, see the "Overriding events defined in the .NET Framework" section later in this chapter

Creating the event handler

Now you're ready to create the event handler. The following code declares a class named "MyLabel" derived from the Windows Forms Label class.

In C#:

```
public class MyLabel : Label
{
  public void Localize(object sender, LocalizeEventArgs e)
  {
      // Localize the label's text
      MessageBox.Show("Localizing the control to language: " +
          e.Language);
  }
}
```

And in Visual Basic .NET:

```
Public Class MyLabel
    Inherits Label

    Public Sub Localize(ByVal sender As Object, _
        ByVal e As LocalizeEventArgs)
        ' Localize the label's text
        MessageBox.Show(("Localizing the control to language: " & _
            e.Language.ToString()))
    End Sub 'Localize
End Class 'MyLabel
```

Notice the Localize method has the same signature as defined in the LocalizeEventArgs delegate. This allows you to use LocalizeDelegate to hold a reference to this method as shown in the next section.

Registering the event handler with the event transmitter

Now that you've defined all the pieces, you're ready to register the MyLabel.Localize event handler method with the event transmitter.

The following code first instantiates the LanguageMgr class, which is the event transmitter. Next, it instantiates the MyLabel class, which is the event handler. The third line of code is a bit different in C# versus VB .NET. In C#, this line of code instantiates an instance of the custom LocalizeDelegate, passing a reference to the LabelObj's Localize method in its constructor. It uses the += operator to register the delegate with the Localize event of the language manager.

In C#:

```
// Instantiate the event transmitter
LanguageMgr LangMgr = new LanguageMgr();

// Instantiate the event handler
MyLabel LabelObj = new MyLabel();

// Register the delegate with the event
LangMgr.Localize += new LocalizeDelegate(LabelObj.Localize);

// Fire the Localize event by setting a new language
LangMgr.SetNewLanguage(1);
```

In Visual Basic .NET, you don't need to explicitly "wire-up" to a delegate, because it's done automatically for you. The third line of VB .NET code uses the `AddHandler` statement to associate the Localize event with the LabelObj.Localize event handler:

```
' Instantiate the event transmitter
Dim LangMgr As New LanguageMgr()

' Instantiate the event handler
Dim LabelObj As New MyLabel()

' Register the delegate with the event
AddHandler LangMgr.Localize, AddressOf LabelObj.Localize

' Fire the Localize event by setting a new language
LangMgr.SetNewLanguage(1)
```

For details on how this works in VB .NET, see the .NET Help topic "Delegates and the AddressOf Operator".

The last line of code triggers the language manager's Localize event, by calling the SetNewLanguage method. The UML sequence diagram in **Figure 14** shows the basic message flow between the LanguageMgr, LocalizeDelegate, and MyLabel objects. Notice the event transmitter (LanguageMgr) never talks directly to the event handler (MyLabel). All communication takes place through the delegate (LocalizeDelegate).

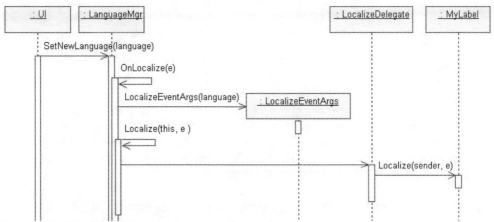

Figure 14. *This diagram demonstrates the basic message flow between event transmitter, delegate, and event handler objects.*

Overriding events defined in the .NET Framework

In the .NET Help topic "Event Usage Guidelines", Microsoft recommends creating a protected, virtual method for raising an event so subclasses can handle the event by overriding the method.

Microsoft followed this standard when defining events in the .NET Framework classes. This means you can override events defined in the .NET Framework by overriding the event's associated On*EventName* method. For example, the .NET Help topic "Overriding the Paint Event" contains the following sample code for overriding the Paint event of the System.Windows.Forms.Control class.

In C#:

```
public class FirstControl : Control{
    {
        protected override void OnPaint(PaintEventArgs e)
            // Call the OnPaint method of the base class.
            base.OnPaint(e);

        // Call methods of the System.Drawing.Graphics object.
        e.Graphics.DrawString(Text, Font, new SolidBrush(ForeColor),
          ClientRectangle);
    }
}
```

In Visual Basic .NET:

```
Public Class FirstControl
    Inherits Control

    Protected Overrides Sub OnPaint(e As PaintEventArgs)
        ' Call the OnPaint method of the base class.
        MyBase.OnPaint(e)
        ' Call methods of the System.Drawing.Graphics object.
        e.Graphics.DrawString(Text, Font, New SolidBrush(ForeColor), _
            RectangleF.op_Implicit(ClientRectangle))
    End Sub
End Class
```

This code defines a class named "FirstControl" derived from the .NET Framework's System.Windows.Forms.Control class. The code shown in grey overrides the OnPaint method of the Control class. Notice the method first calls the base class's OnPaint method before it performs its own processing. You must call the On*EventName* method of the base class in this way to ensure registered delegates receive the event.

Event handling using `WithEvents` in Visual Basic .NET

Although you can use the same technique for creating events in Visual Basic .NET as in C#, VB .NET provides an alternate method using the `WithEvents` and `Handles` keywords. This methodology isn't as flexible as the one described in the previous section, but if your needs are more basic, it provides an easy way to raise and respond to events in VB .NET.

A great place to see `WithEvents` at work is the VB .NET user interface code. For example, the Visual Basic .NET source code for this book has a Windows Form code-behind file named SampleCodeForm.vb. A search for the phrase "WithEvents" takes you to several form-level variables declared using the `WithEvents` keyword. The following code declares a variable named "cmdClose" of the type System.Windows.Forms.Button. The `WithEvents` keyword specifies this variable contains an object that is a source of events.

```
Friend WithEvents cmdClose As System.Windows.Forms.Button
```

Further down in the source code is the following handler code for this event. The `Handles` keyword specifies this method handles the `cmdClose.Click` event.

```
Private Sub cmdClose_Click(ByVal sender As System.Object, _
    ByVal e As System.EventArgs) Handles cmdClose.Click
    Me.Close()
End Sub
```

This is extremely easy and straightforward, eliminating the need to work with delegates directly—Visual Basic .NET handles delegate registration for you behind the scenes. Although `WithEvents` can be used for many VB .NET event handling situations, the .NET Help topic "WithEvents and the Handles Clause" lists the following restrictions on the use of `WithEvents` variables:

- You cannot use a `WithEvents` variable as a generic object variable. You must specify a class name when you declare the variable.

- You cannot use `WithEvents` to declaratively handle shared events, because they are not tied to an instance that can be assigned to a `WithEvents` variable.

- You cannot create arrays of `WithEvents` variables.

- `WithEvents` variables allow a single event handler to handle one or more kind of event, or one or more event handlers to handle the same kind of event.

For more information on using `WithEvents`, see the .NET Help topic "Writing Event Handlers".

Event handling made easy in Visual Studio .NET

As shown in the previous section, creating your own custom events, event handlers, and delegates takes a bit of effort. Fortunately, Visual Studio .NET makes plugging into events much easier than this. Take a quick look at a simple example.

Say you have a button on a Windows form named "cmdClose". If you open this form in design mode in Visual Studio .NET and double-click the button, it automatically adds an event handler method behind the scenes. You can add custom code to this method that automatically executes when the event fires. For example, the following event handler method contains code to close the form.

In C#:

```
private void cmdClose_Click(object sender, System.EventArgs e)
{
    this.Close();
}
```

And in Visual Basic .NET:

```
Private Sub cmdClose_Click(ByVal sender As System.Object, _
    ByVal e As System.EventArgs) Handles cmdClose.Click
    Me.Close()
End Sub
```

However, this code is only half the story. If you expand the "Windows Form Designer Generated Code" section, you will see the following code.

In C#:

```
this.cmdClose.Click += new System.EventHandler(this.cmdClose_Click);
```

In Visual Basic .NET:

```
Friend WithEvents cmdClose As System.Windows.Forms.Button
```

This code should look somewhat familiar! As discussed previously, the C# code instantiates a delegate of the type EventHandler, passing a reference to the cmdClose_Click event handler method. In Visual Basic .NET, the code is even easier, because there are no delegates involved. The `WithEvents` keyword declares the cmdClose variable contains an object that is a source of events.

Double-clicking a user interface element in Visual Studio .NET automatically creates an event handler for the object's default event. So, how do you create event handlers in VS .NET for other events?

Automatically creating event handlers in C#

If you're working with C#, you automatically create event handlers in VS .NET as follows:

1. From within Visual Studio .NET, select the object in design mode.

2. Go to the Properties Window (press F4 if it's not visible).

3. Select the Events button at the top of the dialog (the button with the lightning bolt shown in **Figure 15**).

4. Double-click on the desired event and VS .NET automatically places an event handling method in the form for you.

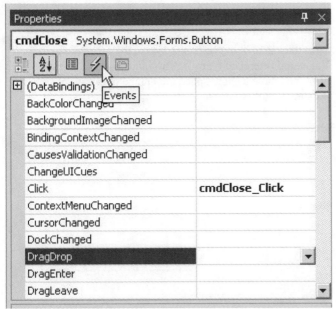

Figure 15. In C#, you can see an object's events by selecting it in design mode and clicking the Events button in the Properties Window.

If you accidentally double-click on an event in the Properties Window, or on a user interface element in design mode, you can easily remove the event handling code automatically added to the form by right-clicking on the event in the Properties Window and selecting Reset from the shortcut menu.

Automatically creating event handlers in Visual Basic .NET

If you're working with Visual Basic .NET, you automatically create event handlers in VS .NET as follows:

1. In Visual Studio .NET's code editor, select the desired `WithEvents` variable from the combo box at the upper left of the code-editing window.

2. Choose the event you want to handle from the combo box at the upper right of the code-editing window.

3. VS .NET automatically places an event-handling method in the file for you.

Structures

Structures are similar to classes, but rather than being reference types, they are value types (For more information, see the "Value and reference types" section in Chapter 3, "Introduction to C#). Because they are value types, they have a slight speed advantage over classes.

Structures are defined in C# as shown in this sample:

```
public struct StructureDemo
{
  public string FirstName;
  public string MiddleName;
  public string LastName;

  public string GetName()
  {
      return FirstName + " " +
          MiddleName + " " +
          LastName;
  }
}
```

And in Visual Basic .NET:

```
Public Structure StructureDemo
    Public FirstName As String
    Public MiddleName As String
    Public LastName As String


    Public Function GetName() As String
        Return FirstName & " " & MiddleName & " " & LastName
    End Function 'GetName
End Structure 'StructureDemo
```

Structures can:

- Have properties and methods.

- Raise and handle events.

- Implement interfaces.

Structures cannot:

- Have subclasses.

- Have protected members (this makes sense because they can't have subclasses).

Copying structures

Because structures are value types, you can copy values from one structure to another by simply assigning one structure variable to another. For example, the following code instantiates two instances of the StructureDemo structure. It sets the properties of the first instance, and then assigns the first structure variable to the second variable. When the last line is executed, it displays a message showing the second structure now has the same property values as the first.

In C#:

```
StructureDemo StructDemo1 = new StructureDemo();
StructureDemo StructDemo2 = new StructureDemo();

StructDemo1.FirstName = "Alexander";
StructDemo1.MiddleName = "James";
StructDemo1.LastName = "McNeish";

StructDemo2 = StructDemo1;
MessageBox.Show("Structure2 Name: " + StructDemo2.GetName(), "Structure demo");
```

In Visual Basic .NET:

```
Dim StructDemo1 As New StructureDemo()
Dim StructDemo2 As New StructureDemo()

StructDemo1.FirstName = "Alexander"
StructDemo1.MiddleName = "James"
StructDemo1.LastName = "McNeish"

StructDemo2 = StructDemo1
MessageBox.Show("Structure2 Name: " & StructDemo2.GetName(), "Structure demo")
```

Deciding between classes and structures

Structures are value types, so their data is stored on the stack rather than the heap. This means you should use a structure only if the object you create has a small instance size. Objects large in size should be classes.

One common use for structure is as a device for passing parameters. If you have several parameters you need to pass to a method, you can create a structure with a different property to hold each parameter value.

Behind the scenes, all value data types such as Boolean, Byte, Int32, and Decimal are actually structures!

Attributes

.NET attributes allow you to place extra descriptive information in your code that the compiler turns into metadata within your project's assembly. Attributes are useful at a variety of levels, such as an assembly, a class, or a class member. They can also be applied for a variety of reasons, as you'll see in this section.

When you create a new project in Visual Studio .NET, a file named Assembly.cs (or Assembly.vb) is automatically added to your project. This file contains attributes that apply to the entire assembly.

Here is an excerpt from a C# Assembly.cs file:

```
[assembly: AssemblyTitle("")]
[assembly: AssemblyDescription("")]
[assembly: AssemblyCompany("")]
[assembly: AssemblyProduct("")]
[assembly: AssemblyCopyright("")]
[assembly: AssemblyTrademark("")]
```

And from a Visual Basic .NET Assembly.vb file:

```
<Assembly: AssemblyTitle("")>
<Assembly: AssemblyDescription("")>
<Assembly: AssemblyCompany("")>
<Assembly: AssemblyProduct("")>
<Assembly: AssemblyCopyright("")>
<Assembly: AssemblyTrademark("")>
```

The keyword `assembly` indicates these attributes are applied at the assembly level. If you enter a description between the double quotes for each attribute, the compiler turns the description into metadata within your project's assembly. If you want a quick way to view this attribute information, you can use the Intermediate Language Disassembler (IL DASM) discussed in Chapter 1, "Introduction to .NET". This tool is located in the FrameworkSDK\ Bin folder below the directory on your machine containing the .NET Framework.

To launch the disassembler, just double-click the ildasm.exe file. To open an assembly, select File | Open from the menu. Use the Open dialog for navigating to and opening the desired assembly. Once the assembly is open, double-click the MANIFEST node (**Figure 16**).

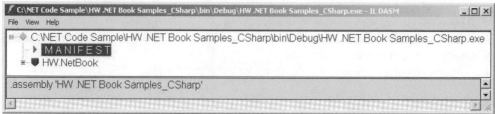

Figure 16. *You can view assembly-level attributes using the Intermediate Language Disassembler.*

This opens a window containing IL code, along with comments displaying the attribute text. Although this is interesting, the most practical way to examine attributes is at runtime by means of *reflection*. For more information, see the "Reflection" section later in this chapter.

Believe it or not, attributes are actually classes. The .NET Framework class library contains a few hundred attribute classes for all occasions! All attribute classes are derived from the System.Attribute class.

Here is an example of an attribute applied at the method level. The `Obsolete` attribute allows you to specify a method is going to eventually be removed.

In C#:

```
public class AttributeDemo
{
  [Obsolete("Method will be removed in the next version")]
  public void YourFavoriteMethod()
  {
  }
}
```

And in Visual Basic .NET:

```
Public Class AttributeDemo

    <Obsolete("Method will be removed in the next version")> _
    Public Sub YourFavoriteMethod()
    End Sub 'YourFavoriteMethod
End Class 'AttributeDemo
```

If any code in your application calls this method, the compiler displays the warning message specified in the attribute declaration:

```
..YourFavoriteMethod()' is obsolete: 'Method will be removed in the next
version'
```

You will see more examples of how attributes are used in Chapter 12, "XML Web Services". For more general information, see the .NET Help topic "Extending Metadata Using Attributes". For information on creating your own custom attributes, see the .NET Help topic "Writing Custom Attributes".

Indexers

The use of Indexers is an object-oriented convenience feature that allows you to access an object as if it is an array. Indexers are similar to properties, but their accessors take parameters.

For example, the following code declares a class named "Address" with three public string fields named "Street", "CityState", and "Zip". Indexers give users the option of accessing instances of the class as an array, with each of these fields representing a different row in the array. The code highlighted in grey is the indexer declaration. This particular indexer specifies instances of the Address class can be treated as a one-dimensional array with an `int` index.

In C#:

```
public class Address
{
  public string Street, CityState, Zip;

  /// Indexer for the Street, CityState & Zip fields
  public string this[int index]
  {
```

```
get
{
   switch (index)
   {
      case 0:
        return Street;
      case 1:
        return CityState;
      case 2:
        return Zip;
      default:
        throw new IndexOutOfRangeException(
          "Invalid Address element specified " + index);
   }
}
set
{
   switch (index)
   {
      case 0:
        Street = value;
        break;
      case 1:
        CityState = value;
        break;
      case 2:
        Zip = value;
        break;
      default:
        throw new IndexOutOfRangeException(
          "Invalid address element specified " + index);
   }
}
}

/// Initialize the address properties
public Address()
{
   this[0] = "952 Rockledge Drive";
   this[1] = "Charlottesville, VA";
   this[2] = "22903";
}
}
```

And in Visual Basic .NET:

```
Public Class Address
  Public Street, CityState, Zip As String

    ' Indexer for the Street, CityState & Zip fields
    Default Public Property Item(ByVal index As Integer) As String
      Get
        Select Case index
          Case 0
            Return Street
          Case 1
            Return CityState
          Case 2
            Return Zip
```

```
         Case Else
           Throw New IndexOutOfRangeException("Invalid element specified " & _
           index.ToString())
      End Select
   End Get

   Set(ByVal Value As String)
     Select Case index
       Case 0
         Street = Value
       Case 1
                 CityState = Value
       Case 2
         Zip = Value
       Case Else
         Throw New IndexOutOfRangeException("Invalid element specified " & _
         index.ToString())
     End Select
   End Set
 End Property

 ' Initialize the address properties
 Public Sub New()
   Me(0) = "952 Rockledge Drive"
   Me(1) = "Charlottesville, VA"
   Me(2) = "22903"
 End Sub 'New
End Class 'Address
```

Within the body of the indexer declaration the get and set accessors use the integer index to access values in the Street, CityState, and Zip fields.

Here is an example of code used to access an instance of this class as an array.

In C#:

```
Address AddressObj = new Address();
MessageBox.Show("Indexer address: \n\n" +
  AddressObj[0] + "\n" +
  AddressObj[1] + "\n" +
  AddressObj[2] + "\n");
```

And in Visual Basic .NET:

```
Dim AddressObj As New Address()
MessageBox.Show(("Indexer address: " & ControlChars.Lf & _
ControlChars.Lf & AddressObj(0) & ControlChars.Lf & _
AddressObj(1) & ControlChars.Lf & AddressObj(2) & ControlChars.Lf))
```

Notice how similar this is to accessing an array. You simply reference the object name followed by brackets or parentheses containing the index of the element you want to access.

Garbage Collection

If the phrase "memory leak" makes your skin crawl, you'll be happy to learn about the .NET Framework's garbage collector. In Visual FoxPro, you have to be extremely careful about cleaning up after objects when you are done using them. When you release an object, its Destroy method is fired, and the memory allocated for it is freed up—if all goes well.

In .NET, as you instantiate objects, the runtime allocates memory for them on the heap. However, rather than having to worry about releasing objects yourself, the .NET runtime takes care of this for you. Periodically, .NET's garbage collector checks for objects in the heap no longer being used and reclaims their memory.

Because the garbage collector periodically releases objects from memory on an "as-needed" basis, you can't count on an object being released at a specific time. Although it may take a while to get used to giving up this control, you'll find this works well in most cases.

Dispose methods

Because there is a delay between the time you are finished with an object and when the garbage collector physically releases it, if your object uses system resources such as database connections, you may want to provide clients with a method they can call to release these resources whenever they choose.

The .NET Framework's IDisposable interface supplies a Dispose method that consumers of your object can call to release resources acquired by your object. For more information on implementing the IDisposable interface, see the .NET Help topics "Implementing a Dispose Method" and "Initialization and Termination of Components".

Destructors and Finalize methods

All classes inherit the Finalize method from the System.Object class. This method automatically fires when the garbage collector releases an object. The Finalize method also automatically calls the Dispose method on classes that implement the IDisposable interface. Because this is the case, you should always call GC.SuppressFinalizeMethod from your Dispose method.

Normally, you don't have to worry about the Finalize method. However, if your object is using unmanaged resources, you may want to add code to your object to clean up these resources when the object is destroyed.

If you're using C#, you accomplish this by declaring a destructor method for your class. In the same way C# constructors are named the same as their containing class, destructors are also given the name of their containing class preceded by a tilde (~). For example, if you have a class named "Customer", you would create a destructor as follows:

```
~ Customer()
{
  // Cleanup Code
}
```

C# destructors are designed to automatically call the object's Finalize method.

If you're using Visual Basic .NET, you don't create destructors as in C#. Instead, you create an override of the Finalize method in your class, placing the necessary cleanup code directly in this method. For example:

```
Protected Override Sub Finalize()
   ' Cleanup Code
   MyBase.Finalize()
End Sub
```

Although placing cleanup code in destructor or Finalize methods is useful when you need it, be forewarned that doing so can impact application performance. Also, as mentioned previously, you can't guarantee when the Finalize method of an object will execute, so do not rely on the timing of any code placed in the Finalize method. For details, see the .NET Help topics "Finalize Methods and Destructors" and "Automatic Memory Management".

C#'s using statement

C#'s using statement has a convenience feature not available in Visual Basic .NET. In this context, using is something completely different than when you are "using" a namespace. The using statement provides a more automatic way of calling the Dispose method of an object. For example, the using statement in the code shown below instantiates a class named "UnmanagedResource". Within the curly braces of the using statement, you place code that uses the MyRes object. When the object loses scope at the bottom of the using statement, the object's Finalize method is automatically called.

```
public class UsingDemo
{
   public void MyMethod()
   {
        using (UnmanagedResource MyRes = new UnmanagedResource())
        {
            // Use the MyRes object
        }
   }
}
```

Note the class you instantiate in the using statement must implement the IDisposing interface.

Operator Overloading

The C# language has an advanced object-oriented feature called *operator overloading* that is not available in Visual Basic .NET. Earlier in this chapter, you learned about *method* overloading—an object-oriented technique that allows you to create multiple methods with the same name.

Operator overloading allows you to do something similar with operators. You can provide new meaning for operators such as +, -, !, ++, and --, by defining static methods in classes using the operator keyword.

Although this is an interesting feature, it's probably not one you will use often. Rather than going into detail here, you can check out two good examples of operator overloading in the .NET Help topic "Operator Overloading Tutorial". For a list of operators that can be overloaded, see the .NET Help topic "Overloadable Operators".

Reflection

In Visual FoxPro, there is a certain freedom and flexibility that comes from specifying the class of an object be instantiated at run time. For example, I use an abstract factory in my Visual FoxPro applications allowing me to data drive my class instantiation. I call the abstract factory's GetClassName method, passing a token specifying the kind of class I want to instantiate. The abstract factory looks up this token in a table, returning the name of the class I should use. I then pass the class name to the CREATEOBJECT command, which instantiates an object from the specified class.

```
lcClassName = goApp.oFactory.GetClassName("SecurityMgr")
loSecurityMgr = CREATEOBJECT(lcClassName)
```

If you are using the new command in C# or in Visual Basic .NET (assuming Option Strict is "On"), you are required to specify the type of the class you will instantiate at compile time.
In C#:

```
Customer CustomerObj = new Customer();
```

In Visual Basic .NET:

```
Dim CustomerObj As New Customer()
```

Fortunately, there is a way to achieve Visual FoxPro's object creation flexibility in C# and VB .NET by using *reflection*. .NET reflection supplies objects that encapsulate assemblies, modules, and classes, allowing you to dynamically create an instance of a class. Some other things you can do with reflection are:

- Load assemblies and modules.

- Retrieve information about class constructors.

- Retrieve information about class methods and invoke them.

- Retrieve information about class fields and get/set their values.

- Retrieve information about class events and add/remove event handlers.

- Retrieve information about class properties and get/set their values.

- Retrieve information about method parameters.

- Generate MSIL code on the fly.

Accessing type information

You get type (class) information from assemblies already loaded in memory by calling the static Type.GetType method. This and other reflection methods return a System.Type object you use to derive information about classes.

For example, the following code calls the GetType method, passing a string containing the fully qualified name of the Client class declared in this chapter's sample code.

In C#:

```
Type ClientType = Type.GetType("HW.NetBook.Samples.Client");
```

In Visual Basic .NET:

```
Dim ClientType As Type = Type.GetType("HW.NetBook.Samples.Client")
```

After running this code, you can examine the ClientType object to discover information about the Client class. Because it is a Type object, it has a number of properties and methods you can use to get information about the Client class. **Table 4** lists some of the more interesting properties and methods.

Table 4. *Type objects have a good number of properties and methods you can use to find out information about classes.*

Properties	Description
Assembly	The assembly where the type is declared.
BaseType	The type from which the current type directly inherits.
FullName	The fully qualified name of the type, including the namespace.
GUID	The GUID associated with the type.
IsAbstract	Specifies if the type is abstract.
IsClass	Specifies if the type is a class.
IsCOMObject	Specifies if the type is a COM object.
IsEnum	Specifies if the type is an enumeration.
IsInterface	Specifies if the type is an interface.
Name	The name of the type
Namespace	The namespace of the type
UnderlyingSystemType	Specifies the .NET Framework base class the type is based on. Even if you have several layers of inheritance in your class hierarchy, this property displays the first .NET Framework base class in the hierarchy.

Methods	Description
FindInterfaces	Returns an array of Type objects representing a list of interfaces implemented or inherited by the current type.
FindMembers	Returns an array of FilterMember objects of the specified member type (i.e. constructor, property, event, method).
GetEvent	Gets a specific event inherited or declared by the current type.
GetField	Gets a specific field of the current type.
GetInterface	Gets a specific interface implemented or inherited by the current type.
GetMember	Gets the specified members of the current type.
GetMethod	Gets a specific method of the current type.
GetProperty	Gets a specific property of the current type.
InvokeMember	Invokes a specific member of the current type.

To obtain information about types located in assemblies that are *not* loaded, you can use the Assembly.GetType or Assembly.GetTypes methods.

Late binding with reflection

When the type of an object is determined at run time rather than compile time, this is known as late binding. This is the type of binding used with Visual FoxPro's CREATEOBJECT command. Following is some code that simulates CREATEOBJECT.

The code declares a class you instantiate using late binding.
In C#:

```csharp
public class Message
{
  public void ShowMessage(string msg)
  {
      MessageBox.Show(msg, "Message class");
  }
}
```

And in Visual Basic .NET:

```vb
Public Class Message

    Public Sub ShowMessage(ByVal msg As String)
        MessageBox.Show(msg, "Message class")
    End Sub 'ShowMessage

End Class 'Message
```

The following code instantiates the Message class and calls its ShowMessage method.
In C#:

```csharp
// Get the type to use from the assembly.
Type MessageType = Type.GetType("HW.NetBook.Samples.Message");

// Get the method to call from the type.
MethodInfo ShowMessageMethod = MessageType.GetMethod("ShowMessage");

// Create an instance of the Message class.
Object MessageObj = Activator.CreateInstance(MessageType);

// Create the arguments array.
Object[] args = new Object[1];

// Set the arguments
args[0] = "I'm using late binding!!!";

// Invoke the PrintHello method.
ShowMessageMethod.Invoke(MessageObj, args);
```

In Visual Basic .NET:

```vb
' Get the type to use from the assembly.
Dim MessageType As Type = Type.GetType("HW.NetBook.Samples.Message")

' Get the method to call from the type.
Dim ShowMessageMethod As MethodInfo = MessageType.GetMethod("ShowMessage")
```

```
' Create an instance of the Message class.
Dim MessageObj As Object = Activator.CreateInstance(MessageType)

' Create the arguments array.
Dim args(0) As Object

' Set the arguments
args(0) = "I'm using late binding!!!"

' Invoke the PrintHello method.
ShowMessageMethod.Invoke(MessageObj, args)
```

The first line of code uses the static Type.GetType method to retrieve a Type object that contains information about the HW.NetBook.Samples.Message class. You can use Type.GetType because the Message class is contained in an assembly already loaded.

The second line of code calls the Type object's GetMethod requesting information on the Message.ShowMessage method. GetMethod returns a MethodInfo object you can use to invoke the ShowMessage method.

The third line of code uses the static Activator.CreateInstance method to create an instance of the Message class. Next, an array of type Object is created to pass a parameter to the Message.ShowMessage method when it is invoked. Even if the method you are calling does not have any parameters, you still need to declare an empty Object array as follows.

In C#:

```
Object[] args = new Object[1];
```

And in Visual Basic .NET:

```
Dim args(0) As Object
```

Finally, the last line of code invokes the Message.ShowMessage method.

If you need to get type information for a class not in a loaded assembly, you use the static Assembly.Load method. For example, the following code loads the MyOtherAssembly file and retrieves the HW.NetBook.Samples.MyClass type from the assembly.

In C#:

```
Assembly assem = Assembly.Load("MyOtherAssembly");
// Get the type to use from the assembly.
Type helloType = assem.GetType("HW.NetBook.Samples.MyClass");
```

In Visual Basic .NET:

```
Dim assem As [Assembly] = [Assembly].Load("MyOtherAssembly")
' Get the type to use from the assembly.
Dim helloType As Type = assem.GetType("HW.NetBook.Samples.MyClass")
```

Late binding in Visual Basic .NET

In addition to the methodology shown in the previous section, there's an easier way to implement late binding in Visual Basic .NET using the Object data type.

VB .NET treats the Object data type in special way. Unlike C#, VB .NET allows you to store an object reference into a variable of type Object and call methods on the object even though the .NET Object class does not implement those methods.

For example, the following code declares a class with a method named "CallMethod" that accepts an Object parameter. In this method there is a single line of code that calls a DisplayMessage method on this object.

```
Public Class ObjectLateBindingDemo
    Public Sub CallMethod(ByVal obj As Object)
        obj.DisplayMessage()
    End Sub
End Class
```

In order to get this code to compile, you must set VB .NET's Option Strict setting to "Off" (for more information on Option Strict, see Chapter 4, "Introduction to Visual Basic .NET"). This tells the compiler to ignore the rules of strict typing.

Turning strict typing off allows you to pass an object reference of any type to CallMethod. The compiler blissfully ignores the fact you declared a variable of type Object and are calling a method (DisplayMessage) not implemented in the Object class.

If you pass an object to CallMethod that implements the DisplayMessage method, everything goes smoothly at run time. However, if you pass an object that does *not* implement this method, you get a runtime error.

The fact that you have to turn off strict typing in order to use this feature should make you think twice before using it. As I recommended in Chapter 4, "Introduction to Visual Basic .NET", you should never turn Option Strict off because you miss the benefit of catching errors at compile time rather than run time.

Performance and late binding

Although late binding provides flexibility, a substantial price is paid in performance. This is because the compiler does not know at compile time the class being used, so binding must be performed at runtime instead.

I suggest using late binding only when you absolutely need it. You should stick to early binding as a general rule. If you are designing your applications well, you can achieve a similar effect by means of abstract classes and interfaces as described earlier in this chapter—and without incurring a performance penalty.

Conclusion

This chapter gives a good overview of C# and Visual Basic .NET's object-oriented features. Again, this is not an exhaustive list of all features, but an introduction to object-orientation in .NET. In the final analysis, both C# and Visual Basic .NET go beyond the OO capabilities of Visual FoxPro and provide a number of advanced features to help you create flexible, well-designed software applications.

Chapter 6
Tour of the .NET Base Classes

Although a lot of heat is generated over which .NET programming language is easier to use and learn, ultimately THE biggest learning curve is not C# or Visual Basic .NET—it's the .NET Framework. This chapter takes you on a tour of some of the more interesting and useful classes and shows you how to use them in your applications.

There are over 2,000 classes in the .NET Framework (compared to Visual FoxPro's 35 base classes), making for a fairly steep learning curve when you are first learning about .NET. Many of the most important .NET classes are covered in detail in other chapters of this book. However, in this chapter, you will learn some details about classes that are also very important, but are not covered in detail elsewhere.

This chapter will cover the classes by namespace so you also get a feel for the organization of classes in .NET, but it will not cover every namespace in the framework. First of all, there's only so much I can cover in a chapter within the scope of this book, and secondly, a number of namespaces contain classes you will not normally use on a regular basis (for example the .NET classes you can use to write your own compiler).

As mentioned in Chapter 1, "Introducing .NET", before you can use a class in your code, first you need to make sure you reference its associated namespace (by means of the "using" directive in C# and the "Imports" directive in Visual Basic .NET).

The System namespace

The System namespace contains quite a few classes that you use frequently and have already been introduced in previous chapters, such as the base value types—Boolean, Byte, Char, Decimal, Integer, and so on (**Figure 1**). The following sections shows a few other classes belonging to the System namespace that are also of interest.

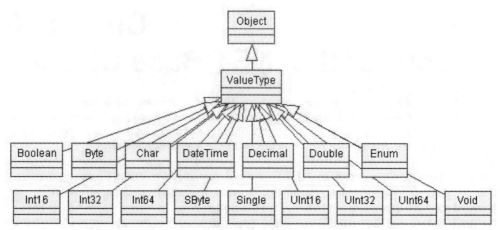

Figure 1. *The System namespace contains many frequently used classes such as the base value type classes shown in this UML class diagram.*

The String class—working with strings

Chapter 3, "Introduction to C#" and Chapter 4, "Introduction to Visual Basic .NET", provide some basic information regarding the string data type. This section further explores its capabilities.

> *The string alias in C# and the String alias in Visual Basic .NET are both shortcuts that refer to the System.String class.*

Parsing strings

The String class provides a number of methods that allow you to parse strings. This is different than Visual FoxPro, which has a variety of independent functions you use to parse strings. The String class brings all of this functionality together in a single class.

To determine the starting position of one or more characters within a string, you use the String class's IndexOf method, which finds the first occurrence or the LastIndex method, which finds the last occurrence. You can also specify the starting character position and number of characters searched.

Here's an example in C#:

```
string MyString = "<GBAddress>Four score and seven years ago...</GBAddress>";
int DotsIndex = MyString.IndexOf("...");     // returns 41
int LastIndex = MyString.LastIndexOf('<');   // returns 44
```

And in Visual Basic .NET:

```
Dim MyString As String = _
  "<GBAddress>Four score and seven years ago...</GBAddress>"
Dim DotsIndex As Integer = MyString.IndexOf("...") ' returns 41
Dim LastIndex As Integer = MyString.LastIndexOf("<"c) ' returns 44
```

You can also determine if a string starts or ends with a specified string.
In C#:

```
string MyString = "<GBAddress>Four score and seven years ago...</GBAddress>";
bool IsStart = MyString.StartsWith("<GBAddress>");  // returns true
bool IsEnd = MyString.EndsWith("</GBAddress>");      // returns true
```

In Visual Basic. NET:

```
Dim MyString As String = _
   "<GBAddress>Four score and seven years ago...</GBAddress>"
Dim IsStart As Boolean = MyString.StartsWith("<GBAddress>") ' returns True
Dim IsEnd As Boolean = MyString.EndsWith("</GBAddress>")    ' returns True
```

To retrieve a substring of another string, you use the String class's Substring method. You specify just a starting position or both a starting position and number of characters.
In C#:

```
string MyString = "<GBAddress>Four score and seven years ago...</GBAddress>";

// Returns "Four score"
string SubString = MyString.Substring(MyString.IndexOf('>')+1, 10);
```

In Visual Basic .NET:

```
Dim MyString As String = _
  "<GBAddress>Four score and seven years ago...</GBAddress>"

' Returns "Four score"
Dim SubString As String = MyString.Substring(MyString.IndexOf(">"c) + 1, 10)
```

Padding and Trimming strings

You pad strings by using the String class's PadLeft and PadRight methods. By default, these methods pad a string with spaces on the left or the right to make the string the total specified length. Alternately, you can pass a second character parameter that specifies a different pad character. In the following example, the PadLeft method is used to add five spaces to the left side of the Unpadded string. The PadRight method is then used to add five periods to the right of the string.
Here's the code in C#:

```
string Unpadded = "Once upon a time";

// Returns "     Once upon a time"
```

```
string PadLeft = Unpadded.PadLeft(Unpadded.Length + 5);

// Returns "Once upon a time     ."
string PadRight = Unpadded.PadRight(Unpadded.Length + 5)+ ".";
```

Here's the code in Visual Basic .NET:

```
Dim Unpadded As String = "Once upon a time"

' Returns "     Once upon a time"
Dim PadLeft As String = MyString.PadLeft((MyString.Length + 5))

' Returns "Once upon a time     ."
Dim PadRight As String = MyString.PadRight((MyString.Length + 5)) + "."
```

You trim characters from the beginning or end of a string (or from both) by using the String class's TrimStart, TrimEnd, and Trim methods. If you don't pass a parameter to these trim methods, they trim spaces from the string. Otherwise, you specify an array of one or more characters to be trimmed from the string.

Here's an example in C#:

```
string MyPaddedStr = "    I've been padded!!!!!";

// Returns "I've been padded!!!!!"
string TrimStart = MyPaddedStr.TrimStart();

char[] TrimChr = {'!'};

// Returns "    I've been padded"
string TrimEnd = MyPaddedStr.TrimEnd(TrimChr);

MyPaddedStr = "    I've been padded    ";

// Returns "I've been padded"
string TrimAll = MyPaddedStr.Trim();
```

And here it is in Visual Basic .NET:

```
Dim MyPaddedStr As String = "    I've been padded!!!!!"

' Returns "I've been padded!!!!!"
Dim TrimStart As String = MyPaddedStr.TrimStart()

Dim TrimChr As Char = "!"c

' Returns "    I've been padded"
Dim TrimEnd As String = MyPaddedStr.TrimEnd(TrimChr)

MyPaddedStr = "    I've been padded    "

' Returns "I've been padded"
Dim TrimAll As String = MyPaddedStr.Trim()
```

Manipulating strings

You can insert, remove, and replace characters in a string or convert a string to uppercase or lowercase by using the corresponding Remove, Replace, Convert, ToUpper, and ToLower methods as shown in the following example.

In C#:

```
string MyString = "<GBAddress>Four score and seven years ago...</GBAddress>";
int DotsIndex = MyString.IndexOf("...");      // Returns 41

// Returns "<GBAddress>Four score and seven years ago our
fathers...</GBAddress>"
string NewString = MyString.Insert(DotsIndex, " our fathers");

// Returns "<GBAddress>Four score and seven years ago</GBAddress>"
string RemoveStr = MyString.Remove(DotsIndex, 3);

// Returns "<GBAddress>Four score and seven years ago etc.</GBAddress>"
string ReplaceStr = MyString.Replace("...", " etc.");

// Returns "<gbaddress>four score and seven years ago...</gbaddress>"
string Lower = MyString.ToLower();

// Returns "<GBAddress>FOUR SCORE AND SEVEN YEARS AGO...</GBAddress>"
string Upper = MyString.ToUpper();
```

And in Visual Basic .NET:

```
Dim MyString As String = _
  "<GBAddress>Four score and seven years ago...</GBAddress>"
Dim DotsIndex As Integer = MyString.IndexOf("...")   ' Returns 41

' Returns "<GBAddress>Four score and seven years ago our
fathers...</GBAddress>"
Dim NewString As String = MyString.Insert(DotsIndex, " our forefathers")

' Returns "<GBAddress>Four score and seven years ago</GBAddress>"
Dim RemoveStr As String = MyString.Remove(DotsIndex, 3)

' Returns "<GBAddress>Four score and seven years ago etc.</GBAddress>"
Dim ReplaceStr As String = MyString.Replace("...", " etc.")

' Returns "<gbaddress>four score and seven years ago...</gbaddress>"
Dim Lower As String = MyString.ToLower()

' Returns "<GBAddress>FOUR SCORE AND SEVEN YEARS AGO...</GBAddress>"
Dim Upper As String = MyString.ToUpper()
```

The Environment class – platform and environment information

The Environment class has some very useful static properties and methods for retrieving information about the current environment and platform where your application is running. For example, the following code gets the current directory, machine name, operating system version, system directory, domain name, and user name from properties of the Environment class, and then displays them in a message box.

In C#:

```
string EnvironMsg;
EnvironMsg = "Current Directory: " +
  Environment.CurrentDirectory + "\n" +
  "MachineName: " + Environment.MachineName + "\n" +
  "OS Version: " + Environment.OSVersion + "\n" +
  "System Directory: " + Environment.SystemDirectory + "\n" +
  "Domain name: " + Environment.UserDomainName + "\n" +
  "User name: " + Environment.UserName + "\n";

MessageBox.Show(EnvironMsg, "Environment class");
```

In Visual Basic .NET:

```
Dim EnvironMsg As String
EnvironMsg = "Current Directory: " & Environment.CurrentDirectory & _
  ControlChars.Lf & "MachineName: " & Environment.MachineName & _
  ControlChars.Lf & "OS Version: " & Environment.OSVersion.ToString() & _
  ControlChars.Lf & "System Directory: " & Environment.SystemDirectory & _
  ControlChars.Lf & "Domain name: " & Environment.UserDomainName & _
  ControlChars.Lf & "User name: " & Environment.UserName & ControlChars.Lf

MessageBox.Show(EnvironMsg, "Environment class")
```

You can also use the Environment class to retrieve a list of logical drives.
In C#:

```
string DriveList = "Logical drives: \n";
string[] Drives = Environment.GetLogicalDrives();
foreach (string Drive in Drives)
{
  DriveList += Drive + "\n";
}
MessageBox.Show(DriveList, "Environment class");
```

In Visual Basic .NET:

```
Dim DriveList As String = "Logical drives: " + ControlChars.Lf
Dim Drives As String() = Environment.GetLogicalDrives()
Dim Drive As String
For Each Drive In Drives
  DriveList += Drive + ControlChars.Lf
Next Drive

MessageBox.Show(DriveList, "Environment class")
```

The Environment class also contains methods that allow you to retrieve command line arguments and environment variables. For more information on the Environment class, see the .NET Help topic "Environment Class".

DateTime structure

The DateTime structure is used to represent a date and time-of-day. DateTime has a number of static properties and methods you use to get date and time-related information. For example, the following code uses the DateTime structure to get the current date, current time, number of days in October 1960 (my birth month/year), and to determine if 2002 is a leap year.

In C#:

```
string DateTimeMsg;
DateTimeMsg = "Current Date: " + DateTime.Today + "\n" +
  "Current DateTime: " + DateTime.Now + "\n" +
  "Days in month for Oct '60: " + DateTime.DaysInMonth(1960,10) + "\n" +
  "Is 2002 a leap year: " + DateTime.IsLeapYear(2002);
```

And in Visual Basic .NET:

```
Dim DateTimeMsg As String
DateTimeMsg = "Current Date: " + DateTime.Today.ToString() + _
  ControlChars.Lf + "Current DateTime: " + _
  DateTime.Now.ToString() + ControlChars.Lf + _
  "Days in month for Oct '60: " + _
  DateTime.DaysInMonth(1960, 10).ToString() + ControlChars.Lf + _
  "Is 2002 a leap year: " + DateTime.IsLeapYear(2002).ToString()
```

You can also instantiate an instance of the DateTime structure, passing a date and time that you want to work with in the constructor. The following code passes my birth date and time, October 9, 1960, 1:10 am (huge hint to readers who don't want to miss an opportunity to send the author a birthday present) to the constructor of the DateTime structure. It then builds a string that contains the date, day, day-of-week, day-of-year, month, time-of-day, and year of my birthday. The second section of this code uses the DateTime structure's AddYears method to return a new DateTime object that represents my 64th birthday (for you Beatle fans).

Here's the code in C#:

```
DateTime DateTimeObj = new DateTime(1960,10,9,1,10,0,0);
DateTimeMsg = "October 9, 1960, 1:10am\n\n";
DateTimeMsg += "Date: " + DateTimeObj.Date + "\n" +
  "Day: " + DateTimeObj.Day + "\n" +
  "Day-of-week: " + DateTimeObj.DayOfWeek + "\n" +
  "Day-of-year: " + DateTimeObj.DayOfYear + "\n" +
  "Month: " + DateTimeObj.Month + "\n" +
  "Time-of-Day: " + DateTimeObj.TimeOfDay + "\n" +
  "Year: " + DateTimeObj.Year + "\n";

DateTime DateTime64 = DateTimeObj.AddYears(64);
DateTimeMsg += "When I'm 64: " + DateTime64.Year;
MessageBox.Show(DateTimeMsg, "DateTime structure");
```

Here's the code in Visual Basic .NET:

```
Dim DateTimeObj As New DateTime(1960, 10, 9, 1, 10, 0, 0)
DateTimeMsg = "October 9, 1960, 1:10am" + ControlChars.Lf + ControlChars.Lf
DateTimeMsg += "Date: " + DateTimeObj.Date.ToString() + _
    ControlChars.Lf + "Day: " + DateTimeObj.Day.ToString() + _
```

```
        ControlChars.Lf + "Day-of-week: " + DateTimeObj.DayOfWeek.ToString() + _
        ControlChars.Lf + "Day-of-year: " + DateTimeObj.DayOfYear.ToString() + _
        ControlChars.Lf + "Month: " + DateTimeObj.Month.ToString() + _
        ControlChars.Lf + "Time-of-Day: " + DateTimeObj.TimeOfDay.ToString() + _
        ControlChars.Lf + "Year: " + DateTimeObj.Year.ToString() + _
        ControlChars.Lf

Dim DateTime64 As DateTime = DateTimeObj.AddYears(64)
DateTimeMsg += "When I'm 64: " + DateTime64.Year.ToString()

MessageBox.Show(DateTimeMsg, "DateTime structure")
```

The DateTime structure has many other methods you can use to add and subtract dates and times, as well as methods for converting to other data types.

You can also check out the System.TimeSpan structure when working with time intervals rather than a specific date and time.

The Math class

The Math class performs common mathematical as well as logarithmic and trigonometric functions. The following code demonstrates using the Math class to round numbers (Round), determine the larger of two numbers (Max), the smaller (Min), and raise a number to a specified power (Pow).

Here's the code in C#:

```
string MathMsg;
double Value, Result;
int MaxValue, MinValue;

Value = Math.Round(1.23, 1);    // Returns 1.2
MaxValue = Math.Max(7, 5);      // Returns 7
MinValue = Math.Min(7, 5);      // Returns 5
Result = Math.Pow(12, 3);       // Returns 1728.0
```

Here's the code in Visual Basic .NET:

```
Dim MathMsg As String
Dim Value, Result As Double
Dim MaxValue, MinValue As Integer

Value = Math.Round(1.23, 1)     ' Returns 1.2
MaxValue = Math.Max(7, 5)       ' Returns 7
MinValue = Math.Min(7, 5)       ' Returns 5
Result = Math.Pow(12, 3)        ' Returns 1728.0
```

There are many other math functions you can perform using the Math class such as determining sign, cosine, logarithm, square root, and so on.

The System.Collections namespace

The System.Collections namespace contains classes that contain collections of objects. **Figure 2** shows some of the classes that define collections of queues, arrays, hash tables, and dictionaries.

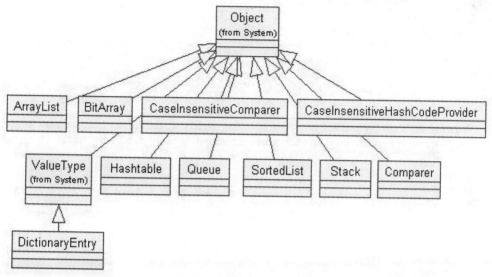

Figure 2. *The System.Collections namespace contains classes that contain collections of objects such as queues, arrays, hash tables, and dictionaries.*

The ArrayList class

The ArrayList class is an object-oriented array that can be dynamically resized at runtime. This is particularly useful in C# where an array's dimensions cannot be changed. The ArrayList contains a variety of methods you use to manipulate array elements.

To add elements to an ArrayList, you use the Add method, specifying the item to be added. You can also use the Insert method to insert an element at a specified index.

Here's the code in C#:

```
ArrayList ArryList = new ArrayList();
ArryList.Add("Moe");
ArryList.Add("Larry");
ArryList.Add("Curly");
ArryList.Insert(2, "Bob");
```

And in Visual Basic .NET:

```
Dim ArryList As New ArrayList()
ArryList.Add("Moe")
ArryList.Add("Larry")
ArryList.Add("Curly")
ArryList.Insert(2, "Bob")
```

This code produces elements in the following order:

```
Moe
Larry
Curly
Bob
```

You use the Remove method or the RemoveAt (specifying the index of the element to be removed) methods to remove elements from an ArrayList.
In C#:

```
ArryList.Remove("Bob");
ArryList.RemoveAt(2);
```

In Visual Basic .NET:

```
ArryList.Remove("Bob")
ArryList.RemoveAt(2)
```

This code produces elements in the following order:

```
Moe
Larry
```

You can access an element (get its value or set its value) at a specified index.
In C#:

```
ArryList[1] = "Shemp";
```

In Visual Basic .NET:

```
ArryList(1) = "Shemp"
```

This code sets the ArrayList elements to the following:

```
Moe
Shemp
```

You find the index of the first occurrence of a value by calling the IndexOf method. You find the index of the last occurrence of a value by calling the LastIndexOf method. The following code adds two duplicate values to an ArrayList, one at the beginning and one at the end, and then uses IndexOf and LastIndexOf to get their indexed location.

Here's the code in C#:

```
ArryList.Insert(0, "Curly");
ArryList.Add("Curly");
int FirstIndex = ArryList.IndexOf("Curly");
int LastIndex = ArryList.LastIndexOf("Curly");
```

And here's the code in Visual Basic .NET:

```
ArryList.Insert(0, "Curly")
ArryList.Add("Curly")
Dim FirstIndex As Integer = ArryList.IndexOf("Curly")
Dim LastIndex As Integer = ArryList.LastIndexOf("Curly")
```

This code produces elements in the following order:

```
Curly
Moe
Shemp
Curly
```

You sort the elements in an ArrayList by calling the Sort method. You can reverse the order by calling the Reverse method. This code is the same in C# and Visual Basic .NET:

```
ArryList.Sort();
ArryList.Reverse();
```

The Capacity property specifies the number of elements an ArrayList can contain (the default value is 16). The Count property specifies the actual number of elements in the array. If the Count exceeds the Capacity, the Capacity is automatically doubled to accommodate the new array element. If you want to set the capacity to the actual number of elements, you use the TrimToSize method.

For more information on the capabilities of the ArrayList class, see the .NET Help topic "ArrayList Class".

Comparer and CaseInsensitiveComparer classes

The Comparer class performs a case-sensitive comparison of two objects of the same type. The CaseInsensitiveComparer class performs a case-insensitive comparison of two objects of the same type. Each class has a Compare method you call and pass the two objects to be compared. It returns a -1 if the first value is less than the second value, a zero if the two objects are equal, and a 1 if the first value is greater than the second value.

The following example shows the comparison of the same two strings using each class. In C#:

```
int CompValue1 = Comparer.Default.Compare("new york", "New York");
int CompValue2 = CaseInsensitiveComparer.Default.Compare("new york", "New York");
```

In Visual Basic .NET:

```
Dim CompValue1 As Integer = Comparer.Default.Compare("new york", "New York")
Dim CompValue2 As Integer = CaseInsensitiveComparer.Default.Compare("new york",
"New York")
```

The Comparer class returns a minus 1 indicating that "new york" is less than "New York". The CaseInsensitiveComparer class returns a zero indicating that "new york" is the same as "New York".

The HashTable class

So far, the collections you have examined only allow you to store the equivalent of a single array column. This can be somewhat limiting when you have multiple elements of the same value you want to distinguish in a unique way. This is where the HashTable class comes to the rescue.

The HashTable class allows you to create a collection of key-and-value pairs organized based on the hash of the key. The following example creates a HashTable and adds three key-value pairs to it. Afterwards, it retrieves the value "Oranges" using the key "A2".

Here's the code in C#:

```
// Create the Hash Table and add three key-value pairs
Hashtable HTable = new Hashtable();
HTable.Add("a1", "Apples");
HTable.Add("a2", "Oranges");
HTable.Add("a3", "Pears");

// Get a value based on a key
string Item = (string)HTable["a2"];
```

And here it is in Visual Basic .NET:

```
' Create the Hash Table and add three key-value pairs
Dim HTable As New Hashtable()
HTable.Add("a1", "Apples")
HTable.Add("a2", "Oranges")
HTable.Add("a3", "Pears")

' Get a value based on a key
Dim Item As String = CStr(HTable("a2"))
```

Notice when the string value is retrieved from the HashTable in the last line of code, it must be cast to a string. Why is this necessary since it was added to the HashTable as a string? Because each key-value *pair* comprises a *single* element of a HashTable and the element is of the type DictionaryEntry.

The Queue class

The Queue class provides a first-in, first-out collection of objects. For example, you can use this class to process messages in the order they were received. The following code adds messages to the Queue class using the Enqueue method and retrieves *and removes* objects in first-in, first-out order using the Dequeue method.

In C#:

```
Queue QueueTest = new Queue();
QueueTest.Enqueue("9:00 am - Your mother called, don't be a stranger!");
QueueTest.Enqueue("9:10 am - Your wife called, pick up haggis for dinner");
QueueTest.Enqueue("10:40am - Ed McMahon called, your ship has come in");

string MessageList = "You have " + QueueTest.Count + " messages:\n\n";
while (QueueTest.Count > 0)
{
  MessageList += QueueTest.Dequeue() + "\n";
}

MessageBox.Show(MessageList, "Queue class");
```

In Visual Basic .NET:

```
Dim QueueTest As New Queue()
QueueTest.Enqueue("9:00 am - Your mother called, don't be a stranger!")
QueueTest.Enqueue("9:10 am - Your wife called, pick up haggis for dinner")
QueueTest.Enqueue("10:40am - Ed McMahon called, your ship has come in")

Dim MessageList As String = "You have " & QueueTest.Count.ToString() & _
    " messages:" & ControlChars.Lf & ControlChars.Lf
While QueueTest.Count > 0
    MessageList += QueueTest.Dequeue().ToString() & ControlChars.Lf
End While

MessageBox.Show(MessageList, "Queue class")
```

Figure 3 shows the resulting message box displayed by this code.

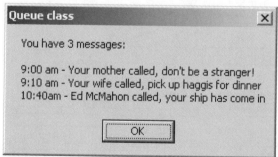

Figure 3. The Queue class is a first-in, first-out collection of objects. You can, for example, use it to process messages in the order they were received.

The Stack and SortedList classes

The Stack and SortedList classes represent two additional types of collections. The Stack class is similar to the Queue class, except it is a last-in, first-out collection. You add items to the Stack class by using the Push method. You retrieve and remove items from the Stack class by using the Pop method.

The SortedList class is a cross between a HashTable and an Array. You access an item in a SortedList using its key, as you do in HashTables. You can also access an item by passing its index to the GetByIndex and SetByIndex methods, as you do in an Array.

The System.Collections.Specialized namespace also contains more specialized collections such as a string collection, a linked list dictionary, and other strongly-typed collections.

The System.EnterpriseServices namespace

If you're building n-tier, distributed .NET applications, you'll definitely use some of the classes found in the System.EnterpriseServices namespace. These classes provide access to COM+ services, including queued components, COM+ events, transaction services, and something you can't get with either Visual FoxPro or Visual Basic 6—object pooling.

COM+ services is still the primary Microsoft technology for hosting components, both COM and .NET, and the .NET Framework fully supports COM+. For more information on COM+, see the Hentzenwerke book "What's New in Visual FoxPro 7" (chapter 14, "Playing in the COM+ Sandbox").

The main classes in the System.EnterpriseServices namespace are show in **Figure 4**.

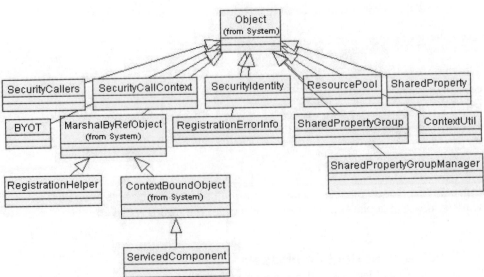

Figure 4. The classes in the System.EnterpriseServices namespace provide COM+ services access to your .NET components.

A description of all the enterprise services classes is beyond the scope of this book, but the following sections show you the basics of using some of the classes to configure an assembly for COM+ services and specifically, object pooling. This involves the following steps:

- Configuring an assembly to use COM+ services – Before an assembly can use COM+ services, you need to set some special attributes on the assembly.

- Deploying the assembly – You must install the assembly in the Global Assembly Cache (GAC).

- Configuring a class to use object pooling – You must specify special attributes for each class that you want to pool.

The following sections explain each of these steps in detail.

Configuring an assembly for COM+ services

To configure an assembly to use COM+ services requires that you set four assembly attributes: ApplicationActivation, ApplicationID, ApplicationName, and Description. These attributes are set in your solution's AssemblyInfo.cs file (C#) or AssemblyInfo.vb file (VB .NET).

Here's an example in C#:

```
using System.EnterpriseServices;

[assembly: ApplicationActivation(ActivationOption.Server)]
[assembly: ApplicationName(".NET for VFP Developers samples")]
[assembly: Description(".NET for VFP Developers book samples")]
[assembly: ApplicationID("1B55DB81-11CC-46b9-B989-11A5784D8E26")]
```

And in Visual Basic .NET:

```
Imports System.EnterpriseServices

<Assembly: ApplicationActivation(ActivationOption.Server)>
<Assembly: ApplicationID("1B55DB81-11CC-46b9-B989-11A5784D8E26")>
<Assembly: ApplicationName(".NET for VFP Developers samples")>
<Assembly: Description(".NET for VFP Developer book samples")>
```

First of all, notice that you need to add a reference to the System.EnterpriseServices namespace to your AssemblyInfo file as shown in the first line of the sample code. However, before you can do this, you must first add a reference to the System.EnterpriseServices .NET component in the Solution Explorer (this DLL is not automatically added to a project by VS .NET). To add this reference, right-click on your project's References node in the Solution Explorer, and select Add Reference... from the shortcut menu. In the Add Reference dialog, select "System.EnterpriseServices" from the list of components on the .NET tab, click the Select and the OK button.

The ApplicationActivation attribute needs to be set to either Library or Server (using the ActivationOption enumeration) depending on the type of COM+ application you are creating.

The ApplicationName and Description attributes can be set to whatever descriptive text you want to give them.

The ApplicationID attribute must be set to globally unique identifier (GUID). You can generate your own GUID by using the GuidGen.exe tool that comes with Visual Studio .NET (located in the Common7\Tools folder). Just run GuidGen.exe and in the Create Guid dialog (**Figure 5**), select 4. Registry Format. Click the Copy button, to copy the new GUID to the clipboard, and then paste this new value into your AssemblyInfo file. You need to remove the curly braces that bracket the GUID.

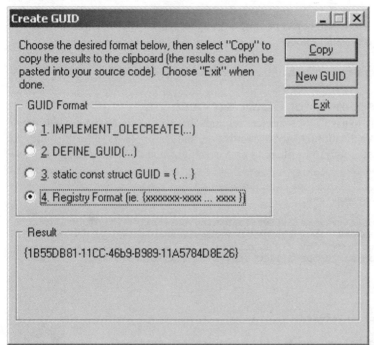

Figure 5. The GuidGen.exe tool allows you to generate globally unique identifiers (GUIDs) that you can use to create unique application IDs for your assemblies.

Deploying the assembly

Deploying an assembly that uses COM+ services involves the following steps:

- Create a strong name for the assembly

- Register the assembly in the global assembly cache (GAC)

- If your assembly is going to be used by non .NET clients, you need to register the assembly with COM+ services using the RegSvcs.exe tool that comes with Visual Studio .NET.

Detailed instructions on creating a strong name for an assembly and registering it in the GAC are covered in Chapter 1, "Introducing .NET" under the "Creating and installing shared assemblies" section. If you need to register your assembly using RegSvcs.exe, you do so using the following command line syntax:

```
RegSvcs <component name> [COM+ Application name] [TypeLibrary.tlb]
```

The first parameter is the name of your .NET component. The second parameter (optional) allows you to assign a name to your COM+ application. The third parameter (also optional) allows you to specify the name of the type library generated by RegSvcs.

Configuring a class for object pooling

To indicate that you want an object to be pooled, there are three main steps you need to take. The first step is to derive your class from the .NET ServicedComponent class that belongs to the System.EnterpriseServices namespace. All classes that use COM+ services must be derived from this class.

The second step is to specify an ObjectPool attribute for the class you want to pool. The following example specifies that object pooling is enabled, the minimum pool size is 1, the maximum pool size is 75, and the creation timeout is 45 seconds (if you don't specify values for these parameters, they are set to the COM+ defaults—minimum pool size of 0, a maximum pool size of 1,048,576, and a creation timeout of 60 seconds).

Here's the code in C#:

```
[ObjectPooling (Enabled=true, MinPoolSize=1, MaxPoolSize=75,
CreationTimeout=45)]
public class Executant : ServicedComponent
{
}
```

And here's the code in Visual Basic .NET:

```
<ObjectPooling(Enabled:=True, MinPoolSize:=1, MaxPoolSize:=75, _
CreationTimeout:=45)> Public Class Executant
    Inherits ServicedComponent
End Class 'Executant
```

The third step is implementing the three methods inherited from the ServicedComponent class—CanBePooled, Activate, and Deactivate. Clients use the CanBePooled method to determine if an object can be pooled. The Activate method is called by COM+ whenever an object is taken from the pool and activated, so you can place initialization code in here. The Deactivate method is called by COM+ whenever an object is placed back on the pool, so you can place cleanup code in here.

Here's an example in C#:

```
[ObjectPooling (Enabled=true, MinPoolSize=1, MaxPoolSize=75,
CreationTimeout=45)]
public class Executant : ServicedComponent
{
   /// Returns a boolean value indicating if the object can be pooled
```

```csharp
protected override bool CanBePooled()
{
    return true;
}

/// This method is called by COM+ services each time the object
/// is taken from the pool and activated
protected override void Activate()
{
}

/// This method is called by COM+ services each time the object
/// is placed back into the pool
protected override void Deactivate()
{
}

public DataSet ReadXmlFileToDataSet(string xmlFile)
{
    DataSet ds = new DataSet();
    ds.ReadXml(xmlFile);
    return ds;
}
}
```

And here it is in Visual Basic .NET:

```vb
<ObjectPooling(Enabled:=True, MinPoolSize:=1, MaxPoolSize:=75, _
CreationTimeout:=45)> Public Class Executant
    Inherits ServicedComponent

    '/ Returns a boolean value indicating if the object can be pooled
    Protected Overrides Function CanBePooled() As Boolean
        Return True
    End Function 'CanBePooled


    '/ This method is called by COM+ services each time the object
    '/ is taken from the pool and activated
    Protected Overrides Sub Activate()
    End Sub 'Activate


    '/ This method is called by COM+ services each time the object
    '/ is placed back into the pool
    Protected Overrides Sub Deactivate()
    End Sub 'Deactivate


    Public Function ReadXmlFileToDataSet(ByVal xmlFile As String) As DataSet
        Dim ds As New DataSet()
        ds.ReadXml(xmlFile)
        Return ds
    End Function 'ReadXmlFileToDataSet
End Class 'Executant
```

The System.IO namespace

The System.IO namespace contains classes that allow you to read and write to files and data streams, as well as classes for working with directories and paths (**Figure 6**).

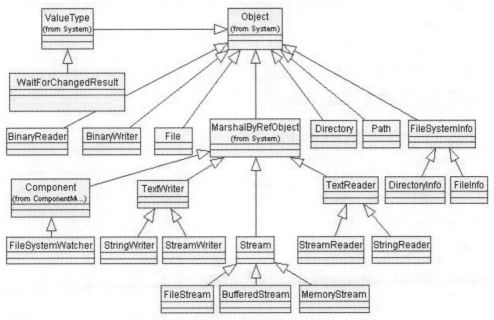

Figure 6. They System.IO namespace contains classes that allow you to read and write files and data streams.

The Directory and DirectoryInfo classes

If you need to create, manipulate, or retrieve directory information, the Directory class provides this capability. The Directory class has static methods that allow you to:

- Create directories

- Get and set the current working directory

- Delete a directory and its contents

- Determine whether a directory exists

- Retrieve a list of subdirectories

- Retrieve a list of files in a specified directory

- Move a file or directory and its contents to a new location

For example, the following code retrieves and displays the current working directory, sets the current directory to "c:\" and displays it, and then restores the original directory.

Here's the code in C#:

```
string SaveDir;
// Save the current directory
SaveDir = Directory.GetCurrentDirectory();
MessageBox.Show("The current directory is: " + SaveDir);

// Set the current directory to c:\ and display the current directory
Directory.SetCurrentDirectory("c:\\");
MessageBox.Show("The current directory now is: " +
  Directory.GetCurrentDirectory());

// Restore the original directory
Directory.SetCurrentDirectory(SaveDir);
```

And here it is in Visual Basic .NET:

```
Dim SaveDir As String
' Save the current directory
SaveDir = Directory.GetCurrentDirectory()
MessageBox.Show(("The current directory is: " + SaveDir))

' Set the current directory to c:\ and display the current directory
Directory.SetCurrentDirectory("c:\")
MessageBox.Show(("The current directory now is: " + _
    Directory.GetCurrentDirectory()))

' Restore the original directory
Directory.SetCurrentDirectory(SaveDir)
```

The DirectoryInfo class performs many of the same functions as the Directory class. The difference between them is the Directory class performs a security check when each method is called (to determine if sufficient permissions exist to execute the requested method), and the DirectoryInfo class does not. If you are going to reuse an object to check directories multiple times, you should consider using the DirectoryInfo class because you may not need to continually recheck security.

The File, FileInfo classes

The File class allows you to manipulate files and create FileStream objects. The File class has static methods that allow you to:

- Copy an existing file to a new file

- Create files

- Delete files

- Determine if a file exists

- Move files

- Open files

- Read and set file attributes

In the following example, the code checks to see if a file exists, and if so, deletes it:
In C#:

```csharp
if (File.Exists("c:\\test.txt"))
{
  File.Delete("c:\\test.txt");
}
```

And in Visual Basic .NET:

```vb
If File.Exists("c:\test.txt") Then
    File.Delete("c:\test.txt")
End If
```

The difference between FileInfo and File is the same as DirectoryInfo vs. Directory. The File class performs the security check and the FileInfo class does not.

Writing and Reading files with StreamWriter and StreamReader

If you want to create a file and add text to it, the StreamWriter class is a great tool for the job. For example, when you use the File class's CreateText method to create a new file, it returns an instance of a StreamWriter class you can use to add text to the file.

In the following code, a new text file named text.txt is created using File.CreateText, which returns a StreamWriter object. This object is then used to write three new lines of text to the file. Afterwards, the StreamWriter's Close method is called, which closes the StreamWriter and the associated text file.

Here's the code in C#:

```csharp
StreamWriter StrWriter = File.CreateText("c:\\test.txt");
StrWriter.WriteLine("Use case diagrams");
StrWriter.WriteLine("Activity diagrams");
StrWriter.WriteLine("Sequence diagrams");
StrWriter.Close();
```

Here's the code in Visual Basic .NET:

```vb
Dim StrWriter As StreamWriter = File.CreateText("c:\test.txt")
StrWriter.WriteLine("Use case diagrams")
StrWriter.WriteLine("Activity diagrams")
StrWriter.WriteLine("Sequence diagrams")
StrWriter.Close()
```

The StreamReader class is great for reading text from a file. In the following code, a text file is opened using File.OpenText, which returns a StreamReader object. You use the methods of the StreamReader to read the text from the file. In this case, the ReadToEnd method is used to read all of the text in the file into the FileText variable.

Here's the code in C#:

```csharp
StreamReader StrReader = File.OpenText("c:\\test.txt");
string FileText = StrReader.ReadToEnd();
```

Here's the code in Visual Basic .NET:

```
Dim StrReader As StreamReader = File.OpenText("c:\test.txt")
Dim FileText As String = StrReader.ReadToEnd()
```

You can use other methods in the StreamReader class to read just a portion of the text from a file. For example, the Read method reads the next character or set of characters from the stream, and the ReadLine method reads a line of characters from the stream.

The Path class

The Path class allows you to manipulate file or directory path strings including functionality similar to Visual FoxPro's JustPath(), JustStem(), JustExt(), and JustFName() functions. With the Path class you can do the following to a file or path string (among other things):

- Change a file extension

- Get just the directory

- Get just the extension

- Get just the file name

- Get a full path

- Generate a unique file name and create a zero-byte file with that name on disk

The following code takes a fully qualified path and file name, breaks it down into each of its parts, and displays it.

In C#:

```
string PathString = @"c:\Program Files\Microsoft Visual Studio
.NET\readme.htm";
string Dir = Path.GetDirectoryName(PathString);
string Ext = Path.GetExtension(PathString);
string FileName = Path.GetFileName(PathString);
string Stem = Path.GetFileNameWithoutExtension(PathString);

MessageBox.Show("Path: " + PathString + "\n\n" +
  "Directory: " + Dir + "\n" +
  "Extension: " + Ext + "\n" +
  "File Name: " + FileName + "\n" +
  "Stem: " + Stem);
```

In Visual Basic .NET:

```
Dim PathString As String = _
  "c:\Program Files\Microsoft Visual Studio .NET\readme.htm"
Dim Dir As String = Path.GetDirectoryName(PathString)
Dim Ext As String = Path.GetExtension(PathString)
Dim FileName As String = Path.GetFileName(PathString)
Dim Stem As String = Path.GetFileNameWithoutExtension(PathString)

MessageBox.Show(("Path: " + PathString + ControlChars.Lf + _
```

```
ControlChars.Lf + "Directory: " + Dir + ControlChars.Lf + _
"Extension: " + Ext + ControlChars.Lf + "File Name: " + _
FileName + ControlChars.Lf + "Stem: " + Stem))
```

The output of this message box is shown in **Figure 7**.

Path: c:\Program Files\Microsoft Visual Studio .NET\readme.htm

Directory: c:\Program Files\Microsoft Visual Studio .NET
Extension: .htm
File Name: readme.htm
Stem: readme

[OK]

Figure 7. The Path class allows you to extract the directory, extension, file name, and stem from a path string.

The FileSystemWatcher class

Many applications have a need to perform a particular action when something changes in the file system. Often, this takes the form of waiting for a particular file to appear in a specified directory. The FileSystemWatcher class is a great class for this and other scenarios. Not only can you watch the file system of a local computer, you can also watch files on a network drive or a remote computer.

You set the Filter property of the FileSystemWatcher class to the name of the file you want to watch. If you set the Filter property to an empty string, it watches for all files. You set the Filter to watch for a specific type of file by specifying an asterisk and a file extension, for example "*.xml".

The FileSystemWatcher class can watch for a variety of changes, including the attributes of a file or folder, the name of a file or directory, the last date/time a file or folder was written to, the size of a file or folder, and so on (**Figure 8**).

```
Watcher.NotifyFilter = NotifyFilters.
```

```
Attributes
CreationTime
DirectoryName
FileName
LastAccess
LastWrite
Security
Size
```

Figure 8. The FileSystemWatcher class can watch for a variety of changes including changes in attributes, the last write date and time, the size of a file or directory, and the name of a file.

The events you can watch for are change, create, delete, and rename. In order to respond to these events, you must add event handlers to the FileSystemWatcher's Changed, Created, Deleted, and Renamed events. For example, in the following code, the WatchForFile method configures a FileSystemWatcher to watch for any .xml files created in the c:\ directory. It adds an event handler named OnCreated to the FileSystemWatcher's Created event. Also notice the watcher's EnableRaisingEvents property must be set to true before it begins watching.

Here's the code in C#:

```csharp
public class FileSystemWatcherDemo
{
  public void WatchForFile()
  {
      // Configure the FileSystemWatcher
      FileSystemWatcher Watcher = new FileSystemWatcher();
      Watcher.Path = "c:\\";
      Watcher.Filter = "*.xml";
      Watcher.NotifyFilter = NotifyFilters.FileName

      // Add an event handler to the Created event
      Watcher.Created += new FileSystemEventHandler(OnCreated);

      // Start watching!
      Watcher.EnableRaisingEvents = true;
  }

  // Event handler for FileSystemWatcher Created event
  public static void OnCreated(object source, FileSystemEventArgs e)
  {
      MessageBox.Show("New file created: " + e.Name);
  }
}
```

Here's the code in Visual Basic .NET:

```vbnet
Public Sub WatchForFile()
    ' Configure the FileSystemWatcher
    Dim Watcher As New FileSystemWatcher()
    Watcher.Path = "c:\"
    Watcher.Filter = "*.xml"
    Watcher.NotifyFilter = NotifyFilters.FileName

    ' Add an event handler to the Created event
    AddHandler Watcher.Created, AddressOf OnCreated

    ' Start watching!
    Watcher.EnableRaisingEvents = True
End Sub 'WatchForFile

' Event handler for FileSystemWatcher Created event
Public Shared Sub OnCreated(ByVal [source] As Object, _
  ByVal e As FileSystemEventArgs)
    MessageBox.Show(("New file created: " + e.Name))
End Sub 'OnCreated
```

You can implement the FileSystemWatcher class in a wide variety of places. For example, you can creat a console application that sits on a server, waiting for XML files to be copied into a specific directory. These XML files might contain data that needs to be imported into your system. When an XML file is copied into the directory, the FileSystemWatcher object alerts the event handler, which imports the XML data, and then moves the file to a "processed" directory.

The System.Net namespace

The System.Net namespace contains a wide variety of classes to Web-enable your .NET applications (**Figure 9**). I can't do justice to these classes in this short section, but I will go over a few of the main classes.

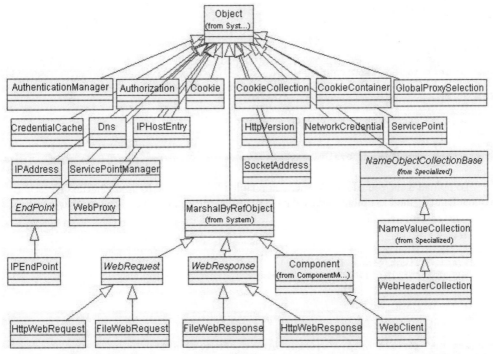

Figure 9. *The System.Net namespace contains classes that allow you to Web-enable your .NET applications.*

Downloading and uploading with the WebClient class

You can use the WebClient class to upload and download data from the Internet. The following example shows how to use the WebClient's OpenRead method to open a file (in this case, the default web page on a web site) and read through the text with a stream reader.

In C#:

```
string Text = "Downloaded text:\n\n";
int i;

WebClient WClient = new WebClient();
Stream strm = WClient.OpenRead("http://www.oakleafsd.com");
StreamReader StrmReader = new StreamReader(strm);
for (i=0; i < 10; i++)
{
  Text += StrmReader.ReadLine() + "\n";
}
strm.Close();
MessageBox.Show(Text, "System.Net classes");
```

In Visual Basic .NET:

```
Dim Text As String = "Downloaded text:" & ControlChars.Lf & ControlChars.Lf
Dim i As Integer

Dim WClient As New WebClient()
Dim strm As Stream = WClient.OpenRead("http://www.oakleafsd.com")
Dim StrmReader As New StreamReader(strm)
For i = 0 To 9
    Text += StrmReader.ReadLine() & ControlChars.Lf
Next i
strm.Close()
MessageBox.Show(Text, "System.Net classes")
```

To upload data, you use the WebClient's UploadFile method to upload a file or UploadData method to upload binary data. The following example uses UploadFile to upload a file named MyFile.xml.

In C#:

```
WebClient WClient = new WebClient();
WClient.UploadFile("http://mywebsite.com", "MyFile.xml");
```

In Visual Basic .NET:

```
Dim WClient As New WebClient()
WClient.UploadFile("http://mywebsite.com", "MyFile.xml")
```

Note that you can only upload files using this method if you have permissions on the server. If you don't have permissions, you will get a WebException error when you try to upload.

The Dns and IPHostEntry classes

The Dns class communicates with your default DNS server to provide some basic domain name functionality. In the following example, the Dns class's Resolve method is called, passing a domain name, and an IPHostEntry object is returned. The IPHostEntry class acts as a container for host address information. As shown in the code below, you iterate through the IPHostEntry's AddressList to get information on the addresses it contains.

Here's the code in C#:

```
IPHostEntry IPHost = Dns.Resolve("www.oakleafsd.com");
string IPList = "";
foreach (IPAddress IP in IPHost.AddressList)
{
  IPList += IP.Address + "\n";
}
MessageBox.Show("www.oakleafsd.com\n\n" +
  "Address List: " + IPList +
  "Host name: " + IPHost.HostName);
```

Here's the code in Visual Basic .NET:

```
Dim IPHost As IPHostEntry = Dns.Resolve("www.oakleafsd.com")
Dim IPList As String = ""
Dim IP As IPAddress
For Each IP In IPHost.AddressList
    IPList += IP.Address.ToString() & ControlChars.Lf
Next IP
MessageBox.Show(("www.oakleafsd.com" & ControlChars.Lf & ControlChars.Lf & _
    "Address List: " & IPList & "Host name: " & IPHost.HostName))
```

The System.Timers namespace

The System.Timers namespace contains only three classes—the main class is the Timer class, which functions similar to timers in Visual FoxPro.

> *There is a Timer class in each of the System.Timers, System.Threading, and System.Windows.Forms namespaces, so you need to qualify the Timer class name with the namespace if you have referenced more than one of these in your code. The System.Timers Timer class is used to generate recurring events in your application. The System.Threading Timer class is used to call methods at specified intervals. The System.Windows.Forms Timer should be used in Windows Forms applications. See the .NET Help file for more information on each of these classes.*

In the following code, the StartTimer method sets the Interval of the timer to 2000ms (2 seconds), registers an event handler named OnElapsed with the timer's Elapsed event, and then sets the timer's Enabled property to true. After two seconds, the Elapsed event fires, calling the OnElapsed event handler which shuts off the timer by setting its Enabled property to false, and then displays a message to the user.

Here is the code in C#:

```
public class TimerDemo
{
  System.Timers.Timer MyTimer = new System.Timers.Timer();
```

```csharp
public void StartTimer()
{
    this.MyTimer.Interval = 2000;
    this.MyTimer.Elapsed += new ElapsedEventHandler(OnElapsed);
    this.MyTimer.Enabled = true;
}

/// <summary>
/// Event handler for the timer's Elapsed event
/// </summary>
public void OnElapsed(object source, ElapsedEventArgs e)
{
    MyTimer.Enabled = false;
    MessageBox.Show("Timer has fired at: " + e.SignalTime, "Timer class");
}
}
```

And here is the code in Visual Basic .NET:

```vbnet
Public Class TimerDemo
    Private MyTimer As New System.Timers.Timer()

    Public Sub StartTimer()
        Me.MyTimer.Interval = 2000
        AddHandler Me.MyTimer.Elapsed, AddressOf OnElapsed
        Me.MyTimer.Enabled = True
    End Sub 'StartTimer


    '/ <summary>
    '/ Event handler for the timer's Elapsed event
    '/ </summary>
    Public Sub OnElapsed(ByVal source As Object, ByVal e As ElapsedEventArgs)
        MyTimer.Enabled = False
        MessageBox.Show("Timer has fired at: " + e.SignalTime, "Timer class")
    End Sub 'OnElapsed
End Class 'TimerDemo
```

Conclusion

This chapter really just scratches the surface of the .NET Framework's namespaces and base classes. To learn more about each namespace and their associated classes, check out the .NET Help topic ".NET Framework Class Library in Visual Studio", which covers different categories of namespaces.

Chapter 7
Data Access with ADO.NET

To a Visual FoxPro developer, one of the most important aspects of software development is data access. This chapter shows you how to use Microsoft's new universal data access technology, ADO.NET, to access and manipulate a wide variety of data—including VFP data. Because there are a number of different ways to access data from ADO.NET, this chapter offers information on the best practices for data access.

If there's one thing that a Visual FoxPro developer is proud of, it's VFP's data access capabilities. From accessing FoxPro data, to client-server data, and XML, VFP is a great tool for building data-centric applications. Based on this, I'm sure most VFP developers are very interested in .NET's data access model.

This chapter does not attempt to cover all the idiosyncrasies of data access with ADO.NET—there are already plenty of books on the market that do this. Rather, to help you get up and running quickly, this chapter provides an overview of ADO.NET's capabilities.

However, before diving directly into ADO.NET, the following section gives a brief history of data access from the perspective of FoxPro, because it's easier to see where you're going if you know where you've been. If you are already familiar with this information, I recommend you skip ahead to the "Introducing ADO.NET" section.

A brief history of data access

Unlike most other software development tools, FoxPro is both a language *and* a database—you do not need any external technology to access native FoxPro data. This differs from other tools such as Visual Basic where you must rely on external data access technology to retrieve and manipulate data. However, when you need to access non-FoxPro data (such as SQL Server and Oracle) from within FoxPro, you *do* need external technology to connect to, access, and manipulate that data.

> *In FoxPro terminology, FoxPro data accessed natively is referred to as "local data". Data accessed in any other way is known as "remote data".*

Initially, the technology used to access remote data was Microsoft's Open Database Connection (ODBC).

ODBC—A first attempt at universal data access

ODBC was one of Microsoft's first attempts at creating a uniform way to access data from FoxPro and other programming tools. To access a particular type of data from within FoxPro (such as SQL Server, Oracle, or Sybase), you had to use an ODBC driver specifically designed to access that type of data. As long as the driver was installed on your computer, you could easily access remote data using remote views or SQL pass through. ODBC was a great tool for accessing just about any type of relational data.

OLE DB and ADO—The successors to ODBC

A few years back, Microsoft introduced OLE DB as its new-and-improved solution to universal data access and as the successor to ODBC. While ODBC allowed you to access most types of relational data, OLE DB went a step further and provided a way to access both relational *and* non-relational data in a standard way using a COM (Component Object Model) programming interface.

> *COM defines a software interface standard that specifies, at the binary level, how software components interact. COM acts as a common layer through which all COM-capable tools can communicate.*

In OLE DB, the equivalent to ODBC drivers is OLE DB *data providers*. Again, you need to use an OLE DB data provider designed to access a particular type of data. Visual FoxPro 7 supplied an OLE DB provider that allows non-Fox clients to access Visual FoxPro data.

Microsoft designed OLE DB with C++ in mind, trading ease-of-use for performance. However, in order to make OLE DB accessible to the masses, Microsoft created ActiveX Data Objects (ADO). ADO supplied a high-level COM interface, built on top of OLE DB, and easily used by languages such as Visual FoxPro and Visual Basic.

Rather than using cursors (as in Visual FoxPro) ADO provided data access through a set of COM objects—the object most frequently used being the Recordset. A good number of VFP developers tried their hand at data access using ADO. Although it was relatively easy to retrieve data using ADO, there was a huge performance hit when you tried to "scan" through the records in a Recordset. In addition, it was difficult to integrate an ADO Recordset into a Visual FoxPro application with Visual FoxPro's data model and user interface based on cursors, rather than data objects. In order to make an ADO Recordset available to the user for viewing and manipulating in a VFP application, you either had to convert it to a VFP cursor, or bind the Recordset to an ActiveX grid.

All of this said, ADO was a big step in the right direction—it did provide universal access to both relational and non-relational data. However, it also had its limitations—especially with n-tier architectures.

Data access and the n-tier architecture model

So, what is n-tier architecture and what impact does it have on data access?

Before answering this question, you should first understand *single tier* system architecture. In a single tier architecture, all of the application processing takes place on a single computer—this includes user interface, business logic, and data processing. For example, when you have a Visual FoxPro desktop application access FoxPro data (see **Figure 1**), whether the data is located on your local machine or a machine across your network, all the processing takes place on your workstation. This is because the VFP data engine resides on your workstation.

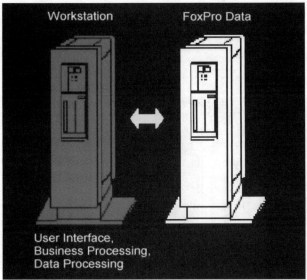

Figure 1. In a single-tier architecture, all processing occurs on a single computer

In a *two-tier* system architecture (see **Figure 2**), the database engine moves from the workstation to a database server. A good example of this is accessing a client-server database such as SQL Server from a Visual FoxPro desktop application. In this scenario, the workstation running the VFP application sends requests to SQL Server. The data processing occurs on the server and the results return back to the VFP application. ADO was originally designed for this client-server, two-tier architecture—where a workstation is continuously connected to a back end data server.

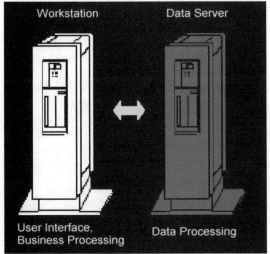

Figure 2. In a two-tier architecture, the database engine moves to a different computer. This is the client-server model.

In a *three-tier* system architecture (see **Figure 3**), the application's business logic is separated from the user interface and placed in business components, creating three unique tiers—user interface (tier 1), business logic (tier 2), and data (tier 3). In this context, business logic includes all application code that performs processing and retrieves or manipulates data. For a more detailed explanation, see Chapter 8, ".NET Business Objects" for details.

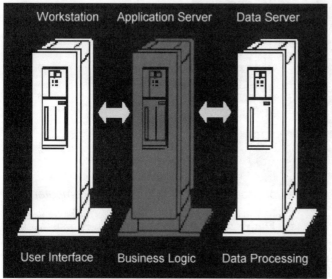

Figure 3. *In a three-tier architecture, both the data processing and the business logic are separated from the user interface.*

So, where does the phrase n-tier architecture come from? A three-tier architecture can be broken down into additional sub-tiers. However, in the final analysis, n-tier architecture is really the same as three-tier architecture.

Passing data between tiers
In an n-tier architecture, data must be passed between each tier of the application—from the data tier to the business tier to the user interface tier and back again. In a distributed Internet environment there are inherent difficulties with passing ADO Recordsets between tiers.

For example, COM technology used to return an ADO Recordset from a web server relies on Remote Procedure Calls (RPCs), which make a server vulnerable to security breaches including denial-of-service attacks. One solution is converting the ADO Recordset to XML, which easily passes through firewalls. Although this is possible, ADO's XML capabilities are somewhat limited.

Connected and disconnected data
It's often desirable for n-tier applications to operate in a disconnected fashion. Rather than maintaining an active connection to the back end data, each new data access causes the application to create a new connection, retrieve or update data, then disconnect. This helps free up valuable resources on the data server. Maintaining many active connections consumes a

tremendous amount of resources on a data server and bogs down your application's performance. Freeing up a connection as soon as a transaction completes allows your database to serve many more users.

The architecture of the Internet is inherently disconnected. As you surf the Internet, each request you make from your browser (navigating to a different site, requesting data, sending data, and so on) makes a brand new connection to the web server, rather than maintaining a continuous connection. Although ADO *can* work in a disconnected architecture, ADO was primarily designed for connected data access.

Introducing ADO.NET

Based on the needs of more modern n-tier and Internet architectures, Microsoft completely reworked ADO for its .NET initiative, and introduced ADO.NET.

When accessing data from Visual FoxPro, you should still use either ODBC or ADO, because VFP is not a .NET language. When accessing data from a .NET application, you can still use ADO, but it's far better to use ADO.NET. If you are using C++, you can bypass the overhead of both ADO and ADO.NET and use OLE DB directly.

Conceptually, ADO and ADO.NET are similar. They both provide universal access to relational and non-relational data, however ADO.NET does a much better job! ADO.NET is ADO supercharged—in short, it allows you to work with any software component on any platform that understands XML.

.NET data providers

.NET data providers are not a single class—they are comprised of a set of classes in the .NET Framework optimized for connecting to specific types of data. As of this writing, there are four main data providers in .NET:

- SQL Server Managed Data Provider– designed for accessing SQL Server 7.0 or later. The classes in this provider are all located in the System.Data.SqlClient namespace.

- Oracle Managed Data Provider – designed for accessing Oracle data. The classes in this provider are all located in the System.Data.OracleClient namespace.

- OLE DB Managed Data Provider – designed for accessing any data source available by means of a classic OLE DB provider. The classes in this provider are all located in the System.Data.OleDbClient namespace.

- ODBC Managed Data Provider – designed for accessing native ODBC drivers. The classes in this provider are all located in the System.Data.Odbc namespace.

The SQL Server Managed data provider delivers fast performance because it bypasses the overhead imposed by both ADO.NET and OLE DB (See **Figure 4**). It does this by using the native protocol of SQL Server—Tabular Data Stream (TDS). If your application accesses data in SQL Server 7.0 or later, you should definitely use these classes rather than the generic OLE DB classes.

The Oracle Managed data provider delivers fast access to Oracle data using the Oracle Call Interface (OCI). To use this provider, you must have Oracle 8i Release 3 (8.1.7) Client or later installed. If your application accesses Oracle data, you should use the Oracle Managed Provider rather than the OLE DB Managed provider. This data provider was made available after the release of .NET, so you may need to download it from Microsoft's Web site.

The OLE DB Managed data provider is used to access any other type of data available using a classic OLE DB provider. As shown in Figure 4, using the OLE DB managed provider is slower because an extra level of translation occurs between the data source and the client. This is the way you access Visual FoxPro data from .NET. The .NET client program uses the OLE DB Managed Provider, which in turn accesses data through the Visual FoxPro classic OLE DB Provider.

The ODBC Managed Data Provider provides access to native ODBC drivers. This is useful in situations where you work with legacy data with no OLE DB Provider available. This data provider was made available after the official release of .NET, so if you need to use this provider, you need to download it from Microsoft's web site.

Although SQL Server is currently the only data-specific managed provider for .NET, other data-specific managed providers will be written to access other popular databases such as Oracle.

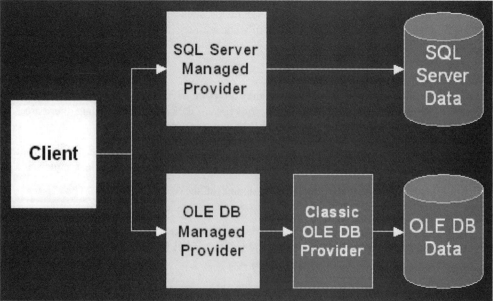

Figure 4. The SQL Server Managed Provider provides fast, direct access to SQL Server 7.0 and higher data. The OLE DB Managed Provider allows you to access any data source available using a classic OLE DB provider.

Although these classes will be discussed later in this chapter, for now, all you need to know is the classic OLE DB data providers return data as COM objects, which can be translated into the higher level ADO Recordset. .NET managed data providers return data as an XML stream, which provides many benefits over COM.

Disconnected DataSets

In ADO.NET, the *DataSet* is analogous to the ADO Recordset. Unlike the ADO Recordset, the ADO.NET DataSet is designed for disconnected data access (no active connection to a database), which is optimal for distributed, Internet applications.

ADO.NET and XML

In contrast to ADO that had some basic XML functionality, ADO.NET was built from the ground up with advanced XML capabilities.

As mentioned previously, XML is a great data format for passing data between layers of an n-tier application—especially when a web server and firewall are involved—and ADO.NET does this with ease. In addition to passing XML between tiers, the ADO.NET DataSet also allows you to read XML data from a wide variety of data sources as easily as you can read data from a database.

ADO.NET's XML integration also improves its ability to work with non-relational data. While ADO touted the capability to work with both relational and non-relational data, in reality it was not very straightforward. In contrast, ADO.NET allows you to read XML as easily as reading data from a database, making it much easier to work with non-relational data. You can think of it this way—ADO is designed to be database-centric, working best with data stored in databases. ADO.NET is data-centric, designed to work well with data regardless of where it is stored.

ADO.NET performance

Another improvement ADO.NET gives you is greater performance. ADO is based on COM, which incurs an inherent performance hit. This is because your application communicates with ADO in a non-native way through COM interfaces, adding extra overhead. In addition, because COM objects are not native to the language you're using, performance suffers when converting native data types in your programming language of choice to COM's data types.

Because .NET managed data providers are written on top of the Common Language Runtime and Common Type System (see Chapter 1 "Introducing .NET" for details), the need for conversion between data types disappears, providing a great improvement in speed. This is the case with the SQL Server managed data provider (which was also tuned to work specifically with SQL Server data, offering even greater performance). However, in scenarios that use the classic OLE DB Provider, as with the OLE DB Managed Data Provider, this conversion between data types must still occur.

The .NET data classes

The .NET Framework provides a wide variety of classes for accessing data. These can be found in the following namespaces:

- System.Data – the ADO.NET data access classes.

- System.Data.Common – common classes shared by all .NET data providers.

- System.XML – XML processing classes.

- System.Data.OleDb – classes comprising the .NET data provider for OLE DB-compatible data sources.

- System.Data.SqlClient – classes comprising the .NET data provider for SQL Server 7.0 and later.

- System.Data.OracleClient – classes comprising the .NET data provider for Oracle.

- System.Data.SqlTypes – classes representing SQL Server native data types.

- System.Data.Odbc – classes comprising the .NET data provider for ODBC.

In the sections that follow, you will learn more about the classes found in each of these namespaces.

Data-specific classes

Table 1 lists data classes used when working with specific kinds of data. The classes in the first column are used when accessing SQL Server 7.0 and higher. The classes in the second column are used when accessing any type of data by means of OLE DB (the Oracle and ODBC data provider classes are not listed in this table). Each of the classes is described in detail throughout this chapter.

Table 1. This table contains a list of .NET classes used for a specific type of data.

SQL Server classes	Generic OLE DB classes	Description
SqlCommand	OleDbCommand	Represents a SQL statement or stored procedure
SqlCommandBuilder	OleDbCommandBuilder	Automatically generates single-table SQL statements from a SELECT clause for updating, inserting and deleting data
SqlConnection	OleDbConnection	Represents an open connection to a database
SqlDataAdapter	OleDbDataAdapter	Represents a set of data commands (select, update, insert, delete) and a database connection used to fill a DataSet and update the data source
SqlDataReader	OleDbDataReader	Reads a forward-only stream of data from a data source
SqlParameter	OleDbParameter	Represents a parameter to a SQL statement or stored procedure
SqlTransaction	OleDbTransaction	Represents a database transaction

Accessing data with ADO.NET

It's important to understand that ADO.NET provides two main ways to access data:

1. Using a DataReader and a data command object

2. Using a DataSet

In either case, the ADO.NET data access model assumes you connect to the database, retrieve data (or perform an operation), and then close the connection.

> *You might think that constantly creating, opening, and closing connections would slap a huge performance penalty on your application—after all, it does take time to create new connections. Fortunately, behind the scenes, ADO.NET manages a pool of connections from which new connection requests can be tapped. This significantly increases the performance and scalability of your applications.*

Choosing between DataReaders and DataSets

Deciding whether to use a DataReader or a DataSet for accessing data depends on a number of factors. There is a great topic in the .NET Help file titled "Recommendation for Data Access Strategies" to help you decide which methodology to use in a wide variety of situations. The following sections give you the quick lowdown.

Choosing DataReaders and data command objects

When using a DataReader, you first work with a data command object that executes a SQL SELECT statement or stored procedure and returns a DataReader object. You then use the DataReader to retrieve records in the result set.

DataReaders provide forward-only, read-only access to data. They are "forward-only" in the sense that only one record is present in the DataReader at any given time. Each time you read the next record, it replaces the previous record, and you can't go back to the previous record. Based on this, DataReaders work in a connected fashion—you need to explicitly close the DataReader and the connection after you finish retrieving data.

DataReaders have a performance advantage over DataSets because they communicate directly with the data source, incurring less overhead (in contrast with a DataSet where you manipulate a disconnected "image" of data). This makes a big difference in Web applications. In addition, command objects give you a little more control over SQL SELECT and stored procedure execution. DataSets sacrifice a measure of control for ease-of-use.

If you need to perform tasks such as creating, editing and removing tables, and executing stored procedures, you can't use a DataSet—you must use a data command object.

One downside of DataReaders is you can't bind a Windows Forms DataGrid directly to a DataReader object—you can only do this with a DataSet (although you *can* bind DataReaders directly to a Web Forms DataGrid). Although you can't bind directly to a DataReader, you can programmatically load data from a DataReader into the DataGrid.

Choosing DataSets

In a number of ways, DataSets are more capable than DataReaders. DataSets can range from containing data from a single table to representing an in-memory database containing multiple tables, relationships, and constraints.

Figure 5 shows a conceptual model of the DataSet. As you can see, a DataSet contains tables that in turn contain DataRows and DataColumns. The DataRow is equivalent to a Visual FoxPro record and a DataColumn is equivalent to a Visual FoxPro field. The DataSet also allows you to create relationships between the DataTables and constraints on the DataColumns.

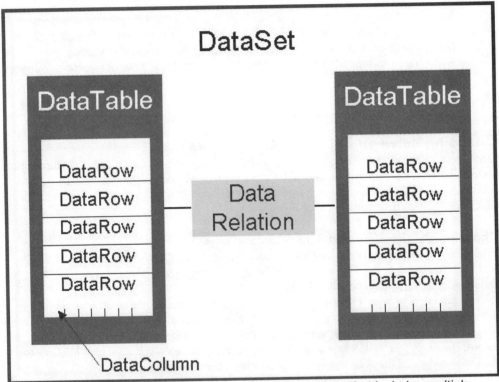

Figure 5. A DataSet can represent an in-memory database that includes multiple tables, relations, and even constraints.

DataSets are connectionless by default—an initial connection is opened, all requested data is retrieved from the data source, and then the connection is automatically closed. When you are ready to save changes, you reconnect the DataSet, update the data source with changes you have made, and the DataSet gets updated with changes made by others. Exception (error) handling is an important consideration when creating connections to the data source. For more information on handling exceptions see Chapter 13, "Error Handling and Debugging in .NET".

As discussed in the .NET Help file, DataSets are good for situations where you are working with multiple tables, multiple data sources, moving data between application tiers, exchanging data with other applications, and binding to user interface controls.

Accessing data with a DataReader

As mentioned earlier, when you use a DataReader object, you first work with a data command object that returns a DataReader to you.

Depending on the type of data you're working with, there are three main .NET data command classes to choose from—the SqlCommand class (for accessing SQL Server data), the OracleCommand class (for accessing Oracle data), and the OleDbCommand class (for accessing OLE DB data sources).

The basic steps for accessing data using this a DataReader and Command object are:

1. Create a connection to the data source.

2. Configure a data command object with a SQL statement or the name of a stored procedure to be executed.

3. Execute the data command.

4. If the command returns a DataReader, use it to retrieve the result set.

5. Close the DataReader and the connection.

The following sections provide details for each of these steps. Rather than giving samples using SQL Server, Oracle, and OLE DB data sources, the sample code in the following sections just demonstrates accessing SQL Server. To translate the samples into code that works with OLE DB, you simply replace the "Sql" prefix of all class names with "OleDb" instead. To translate the samples into code that works with Oracle, substitute the "Sql" prefix with "Oracle".

> *Because you haven't learned about error handling yet, (and to make the samples easier to read), I haven't included any error handling code—which you should definitely include in your real-world data access code. For details on error handling, see Chapter 13, "Error Handling and Debugging in .NET".*

In all of the sample code throughout this chapter, you need to specify you are using classes from the following namespaces:
In C#:

```
using System;
using System.Data;
using System.Data.SqlClient;
using System.Data.SqlTypes;
using System.Windows.Forms;
```

And in Visual Basic .NET:

```
Imports System.Data.SqlClient
Imports System.Data.SqlTypes
```

Why are there fewer namespaces listed for Visual Basic .NET than for C#? When you build a new Visual Basic .NET Windows application using VS .NET, it automatically imports several namespaces at the project level, including the System, System.Data, and System.Windows.Forms namespaces. This means you don't have to explicitly import these in your code files. For more information, check out the "Namespaces" section in Chapter 4, "Introduction to Visual Basic .NET".

Creating a connection to the data source

The first step in accessing data with a command object is creating a connection to the data. You use the .NET SqlConnection class to make this connection to SQL Server data. The following C# code shows how to connect to the SQL Server Northwind database:

> *The following code specifies a connection to the SQL Server Northwind database, with a user id of "sa" and no password. If you have SQL Server set up differently (a machine other than your local machine with a different user id and password), you need to adjust the connection string values accordingly.*

```
// Build the connection string
string ConnectionString = "server=(local);"+
    "uid=sa;pwd=;"+
    "database=Northwind";

// Create and open the connection
SqlConnection Connection = new SqlConnection(ConnectionString);
Connection.Open();
```

And here's the code in Visual Basic .NET:

```
' Build the connection string
Dim ConnectionString As String = "server=(local);" + _
  "uid=sa;pwd=;" + _
  "database=Northwind"

' Create and open the connection
Dim Connection As SqlConnection = New SqlConnection(ConnectionString)
Connection.Open()
```

Configuring a data command object

Once you create and open a connection, you define and execute commands against the back end data. For example, the following C# code *configures* the data command object with a SQL

SELECT command for retrieving the first name, last name, and title from the Northwind database Employees table (you actually *execute* the data command in the next step):

```
// Configure the data command object
string SelectCmd = "SELECT TOP 3 LastName, FirstName, Title FROM Employees";
SqlCommand Command = new SqlCommand(SelectCmd, Connection);
```

And here's the code in Visual Basic .NET:

```
' Configure the data command object
Dim SelectCmd As String = "SELECT TOP 3 LastName, FirstName, Title FROM
Employees"
Dim Command As SqlCommand = New SqlCommand(SelectCmd, Connection)
```

Executing a data command

Once you have configured the data command object, there are a few methods you can call on the object to actually *execute* the command associated with the object. The method you choose is based on the type of command you are executing. Here are the primary methods you can call:

- ExecuteReader – Used to execute a command and return a DataReader object (i.e. SqlDataReader, OleDbDataReader). This method is normally used to execute SQL SELECT statements or stored procedures that return data.

- ExecuteNonQuery – Used to execute a SQL statement and return the number of rows affected. Often used for UPDATE, INSERT, or DELETE commands.

- ExecuteScalar – Used to execute a command and return a single value (such as a record count).

- ExecuteXmlReader (available only on the Sql Provider) – Used to execute a command and return an XmlReader object

For this example, I use the ExecuteReader method to retrieve records from the data source. Here's the code in C#:

```
// Execute the command which returns a SqlDataReader object
SqlDataReader Reader = Command.ExecuteReader();
```

And in Visual Basic .NET:

```
' Execute the command which returns a SqlDataReader object
Dim Reader As SqlDataReader = Command.ExecuteReader()
```

Processing the return value

As mentioned in the previous section, different types of values are returned depending on the type of command executed. In the following example, executing the command returns a DataReader object.

Unlike a DataSet, which returns all requested records from the data source, a DataReader object only contains one row at a time. You could compare it to a cursor with a single row of data. When a data command object first returns a DataReader, it doesn't contain any data. You must call the DataReader's Read method to get the first record in the result set, call it again to get the second row, and so on. Each time you call the Read method, the row previously stored in the DataReader is replaced by the new row.

The following C# code cycles through the rows in the result set and displays them in a message box. In this example, I am using the DataReader's GetString method to access the three columns (0 = LastName, 1 = FirstName, and 2 = Title):

```
string Employees = "";
// Get the next record
while (Reader.Read())
{
  // Access the data in the current row
  Employees += Reader.GetString(0) + ", " +
    Reader.GetString(1) + " - " + Reader.GetString(2) + "\n";
}
MessageBox.Show(Employees, "DataReader Demo");
```

The code in Visual Basic .NET:

```
Dim Employees As String = ""
' Get the next record
While Reader.Read()

  ' Access the data in the current row
  Employees += Reader.GetString(0) + ", " + _
    Reader.GetString(1) + " - " + Reader.GetString(2) + Chr(13) + Chr(10)

End While

MessageBox.Show(Employees, "DataReader Demo")
```

Rather than using the DataReader's GetString method to retrieve the column values, you could simply access each column by using the syntax Reader[0], Reader[1], and Reader[2]. However, if you know the type of the data in a particular column, you'll get better performance retrieving the data by using the DataReader method that corresponds to the value type of the column. The DataReader class has a number of additional type-specific "Get" methods such as GetBoolean, GetByte, GetDateTime, and GetDecimal for this purpose.

In Chapter 9, "Building .NET Windows Forms Applications" and Chapter 10, "Building Web Applications with ASP.NET", you will see a more meaningful use for the data returned from a DataReader object.

Closing the connection

Because the DataReader is a connected object, you need to wait until you are done with the DataReader before closing the connection. When you're ready, close the DataReader first, then close the connection (this code is the same in C# and Visual Basic .NET):

```
Reader.Close()
Connection.Close()
```

Pulling it all together

So you can get a sense for the entire flow, here's all the code snippets pulled together. Here's the C# code:

```csharp
// Build the connection string
string ConnectionString = "server=(local);"+
    "uid=sa;pwd=;"+
    "database=Northwind";

// Create the connection
SqlConnection Connection = new SqlConnection(ConnectionString);

// Open the connection
Connection.Open();

// Configure the data command object
string SelectCmd = "SELECT TOP 3 LastName, FirstName, Title FROM Employees";
SqlCommand Command = new SqlCommand(SelectCmd, Connection);

// Execute the command which returns a SqlDataReader object
SqlDataReader Reader = Command.ExecuteReader();

// Display the records
string Employees = "";
// Get the next record
while (Reader.Read())
{
  // Access the data in the current row
  Employees += Reader.GetString(0) + ", " +
    Reader.GetString(1) + " - " + Reader.GetString(2) + "\n";
}
MessageBox.Show(Employees, "DataReader Demo");

Reader.Close()
Connection.Close()
```

And in Visual Basic .NET:

```vbnet
' Build the connection string
Dim ConnectionString As String = "server=(local);" + _
   "uid=sa;pwd=;" + _
   "database=Northwind"

' Create the connection
Dim Connection As SqlConnection = New SqlConnection(ConnectionString)

' Open the connection
Connection.Open()

' Configure the data command object
```

```
Dim SelectCmd As String = "SELECT TOP 3 LastName, FirstName, Title FROM
Employees"
Dim Command As SqlCommand = New SqlCommand(SelectCmd, Connection)

' Execute the command which returns a SqlDataReader object
Dim Reader As SqlDataReader = Command.ExecuteReader()

' Display the records
Dim Employees As String = ""
' Get the next record
While Reader.Read()

  ' Access the data in the current row
  Employees += Reader.GetString(0) + ", " + _
    Reader.GetString(1) + " - " + Reader.GetString(2) + Chr(13) + Chr(10)

End While

MessageBox.Show(Employees, "DataReader Demo")



Reader.Close()
Connection.Close()
```

Accessing data using DataSets

There are two main ways to insert data into a DataSet—you either use a data adapter to
fill the DataSet or you read XML directly into the DataSet. First, I will demonstrate using a
data adapter.

Loading a DataSet with a data adapter

The basic steps for loading data using a data adapter are:

1. Configure a data adapter with a command string and a connection string

2. Fill the DataSet using the data adapter

Configuring a data adapter

A data adapter serves as a conduit between the DataSet and the data source. Its primary
purpose is to populate the DataSet with data retrieved from the data source and return changed
data back to the data source. Using a data adapter prevents the DataSet from being coupled too
tightly to a specific type of database.

Here is the code in C# for configuring a data adapter with a command string and a
connection string:

```
// Build the connection string
string ConnectionString = "server=(local);"+
   "uid=sa;pwd=;"+
   "database=Northwind";
```

```
// Build the command string
string CommandString = "SELECT TOP 3 LastName, FirstName, Title FROM
Employees";

// Create the data adapter, passing the command and connection strings
SqlDataAdapter DataAdapter = new SqlDataAdapter(CommandString,
ConnectionString);
```

And in Visual Basic .NET:

```
' Build the connection string
Dim ConnectionString As String = "server=(local);" + _
  "uid=sa;pwd=;" + _
  "database=Northwind"

' Build the command string
Dim CommandString As String = "SELECT TOP 3 LastName, FirstName, Title FROM
Employees"

' Create the data adapter, passing the command and connection strings
   Dim DataAdapter As SqlDataAdapter = New SqlDataAdapter(CommandString,
ConnectionString)
```

At this point the data adapter is configured, but no data has been read from the back end yet.

Fill the DataSet using the data adapter

In this next step, a DataSet object is instantiated, and then the data adapter's Fill method is called. When Fill is executed, the data adapter converts the SQL SELECT string into a SqlCommand object, creates a SqlConnection from the connection string you specified, executes the command, and fills the DataSet with records returned in the result set.

```
// Instantiate a DataSet object
DataSet ds = new DataSet();

// Fill the DataSet
DataAdapter.Fill(ds);
```

And in Visual Basic .NET:

```
' Instantiate a DataSet object
Dim ds As DataSet = New DataSet()

' Fill the DataSet
DataAdapter.Fill(ds)
```

Pulling it all together

Here is all the code pulled together in one place, with the addition of code that displays the result set in a message box:

```
// Build the connection string
string ConnectionString = "server=(local);"+
   "uid=sa;pwd=;"+
   "database=Northwind";

// Build the command string
string CommandString = "SELECT TOP 3 LastName, FirstName, Title FROM
Employees";

// Create the data adapter, passing the command and connection strings
SqlDataAdapter DataAdapter = new SqlDataAdapter(CommandString,
ConnectionString);
// Instantiate a DataSet object
DataSet ds = new DataSet();

// Fill the DataSet
DataAdapter.Fill(ds);

//  Get the table from the DataSet
DataTable DTable = ds.Tables[0];

// Display the records
string Employees = "";
foreach (DataRow DRow in DTable.Rows)
{
  Employees += DRow[0] + ", " +
       DRow[1] + " - " + DRow[2] + "\n";
}
MessageBox.Show(Employees, "DataSet Demo");
```

Here is the Visual Basic .NET equivalent:

```
Dim ConnectionString As String = "server=(local);" + _
   "uid=sa;pwd=;" + _
   "database=Northwind"

' Build the command string
Dim CommandString As String = "SELECT TOP 3 LastName, FirstName, Title FROM
Employees"

' Create the data adapter, passing the command and connection strings
Dim DataAdapter As SqlDataAdapter = New SqlDataAdapter(CommandString,
ConnectionString)
' Instantiate a DataSet object
Dim ds As DataSet = New DataSet()

' Fill the DataSet
DataAdapter.Fill(ds)

'  Get the table from the DataSet
Dim DTable As DataTable = ds.Tables(0)
```

```
' Display the records
Dim Employees As String = ""
Dim DRow As DataRow
For Each DRow In DTable.Rows
  Employees += DRow(0) + ", " + _
  DRow(1) + " - " + DRow(2) + Chr(13) + Chr(10)
Next

MessageBox.Show(Employees, "DataSet Demo")
```

As you can see in this code, once you fill a DataSet with data, you access the data using the different DataSet collections. For example, you can access tables in a DataSet by using the Tables collection. In the previous example, there was only one table in the DataSet and I referenced it using the following syntax (where `ds` references a DataSet):

```
ds.Tables[0]
```

The sample code accesses DataRows in the DataSet by using the foreach command. You can also reference a DataRow by means of the DataTable's Rows collection. For example, you access the first row in a DataTable this way (where `dt` references a DataTable):

```
dt.Rows[0]
```

You can also reference the different DataSet elements by using "friendly" names. For example, if you want to access a table named "Employee" within a DataSet, you use the syntax:

```
ds.Tables["Employees"]
```

If you want to access a DataColumn named "Address", you use the following syntax (where `dt` references a DataTable):

```
dt.Rows[0]["Address"]
```

Although friendly names are easier to read, using them in your applications incurs a measurable performance hit due to the extra lookup the DataSet needs to do to convert the friendly name into an index. For an alternate way to access data using friendly names, see the "Typed DataSets" section later in this chapter.

Loading XML into a DataSet

The DataSet's overloaded ReadXml method makes it very easy to read native XML into a DataSet from a wide variety of sources. The following sample shows how to use the DataSet to read XML from a file on disk and afterwards display the data in a message box.

In C#:

```
DataSet ds = new DataSet();
ds.ReadXml("chapters.xml");

DataTable DTable = ds.Tables[0];
```

```
// Display the records
string Chapters = "";
foreach (DataRow DRow in DTable.Rows)
{
  Chapters += DRow[1] + "\n";
}
MessageBox.Show(Chapters, "DataSet XML Demo");
```

In Visual Basic .NET:

```
Dim ds As DataSet = New DataSet()
ds.ReadXml("chapters.xml")

Dim DTable As DataTable = ds.Tables(0)

' Display the records
Dim Chapters As String = ""
Dim DRow As DataRow
For Each DRow In DTable.Rows
  Chapters += DRow(1) + Chr(13) + Chr(10)
Next

MessageBox.Show(Chapters, "DataSet XML Demo")
```

The chapters.xml file is actually used in this book's sample application to data drive the combo box on the Samples form.

Invoking stored procedures

In most database applications, you need to execute stored procedures. For example, you may use a stored procedure to generate primary keys for your tables. You may also use stored procedures to insert, update, and delete data. In .NET, you can execute stored procedures by means of a data command object. This section shows you a simple example of how to execute a stored procedure. Here are the basic steps:

- Create and open a connection to the data source.

- Create a data command object, passing the name of the stored procedure and the connection object.

- Configure the data command object.

- Execute the command.

Here is an example of code you can use to create a connection and a data command object. Again, the example uses the SQL Server Northwind database.

First, you need to build the connection string. Here it is in C#:

```
string ConnectionString = "server=(local);"+
   "uid=sa;pwd=;"+
   "database=Northwind";
```

And in Visual Basic .NET:

```
Dim ConnectionString As String = "server=(local);" + _
  "uid=sa;pwd=;" + _
  "database=Northwind"
```

Next, you instantiate a SqlConnection object, passing the connection string to the constructor. Afterwards, you can open the connection.

In C#:

```
SqlConnection Connection = new SqlConnection(ConnectionString);
Connection.Open();
```

In Visual Basic .NET:

```
Dim Connection As SqlConnection = New SqlConnection(ConnectionString)
Connection.Open()
```

The next step involves instantiating a SqlCommand object and passing the name of the stored procedure to be executed (in this case, CustOrderHist) and the connection object.

In C#:

```
SqlCommand Command = new SqlCommand("CustOrderHist", Connection);
```

In Visual Basic .NET:

```
Dim Command As SqlCommand = New SqlCommand("CustOrderHist", Connection)
```

You also need to tell the data command object that the type of command to be executed is a stored procedure. You do this by setting its CommandType property to the enumeration value CommandType.StoredProcedure.

```
Command.CommandType = CommandType.StoredProcedure;
```

If the stored procedure you are executing accepts parameters, you need to tell the data command object details about each one. In this case, the CustOrderHist stored procedure accepts a single parameter named CustomerID, whose type is NChar and size is 5.

```
Command.Parameters.Add(new SqlParameter ("@CustomerID",
  SqlDbType.NChar,
  5));
```

Next, you need to set the value that you want to pass in the parameter to the stored procedure. In the example, I have hard-coded the customer ID value of "ALFKI", the ID of the first customer in the Northwind database (typically, you store a user-specified value in the Value property instead)

```
Command.Parameters[0].Value = "ALFKI";
```

Finally, you are ready to execute the command. As mentioned previously in the "Executing a data command" section, there are a few different methods that can be called on the data command object, depending on the type of command you are executing. In this case, I call the ExecuteReader method because I want to return a data reader object I can use to view the result set. Alternately, I could have filled a DataSet with the result set by assigning the data command object to a data adapter and running its Fill method.

In C#:

```
SqlDataReader DataReader = Command.ExecuteReader();
```

And in Visual Basic .NET

```
Dim DataReader As SqlDataReader = Command.ExecuteReader()
```

The following code simply iterates through the result set and displays it in a message box. Afterwards, the DataReader and Connection are closed.

Pulling it all together

Here is all the C# code used to execute this stored procedure. I have added code at the end to display the result set stored in the DataReader, as well as code to close the DataReader and the Connection.

```
// Build the connection string
string ConnectionString = "server=(local);"+
  "uid=sa;pwd=;"+
  "database=Northwind";

// Open the connection
SqlConnection Connection = new SqlConnection(ConnectionString);
Connection.Open();

// Create a data command object passing the name
// of the stored procedure and the connection object
SqlCommand Command = new SqlCommand("CustOrderHist", Connection);

// Specify that the command type is a stored procedure
Command.CommandType = CommandType.StoredProcedure;

// Specify a single stored procedure parameter
// named CustomerID, of type NChar and size of 5
Command.Parameters.Add(new SqlParameter ("@CustomerID",
  SqlDbType.NChar,
  5));
// Specify the value of the parameter
Command.Parameters[0].Value = ALFKI;

// Execute the command
SqlDataReader DataReader = Command.ExecuteReader();
```

```csharp
// Get the next record in the result set
string OrderHist = "";
while (DataReader.Read())
{
  // Access the data in the current row
  OrderHist += DataReader.GetString(0) + ", " +
       DataReader.GetInt32(1) + "\n";
}

// Display the order history`
MessageBox.Show("Order History for customer " +
  customerID + "\n\n" +
  OrderHist, "Stored Procedure Demo");

DataReader.Close();
Connection.Close();
```

And here it is in Visual Basic .NET:

```vbnet
' Build the connection string
Dim ConnectionString As String = "server=(local);" + _
  "uid=sa;pwd=;" + _
  "database=Northwind"

' Open the connection
Dim Connection As SqlConnection = New SqlConnection(ConnectionString)
Connection.Open()

' Create a data command object passing the name
' of the stored procedure and the connection object
Dim Command As SqlCommand = New SqlCommand("CustOrderHist", Connection)

' Specify that the command type is a stored procedure
Command.CommandType = CommandType.StoredProcedure

' Specify a single stored procedure parameter
' named CustomerID, of type NChar and size of 5
Command.Parameters.Add(New SqlParameter("@CustomerID", _
  SqlDbType.NChar, _
  5))
' Specify the value of the parameter
Command.Parameters(0).Value = customerID

' Execute the command
Dim DataReader As SqlDataReader = Command.ExecuteReader()
' Command.Exec

' Get the next record in the result set
Dim OrderHist As String = ""
While DataReader.Read()

  ' Access the data in the current row
  DataReader.GetInt32(1).ToString() + Chr(13) + Chr(10)

End While
```

```
' Display the order history`
MessageBox.Show("Order History for customer " + _
  customerID + Chr(13) + Chr(10) + Chr(13) + Chr(10) + _
  OrderHist, "Stored Procedure Demo")

DataReader.Close()
Connection.Close()
```

In addition to using stored procedures to retrieve data, you can also create and execute stored procedures that perform functions such as inserting, updating, and deleting records. In the next section, you will see how to perform these tasks using a DataSet.

Updating Data Using DataSets

In the "Accessing data using DataSets" section, you saw how a DataSet works in conjunction with a data adapter to retrieve data. This same sort of relationship is used when updating data. To understand how this works, you need to learn more about data adapters.

Understanding data adapters

Data adapters need to be given specific instructions on how to handle selects, updates, inserts, and deletes. The data adapter has four properties that allow you to do this:

- SelectCommand

- UpdateCommand

- InsertCommand

- DeleteCommand

You configure and store in each of these properties an instance of a data command object that tells the data adapter how to carry out each type of data manipulation (update, insert, and delete). Previously, in the examples on accessing data using DataSets, you used the data adapter to retrieve data. The sample code passed a command string and connection string to the constructor of the data adapter. For example in C#:

```
SqlDataAdapter DataAdapter = new SqlDataAdapter(CommandString,
ConnectionString);
```

And in Visual Basic .NET:

```
Dim DataAdapter As SqlDataAdapter = New SqlDataAdapter(CommandString,
ConnectionString)
```

The data adapter takes the command string, automatically creates a data command object, and stores it in the SelectCommand property.

To update data using a data adapter, you should set the other three properties. Technically, you don't need to set all three (for example, if there are no new records, you wouldn't need to specify an InsertCommand object). However, because you may not know if a user has inserted, deleted, or updated records, you simply set all three properties.

If you use stored procedures for updating, inserting, and deleting data, you can manually configure data command objects to execute these stored procedures as demonstrated in the "Invoking stored procedures" section. This can be quite an involved process! However, given the right conditions, you can use a command builder to create the data command objects for you, rather than using stored procedures.

Using command builders

The .NET Framework's SqlCommandBuilder or OleDbCommandBuilder are command objects you instantiate and use to automatically create update, insert, and delete command objects. However, a command builder can only be used in the following situations:

- The DataSet being updated must only contain data from a single source table.

- You must specify at least one primary key or unique value column in the source table.

- The DataSet table must contain the primary key or unique value column.

- There can be no special characters in the table name.

Once you verify that all these conditions are true, it's very easy to use the command builder. The following code demonstrates retrieving a record from the Northwind database's Supplier table, changing the supplier name, and then updating the data.

I've shown the retrieval and update code as two methods contained within a Supplier class. The GetSupplierID method should be familiar because you've already seen similar code for filling a DataSet with SQL Server data. The Save method contains the new code that implements a command builder. As you can see, all you need to do is instantiate a command builder, call its GetDeleteCommand, GetUpdateCommand and GetInsertCommand methods, and then store the returned command object in the corresponding data adapter's properties. Afterwards, you simply call the data adapter's Update method and the data is persisted back to SQL Server. Here's the C# code:

```
public class Supplier
{
  protected SqlDataAdapter DataAdapter;

  public DataSet GetSupplierByID(int supplierID)
  {
    // Build the connection string
    string ConnectionString = "server=(local);"+
      "uid=sa;pwd=;"+
      "database=Northwind";

    // Build the command string
    string CommandString = "SELECT supplierid, CompanyName" +
      " FROM Suppliers WHERE supplierid = " + supplierID;

    // Create the data adapter, passing the command and connection strings
    DataAdapter = new SqlDataAdapter(CommandString, ConnectionString);

    // Instantiate a DataSet object
    DataSet ds = new DataSet();
```

```
    // Fill the DataSet
    DataAdapter.Fill(ds);

    return ds;
  }

  /// Save the specified DataSet
  public int Save(DataSet ds)
  {
    // Create a Command Builder and build the delete, update and insert
commands
    SqlCommandBuilder CommandBuilder = new SqlCommandBuilder(DataAdapter);
    DataAdapter.DeleteCommand = CommandBuilder.GetDeleteCommand();
    DataAdapter.UpdateCommand = CommandBuilder.GetUpdateCommand();
    DataAdapter.InsertCommand = CommandBuilder.GetInsertCommand();

    // Update the data in thet DataSet
    int RowsUpdated = DataAdapter.Update(ds, ds.Tables[0].ToString());

    return RowsUpdated;
  }
}
```

And here it is in Visual Basic .NET:

```
Public Class Supplier
  Protected DataAdapter As SqlDataAdapter

  Function GetSupplierByID(ByVal supplierID As Integer) As DataSet
        ' Build the connection string
        Dim ConnectionString As String = "server=(local);" + _
            "uid=sa;pwd=;" + _
            "database=Northwind"

        ' Build the command string
        Dim CommandString As String = "SELECT supplierid, CompanyName" + _
            " FROM Suppliers WHERE supplierid = " + supplierID.ToString()

        ' Create the data adapter, passing the command and connection strings
        DataAdapter = New SqlDataAdapter(CommandString, ConnectionString)

        ' Instantiate a DataSet object
        Dim ds As DataSet = New DataSet()

        ' Fill the DataSet
        DataAdapter.Fill(ds)

        Return ds

  End Function

  '/ <summary>
  '/ Save the specified DataSet
  '/ </summary>
  '/ <param name="ds"></param>
  Public Function Save(ByVal ds As DataSet) As Integer
        ' Create a Command Builder and build the delete, update and insert
commands
```

```
        Dim CommandBuilder As SqlCommandBuilder = New
SqlCommandBuilder(DataAdapter)
        DataAdapter.DeleteCommand = CommandBuilder.GetDeleteCommand()
        DataAdapter.UpdateCommand = CommandBuilder.GetUpdateCommand()
        DataAdapter.InsertCommand = CommandBuilder.GetInsertCommand()

        ' Update the data in thet DataSet
        Dim RowsUpdated As Integer = DataAdapter.Update(ds,
ds.Tables(0).ToString())

        Return RowsUpdated

   End Function
End Class
```

The data adapter returns the number of rows that were updated, including deleted, updated, and inserted records.

Typed DataSets

There are two main types of DataSets in .NET—typed and untyped DataSets. This chapter has only looked at untyped DataSets created on the fly by executing SQL SELECT statements. You can also create typed DataSets whose structures are defined by using Visual Studio .NET design tools. Based on the fact that typed DataSets make coding much easier, they may be your best choice for data access.

For more information on typed DataSets, see Chapter 11, ".NET XML" for details.

Deploying a .NET application with data access

When deploying a .NET application that accesses data, you must be sure to have Microsoft Data Access Components (MDAC) version 2.7 or higher installed on the target machine.

You do this by adding a *launch condition* to your .NET project in the Solution Explorer. For more information, see the .NET Help topic "Adding a Launch Condition for Microsoft Data Access Components".

Accessing Visual FoxPro Data from ADO.NET

This chapter wouldn't be complete without an overview of how to access Visual FoxPro data using ADO.NET.

To access VFP data, you need to use the OLE DB Managed Data Provider (vfpoledb.dll). Using this provider you can retrieve and update data, as well as run stored procedures. The following example demonstrates how to load VFP data into a Data Reader. I've taken the code used previously to load SQL Server data into a DataReader and adapted it for Visual FoxPro.

The first change I made was adding a reference to the System.Data.OleDb namespace, the namespace of the OLE DB Data Provider classes. The next change I made was to search for class names beginning with the string "Sql" and replace it with "OleDb". The next obvious change was to the connection string. The OLE DB connection string is slightly different than that of SQL Server. For Visual FoxPro data, you simply need to specify the Provider (vfpoledb.1) and the Data Source (in this case, samples.dbc).

There was one other subtle change that the SELECT statement needed. In Visual FoxPro, when you use the TOP keyword, you must specify an ORDER, so I added "ORDER BY employeeid" to the end of the SQL SELECT string. These changes demonstrate the need to be aware of the idiosyncrasies of each type of data used by your application.

Here's the C# code in its entirety:

```
using System.Data.OleDb;

/// Build the connection string
string ConnectionString = "Provider=vfpoledb.1;Data Source=samples.dbc";

/// Create the connection
OleDbConnection Connection = new OleDbConnection(ConnectionString);

/// Open the connection, access the data and close the connection
Connection.Open();

string SelectCmd = "SELECT TOP 3 LastName, FirstName, Title FROM Employees
   ORDER BY employeeid";
OleDbCommand Command = new OleDbCommand(SelectCmd, Connection);

OleDbDataReader Reader = Command.ExecuteReader();

// Get the next record in the result set
string Employees = "";
while (Reader.Read())
{
  // Access the data in the current row
  Employees += Reader.GetString(0) + ", " +
       Reader.GetString(1) + " - " + Reader.GetString(2) + "\n";
}
MessageBox.Show(Employees, "Data Reader Demo");

Reader.Close();
Connection.Close();
```

And here's the Visual Basic .NET code:

```
Imports System.Data.OleDb

'/ Build the connection string
Dim ConnectionString As String = "Provider=vfpoledb.1;Data Source=samples.dbc"

'/ Create the connection
Dim Connection As OleDbConnection = New OleDbConnection(ConnectionString)

'/ Open the connection, access the data and close the connection
Connection.Open()

Dim SelectCmd As String = "SELECT TOP 3 LastName, FirstName, Title FROM
Employees ORDER BY employeeid"
Dim Command As OleDbCommand = New OleDbCommand(SelectCmd, Connection)

Dim Reader As OleDbDataReader = Command.ExecuteReader()

' Get the next record in the result set
Dim Employees As String = ""
While Reader.Read()
  ' Access the data in the current row
```

```
    Employees += Reader.GetString(0) + ", " + _
    Reader.GetString(1) + " - " + Reader.GetString(2) + Chr(13) + Chr(10)
End While

MessageBox.Show(Employees, "Data Reader Demo")

Reader.Close()
Connection.Close()
```

As of the writing of this chapter, the Visual FoxPro OLE DB Provider does not work properly with the Command Builder. The Fox team was made aware of the problem, so there should hopefully be an updated version of the provider available by the time you read this.

Conclusion

As you can see, accessing data with ADO.NET is quite a bit more complex than using Visual FoxPro! There are a variety of ways available for accessing data—primarily by using DataSets or DataReaders and command objects. Be sure to evaluate your needs carefully before deciding which data access method to use in any given situation.

Chapter 8
.NET Business Objects

The VFP community has known about the importance of business objects for several years now. They continue to be extremely important in all types of .NET applications including Web Forms, Window Forms, and Web Services. This chapter explains what business objects are, why you should use them, and how to implement them in .NET.

In most .NET books, documentation, white papers, and Internet resources available these days, you hear little mention of business objects. This isn't because business objects are unimportant—just the opposite; they are extremely important in building flexible applications that are scalable and easy to maintain. Rather, I think this omission is because business objects are perceived as being too advanced when first learning a new technology. While there may be some truth to that, hopefully this chapter will help you grasp the concept of business objects and take your software development to a new level.

In this chapter you'll learn the basic mechanics of creating and using business objects. In subsequent chapters, you'll see how they can be used in Windows Forms, Web Forms, and XML Web Services.

What is a business object?

A business object is an object that represents a real-world entity such as a person, place, or business process (**Figure 1**).

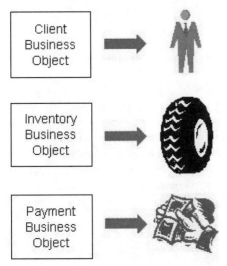

Figure 1. *Business objects can represent real world entities such as a person, place, or business process.*

For example, in the real world, you have clients. You can create a business object that represents clients. In the real world, you have inventory and payments. You can create business objects that represent inventory and payments.

This concept isn't completely foreign to Visual FoxPro developers. When you design a data model, you often create data that represents the characteristics of real-world entities. For example, you create a client table that represents the characteristics of a client in the real world—a name, address, phone number, e-mail address, and so on. You can create an inventory table that represents the characteristics of different inventory items, a payment table that represents the characteristics of payments, and so on (**Figure 2**).

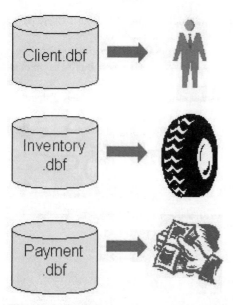

Figure 2. *Data can represent the characteristics of real world entities, but this is only half the picture.*

Modeling the characteristics of a real-world entity by means of data is only half the story. The other half is modeling its behavior—and you do that by means of code. This includes data manipulation code as well as any business logic (or application logic) code associated with the entity. For example, you may have code that calculates the tax on an invoice, totals the payments made by a client, or calculates a client's credit limit. Business objects bring together both the characteristics and behavior of a particular entity (**Figure 3**).

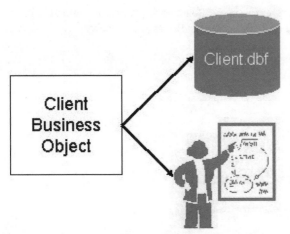

Figure 3. *Business objects bring together both the characteristics and behavior of a single real-world entity.*

In an application that uses business objects, all the code for a particular entity is stored in the corresponding business object. For example, all the code that has something to do with clients is stored in the client business object; all the code that has something to do with inventory is in the inventory business object; and yes, all the code that has something to do with payments is stored in the payments business object.

The simplest aspect of modeling an entity's behavior is data manipulation. Just about every business object needs methods that allow you to add, edit, retrieve, save, and delete records—these translate to actions that occur in the real world. For example, when you acquire a new client, this corresponds to the ability of a business object to add a new record. When you lose a client, this may correspond to the ability of a business object to delete a record (or possibly mark it as "inactive"). When some attribute of a client changes (address, phone number, e-mail address), this corresponds to the ability of a business object to retrieve, edit, and save a client record.

Examining business objects in popular software applications

The concept of using business objects in software applications is very common among popular off-the-shelf software packages. Examining the business objects in these applications can help you better understand how to implement business objects in the software you create.

A good place to start is by exploring the business object model of Microsoft Word. The primary business object in this model is the Document object, which represents a real-world Microsoft Word document. You can view Word's object model by using Visual Studio .NET's Object Browser. To launch the Object Browser, select View | Other Windows | Object Browser from the menu. To open up the Microsoft Word object model, click the Customize button at the top of the Object Browser, which launches the Selected Components dialog. Click the Add button, which launches the Component Selector dialog (**Figure 4**). Click the COM tab and select Microsoft Word 9.0 Object Library in the component list (the version number differs depending on which version of Microsoft Word is on your computer). Click the Select button to add Microsoft Word to the Selected Components list, and then click OK to close the

Component Selector dialog. Click the OK button in the Selected Components dialog to add it to the Object Browser. This adds a Word node to the Object Browser tree view.

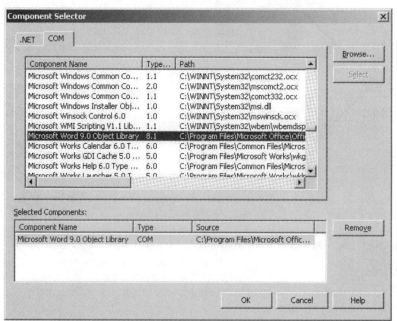

Figure 4. *The Component Selector allows you to add components to the Object Browser for viewing.*

If you expand the Word node, you see quite a few items listed. If you select the Document business object in the left pane, it displays the members of the Document object in the right pane (**Figure 5**).

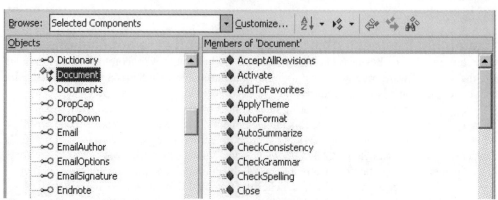

Figure 5. *You display the members of a business object by selecting the object in the left pane of the Object Browser.*

You can determine which items are business objects in the Object Browser because they have the same icon as shown to the left of the Document business object shown in Figure 5.

You can get quite an education by examining the methods of the Document business object. For example, in the real world you can perform a wide variety of actions against a document such as:

- Check grammar

- Check spelling

- Print it

- Undo changes

- Close It

In the Document business object the methods represent these different actions:

- CheckGrammar

- CheckSpelling

- PrintOut

- Undo

- Close

For another example, open up the Microsoft Internet Controls object library in the VS .NET Object Browser (**Figure 6**).

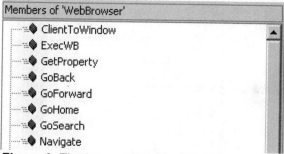

Figure 6. The Internet Explorer WebBrowser business object represents a real-world web browser.

This library contains a WebBrowser business object that represents a real-world browser. It contains methods such as GoBack, GoForward, GoHome, Navigate, Refresh, and so on. Each one represents real-world actions you can perform with a web browser.

One of the main points to realize from looking at these object models is when Microsoft created these tools they did not put the application logic in the user interface of Microsoft Word and Internet Explorer. Instead, they created business objects possessing events and methods that contain the business logic. The methods are intuitive and perform a discrete action that accomplishes a well-defined objective. If they change the interface of the tool, they don't have to move or rewrite all of the internal code that handles operations like SpellCheck and GoHome.

Monolithic vs. three-tier applications

A *monolithic* application is a software application where the user interface, business logic, and data are inextricably bound to each other. Typically this type of application does not use business objects. Despite the benefits that business objects can provide, most developers (Visual FoxPro and otherwise) continue to build monolithic applications. This should come as no surprise, because most of the software development tools on the market actually encourage you to build applications this way.

For example, think about the Data Environment builder in Visual FoxPro. The Form Designer and Report Designer allow you to use the Data Environment builder (**Figure 7**) to specify the data to be loaded by a form or report.

Although these tools can help you build applications rapidly, they don't provide the most scalable solution. For example, if you load Visual FoxPro tables into the data environment of a form, what happens when you want to move to SQL Server or Oracle? You have to spend weeks or months tearing apart your application and putting it back together again.

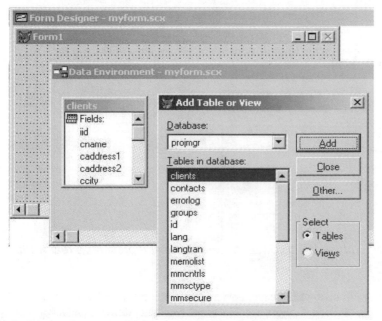

Figure 7. The Data Environment builder in Visual FoxPro 7 encourages you to create monolithic applications by binding your user interface directly to your data.

As mentioned at the beginning of this chapter, most .NET documentation, books, and periodicals also demonstrate creating monolithic applications. Not using business objects means the data access code is placed directly in the user interface, making for a very monolithic application.

In contrast, **Figure 8** shows a three-tier system architecture that includes business objects. This is a far more flexible architecture where any tier can be swapped out (for more information on three-tier architecture, see Chapter 7, "Data Access with ADO.NET").

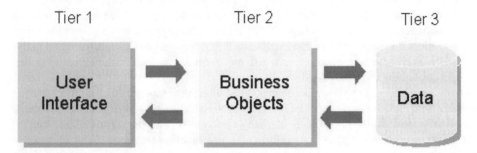

Figure 8. Business objects allow you to create a three-tier architecture that is far more scalable than a monolithic architecture.

For example, you can create a smart client Windows desktop application for tier 1, and then later you can swap it out with a thin client Web browser interface, without affecting the rest of the application (**Figure 9**). You can also change the data tier from Visual FoxPro to SQL Server without changing your application logic.

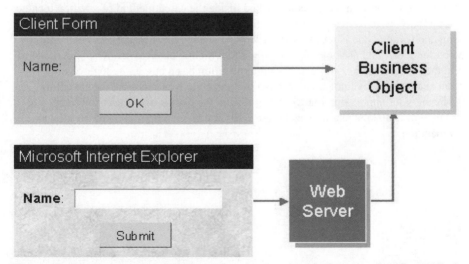

Figure 9. Three tier architectures allow you to swap between a fat client Windows desktop front end and a thin client Web browser front end without changing the application logic.

Additional business object benefits

In addition to the scalability gained with business objects, there are other benefits that come from using them.

Normalizing application logic

One benefit of using business objects is normalizing your application logic. As a Visual FoxPro developer, you know all about normalizing data—eliminating redundancies in the data structure. But how conscious are you of eliminating redundancies in your application logic? When you work with a team of developers, the chances of creating duplicate application logic increases dramatically—especially when creating a monolithic application. You can have five different developers create the same routine five different times when the code is stored in the user interface. Each developer working on a different form has no idea that another developer has already created the code they need.

In contrast, when you use business objects, even when developers work on different forms, each form uses the same set of business objects. Each business object acts as a common repository for code that relates to a particular real-world entity. The chances of adding two or more methods to a business object that perform the same function are pretty slim—especially if you give your methods meaningful names!

Normalizing your application logic means you write, debug, and maintain less code. When a change request comes through there's only one place in your application that needs to change.

Solving the "where's the code" syndrome

Have you ever played "where's the code?" with your software applications? When you create a monolithic application, the code can be located just about anywhere—and Murphy's law predicts that the code you want is probably tucked inside the Click method of a button located on page 3 of a "sub" page frame contained within another page frame.

Finding application code is much easier when you use business objects. For example, if you search for code that has something to do with invoicing, chances are *very* high it can be found in the Invoice business object. If your application has a bug in the logic that performs calculations on inventory, you can bet that the code is probably in the Inventory object. Surfacing your application logic (raising it from the depths of the user interface) and exposing it in high level business objects (**Figure 10**) makes your application far easier to debug and maintain.

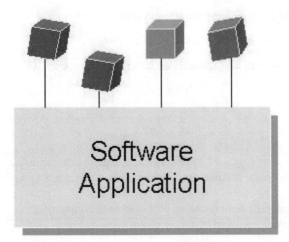

Figure 10. *Surfacing your application logic into business objects (represented by the colored cubes) makes it easier to find the code you're looking for, helps normalize your application logic, and lets you conceive and create complex software systems.*

Ease of conceiving and creating complex software systems

When your code is stuck "in the weeds" of your application's user interface, it can be very difficult to step back and see the big picture of a complex software system.

However, when you place your application logic in business objects, it's far easier to see the big picture and think "big thoughts". Rather than poring through a morass of methods within your user interface code, you can conceptualize complex processes as high-level business objects representing real-world entities and interacting with each other.

I have the same experience over and over again when I visit software development companies to help them solve some of their more thorny issues. As soon as they lay out business objects on a diagram and begin conceptualizing at a higher level, problems that were previously impossible to wrap their minds around can be grasped and solved.

Once you learn how to use business objects, you'll never go back again!

A simple example

So, how do you transform a monster Click event into a business object model? Although this isn't a book about analysis and design, here is a simple example of how this works.

Consider the example of a point-of-sale invoicing application. If you're creating a monolithic application, you might have an Invoice form that has a Save button. Within the Click event of the Save button, you might have code that does the following:

- Scans through each invoice item calculating the tax (if any) on each item.

- Adds the tax and item cost to the invoice header total.

- Subtracts the invoice item quantity from the "quantity on hand" in inventory.

- Saves the invoice items.

- Saves the invoice header

How would you handle this using business objects? Typically, you should create a different business object for each table in your back end database (this is a guideline, not a "set in stone" rule). In this example, you might create Invoice, InvoiceItem, Tax, and Inventory business objects.

Figure 11 shows a UML sequence diagram demonstrating how you might implement business objects to handle all of the processes involved in saving an invoice.

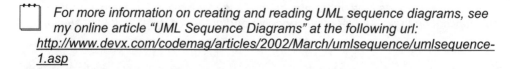

For more information on creating and reading UML sequence diagrams, see my online article "UML Sequence Diagrams" at the following url: http://www.devx.com/codemag/articles/2002/March/umlsequence/umlsequence-1.asp

The stick figure at the top left of diagram represents the Sales Rep who interacts with the application to save an invoice. To the immediate right of the SalesRep a box labeled "UI" is a generic representation of the application's user interface. The Save() message line pointing from the SalesRep to the UI represents the SalesRep pressing the Save button.

The rest of the boxes to the right of the UI box represent the application's business objects. Notice the arrow labeled "Save()" between the UI object and the Invoice object. This indicates the Invoice object has a Save() method being called by the user interface. The Invoice object in turn sends a Save() message to the InvoiceItems object. The InvoiceItems object calls a method on itself named SaveItem(). The asterisk preceding the SaveItem() method indicates this method is called multiple times—in this case, once for each invoice item. From within the SaveItem() method, a call is made to the Tax object (CalcTax) to calculate tax on the item and to the Inventory object (RemoveFromStock) to remove each item from stock.

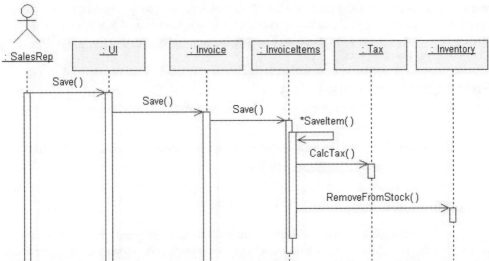

Figure 11. *This sequence diagram shows how you might place application logic in business objects to save an invoice.*

Note that I haven't included any parameters in this diagram. I did this to make it easier to read. However, in reality most methods in this diagram would receive parameters. For example, the RemoveFromStock() method might receive an inventory item primary key and a quantity, so it can determine which inventory item to adjust and by how much.

The main purpose of this example is to show you the big picture of how to use business objects in applications. You will see more detailed examples of using business objects in Chapter 9, "Building .NET Windows Forms Applications", Chapter 10, "Building Web Applications with ASP.NET", and Chapter 12, "XML Web Services".

Making .NET data access easy

If nothing I've mentioned so far strikes you as a compelling reason to use business objects, the fact that business objects make it much easier to use ADO.NET may be the reason you are looking for.

As Chapter 7, "Data Access with ADO.NET" explained, ADO.NET is very flexible, very scalable, and very object-oriented, but it can be difficult to learn and use. Business objects change all that by creating a high-level interface to ADO.NET that doesn't require all developers on your team to be familiar with creating connections or manipulating and coordinating data objects.

You write your data access logic once, store the code in a family of data access classes used by your business objects, and never worry about the specifics of ADO.NET again—until Microsoft changes the ADO.NET object model.

This actually brings up another compelling reason to create a layer of abstraction between your application and ADO.NET. Microsoft is notorious for changing its data access model every few years. If you follow the pattern set by many .NET code samples found in books, magazines, and online articles, you'll end up sprinkling lots of data access code throughout your user interface. This becomes a problem if Microsoft makes changes to ADO.NET. It will force you to update all of this data access code accordingly. However, if you use business objects, you have only one place to change your data access code—within the data access classes of the business object.

Enforcing business rules

One of the primary jobs of a business object is to enforce business rules. Business rules fall into two broad categories:

1. Data integrity rules – This encompasses rules that enforce things such as required fields, field lengths, ranges, and so on.

2. Domain rules – This refers to high-level business rules such as "You can't create an invoice for a client who is over their credit limit".

Typically, an application checks business rules at two different points in time. The first is when trying to save a record. After a user clicks the Save button (Windows Forms application) or the Submit button (Web Forms application), the system needs to check if any rules pertaining to the record being saved are broken, and if so, display a message with showing the broken rules.

The second place rules are often checked is when the user leaves a data entry control. For example, when the user leaves an e-mail text box, you may want to immediately check if the e-mail is valid. You can call a business rule method to verify this. For details, check out the section, "The BusinessRules class", below.

.NET business object architecture

To help you grasp the concept of business objects, the sample code that comes with this book provides a simple business object class you can use to access either FoxPro or client-server data. **Figure 12** shows a UML class diagram documenting the basic architecture of this business object class.

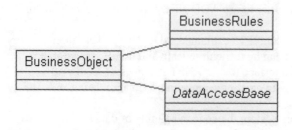

Figure 12. Good business object architecture gives you a lot of flexibility—especially in the area of data access.

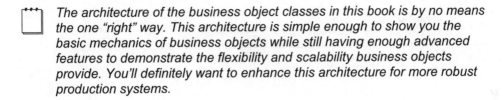

The architecture of the business object classes in this book is by no means the one "right" way. This architecture is simple enough to show you the basic mechanics of business objects while still having enough advanced features to demonstrate the flexibility and scalability business objects provide. You'll definitely want to enhance this architecture for more robust production systems.

Each of these objects is covered in detail in the following sections.

The BusinessObject class

The BusinessObject class, shown in Figure 12, is the primary class in the business object architecture that the user directly interfaces with.

The sample code in this chapter is set to use the SQL Server Northwind database by default.

Creating subclasses of the BusinessObject class

You create subclasses of the BusinessObject class that represent entities in your application domain. For example, in this book's sample code, four business objects have been subclassed from BusinessObject:

- Employee
- Customer
- Orders
- OrderDetail

When you create a subclass of BusinessObject, two important properties should be set right away—the TableName and FieldList. The TableName property specifies the primary table in the database with whichwhere the business object retrieves and manipulates data. The FieldList property specifies the default list of fields included in the DataSet when you retrieve data from the back end. This property is set to "*" by default, which specifies that all fields in the table are returned.

You can easily change the value of these properties in your custom business object's constructor method. For example, the following code defines a Customer class derived from BusinessObject and sets the value of TableName and FieldList.

In C#:

```csharp
public class Customer : BusinessObject
{
  /// <summary>
  /// Customer constructor
  /// </summary>
  public Customer()
```

```
    {
        this.TableName = "Customer";
        this.FieldList = "CustomerID, CompanyName, " +
            "Address, City, PostalCode, Country, Phone";
        this.BusinessRuleObject = new CustomerRules();
    }
}
```

And in Visual Basic .NET:

```
Public Class Customer
    Inherits BusinessObject

    '/ <summary>
    '/ Customer constructor
    '/ </summary>

    Public Sub New()

        Me.TableName = "Customer"
        Me.FieldList = "CustomerID, CompanyName, " & _
            Address, City, PostalCode, Country, Phone"
        Me.BusinessRuleObject = New CustomerRules()

    End Sub 'New

End Class 'Customer
```

Retrieving data with the GetDataSet method

The BusinessObject class has a GetDataSet method that executes a SQL SELECT statement and returns a DataSet containing the result set. This method has two overloads.

In C#:

```
protected DataSet GetDataSet()
{
  string Command = "SELECT " + this.FieldList + " FROM " + this.TableName;
  return this.GetDataSet(Command);
}

protected DataSet GetDataSet(string command)
{
  return DataAccessObject.GetDataSet(command, this.TableName);
}
```

And in Visual Basic .NET:

```
Protected Function GetDataSet() As DataSet

    Dim Command As String = "SELECT " & Me.FieldList & " FROM " & Me.TableName
    Return Me.GetDataSet(Command)

End Function 'GetDataSet
```

```
Protected Function GetDataSet(command As String) As DataSet

  Return DataAccessObject.GetDataSet(command, Me.TableName)

End Function 'GetDataSet
```

The first method signature accepts zero parameters. It simply uses the FieldList and TableName properties to automatically build a SELECT command that it passes to the second overload of the GetDataSet method. The second overload accepts a single "command" parameter that it passes to the data access object (discussed below) for execution. It also passes the TableName property, used to specify the name of the main DataTable within the DataSet.

The GetDataSet methods are marked as protected, because you typically don't want to open your back end database to this sort of carte blanche querying capability. For example, if the second GetDataSet method was public, there's nothing stopping someone from issuing a SELECT * that returns all fields and records in a table with millions of records.

To retrieve data from a custom business object, you typically create methods that build a SELECT string and pass it to the second overload of GetDataSet. For example, the following methods of the Customer business object retrieve a customer by ID and phone number.

In C#:

```csharp
public DataSet GetCustomerByID(string customerID)
{
  return this.GetDataSet("SELECT " + this.FieldList + " FROM " + this.TableName +
        " WHERE customerID='" + customerID + "'");
}

public DataSet GetCustomerByPhone(string phone)
{
  return this.GetDataSet("SELECT " + this.FieldList + " FROM " + this.TableName +
        " WHERE Phone = '" + phone + "'");
}
```

In Visual Basic .NET:

```vbnet
Public Function GetCustomerByID(ByVal customerID As String) As DataSet

  Return Me.GetDataSet(("SELECT " & Me.FieldList & " FROM " & Me.TableName & _
        " WHERE customerID='" & customerID + "'"))

End Function 'GetCustomerByID

Public Function GetCustomerByPhone(ByVal phone As String) As DataSet

  Return Me.GetDataSet(("SELECT " & Me.FieldList & " FROM " & Me.TableName & _
        " WHERE Phone = '" & phone & "'"))

End Function 'GetCustomerByPhone
```

Here is an example of how you call the GetCustomerByPhone method from client code. In C#:

```
Customer CustomerObj = new Customer();
DataSet dsCustomers = CustomerObj.GetCustomerByPhone("555-3425");
```

And in Visual Basic .NET:

```
Dim CustomerObj As New Customer()
Dim dsCustomers As DataSet = CustomerObj.GetCustomerByPhone("555-3425")
```

Saving data with the SaveDataSet method

The SaveDataSet method accepts a single DataSet parameter and updates the back end database with any changes (updates, inserts, deletes) found in the DataSet.

Here is an example of how you call the SaveDataSet method to update a DataSet. In C#:

```
Employee EmployeeBizObj = new Employee();

// Retrieve an Employee record
DataSet dsEmployee = EmployeeBizObj.GetEmployeeByID(1);
DataRow drEmployee = dsEmployee.Tables[0].Rows[0];

// Change a value
drEmployee["Title"] = "Vice president";

// Save the change
int RowsUpdated = EmployeeBizObj.SaveDataSet(dsEmployee);
```

And in Visual Basic .NET:

```
Dim EmployeeBizObj As New Employee()

' Retrieve an Employee record
Dim dsEmployee As DataSet = EmployeeBizObj.GetEmployeeByID(1)
Dim drEmployee As DataRow = dsEmployee.Tables(0).Rows(0)

' Change a value
drEmployee("Title") = "Vice president"

' Save the change
Dim RowsUpdated As Integer = EmployeeBizObj.SaveDataSet(dsEmployee)
```

Before the actual update occurs, this method checks to see if there is a business rule object attached and, if so, calls that object's CheckRules method. If this method is successful, it returns the number of records containing changes that were persisted to the back end (zero or more). If any business rules are broken, this method returns a –1. For details on how to handle broken business rules, see the next section.

The BusinessRules class

The BusinessRules class enforces business rules and keeps track of any rules that are broken. Typically, you should create a subclass of the BusinessRules class for each of your business objects. For example, in the samples for this book, the Customer business object has a CustomerRules object, the Employee object has an EmployeeRules object, and so on.

To associate a business rule class with a business object, you need to instantiate it in the constructor of the business object. For example, you add the following code to the constructor of the Customer business object to instantiate and associate the CustomerRule object with it.

In C#:

```csharp
public Customer()
{
  this.BusinessRuleObject = new CustomerRules();
}
```

And in Visual Basic .NET:

```vbnet
Public Sub New()
  Me.BusinessRuleObject = New CustomerRules()
End Sub 'New
```

Typically, you create a separate method in the rules object for each different business rule. For example, the CustomerRules object has IsCompanyNameValid, IsPostalCodeValid, and IsPhoneValid methods. Breaking these methods out allows you to call each method individually (for example, from the event of a user interface control).

In most cases, you also need to check all business rules when you try to save a record. How can this be done if you have each rule in a separate method? The answer is to add a call to each business rule method in the CheckRulesHook method of the BusinessRules class. For example, the CustomerRules object contains the following code in its CheckRulesHook method.

In C#:

```csharp
public override void CheckRulesHook(DataSet ds, string tableName)
{
    DataRow dr = ds.Tables[tableName].Rows[0];    // Get the first DataRow

    this.IsCompanyNameValid(dr["CompanyName"].ToString());
    this.IsPostalCodeValid(dr["PostalCode"].ToString());
    this.IsPhoneValid(dr["Phone"].ToString());
}
```

And in Visual Basic .NET:

```
Public Overrides Sub CheckRulesHook(ds As DataSet, tableName As String)

   Dim dr As DataRow = ds.Tables(tableName).Rows(0) ' Get the first DataRow

   Me.IsCompanyNameValid(dr("CompanyName").ToString())
   Me.IsPostalCodeValid(dr("PostalCode").ToString())
   Me.IsPhoneValid(dr("Phone").ToString())

End Sub 'CheckRulesHook
```

The BusinessObject class automatically calls the CheckRulesHook method before it tries to save a record. It passes the DataSet to be saved as well as the name of the Table within the DataSet. If any rules are broken, the business object does not save the data in the DataSet (the next section shows how you can retrieve and display broken rules).

In this particular implementation, the BusinessRules class only checks the first record in the DataSet. You can enhance this method to check multiple records in a DataTable.

Checking for broken business rules

If the BusinessObject's SetDataSet method returns a –1, you call the GetBrokenRules method of the BusinessObject class to determine the business rules that were broken. This list of broken rules can then be displayed to the user. For example, here's code that checks for broken rules when saving an order.

In C#:

```
Orders OrderObj = new Orders();
DataSet dsOrder = OrderObj.GetOrderByOrderID(10248);
DataRow drOrders = dsOrder.Tables[0].Rows[0];

drOrders["EmployeeID"] = 0;

int RowCount = OrderObj.SaveDataSet(dsOrder);
if (RowCount == -1)
{
  string BrokenRuleList = "";
  foreach (string BrokenRule in OrderObj.BusinessRuleObject.BrokenRules)
  {
      BrokenRuleList += BrokenRule + "\n";
  }
  MessageBox.Show("Broken Rules: \n\n" + BrokenRuleList, "Business Rules");
}
else
{
  MessageBox.Show("Order successfully saved","Business Rules");
}
```

And in Visual Basic .NET:

```
Dim OrderObj As New Orders()
Dim dsOrder As DataSet = OrderObj.GetOrderByOrderID(10248)
Dim drOrders As DataRow = dsOrder.Tables(0).Rows(0)
```

```
drOrders("EmployeeID") = 0

Dim RowCount As Integer = OrderObj.SaveDataSet(dsOrder)
If RowCount = - 1 Then

    Dim BrokenRuleList As String = ""
    Dim BrokenRule As String

    For Each BrokenRule In  OrderObj.BusinessRuleObject.BrokenRules
        BrokenRuleList += BrokenRule + ControlChars.Lf
    Next BrokenRule

    MessageBox.Show("Broken Rules: " + ControlChars.Lf + _
        ControlChars.Lf + BrokenRuleList, "Business Rules")
Else
    MessageBox.Show("Order successfully saved", "Business Rules")
End If
```

This code instantiates the Orders business object, retrieves an order, and saves the DataSet with a broken rule (the Employee ID is empty). It then checks the return value of the SaveDataSet method to see if any rules are broken (indicated by a return value of –1). If any rules are broken, it retrieves all broken rules from the BusinessRule object. A reference to the BusinessRule object is stored in the business object's BusinessRuleObject property. BrokenRules is a string collection contained within the BusinessRule object. The "for each" loop iterates through the string collection building a string containing all broken rules which it then displays in a message box.

Some developers like to display all the broken rules in a single dialog. You can do this by simply concatenating the broken rules together and displaying them. Another option is to have your business object return broken rules as an XML string. You can then display the broken rules in a list box, DataGrid, etc.

Data access classes

Figure 12 showed the BusinessObject class has an associated data access class it uses to retrieve and manipulate data. As shown in **Figure 13**, there is actually a family of data access classes used to access different types of data.

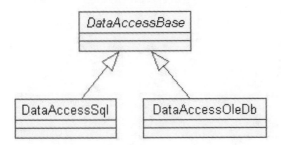

Figure 13. Providing a family of data access classes for your business objects allows you to access different data sources (Visual FoxPro, SQL Server, Oracle) without changing your business object.

The abstract DataAccessBase class defines the interface for the family of data access classes. The DataAccessSql class allows you to access SQL Server 7.0 and later, acting as a wrapper around the .NET SQL Server data provider. The DataAccessOleDb class allows you to access any data with an OleDB Data Provider, acting as a wrapper around the .NET OleDB data provider.

By default, the BusinessObject class uses the DataAccessSql class to access the Northwind SQL Server database. To change the BusinessObject class (and all subclasses) to use the DataAccessOleDb class instead, you change its DataAccessClass property from "DataAccessSql" to "DataAccessOleDb".

Conclusion

You don't have to use business objects in your .NET applications, but doing so makes your applications far more flexible, extensible, and maintainable. In this chapter you've seen how to design and implement business objects. For examples showing how business objects can be used in different types of applications, see Chapter 9, "Building .NET Windows Forms Applications", Chapter 10, "Building Web Applications with ASP.NET", and Chapter 12, "XML Web Services".

Chapter 9
Building .NET Windows Forms Applications

Microsoft has placed a tremendous emphasis on .NET being a platform to create, consume, and deploy XML Web Services. Unfortunately, it caused many developers among the uninitiated to believe that .NET is *only* for building applications that access the Internet. I've heard the question over and over again: "Why should I use .NET if I'm not creating Web applications"? This chapter aims to dispel this notion.

You can use .NET to create standard, Windows desktop applications (known in .NET as Windows Form or WinForm applications). Truth be told, you can quite happily create C# and Visual Basic .NET applications that never think twice about the Internet. However, should you decide to provide Web access to your desktop applications, all the tools are ready and waiting for you.

This chapter shows you how to take advantage of Visual Studio .NET to create Windows Forms Applications. You'll be amazed at how easy it is to do things you could never do in Visual FoxPro (or things you had to kludge). Most importantly, you'll see how to use business objects in a Windows Forms application.

Creating a Windows Forms application

In this chapter you will learn about Windows Forms applications by building a simple Windows Forms application and taking a look behind the scenes each step of the way. Chapter 2, "Visual Studio .NET" showed the very basics of creating a Windows application. This chapter takes you beyond the basics and explores the process in greater detail.

A Windows Forms application typically contains a main application form, a main menu, toolbars, a variety of forms, code files containing business object classes, and references to external .NET assemblies. In this walk-through you'll see how each element is used in a .NET Windows Forms application.

To create a new Windows Forms application:

1. From the Visual Studio .NET Start Page, click the New Project button.

2. In the New Project dialog look in the Project Types pane on the left and select Visual C# to create a C# Windows application or Visual Basic .NET to create a VB .NET Windows application. Then in the Templates pane on the right, select Windows Application.

3. In the Name text box, enter the name you want to give your new Windows application. In this example I'll enter "Simple Windows Application".

4. Make sure the Location box contains the directory you want to create your new application in and click OK.

At this point, VS .NET creates a new application for you, using the Windows Application template you selected. After a few moments, a new form named Form1 is displayed in design mode in the Visual Studio .NET IDE (**Figure 1**).

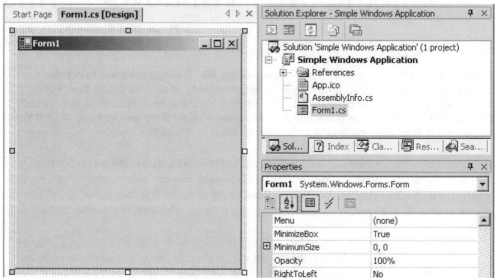

Figure 1. *Visual Studio .NET creates a Windows application from the template you select in the New Project dialog.*

You may be wondering what this form is for—is it supposed to be a login form or maybe just one of the forms in the application? By default, this form is meant to be your main application desktop, more or less equivalent to the main Visual FoxPro window. Take a look behind the scenes by right-clicking on Form1 and selecting View Code from the shortcut menu.

Namespaces in C#

Because namespaces are handled a bit differently in C# versus Visual Basic .NET, I'll talk about namespaces for each language separately. If you're using C#, notice the namespace declaration at the top of the code file:

```
namespace Simple_Windows_Application
```

This is the namespace automatically created by Visual Studio .NET when you created the new project—it's basically the project name with spaces replaced by underscores. Before going any further, change the namespace to something more meaningful. Microsoft recommends that you use the "Company.Product" naming convention for your namespaces. For example, the following namespace specifies the company HW (Hentzenwerke), the product NetBook (.NET for VFP Developers Book), and I've added an extra ".Samples" section to indicate these are the samples for the book:

```
namespace HW.NetBook.Samples
```

Now you need to change the project's *default namespace* to the same namespace. The default namespace specifies the namespace that is used for all new code files added to the project. To change the default namespace, right-click on your project in the Solution Explorer and select Properties from the shortcut menu. In the Property Pages dialog, expand the Common folder in the left pane and select General. Change the Default Namespace (**Figure 2**) to the new namespace, "HW.NetBook.Samples".

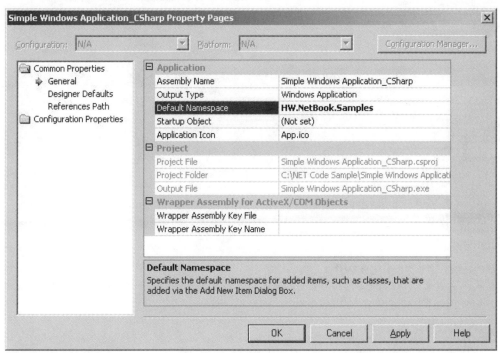

Figure 2. You change your project's default, or root namespace, in the project's Property Pages dialog.

Namespaces in Visual Basic .NET

If you're using Visual Basic .NET, there is no namespace declaration in the Form1.vb code file—that's because VB .NET handles namespaces differently than C#. In VB .NET there is the concept of a *root namespace* for each project, which is different than C#'s *default namespace*. This root namespace acts as a prefix for any namespace you declare within a code file. For example, if the project's root namespace is "HW.NetBook.Samples", and you specify an additional "Business" namespace, the full namespace is "HW.NetBook.Samples.Business".

To set the VB .NET project's root namespace, right-click on the project and select Properties from the shortcut menu to launch the Property Pages dialog (**Figure 3**). In the Root namespace text box, enter "HW.NetBook.Samples", and click OK to save changes.

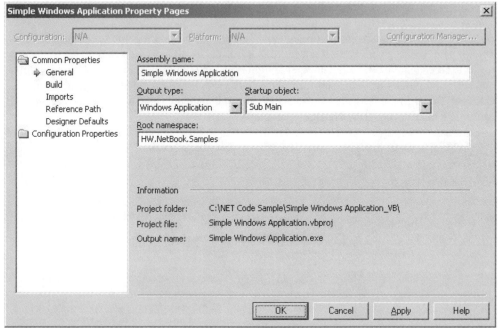

Figure 3. You change a Visual Basic .NET project's root namespace in the Property Pages dialog.

Behind the scenes with C#

If you created a C# Windows Forms application, scroll down to the bottom of the code file and you will see the following method declaration:

```
static void Main()
{
  Application.Run(new Form1());
}
```

As mentioned in chapter 3, "Introduction to C#", all C# programs must have a static method named Main, which is the method called when the program is first executed. By default, the Main method is added to the Form1 class by Visual Studio .NET. If you don't want a form to be the first object instantiated in your application, you can remove the Main method from the form, create a new class, and add the method to it.

If you're using C#, the compiler automatically finds the class with the Main method at compile time. If you're using Visual Basic .NET, you must specify in your project's Property Pages dialog which object in your application is the startup object.

The ability to change your startup object is useful when you are creating a more robust application with an application object that you want to instantiate first. After doing some application startup processing, you can instantiate your main application form. For now, I'll leave this method in the Form1 class.

Within the Main method, there is the following code:

```
Application.Run(new Form1());
```

The Application object belongs to the System.Windows.Forms namespace. Its static Run method runs an application message loop that processes messages from the operating system to your application. In this line of code, a new instance of the Form1 class is passed as a parameter to the Run method. This causes the message processing to begin and the main application form to be made visible. If you leave out this line of code the application will start up and immediately exit—similar to Visual FoxPro's READ EVENTS.

Behind the scenes with Visual Basic .NET

If you created a Visual Basic .NET Windows application, you will not see a Main method declaration in the form's code as you do in C#. What's going on here?

In a VB .NET Windows application, Form1 is specified as the startup object by default; however, a form-level Main method is not exposed in the source code. Behind the scenes, the Visual Basic .NET compiler inserts a Main method into the IL code to satisfy .NET's requirement that all programs must have a Main method. This model was chosen to help simplify VB .NET Windows Forms applications.

If you don't want a form to be the first object instantiated in your VB .NET application, you can create a new class and add a Main method to it. For example:

```
Public Class MainClass
    Shared Sub Main()
        Application.Run(New Form1())
    End Sub
End Class
```

Next, you need to change the startup object from Form1 to your Main method. Right-click on your project and select Properties from the shortcut menu to launch the Property Pages dialog (Figure 3). In the left pane, expand the Common Properties folder and select General. In the Startup object combo box, change the selection from "Form1" to "Sub Main".

Modifying the main application form

To learn more about .NET forms, click Form1 in design mode and bring up the Properties Window. Follow these steps to change some key properties of the form:

1. Change the form's Text property from "Form1" to "My Simple WinForm Application". When you press Enter or move off the Text property, the caption of the form changes to the new text.

2. Scroll to the top of the Properties Window and find the (Name) property to specify the name of the form class. Change the (Name) property to MainAppForm.

3. Go to the Size property in the Properties Window and change the size to 640, 480. Note that if you expand the Size property by clicking on the plus sign (+) you can change just the Height or just the Width of the form.

4.   Select the IsMdiContainer property and set its value to "True". "MDI" stands for Multiple Document Interface. An MDI form can contain child forms. If you don't set this property to "True", any child forms you launch will exist outside of the main application form. Note when you change this property to "True", the back color of the form changes to the "Application Background" color in your Windows color scheme (on my computer, it's dark grey).

5.   Now change the WindowState property. The default value is "Normal", which means when you run the application the form is the same size you see in design mode. Change the value of this property to "Maximized", so the window fills the computer screen at run time.

Before compiling and running the application, you need to make one more change to the Form1 code file. When you changed the name of the form class from "Form1" to "MainAppForm", it changed the name of the class in the code file. However it did *not* change the name of the form class being passed to Application.Run(). Go back to the Main method and change the call to the Application class's Run method as follows.
   In C#:

```
Application.Run(new MainAppForm());
```

In Visual Basic .NET, rather than adding this line of code, right-click on the project and select Properties from the shortcut menu. In the Property Pages dialog's Startup object combo box, select "MainAppForm", and then click OK to close the dialog.
   Next, for the sake of consistency, go to the Solution Explorer, right-click on the Form1 source code file, select Rename from the shortcut menu, and change the name from "Form1.cs" to "MainAppForm.cs" (in C#) or from "Form1.vb" to "MainAppForm.vb" (in Visual Basic .NET).
   Now you're ready to compile the application. To do so, select Build | Build Solution from the main menu. To run the application, select Debug | Start from the menu or press the F5 shortcut key. Your main application form should fill the entire screen. To close the application, click the close button on the upper right side of the form.

Creating a main application menu
At this point, you need to create a main application menu where you launch other application forms you build later on. In Visual Studio .NET, you add a menu to any form in your application. To add a menu to your main application form, select the form in design mode, and then drag and drop a MainMenu class from the VS .NET Toolbox onto the form. If the Toolbox is not visible, select View | Toolbox from the main menu.
   When you drop the menu on the form, rather than showing up on the form's design surface, it is displayed in the component tray beneath the form (**Figure 4**).

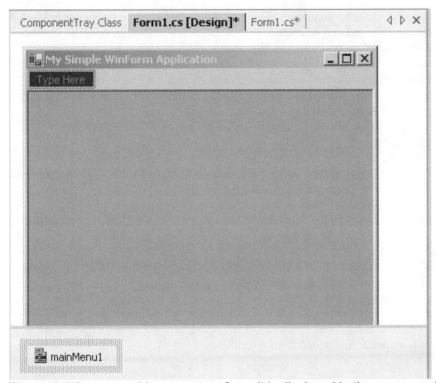

Figure 4. *When you add a menu to a form, it is displayed in the component tray beneath the form rather than on the form's design surface.*

If you've ever struggled with Visual FoxPro's menu designer, you're going to like the menu designer in VS .NET. To kick the tires a bit, add a few menu pads and menu bars using the menu designer.

To create a <u>F</u>ile menu pad, click in the rectangle labeled Type Here at the top of the form, and enter the text "&File" as shown in **Figure 5**. The "&" indicates the "F" is the menu item's access key. At run time, pressing ALT+F selects this menu pad. When you add a new menu item Visual Studio .NET automatically gives it a generic name such as "menuItem1". It's best if you change this name to something more meaningful, such as "FilePad". To do this, select the menu item, bring up the Properties Window, and set the value of the (Name) property to "FilePad".

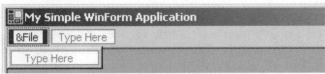

Figure 5. *You indicate the access key of a menu item by placing an ampersand in front of it.*

Next, add an E<u>x</u>it menu bar to the File menu pad. To do this, click in the rectangle labeled Type Here below the File pad and enter the text "E&xit". Next, change the name of the new menu bar to "FileExitBar" in the Properties Window.

Add a second menu pad called <u>C</u>ustomers by clicking in the Type Here box to the right of the File menu pad, entering the text "&Customers", and changing the name of the menu pad to "CustomersPad". Add a menu bar to this pad by clicking in the Type Here box beneath the pad, entering the text "&Orders", and changing the name of the menu bar to "CustomerOrdersBar". This bar will be used to launch a Customer Orders form that you will create later in this chapter.

Most applications have a <u>W</u>indow menu pad containing a list of all forms open on the desktop. In Visual FoxPro, you had to write code adding a menu bar to the Window menu pad whenever a new form was instantiated. In Visual Studio .NET, all you have to do is add a menu bar with the text "Window" and set a single property in the Property Window. To create the Windows menu pad, click in the Type Here box to the right of the Customers menu pad and enter the text "&Window". In the Properties Window, change the name of the menu pad to "WindowsPad". Next, change the value of the MdiList property from False to True. If this property is set to True, when an MDI child form is instantiated at run time, a corresponding menu bar is automatically added to this menu pad.

At this point, your menu system looks good, but doesn't do much (other than the Windows menu pad). Now add some code to the Exit menu bar that closes the application when the user selects it at run time. To do this, double-click on the Exit menu bar and the following code is automatically added to your form.

In C#:

```
private void FileExitBar_Click(object sender, System.EventArgs e)
{

}
```

And in Visual Basic .NET:

```
Private Sub FileExitBar_Click(ByVal sender As System.Object, ByVal e As
System.EventArgs) Handles FileExitBar.Click

End Sub
```

This code is a form-level method acting as an event handler for the FileExitBar's Click() event. Any code you place in this method is automatically executed at run time when a user selects File | Exit from the menu.

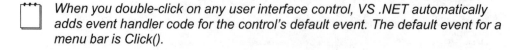

When you double-click on any user interface control, VS .NET automatically adds event handler code for the control's default event. The default event for a menu bar is Click().

What mechanism automatically calls this event handler when the Click event of the menu bar is executed? When you double-clicked the FileExitBar in the menu designer, it actually adds another line of code to your form that is hidden in the code editor. To see this code, scroll up in the code editor until you see a rectangle containing the text "Windows Form Designer generated code" (**Figure 6**), and expand this node.

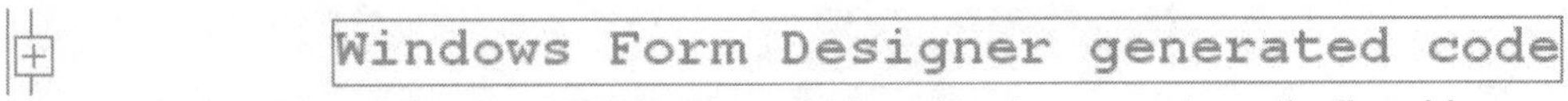

```
Windows Form Designer generated code
```

Figure 6. The Visual Studio .NET Form and Menu Designers automatically add "behind-the-scenes" code to your form

As you can see, the Form and Menu Designer have been adding plenty of "behind-the-scenes" code to your form as you've been creating new menu items and setting form properties. The C# editor hides less of this code than the Visual Basic .NET editor which hides just about everything. Take a look at some of this form-level code to see what's going on.

First, look at the form's constructor code. This code is *not* hidden in C#, but is hidden in Visual Basic .NET.

Here's the C# form constructor code:

```
public MainAppForm()
{
  //
  // Required for Windows Form Designer support
  //
  InitializeComponent();

  //
  // TODO: Add any constructor code after InitializeComponent call
  //
}
```

Here's the Visual Basic .NET form constructor code:

```
Public Sub New()
  MyBase.New()

  'This call is required by the Windows Form Designer.
  InitializeComponent()

  'Add any initialization after the InitializeComponent() call

End Sub
```

In each constructor method, a call is made to a form-level method named InitializeComponent. By default, this method is hidden in both C# and Visual Basic .NET.

Here are the first few lines of code in C#:

```
private void InitializeComponent()
{
  this.mainMenu1 = new System.Windows.Forms.MainMenu();
  this.FilePad = new System.Windows.Forms.MenuItem();
  this.FileExitBar = new System.Windows.Forms.MenuItem();
  private System.Windows.Forms.MenuItem CustomersPad;
  private System.Windows.Forms.MenuItem CustomerOrdersBar;
```

```
this.WindowPad = new System.Windows.Forms.MenuItem();
```

And here they are in Visual Basic .NET:

```
<System.Diagnostics.DebuggerStepThrough()> Private Sub InitializeComponent()
Me.MainMenu1 = New System.Windows.Forms.MainMenu()
Me.FilePad = New System.Windows.Forms.MenuItem()
Me.FileExitBar = New System.Windows.Forms.MenuItem()
Me.CustomersPad = New System.Windows.Forms.MenuItem()
Me.CustomerOrdersBar = New System.Windows.Forms.MenuItem()
Me.WindowsPad = New System.Windows.Forms.MenuItem()
```

As you see by looking at this code, Visual Studio .NET added a form-level, private variable for the main menu and each menu item. When the form is instantiated and the constructor method calls this InitializeComponent method, an instance of each menu class is created and stored in these form-level variables.

As you look down through the rest of the code in the InitializeComponent method, you see code added by the Menu Designer and Form Designer that changes the values of menu and form properties. For example, at the bottom of each method, you find the following code setting various form properties.

In C#:

```
this.AutoScaleBaseSize = new System.Drawing.Size(5, 13);
this.ClientSize = new System.Drawing.Size(640, 480);
this.IsMdiContainer = true;
this.Name = "MainAppForm";
this.Text = "My Simple WinForm Application";
this.WindowState = System.Windows.Forms.FormWindowState.Maximized;
```

In Visual Basic .NET:

```
Me.AutoScaleBaseSize = New System.Drawing.Size(5, 13)
Me.ClientSize = New System.Drawing.Size(640, 480)
Me.IsMdiContainer = True
Me.Menu = Me.MainMenu1
Me.Name = "MainAppForm"
Me.Text = "My Simple WinForm Application"
Me.WindowState = System.Windows.Forms.FormWindowState.Maximized
```

This approach is very different from the Visual FoxPro form and menu designers. In Visual Studio .NET, ultimately, every object you add to a form or a menu is implemented as code in the form's associated code file. In design view, Visual Studio .NET interprets the code into a representation you work with visually on a form.

Getting back to the real reason you began looking at the form's code, if you look at the C# code, you find the following line:

```
this.FileExitBar.Click += new System.EventHandler(this.FileExitBar_Click);
```

This code links the Exit menu bar's Click event with the form-level FileExitBar_Click event handler method shown earlier. The FileExitBar_Click method is registered as an event handler (using the += operator) with the FileExitBar's Click event, establishing a link between the two.

Now, look at the corresponding Visual Basic .NET code. You may be surprised to find this code is not located in the InitializeComponent method. This is because VB .NET establishes event handlers differently by using the "Handles" keyword. The code you're looking for is actually found right in the FileExitBar_Click method declaration:

```
Private Sub FileExitBar_Click(ByVal sender As System.Object, ByVal e As
System.EventArgs) Handles FileExitBar.Click

End Sub
```

The Handles keyword indicates the FileExitBar_Click method handles the FileExitBar.Click event.

Now that you have a basic understanding of how this works, it's time to add code to the event handler that closes the application when the user selects File | Exit from the menu.

Here's the code in C#:

```
private void FileExitBar_Click(object sender, System.EventArgs e)
{
  this.Close();
}
```

And here's the code in Visual Basic .NET:

```
Private Sub FileExitBar_Click(ByVal sender As System.Object, ByVal e As
System.EventArgs) Handles FileExitBar.Click
  Me.Close()
End Sub
```

> *For more information on events, event handlers, and delegates, see Chapter 5, "Object-Orientation in C# and Visual Basic .NET".*

Now it's time to test out your new menu. From the Build menu, select Build Solution. Next, press F5 to start the application. If everything's working properly, your main application form should maximize to fill your computer monitor, and you should have a main menu containing File, Customers, and Window menu pads. When you select File | Exit from the menu, your application should exit. You can also exit the application by clicking the close button [X] at the top right corner of the application window.

When you add another form to the project later in this chapter, you will revisit the menu system to verify the Window menu pad is working properly.

> *For more information on creating menus, see the .NET Help topic "Adding Menu Enhancements to Windows Forms".*

Adding a new form to the project

To demonstrate the capabilities of Windows Forms and Visual Studio .NET, you'll create a "Customer Orders" form that allows you to view, edit, and create customer orders.

First, you need to add a new form to the project. Right-click on the project and select Add | Add Windows Form from the shortcut menu. In the Add New Item dialog, change the form name to "CustomerOrdersForm.cs" (in C#) or "CustomerOrdersForm.vb" (in Visual Basic .NET), and click the Open button. This opens the new form in design mode.

Go to the Properties Window and change the Size to 580, 420 (this makes the form a good size for the controls you will add later on), change the Text property to "Customer Orders", and change the StartPosition property to "CenterScreen" (for information on the other settings of the StartPosition property, see the .NET Help topic "FormStartPosition Enumeration"). "CenterScreen" automatically centers the form in the middle of the screen.

Working with the TabControl

The .NET TabControl is equivalent to Visual FoxPro's page frame control. I recommend adding a TabControl to the form to give yourself an idea of how to use it in your applications. The easiest way to add the control is to double-click on it in the Toolbox, which automatically adds the control to the upper left corner of the form. Next, go to the Properties Window, change the TabControl's Name property to TabControl, change its Size to 580,420, and set its TabStop property to False.

You may have noticed that, by default, the TabControl doesn't have any tabs. To add tabs, select the TabPages property in the Properties Window, click the ellipses button (…) to launch the TabPage Collection Editor (**Figure 7**), and click the Add button to add the first page. This displays a Properties sheet in the right pane of the dialog you can use to edit properties of the tab page.

Change the Text property to "List" and change the Name property to "ListPage". Add a second tab and set its Text property to "Properties" and the Name property to "PropertiesPage". Afterwards, click OK to close the dialog.

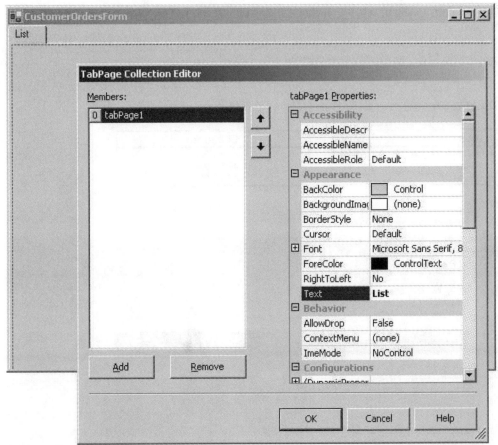

Figure 7. *The TabPage Collection Editor allows you to add, remove, and modify tab pages in the TabControl.*

Adding controls to the List page

In this section, you'll add a few controls to the List page—a text box that allows you to enter a customer ID and a DataGrid that displays all orders for the specified customer. You can drag and drop controls any place on the form that, but if you want to end up with a form looking like the one shown in this chapter's figures, you should set location and size of controls as specified.

First, click on the List page of the tab control. Add a label to the page by double-clicking on the Label item in the Toolbox (or by dragging and dropping it on the form). Go to the Properties Window and change the label's Text property to "Customer ID:" and its Name property to "lblCustomerID". Change its Location property to 25,25.

Next, add a text box control to the form from the Toolbox. Set its Name property to txtCustomerID and remove all characters from its Text property. Set the Location property to 100,22. Finally, set the text box's CharacterCasing property to "Upper". This causes the text box to automatically uppercase all characters as they are typed (the Customer IDs in the Northwind database are all uppercased).

Add a DataGrid control to the form, set its Name property to "grdOrders", its Location property to 25,65, and its Size property to 425, 275.

Finally, add three Buttons to the form and set their properties as shown in **Table 1**.

Table 1. *Properties of Customer Orders form buttons*

Name	Text	Location
btnNew	&New	475, 85
btnDelete	&Delete	475, 125
btnClose	&Close	475, 285

When you're done, the List page should look like **Figure 8**.

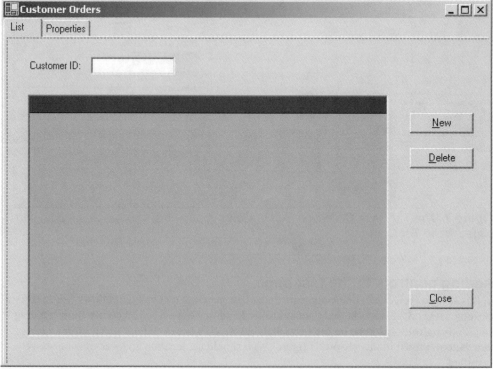

Figure 8. *The Customer Orders form List page allows you to view orders for a specified customer.*

Now add code to respond to the Close button's click event and close the form. First double-click on the Close button, which adds a btnClose_Click event handler method to the form. You just need to add a single line of code to this method to close the form.

In C#:

```
private void btnClose_Click(object sender, System.EventArgs e)
{
  this.Close();
}
```

And in Visual Basic .NET:

```
Private Sub btnClose_Click(ByVal sender As System.Object, _
    ByVal e As System.EventArgs) Handles btnClose.Click
    Me.Close()
End Sub
```

Before adding any controls to the Properties page, I'll first get to something a little more interesting—adding code to the form that displays all orders for a customer when the user enters a Customer ID.

Accessing data by means of business objects

Many of the .NET samples available in books, magazines, and on-line articles place data access code directly in the user interface. As mentioned in Chapter 8, ".NET Business Objects", a far better approach is performing all data access and manipulation using business objects. In this section, you will apply what you learned in the previous chapter and create business objects to use with the Customer Orders form.

First, you need to add two files to your Windows Forms project that are found in the sample code for this book. If you're working with C#, add the files Business.cs and Data.cs to your project. To add these files to your project, open the Solution Explorer, right-click on the project, and select Add | Add Existing item from the shortcut menu. In the Add Existing Item dialog, navigate to the directory containing these files and add them to the project.

If you're working with Visual Basic .NET, copy the existing Business.vb and Data.vb files from the samples directory into your project's root directory using Windows Explorer. Afterwards, add the files to your project as mentioned above. Next, change the namespace in the Business.vb file to:

```
Namespace Business
```

And change the namespace in the Data.vb file to:

```
Namespace Data
```

Now you need to create an Orders business object that retrieves data from the SQL Server Northwind database's Orders table. To do this, open the Solution Explorer, right-click your project, and select Add | Add New Item from the shortcut menu. In the Add New Item dialog's right pane, select Code File. Next, change the code file name to "OrdersBusiness.cs" (in C#) or "OrdersBusiness.vb" (in Visual Basic .NET) and click the Open button. This opens an empty code file in the IDE.

At the top of the code file, enter the following code to define a new Orders business object class.

In C#:

```csharp
using System.Data;

namespace HW.NetBook.Samples.Business
{
  public class Orders : BusinessObject
  {
    public Orders()
    {
      this.TableName = "Orders";
    }

    // Returns a DataSet containing all orders for the specified customer
    public DataSet GetOrdersByCustomerID(string custID)
    {
      custID = custID.ToUpper();
      return this.GetDataSet("SELECT * FROM Orders WHERE CustomerID = '" +
        custID + "'");
    }

    /// Returns a DataSet containing the specified order
    public DataSet GetOrderByOrderID(int orderID)
    {
      return this.GetDataSet("SELECT * FROM Orders WHERE OrderID = " +
        orderID);
    }

  }
}
```

And in Visual Basic .NET:

```vbnet
Imports System.Data

Namespace Business
    Public Class Orders
        Inherits BusinessObject

        Public Sub New()
            Me.TableName = "Orders"
        End Sub 'New


        ' Returns a DataSet containing all orders for the specified customer
        Public Function GetOrdersByCustomerID(ByVal custID As String) _
            As DataSet
            custID = custID.ToUpper()
            Return Me.GetDataSet(("SELECT * FROM Orders WHERE CustomerID = '" _
                + custID + "'"))
        End Function 'GetOrdersByCustomerID

        ' Returns a DataSet containing the specified order
        Public Function GetOrderByOrderID(ByVal orderID As Integer) As DataSet
            Return Me.GetDataSet(("SELECT * FROM Orders WHERE OrderID = " & _
```

```
            orderID.ToString()))
       End Function 'GetOrderByOrderID

   End Class 'Orders
End Namespace 'Business
```

Next, add a reference to the following namespaces to the top of the code file. These references tell the compiler where to find the .NET DataSet class as well as your business object classes.

In C#:

```
using System.Data;
using HW.NetBook.Samples.Business;
```

And in Visual Basic .NET:

```
Imports System.Data
Imports HW.NetBook.Samples.Business
```

Now you need to add code to the form's Load event that instantiates the Orders business object when the form is first loaded. Add the following private field declaration at the top of the CustomerOrdersForm class declaration. This new field will hold a reference to the Orders business object when it's instantiated. While you're at it, also add a private variable named dsOrder to hold the Orders DataSet returned from the Orders business object.

In C#:

```
public class CustomerOrdersForm : System.Windows.Forms.Form
  {
       private Orders OrdersObj;
       private DataSet dsOrders;
```

And in Visual Basic .NET:

```
Public Class CustomerOrdersForm
    Inherits System.Windows.Forms.Form

    Private OrdersObj As Orders
    Private dsOrders As DataSet
```

Next, double-click on the form's title bar in the Form Designer to automatically add event handler code to the form's code file. Next, add code that instantiates the Orders business object.

In C#:

```
private void CustomerOrdersForm_Load(object sender, System.EventArgs e)
{
  /// Instantiate the Orders business object
  this.OrdersObj = new Orders();
}
```

And in Visual Basic .NET:

```
Private Sub CustomerOrdersForm_Load(ByVal sender As Object, _
    ByVal e As System.EventArgs) _
    Handles MyBase.Load

    '/ Instantiate the Orders business object
    Me.OrdersObj = New Orders()
End Sub
```

Now you need to add code to call the Orders business object when a user enters a value in the Customer ID text box. In Visual FoxPro, you may have placed this code in the Valid event of the text box. In .NET, you can place this code in the text box's Validating event.

> *In .NET, user control focus events occur in the following order: Enter, GotFocus, Leave, Validating, Validated, LostFocus*

The text box control's default event is TextChanged, so you can't double-click on the text box to automatically add event handler code to the form. If you're using C#, you do this through the Properties Window. Make sure the Customer Orders form is displayed in design mode and select the text box. Go to the Properties Window and click the button with the lightning bolt icon (the Events button). This displays all the events for the text box.

If you double-click on the Validating event (**Figure 9**), VS .NET automatically adds event handler code to the form and displays the name of the event handler method in the second column of the Properties Window (in this case, txtCustomerID_Validating). Remember, in C# code is added both to the bottom of the form's code file as well as within the "hidden" area of the form's code. If you want to delete both sets of related code, in the Properties Window right-click on the event and select Reset from the shortcut menu. Visual Studio .NET automatically removes both sets of code for you!

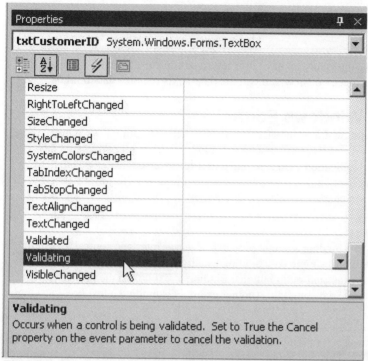

Figure 9. *Double-clicking on a user interface control event in the Properties Window automatically adds event handler code for that event to the form.*

If you are using Visual Basic .NET you can add an event handler to your code by using the combo boxes at the top of the code editor. Just select the control in the left combo box you want to create an event handler for and select the desired event in the right combo box. When you do this, Visual Basic .NET automatically adds event handler code to your form.

At this point, you can add code to the Validating event handler that calls the Orders business object with the specified Customer ID, gets the returned DataSet, and stores it in the form-level private variable dsOrder.

Here's the code in C#:

```
private void txtCustomerID_Validating(object sender,
  System.ComponentModel.CancelEventArgs e)
{
  /// Get all orders for the specified customer
  dsOrders=
this.OrdersObj.GetOrdersByCustomerID(this.txtCustomerID.Text.Trim());
}
```

And here it is in Visual Basic .NET:

```
Private Sub txtCustomerID_Validating(ByVal sender As Object, _
    ByVal e As System.ComponentModel.CancelEventArgs) _
    Handles txtCustomerID.Validating
```

```
'/ Get all orders for the specified customer
dsOrders = Me.OrdersObj.GetOrdersByCustomerID(Me.txtCustomerID.Text.Trim())
End Sub
```

At this point, you have data and you have user interface controls, but now you need to bring the two together so you can display and edit the data—this requires data binding.

Data binding in Windows Forms

In Visual FoxPro, you could bind user interface controls to data by setting the ControlSource, RecordSource, or RowSource of a control to a cursor, field, or object property.

In a Windows Forms application, you can bind a user interface control to a DataSet, Array, ArrayList, or any collection that implements the IList interface (for information on implementing interfaces, see chapter 5, "Object-Orientation in C# and Visual Basic .NET").

Simple data binding

Simple data binding involves binding a single property of a user interface control to a single data value. Controls that support simple data binding usually only display one value at a time such as text boxes, check boxes, and radio buttons. Binding a text box to the property of an object is an example of simple data binding. Another example is binding a text box to a single column in a DataTable.

Simple-bound controls contain a collection of Binding objects stored in a ControlBindingsCollection. Each binding object represents an individual property bound to an individual data source value. This collection is accessible through the control's DataBindings property. You use the DataBindings.Add method to add a Binding object to a control dynamically at run time. You will see an example of this in the "Adding controls to the Properties tab" section later in this chapter.

Complex data binding

Complex data binding involves binding a control to a collection, such as a DataSet, Array, or ArrayList. Controls that support complex data binding can display more than one value at a time—this includes DataGrids, combo boxes, and list boxes. You will see examples of complex data binding with DataGrids and combo boxes later in this chapter.

Data binding controls at run time

You can data bind controls at either design time or run time. Visual Studio .NET has visual tools for adding a data source to a form and binding user interface controls to that data source. However, as you might imagine, using these VS .NET data binding tools creates a hard-coded monolithic application. However, this book is showing you best practices, so I won't use these tools in this chapter, but will show you how to bind data dynamically at run time instead.

The following code sample shows the txtCustomerID_Validating method with two new lines of code (shown in grey). The first new line calls the DataGrid's DataBindings.Clear method. This clears any existing data binding for the grid, which is necessary because this code gets run every time the user enters a new Customer ID. The second new line of code calls the grid's SetDataBinding method, passing the Orders DataSet and the Orders business object's TableName property (which is set to "Orders").

In C#:

```csharp
private void txtCustomerID_Validating(object sender,
  System.ComponentModel.CancelEventArgs e)
{
  /// Get all orders for the specified customer
  dsOrders=
this.OrdersObj.GetOrdersByCustomerID(this.txtCustomerID.Text.Trim());

  /// Clear all data bindings
  this.grdOrders.DataBindings.Clear();

  /// Data bind the grid
  this.grdOrders.SetDataBinding(dsOrders, OrdersObj.TableName);

}
```

And in Visual Basic .NET:

```vbnet
Private Sub txtCustomerID_Validating(ByVal sender As Object, _
    ByVal e As System.ComponentModel.CancelEventArgs) _
    Handles txtCustomerID.Validating
    '/ Get all orders for the specified customer
    dsOrders = Me.OrdersObj.GetOrdersByCustomerID(Me.txtCustomerID.Text.Trim())

    '/ Clear all data bindings
    Me.grdOrders.DataBindings.Clear()
    '/ Data bind the grid
    Me.grdOrders.SetDataBinding(dsOrders, OrdersObj.TableName)

End Sub
```

At this point, you're almost ready to test what you've done so far, but first you need to add code to launch your form when the user selects Customers | Orders from the menu. To do this, open the MainAppForm class in design mode by double-clicking MainAppForm.cs or MainAppForm.vb file in the Solution Explorer (if it's not already open). Next, click on the Customers menu pad and double-click the Orders menu bar below it. This adds a CustomerOrdersBar_Click event handler method to the form (if you remembered to change the name of your menu bar). Add the following code to instantiate and show the form.

In C#:

```csharp
private void CustomerOrdersBar_Click(object sender, System.EventArgs e)
{
  /// Instantiate the form, set its MdiParent and show the form to the user
  CustomerOrdersForm OrdersForm = new CustomerOrdersForm();
  OrdersForm.MdiParent = this;
  OrdersForm.Show();
}
```

And in Visual Basic .NET:

```vbnet
Private Sub CustomerOrdersBar_Click(ByVal sender As System.Object, _
    ByVal e As System.EventArgs) Handles CustomerOrdersBar.Click
```

```
'/ Instantiate the form, set its MdiParent and show the form to the user
Dim OrdersForm As New CustomerOrdersForm()
OrdersForm.MdiParent = Me
OrdersForm.Show()
End Sub
```

The first line of code instantiates the Customer Orders form. The second line of code stores a reference to the main application form in the Order form's MdiParent property. This is necessary if you want the Order form to be contained within the main application form. If you do not set this property, the Order form can be positioned outside the confines of the main form. The last line of code makes the form visible to the user.

Compiling and running the form

Now you're ready to compile and run the form. You can perform each of these steps separately or you can just run the form (which is what I usually do). Press F5 (the shortcut key for the Debug | Start menu bar) and Visual Studio .NET first compiles the solution and then runs the application. If there are any errors, VS .NET displays a warning dialog asking if you still want to run the application. You should select No and fix the problems first before running it again. Although you can select Yes, since the compiler encountered an error, you will be running the last successfully compiled version of the application instead.

When the main application form appears, select Customers | Orders from the menu to launch the form. To test that the form and business object are working properly, enter the text "QUEEN" in the Customer ID box and press the Tab key. The grid should display a list of all orders for the customer (**Figure 10**). If everything works properly, you have permission to pump your fist in the air and do the .NET "dance of joy".

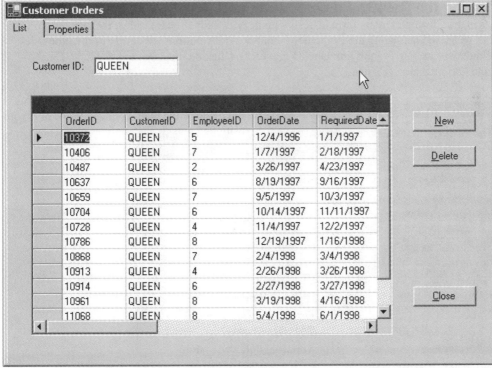

Figure 10. Entering a Customer ID in the text box and pressing Tab sends a request to the Orders business object, which returns a DataSet that displays in the DataGrid.

While you're still flush with the feeling of success, click the Windows menu pad to see that a menu bar for your Customer Orders form has automatically been added (**Figure 11**).

Figure 11. When you set a menu pad's MdiList property to True, a menu bar is added to the pad for each form that is open in the application.

After the initial euphoria wears off, you will probably notice that the data in the grid isn't formatted as nicely as you'd like it to be. First of all, the color scheme of the DataGrid could use some improvement, and secondly, the DataGrid shows all columns in the DataSet (which you probably don't want to do). Select File | Exit to close down the application, and you can take care of these issues.

Designing the DataGrid

There are several very cool features available in Visual Studio .NET that simplify making your DataGrid look great, including a number of features you probably wish were in Visual FoxPro.

Setting the DataGrid's color scheme

Open the CustomerOrders form in design mode (if it isn't already), select the DataGrid on the List page, and then go to the Properties Window. At the bottom left corner of the Properties Window is an <u>Auto Format</u> link label (**Figure 12**). Click on this label to launch the DataGrid Auto Format dialog (**Figure 13**).

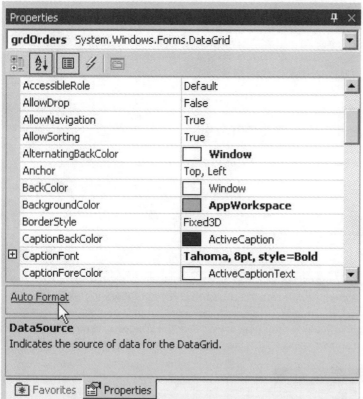

Figure 12. Select the Auto Format link label to launch the DataGrid Auto Format dialog.

The Auto Format dialog gives you over a dozen different DataGrid style formats to select from—similar to Microsoft Word's auto format dialog allowing you to select a style for a table. As you click on different formats in the list box, a preview of the style displays on the right. I've selected the "Professional 4" style, which displays DataGrid elements in different shades of blue *and* displays the grid items in alternating back color! After selecting the desired style, click OK and VS .NET will change several DataGrid properties in the Properties Window to match the style you have selected. The DataGrid on the Customer Orders form also changes appearance accordingly.

> If you want to see the changes that have been made for you, press F4 to give the Properties Window focus, and then press Ctrl+Z repeatedly—this "undoes" each of the property changes one by one. You can then press Ctrl+Y repeatedly to reapply the changes.

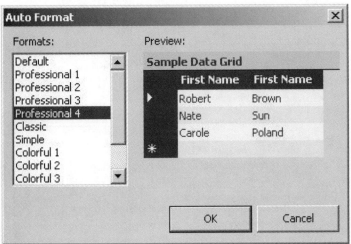

Figure 13. The Auto Format dialog gives you over a dozen different Data Grid styles to select from and automatically sets properties on the DataGrid to match the selected style.

Applying a TableStyle to the DataGrid

While changing the color scheme greatly improves the general appearance of the DataGrid, it hasn't done anything to change the column headers, and for that matter, which columns appear in the DataGrid. To change this, you need to apply a *TableStyle* to the grid. A TableStyle allows you to specify the display format of a given DataSet table (DataTable) in the DataGrid—this includes both visual style as well as which columns appear. You can create a different TableStyle for each different table you want to display in the DataGrid.

To create a TableStyle, select the DataGrid on the Customer Orders form and go to the Properties Window. Select the TableStyles property in the Properties Window and click the ellipses button (...) to launch the DataGridTableStyle Collection Editor (**Figure 14**). Click the Add button to add a new TableStyle to the grid and change the Name property to "OrdersTableStyle". Next, change the MappingName property to "Orders", which specifies that the TableStyle you are creating is only applied to a DataTable named Orders.

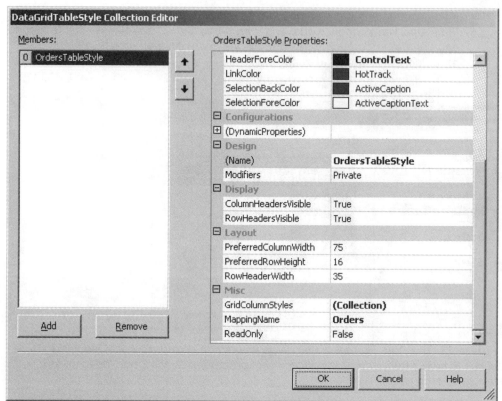

Figure 14. The DataGridTableStyle Collection Editor allows you to create a style for each table displayed in a DataGrid—including which columns should appear.

One down side of creating this TableStyle, is it overrides the style settings you applied to the grid using the Auto Format dialog. To get these back, you must manually set the colors properties to the values shown for the DataGrid in the Properties Window! You can either type these in manually or use the color picker (**Figure 15**). You can find the colors assigned by the Auto Format dialog on the Web tab of the color picker.

Figure 15. *The Web tab of the color picker dialog allows you to pick some of the more interesting colors such as the colors automatically set by the AutoFormat dialog*

There are a number of interesting style properties you can set in this editor, but for now, you will just use it to specify the columns in the DataSet you want to appear in the DataGrid.

Next, scroll to the bottom of the editor's Properties pane on the right and select the GridColumnStyles property. Click the ellipses button (…) to launch the DataGridColumnStyle Collection Editor (**Figure 16**). This editor lets you create a column style for each column you want displayed in the DataGrid.

If you click the small down arrow to the right of the Add button, a shortcut menu displays giving you the option of specifying the type of column you want to add. The "DataGridTextBoxColumn" selection adds a DataGrid column that can host a text box control. The "DataGridBoolColumn" selection adds a DataGrid column that can host a check box control. These are the only two types of column controls available in the editor.

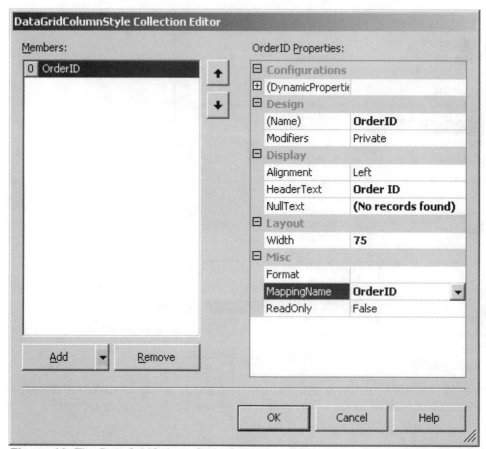

Figure 16. The DataGridColumnStyle Collection Editor lets you specify details about each column you want to appear in a DataGrid.

At this point, click the Add button to add a DataGridTextBoxColumn. In the Properties pane on the right, change the value of the Name property to "OrderID". Change the HeaderText property to "Order ID" and set the NullText property to "(None)". This is the text that appears when no orders are returned in the DataSet for the specified Customer ID. Set the Width Property to 50 and set the MappingName to "OrderID". The MappingName property specifies the name of the DataSet column that the DataGrid column is bound to.

Next, add the three additional columns and set the properties listed in **Table 2**. When you're done, click OK to close each dialog.

Table 2. Properties of DataGrid columns

Name	HeaderText	NullText	Width	MappingName
OrderDate	Date		75	OrderDate
ShipName	Name		175	ShipName
ShipCountry	Country		75	ShipCountry

At this point, compile and run the Customer Orders form again. Your DataGrid should look like **Figure 17**.

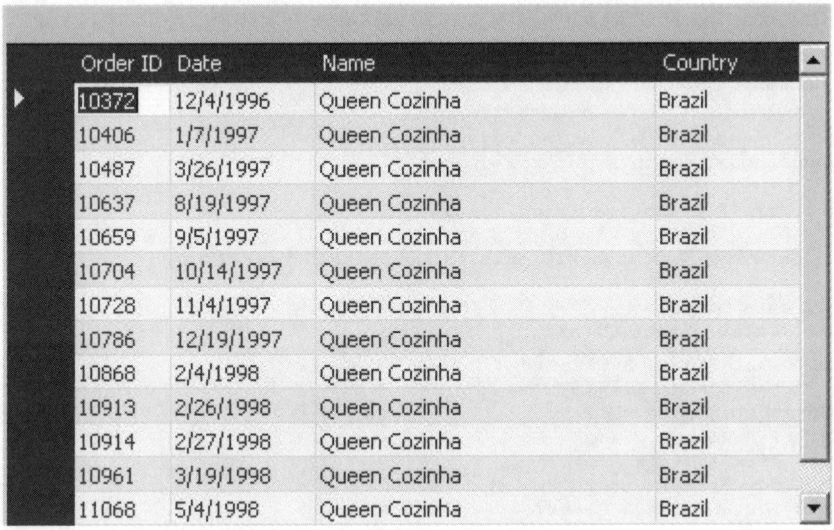

Order ID	Date	Name	Country
10372	12/4/1996	Queen Cozinha	Brazil
10406	1/7/1997	Queen Cozinha	Brazil
10487	3/26/1997	Queen Cozinha	Brazil
10637	8/19/1997	Queen Cozinha	Brazil
10659	9/5/1997	Queen Cozinha	Brazil
10704	10/14/1997	Queen Cozinha	Brazil
10728	11/4/1997	Queen Cozinha	Brazil
10786	12/19/1997	Queen Cozinha	Brazil
10868	2/4/1998	Queen Cozinha	Brazil
10913	2/26/1998	Queen Cozinha	Brazil
10914	2/27/1998	Queen Cozinha	Brazil
10961	3/19/1998	Queen Cozinha	Brazil
11068	5/4/1998	Queen Cozinha	Brazil

Figure 17*. The Visual Studio .NET design tools allow you to easily build professional looking DataGrids.*

Adding controls to the Properties tab

In this section, you're going to add several text boxes to the Properties tab to demonstrate simple data binding in .NET. In design mode, click on the Properties tab of the Customer Orders form and add the label and textbox controls listed in **Table 3**. Note the space left at the top of a form for adding a toolbar later in this chapter.

Table 3*. Name, text, location, and size of controls on Properties tab*

Control	Text	Location	Size
LblOrderID	Order ID:	25,60	Autosize
txtOrderID		100,57	100,20
lblName	Name:	225,60	Autosize
txtName		275,57	260,20
lblAddress	Address:	25,91	Autosize
txtAddress		100,88	328,20
lblCity	City:	25,124	Autosize
txtCity		100,122	175,20
lblRegion	Region:	290,124	Autosize
txtRegion		347,122	185,20
lblPostalCode	Postal Code:	25,160	Autosize
txtPostalCode		100,157	107,20
lblCountry	Country:	290,160	Autosize
txtCountry		347,157	185,20

Next, add the code shown in grey to the txtCustomerID_Validating event handler. This code clears any data binding for the controls and calls the DataBindings.Add method on each text box. The name of the property you want to data bind is the first parameter passed to the Add method; in this case the Text property. The second parameter specifies the DataSet you are binding to and the third parameter indicates the DataTable and column name.

Here's the code in C#:

```csharp
private void txtCustomerID_Validating(object sender,
  System.ComponentModel.CancelEventArgs e)
{
  /// Get all orders for the specified customer
  dsOrders=
this.OrdersObj.GetOrdersByCustomerID(this.txtCustomerID.Text.Trim());

  /// Clear all data bindings
  this.grdOrders.DataBindings.Clear();
  this.txtOrderID.DataBindings.Clear();
  this.txtName.DataBindings.Clear();
  this.txtAddress.DataBindings.Clear();
  this.txtCity.DataBindings.Clear();
  this.txtRegion.DataBindings.Clear();
  this.txtPostalCode.DataBindings.Clear();
  this.txtCountry.DataBindings.Clear();

  /// Data bind the grid
  string OrderTable = OrdersObj.TableName;
  this.grdOrders.SetDataBinding(dsOrders, OrderTable);

  DataTable dtOrders = dsOrders.Tables[OrderTable];
  this.txtOrderID.DataBindings.Add("Text", dsOrders, OrderTable+".OrderID");
  this.txtName.DataBindings.Add("Text", dsOrders, OrderTable+".ShipName");
  this.txtAddress.DataBindings.Add("Text", dsOrders,
OrderTable+".ShipAddress");
  this.txtCity.DataBindings.Add("Text", dsOrders, OrderTable+".ShipCity");
  this.txtRegion.DataBindings.Add("Text", dsOrders, OrderTable+".ShipRegion");
  this.txtPostalCode.DataBindings.Add("Text", dsOrders,
      OrderTable+".ShipPostalCode");
}
```

And here it is in Visual Basic .NET:

```vbnet
Private Sub txtCustomerID_Validating(ByVal sender As Object, _
    ByVal e As System.ComponentModel.CancelEventArgs) _
    Handles txtCustomerID.Validating
    '/ Get all orders for the specified customer
    dsOrders = Me.OrdersObj.GetOrdersByCustomerID(Me.txtCustomerID.Text.Trim())

    '/ Clear all data bindings
    Me.grdOrders.DataBindings.Clear()
    Me.txtOrderID.DataBindings.Clear()
    Me.txtName.DataBindings.Clear()
    Me.txtAddress.DataBindings.Clear()
    Me.txtCity.DataBindings.Clear()
    Me.txtRegion.DataBindings.Clear()
    Me.txtPostalCode.DataBindings.Clear()
    Me.txtCountry.DataBindings.Clear()
```

```
'/ Data bind the grid
Dim OrderTable As String = OrdersObj.TableName
Me.grdOrders.SetDataBinding(dsOrders, OrderTable)
```

```
Dim dtOrders As DataTable = dsOrders.Tables(OrderTable)
Me.txtOrderID.DataBindings.Add("Text", dsOrders, OrderTable + ".OrderID")
Me.txtName.DataBindings.Add("Text", dsOrders, OrderTable + ".ShipName")
Me.txtAddress.DataBindings.Add("Text", dsOrders, OrderTable + _
    ".ShipAddress")
Me.txtCity.DataBindings.Add("Text", dsOrders, OrderTable + ".ShipCity")
Me.txtRegion.DataBindings.Add("Text", dsOrders, OrderTable + _
    ".ShipRegion")
Me.txtPostalCode.DataBindings.Add("Text", dsOrders, OrderTable + _
    ".ShipPostalCode")
Me.txtCountry.DataBindings.Add("Text", dsOrders, OrderTable + _
    ".ShipCountry")
```

```
End Sub
```

Compile and run the application again, and then launch the Customer Orders form. After performing a search, click on the Properties page and the controls should contain the data for the currently selected record in the DataGrid on the List page (**Figure 18**).

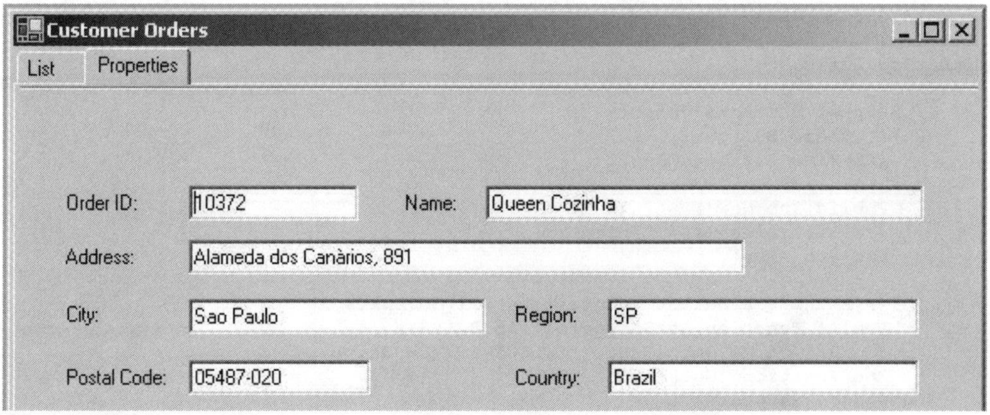

Figure 18. You can bind textbox controls to data using simple binding

Adding a Shipper business object and combo box

In this section, you'll create a new Shipper business object and then you'll add a combo box to the form that displays a list of shippers obtained from the new object.

Right-click on the project and select Add | Add New Item from the shortcut menu. In the Add New Item dialog, select Code File in the Templates pane, change the name of the file to "ShipperBusiness.cs" or "ShipperBusiness.vb", and then click the Open button. This adds the new code file to the project. Next, add the following code to the file. This code defines a new Shipper business object with a single GetShippers method that returns a DataSet containing all shippers.

In C#:

```csharp
using System.Data;

namespace HW.NetBook.Samples.Business
{
  /// Shipper Business Object
  public class Shipper : BusinessObject
  {
      public Shipper()
      {
          this.TableName = "Shippers";
      }

      /// Returns a DataSet containing all Shippers
      public DataSet GetShippers()
      {
          return this.GetDataSet("SELECT * FROM Shippers");
      }
  }
}
```

And in Visual Basic .NET:

```vbnet
Imports System.Data

Namespace Business

    '/ Shipper Business Object
    Public Class Shipper
        Inherits BusinessObject

        Public Sub New()
            Me.TableName = "Shippers"
        End Sub 'New

        '/ Returns a DataSet containing all Shippers
        Public Function GetShippers() As DataSet
            Return Me.GetDataSet("SELECT * FROM Shippers")
        End Function 'GetShippers
    End Class 'Shipper

End Namespace 'Business
```

Now add the following line of code (shown in grey) to the top of the CustomerOrdersForm class definition. The code declares a private field that holds a reference to the Shipper business object. You don't need to store a reference to a Shipper DataSet in a field, because, as you'll see below, the DataSet is only used when the form first instantiates.

In C#:

```csharp
public class CustomerOrdersForm : System.Windows.Forms.Form
{
  private Orders OrdersObj;
  private DataSet dsOrders;
  private Shipper ShipperObj;
```

And in Visual Basic .NET:

```
Public Class CustomerOrdersForm
    Inherits System.Windows.Forms.Form

  Private OrdersObj As Orders
  Private dsOrders As DataSet
  Private ShipperObj As Shipper
```

Now you need to add code to the form's Load method that instantiates the Shipper business object.

Here's the code in C#:

```
private void CustomerOrdersForm_Load(object sender, System.EventArgs e)
{
  /// Instantiate the Orders business object
  this.OrdersObj = new Orders();

  /// Instantiate the Shipper business object
  this.ShipperObj = new Shipper();

}
```

And here it is in Visual Basic .NET:

```
Private Sub CustomerOrdersForm_Load(ByVal sender As Object, _
    ByVal e As System.EventArgs) _
    Handles MyBase.Load

  '/ Instantiate the Orders business object
  Me.OrdersObj = New Orders()

  '/ Instantiate the Shipper business object
  Me.ShipperObj = New Shipper()

End Sub
```

Adding a ComboBox to the form

In this section you will add a combo box control to the Properties tab and learn how to bind data to it. First, select the Customer Orders form Properties tab in the designer, drag a ComboBox control from the Toolbox, and drop it on the form beneath the existing text boxes. Next, drag and drop a label for the combo box onto the form. Set each control's properties as shown in **Table 4**.

Table 4. Name, text, location, and size of the Shippers label and combo box

Control	Text	Location	Size
lblShippers	Shippers:	25,197	Autosize
cboShippers		100,192	175,21

In addition to the properties listed in Table 4, the ComboBox class also has a DropDownStyle property that defines the style of the combo box. The default value of this property is "DropDown" meaning the text box portion of the combo box is editable and the user must click the down arrow to see the other items in the list. In this case, set the value to "DropDownList", which is similar to the "DropDown" setting except it makes the text box portion of the combo box *not* editable. This is similar to setting the Style property of a combo box in Visual FoxPro. Now its time to data bind the combo box. Because the list of available shippers is always the same regardless of the customer or order the user is working with, you add code to the form's CustomerOrdersForm_Load method (which only runs once when the form is first instantiated) to get a DataSet from the Shipper business object and bind it to the Shipper combo box. The new code is highlighted in grey.

Here's the code in C#:

```csharp
private void CustomerOrdersForm_Load(object sender, System.EventArgs e)
{
  /// Instantiate the Orders business object
  this.OrdersObj = new Orders();

  /// Instantiate the Shipper business object
  this.ShipperObj = new Shipper();

  /// Get a DataSet containing all Shippers
  DataSet dsShippers = this.ShipperObj.GetShippers();

  /// Databind the Shippers combo box to the Shippers DataTable
  string ShipperTable = this.ShipperObj.TableName
  this.cboShippers.DataSource = dsShippers.Tables[ShipperTable];
  this.cboShippers.DisplayMember = "CompanyName";
  this.cboShippers.ValueMember = "ShipperID";
}
```

And here it is in Visual Basic .NET:

```vbnet
Private Sub CustomerOrdersForm_Load(ByVal sender As Object, _
    ByVal e As System.EventArgs) _
    Handles MyBase.Load

    '/ Instantiate the Orders business object
    Me.OrdersObj = New Orders()

    '/ Instantiate the Shipper business object
    Me.ShipperObj = New Shipper()
```

```
'/ Get a DataSet containing all Shippers
Dim dsShippers As DataSet = Me.ShipperObj.GetShippers()

'/ Databind the Shippers combo box to the Shippers DataTable
Dim ShipperTable As String = Me.ShipperObj.TableName
Me.cboShippers.DataSource = dsShippers.Tables(ShipperTable)
Me.cboShippers.DisplayMember = "CompanyName"
Me.cboShippers.ValueMember = "ShipperID"
```

```
End Sub
```

The data-binding portion of this code differs from a DataGrid or a text box. Because a combo box can display more than one item at a time, it has complex data binding. The above code sets the DataSource property to the Shippers table (contained within the dsShippers DataSet). The DisplayMember property specifies which column in the DataTable to display in the combo box, and in this case it is set to the CompanyName column. The ValueMember property specifies which column in the DataTable contains the value, which is set to the ShipperID column.

One more combo box property needs to be data bound—the SelectedValue property. You will bind this property to the ShipVia column of the Orders DataSet. This does two things— first, when editing an existing item it specifies which item in the combo box should be selected. Second, if the user selects a different item in the combo box, the value of the selected item is stored into the ShipVia column of the Orders DataSet.

Because you are binding this property to the Orders DataSet, the data binding code should be placed in the form's txtCustomerID_Validating event handler. First place this code at the bottom of the method.

Here it is in C#:

```
this.cboShippers.DataBindings.Add("SelectedValue",dsOrders,
OrderTable+"ShipVia")
```

And here it is in Visual Basic .NET:

```
Me.cboShippers.DataBindings.Add("SelectedValue", dtOrders,
OrderTable+"ShipVia")
```

Now add this code to the txtCustomerID_Validating event handler to clear the combo box's data binding. You can place this code directly beneath the code that clears the data binding from other controls.

In C#:

```
this.cboShippers.DataBindings.Clear();
```

In Visual Basic .NET:

```
Me.cboShippers.DataBindings.Clear()
```

> List boxes are bound the same way as combo boxes, so you can also use the code shown here to bind a list box instead.

Now you're ready to test out your combo box. Compile and run the application again. In the List page, enter a Customer ID of "QUEEN" and press the Tab key. Go to the Properties page and click the Shippers combo box—it should look like the one shown in **Figure 19**.

Figure 19. Combo boxes and List Boxes use complex data binding to displays lists containing multiple items.

Adding an OrderItem business object and a DataGrid

In this section you will create a new OrderItem business object and add a DataGrid to show all the order items for the currently selected order. First, you create the new business object.

Right-click on the project and select Add | Add New Item from the shortcut menu. In the Add New Item dialog, select Code File in Templates pane, change the name of the file to "OrderItemBusiness.cs" or "OrderItemBusiness.vb", and then click the Open button. This adds the new code file to the project. Next, add the following code to the file. This code defines a new OrderItem business object with a single GetOrderItems method that returns a DataSet containing all items for a specific Order ID.

In C#:

```
using System.Data;

namespace HW.NetBook.Samples.Business
{
  /// <summary>
  /// Order Item Business Object
  /// </summary>
  public class OrderItem : BusinessObject
  {
    public OrderItem()
    {
      this.TableName = "OrderItems";
    }

    /// <summary>
    /// Returns all Order items for the specified Order ID
    /// </summary>
    /// <returns>DataSet containing all shippers</returns>
    public DataSet GetOrderItems(int OrderID)
```

```
    {
        return this.GetDataSet("SELECT * FROM [Order Details] WHERE OrderID = "
+
            OrderID);
    }
  }
}
```

And in Visual Basic .NET:

```
Imports System.Data

Namespace Business

    '/ <summary>
    '/ Order Item Business Object
    '/ </summary>
    Public Class OrderItem
        Inherits BusinessObject

        Public Sub New()
            Me.TableName = "OrderItems"
        End Sub 'New

        '/ <summary>
        '/ Returns all Order items for the specified Order ID
        '/ </summary>
        '/ <returns>DataSet containing all shippers</returns>
        Public Function GetOrderItems(ByVal OrderID As Integer) As DataSet
            Return Me.GetDataSet("SELECT * FROM [Order Details] WHERE OrderID =
"  _
                + OrderID.ToString())
        End Function 'GetOrderItems

    End Class 'OrderItem

End Namespace 'Business
```

To add a DataGrid to the Properties tab drag a DataGrid control from the Toolbox and drop it on the Properties page below the Shippers combo box. Change the name of the grid to grdOrderItems, set the Location property to 25,252, and the Size property to 510,95. Also, add a label to the form, set its Name property to lblOrderItems, AutoSize to True, Location to 25,230, and Text to "Order Items".

To make the grid look a bit more attractive, generate a style for the DataGrid as you did with the Orders DataGrid on the List page (select the DataGrid in the Form Designer and click the AutoFormat link label on the Properties Window). For example, I selected the "Colorful 1" format.

Next, create a new DataGridTableStyle by clicking the TableStyles ellipses button (...) in the Properties Window. Change its Name property to OrderItemTableStyle and its MappingName property to OrderItems. If you'd like, you can reapply the colors selected in the previous paragraph because the TableStyle you just created overrides the Auto Format settings.

Now you need to add some ColumnStyles to the new TableStyle. In the DataGridTableStyle Collection Editor dialog, scroll down in the Properties pane to the GridColumnStyles, and click the ellipses button (...). Add the GridColumnStyles shown in **Table 5**.

Table 5. *Order Items DataGrid ColumnStyle properties*

Name	Text	Width	MappingName
ProductColumn	Product		ProductID
UnitPriceColumn	Unit Price		UnitPrice
QuantityColumn	Qty		Quantity
DiscountColumn	Discount		Discount

Now you're ready to add data retrieval and data binding code to the form for the Order Items DataGrid. Although you could place this code in the form's txtCustomerID_Validating method, that wouldn't be efficient. If the code is placed in this method, every time the user selects a new record on the List page by navigating in the DataGrid, the code that retrieves all items for the order would be fired—and the user may never go to the Properties page when a particular order is selected in the DataGrid!

A better place for this code is in an event handler for the Properties page's Enter event, which only fires when the Properties page is activated. Rather than putting the code directly in the Enter event handler, you will put the code in its own form-level method named DisplayOrderItems and simply call it from within the event handler method. This allows the code to be reused from multiple places in the form, which you'll see is important when you add a toolbar later in this chapter.

Before you do anything else, add two new private fields to the top of the class definition. You can add these directly below the other private fields you have already created.

In C#:

```
private OrderItem OrderItemObj;
private DataSet dsOrderItems;
```

In Visual Basic .NET:

```
Private OrderItemObj As OrderItem
Private dsOrderItems As DataSet
```

Now you need to add code to the CustomerOrdersForm_Load event handler that instantiates the OrderItem business object.

In C#:

```
/// Instantiate the Order Item business object
this.OrderItemObj = new OrderItem();
```

And in Visual Basic .NET:

```
'/ Instantiate the Order Item business object
Me.OrderItemObj = New OrderItem()
```

Next, add the following new method to the Customer Order form.
In C#:

```csharp
/// Displays all order items for the currently selected order
public void DisplayOrderItems()
{
  if (dsOrders.Tables[this.OrdersObj.TableName].Rows.Count > 0)
  {
    /// Get the OrderID value of the currently selected DataRow
    DataRowView drView=(DataRowView)this.BindingContext[dsOrders,
      "Orders"].Current;
    int OrderID = (int)drView["OrderID"];

    /// Get all Order Items for the currently selected Order ID
    this.dsOrderItems = this.OrderItemObj.GetOrderItems(OrderID);

    /// Bind the Order Items grid to the Order Items DataSet
    this.grdOrderItems.SetDataBinding(dsOrderItems,
        this.OrderItemObj.TableName);
  }
  else
  {
    // If there are no Orders, clear the Order Items DataSet
    // and DataGrid binding
    if (this.dsOrderItems != null)
    {
      this.dsOrderItems.Clear();
    }
    this.grdOrderItems.DataBindings.Clear();
  }
}
```

In Visual Basic .NET:

```vbnet
'/ Displays all order items for the currently selected order
Public Sub DisplayOrderItems()
    If dsOrders.Tables(Me.OrdersObj.TableName).Rows.Count > 0 Then
        '/ Get the OrderID value of the currently selected DataRow
        Dim drView As DataRowView = CType(Me.BindingContext(dsOrders, _
            "Orders").Current, DataRowView)
        Dim OrderID As Integer = CInt(drView("OrderID"))

        '/ Get all Order Items for the currently selected Order ID
        Me.dsOrderItems = Me.OrderItemObj.GetOrderItems(OrderID)

        '/ Bind the Order Items grid to the Order Items DataSet
        Me.grdOrderItems.SetDataBinding(dsOrderItems, _
            Me.OrderItemObj.TableName)
    Else
        ' If there are no Orders, clear the Order Items DataSet
        ' and DataGrid binding
        If Not (Me.dsOrderItems Is Nothing) Then
            Me.dsOrderItems.Clear()
        End If
        Me.grdOrderItems.DataBindings.Clear()
    End If
End Sub 'DisplayOrderItemsEnd Class
```

This code first checks if there are any rows in the Orders DataSet. If there are, it gets the Order ID of the currently selected row. It does this by getting a DataRowView object from the form's BindingContext object. The BindingContext object is a form-level object that manages data binding in your form. A DataRowView is an object representing the current DataRow of a DataSet bound to a user interface control. This object has methods that allow you to access the columns of a DataRow as a collection (as shown in the above sample code) and, as you'll see later, also allow you to control edits to the DataRow.

The next line of code calls the Order Item business object's GetOrderItems method passing the Order ID of the currently selected order. It then binds the returned Order Item DataSet to the Order Items DataGrid. If there aren't any rows in the Orders DataSet, the Order Item DataSet is cleared and so are the Order Item DataGrid's bindings.

Now you need to add code to the page's Enter event handler to call this method. To do this, click on the Properties page in the Form Designer (make sure you click on the actual page, rather than just on the tab). Next, if you're using C#, go to the Properties Window and click the Events button (the one with the lightning bolt). Double-click on the Enter event (in the first column of the window) and VS .NET automatically adds a new PropertiesPage_Enter event handler method. If you're using Visual Basic .NET, go to the code editing Window and select "PropertiesPage" in the combo box at the upper left side of the code editor. Next, select the "Enter" event from the combo box at the upper right side of the code editor—VS .NET automatically adds a new event handler method named PropertiesPage_Enter. Place the following code in this method to call the new DisplayOrderItems method.

In C#:

```
private void PropertiesPage_Enter(object sender, System.EventArgs e)
{
  this.DisplayOrderItems();
}
```

And in Visual Basic .NET:

```
Private Sub PropertiesPage_Enter(ByVal sender As Object, _
    ByVal e As System.EventArgs) Handles PropertiesPage.Enter
    Me.DisplayOrderItems()
End Sub
```

There's one problem with placing the code in this event handler. In .NET, the TabPage's Enter event does not fire when you click on the appropriate tab. It's not until you set focus to the first control on the TabPage that the Enter event fires. There are a few ways to get around this, but I'm going to demonstrate a tactic that makes use of a .NET class providing functionality near and dear to every Visual FoxPro developer's heart—the SendKeys class.

The SendKey class—a .NET equivalent to VFP's KEYBOARD()

The .NET SendKey class offers functionality similar to Visual FoxPro's KEYBOARD() command. The SendKey class has two static methods for sending keys to an application—the Send method (sends a keystroke to the application and keeps running) and the SendWait method (sends a keystroke to the application and waits for any processes started by the keystroke to be processed before continuing).

In this case you'll use the SendKey.Send method to send a Tab keystroke to the application, and automatically place focus on the first control available to receive focus on the TabPage. This code needs to be run when the TabControl's SelectedIndexChanged event fires.

To create an event handler for this event in C#, click on either the List or the Properties page and select the TabControl in the Properties Window. Click on the Events button (if it's not already selected) to show all events for the TabControl, and then double-click the SelectedIndexChanged event. If you're using VB. NET, go to the code editor and select the "TabControl" from the combo box at the upper left side of the window, then choose the "SelectedIndexChanged" event from the combo box at the upper right side of the window.

When you perform one of these actions, VS .NET automatically adds an event handler method named tabControl_SelectedIndexChanged to the form. Add the following code to send a Tab keystroke to the application.

In C#:

```
private void tabControl_SelectedIndexChanged(object sender, System.EventArgs e)
{
  /// Whenever a new page is selected, TAB to the first control on the page
  SendKeys.SendWait("{TAB}");
}
```

In Visual Basic .NET:
```
Private Sub TabControl_SelectedIndexChanged(ByVal sender As Object, _
    ByVal e As System.EventArgs) Handles TabControl.SelectedIndexChanged
    SendKeys.SendWait("{TAB}")
End Sub
```

Now you're ready to compile and run the form again. If you display orders for a Customer ID of "QUEEN", your form should look like **Figure 20**.

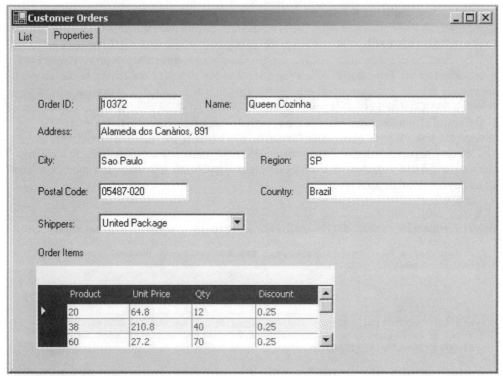

Figure 20. With just a little extra work, you can use business objects for data access in your applications, providing data flexibility and scalability.

Adding a navigation toolbar to the form

Visual Studio .NET makes it very easy to add toolbars to your application. In this section you will add a toolbar to the Properties page of the Customer Orders form allowing you to navigate to different order records.

First, select the Properties tab page. Remember, rather than just clicking the Properties tab itself, you must click in the area below the tab to actually select the page. Next, drag and drop a ToolBar control from the Toolbox onto the form. By default, this docks the empty toolbar at the top of the form. With the toolbar selected, go to the Properties Window and set the toolbar's Name property to "MainToolbar".

To add buttons to the toolbar, in the Properties Window click the ellipses button (…) next to the Buttons property to launch the ToolBarButton Collection Editor (**Figure 21**).

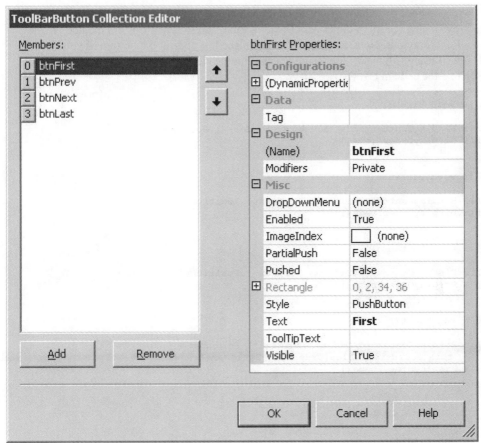

Figure 21. *The ToolBarButton Collection Editor provides a visual means for adding toolbar buttons to your toolbars.*

To add a button to the toolbar, simply click the Add button and specify a Name and Text property. Add four buttons to the toolbar named btnFirst, btnPrev, btnNext, and btnLast. Set the Text property of these buttons to "First", "Prev", "Next", and "Last" respectively. When you're done, click the OK button to close the dialog. You should see the four toolbar buttons displayed in the toolbar (**Figure 22**). Alternately, you can add images to toolbar buttons rather than text, but to make this example easier to work through, you will stick to plain text. For information on adding images to toolbar buttons, see the .NET Help topic "Toolbar Class".

Figure 22. *You can add a navigation toolbar to your form to navigate to different rows in a DataSet.*

Now you need to add code to respond to the Click event of each button and navigate to the corresponding record in the Orders DataSet. First, add four new custom methods to the form—First, Previous, Next, and Last. You can place this code at the bottom of your form's code file (if using C#, make sure the code is within the closing namespace).

Here's the code in C#:

```csharp
public void First()
{
  this.BindingContext[this.dsOrders, "Orders"].Position = 0;
  this.DisplayOrderItems();
}

public void Previous()
{
  this.BindingContext[dsOrders, "Orders"].Position--;
  this.DisplayOrderItems();
}

public void NextRec()
{
  this.BindingContext[dsOrders, "Orders"].Position++;
  this.DisplayOrderItems();
}

public void Last()
{
  this.BindingContext[dsOrders, "Orders"].Position =
       this.dsOrders.Tables[OrdersObj.TableName].Rows.Count - 1;
  this.DisplayOrderItems();
}
```

And here's the code in Visual Basic .NET:

```vbnet
Public Sub First()
    Me.BindingContext(Me.dsOrders, "Orders").Position = 0
    Me.DisplayOrderItems()
End Sub 'First

Public Sub Previous()
    Me.BindingContext(dsOrders, "Orders").Position -= 1
    Me.DisplayOrderItems()
End Sub 'Previous


Public Sub NextRec()
    Me.BindingContext(dsOrders, "Orders").Position += 1
    Me.DisplayOrderItems()
End Sub 'NextRec


Public Sub Last()
    Me.BindingContext(dsOrders, "Orders").Position = _
        Me.dsOrders.Tables(OrdersObj.TableName).Rows.Count - 1
    Me.DisplayOrderItems()
End Sub 'Last
```

Next, add a method to the form to enable and disable the navigation buttons based on the position of the BindingContext object referring to the Orders DataSet. For example, if the current record is the first in the DataSet, the First and Previous buttons should be disabled because you're already at the first record and you can't navigate to any previous records.

Here's the code in C#:

```
public void SetToolbarButtonsEnabled()
{
  int Position = this.BindingContext[this.dsOrders, "Orders"].Position;
  int Count = this.dsOrders.Tables[OrdersObj.TableName].Rows.Count;
  this.btnFirst.Enabled = (Position != 0);
  this.btnPrev.Enabled = (Position != 0);
  this.btnNext.Enabled = (Position != Count-1);
  this.btnLast.Enabled = (Position != Count-1);
}
```

And here it is in Visual Basic .NET:

```
Public Sub SetToolbarButtonsEnabled()
    Dim Position As Integer = _
        Me.BindingContext(Me.dsOrders, "Orders").Position
    Dim Count As Integer = _
        Me.dsOrders.Tables(OrdersObj.TableName).Rows.Count
    Me.btnFirst.Enabled = Position <> 0
    Me.btnPrev.Enabled = Position <> 0
    Me.btnNext.Enabled = Position <> Count - 1
    Me.btnLast.Enabled = Position <> Count - 1
End Sub 'SetToolbarButtonsEnabled
```

Next you need to add a call to this method from the form's DisplayOrderItems method. This should be added *after* the if...else statement so it runs regardless of whether there are rows in the Orders DataSet or not. The following code shows the last half of the method starting with the else statement, with the new line of code shown in grey.

In C#:

```
  else
  {
      // If there are no Orders, clear the Order Items DataSet
      // and DataGrid binding
      if (this.dsOrderItems != null)
      {
          this.dsOrderItems.Clear();
      }
      this.grdOrderItems.DataBindings.Clear();
  }

  this.SetToolbarButtonsEnabled();

}
```

In Visual Basic .NET:

```
Else
   '/ If there are no Orders, clear the Order Items DataSet
   '/ and DataGrid binding
   If Not (Me.dsOrderItems Is Nothing) Then
       Me.dsOrderItems.Clear()
   End If
   Me.grdOrderItems.DataBindings.Clear()
End If
Me.SetToolbarButtonsEnabled()
End Sub 'DisplayOrderItemsEnd Class
```

Now add an event handler for the toolbar's ButtonClick method to the form to call the new form-level navigation methods. To do this, in the Form Designer, double-click the empty portion of the toolbar. This adds a new event handler method named MainToolbar_ButtonClick. Add the following code to this method, which calls the new First, Previous, Next, and Last methods.

In C#:

```
private void MainToolbar_ButtonClick(object sender,
  System.Windows.Forms.ToolBarButtonClickEventArgs e)
{
  // Evaluate the Button property to determine which button was clicked.
  switch(this.MainToolbar.Buttons.IndexOf(e.Button))
  {
      case 0:
          this.First();
          break;
      case 1:
          this.Previous();
          break;
      case 2:
          this.NextRec();
          break;
      case 3:
          this.Last();
          break;
  }
}
```

In Visual Basic .NET:

```
Private Sub MainToolbar_ButtonClick(ByVal sender As System.Object, _
    ByVal e As System.Windows.Forms.ToolBarButtonClickEventArgs) _
    Handles MainToolbar.ButtonClick

    ' Evaluate the Button property to determine which button was clicked.
    Select Case Me.MainToolbar.Buttons.IndexOf(e.Button)
        Case 0
            Me.First()
        Case 1
            Me.Previous()
        Case 2
```

```
        Me.NextRec()
    Case 3
        Me.Last()
End Select


End Sub 'MainToolbar_ButtonClick
```

Now you're ready to compile and run the application so you can test the navigation toolbar. After launching the Customer Orders form, enter "QUEEN" in the Customer ID text box and press the Tab key. Next, select the Properties tab, click the different navigation buttons, and watch the form display each of the orders and their associated order items.

Updating data

So far, the form allows viewing orders for a specified customer, but now in this section, you will add code to update the data. In this example, you will only add code to the form that updates the order header—similar code can be added for saving changes to the order items.

First, select the Properties page on the form and then drag and drop a Button from the Toolbox onto the form. Set its Name property to "btnSave", its Location to 465, 320, and its Text to "&Save". Double-click the button in the Form Designer to add an event handler method for the button's Click event.

In the new btnSave_Click method, add the following code that passes the Orders DataSet back to the SaveDataSet method of the Orders business object and then displays the number of updated records.

Here's the code in C#:

```
/// Update the Orders DataSet
private void btnSave_Click(object sender, System.EventArgs e)
{
    /// Only run this code if there are records in the DataSet
    if (dsOrders.Tables[this.OrdersObj.TableName].Rows.Count != 0)
    {
        /// Get the current DataRowView
        DataRowView drView = (DataRowView)this.BindingContext[dsOrders,
"Orders"].Current;

        /// End the current edit of the DataRowView
        drView.EndEdit();

        /// Send the DataSet to the Orders Business object
        int RowsUpdated = this.OrdersObj.SaveDataSet(this.dsOrders);

        /// Display the number of records updated
        MessageBox.Show("Rows updated: " + RowsUpdated);
    }
}
```

And in Visual Basic .NET:

```
'/ Update the Orders DataSet
Private Sub btnSave_Click(ByVal sender As System.Object, _
    ByVal e As System.EventArgs) Handles btnSave.Click
```

```
     '/ Only run this code if there are records in the DataSet
     If dsOrders.Tables(Me.OrdersObj.TableName).Rows.Count <> 0 Then
         '/ Get the current DataRowView
         Dim drView As DataRowView = _
             CType(Me.BindingContext(dsOrders, "Orders").Current, DataRowView)

         '/ End the current edit of the DataRowView
         drView.EndEdit()

         '/ Send the DataSet to the Orders Business object
         Dim RowsUpdated As Integer = Me.OrdersObj.SaveDataSet(Me.dsOrders)

         '/ Display the number of records updated
         MessageBox.Show(("Rows updated: " & RowsUpdated.ToString()))
     End If
End Sub 'btnSave_ClickEnd Class 'CustomerOrdersForm
```

Now you're ready to test the form's data updating abilities. Compile and run the application again, then launch the Customer Orders form. You can update the Order records in either the DataGrid or in the simple-bound controls on the Properties page. You can use the navigation toolbar to move to other records in the DataSet and make changes to these too. When you're done, click the Save button on the Properties page and you should see a dialog showing how many records have been updated.

Resizing and repositioning user interface controls

Now that the form is functional, it's time to do a little finessing with user interface control positioning and resizing. In Visual FoxPro, if you wanted the controls on a form to be automatically repositioned and resized when the form changed size, you had to write extra logic to do this, which could be somewhat complex. In .NET, it's as simple as setting a property on a control—specifically, the Anchor property.

All .NET user interface controls have an Anchor property. Click the grdOrders DataGrid on the List page of the Customer Orders form, select the Anchor property combo box in the Properties Window, and a graphic is displayed containing a light grey rectangle in the center and four smaller rectangles on each side of it (**Figure 23**). The light grey rectangle represents your user interface control. The four small rectangles represent anchors to the top, bottom, left, and right sides of the control's parent container—which might be a form or a tab page. When one of the smaller rectangles is shown in dark grey, it indicates the user interface control is anchored to the corresponding edge of the parent container.

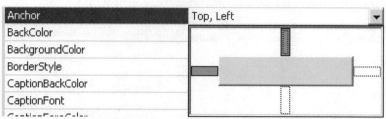

**Figure 23**. The Anchor property allows you to specify where you want to anchor a user interface control in relation to the edges of a form.

By default, controls are anchored to the Top and Left sides of the parent container. With these settings, when a user grabs the bottom right corner of a form, a control remains anchored to the top and left—which means it doesn't move and isn't resized.

On the List page of the Customer Orders form, this is the desired behavior of the Customer ID label and text box. However, you may want different behavior for the New, Delete, and Close buttons. For example, you may want the New and Delete buttons anchored to the Top and Right side of the tab page, and the Close button anchored to the Bottom and Right side of the tab page. In the case of the DataGrid, you probably want it to increase in size rather than change its position when the form is resized.

The first step in setting this up is to specify that the TabControl changes size as the form is resized. To do this, click on either the List or Properties tab in the Form Designer and then click on the Anchor property's combo box. By default, the Top and Left are already anchored. To get the TabControl to change size in tandem with the form, click once on the right and bottom rectangles. When you do this, these rectangles will change color to dark grey.

Now click on the grdOrders DataGrid on the List page. Select the same right and bottom anchors as you did for the TabControl. Next, select the Close button. Deselect the top and left anchors by clicking on them once. When you do this, the rectangles change color to white with a dotted border. Now select the right and bottom anchors.

Finally, select both the New and Delete buttons simultaneously. You do this by clicking on one button, then hold down the Shift key and click on the other button. Deselect the left anchor and select the right anchor instead. This sets the Anchor property to the same value for both controls.

Now you're ready to compile and run the application so you can test these settings. After you launch the Customer Orders form, grab any edge of the form and see how the controls are automatically resized and repositioned on the form.

Conclusion

Not only can you build great Internet applications with .NET, you can also build solid Windows Forms applications. The tools in Visual Studio .NET provide many convenience features for rapid application development. The wide variety of .NET user interface classes gives your application a modern, professional look—and makes your application more usable.

If you incorporate business objects into your desktop applications, these can also be reused in your Web Forms applications as shown in the next chapter.

Chapter 10
Building Web Applications with
ASP.NET

If you've never created a Web application before because you didn't have time to climb the learning curve, ASP.NET could be your big chance. This chapter shows you how to utilize everything you learned in the previous chapter about building Windows Forms applications (plus a few extra twists) in building ASP.NET Web Form Applications. It also demonstrates how to reuse the business objects created in the previous chapter by taking you step-by-step through the process of creating an ASP.NET Web Application.

Microsoft made a mistake a number of years ago underestimating the tremendous impact the Internet would have on our world. After realizing the error of its ways, Microsoft responded by creating Active Server Pages (ASP)—a platform for creating, deploying, and running Web applications. Although ASP contained some interesting technologies, it definitely fell in the category of a "knee jerk" reaction. ASP allowed you to get the job done, but not in the most efficient way.

In contrast, Active Server Pages.NET (ASP.NET) is a vast improvement over ASP. Rather than using scripting languages to write server-side code that is interpreted at run time, ASP.NET allows you to use fully object-oriented languages such as C# and Visual Basic .NET to create code that can be compiled and cached on the server for faster performance. ASP.NET also provides a more robust event-driven model allowing events to be raised on the client and handled on the server. In addition, Microsoft has done a great job making the Windows Forms and Web Application architecture and design tools similar enough so a developer can move from one to the other without incurring a huge learning curve.

ASP.NET actually encompasses two different technologies—Web Forms and Web Services. This chapter focuses on Web Forms. To learn about Web Services, see Chapter 12, "XML Web Services".

> *For information on using ASP.NET with Visual FoxPro 7, check out the white paper by Cathi Gero (this book's technical editor!) at http://msdn.microsoft.com/library/default.asp?url=/library/en-us/dnfoxgen7/html/usingaspnetwithvfp7.asp*

What is a Web Application?

A typical Web application is comprised of Web pages, configuration files, code files containing business object classes, images, and references to external .NET assemblies. In this walk-through, you will see how each element is used in an ASP.NET Web application.

A Web application starts the first time a user requests a page from the server (for example, by entering the URL of the Web site). The application continues to run until the Web server (the physical machine) is restarted, IIS is restarted, or if any of the application's configuration files are edited.

> *There are a number of configuration settings where you specify different conditions for starting a new process in your Web application—percentage of memory used, number of unprocessed requests waiting in the request queue, and so on. Adjusting these settings can help make your Web applications more available and more stable. For more information, see the "Machine.config" and "Web.config" sections later in this chapter.*

What is a Session?

By default, the Web is a stateless environment. If you send multiple requests from your Web browser to a particular Web site, you automatically disconnect and reconnect between each request. A series of successive requests coming from a single browser is known as a *session*. The first request sent from a client browser to a Web application begins a session for that client. By default (you can change this setting), if the client is idle for longer than 20 minutes, the session is automatically ended by the server.

Based on this disconnected model, your Web applications need some way to keep track of all the user sessions. ASP.NET steps in the gap and keeps track of each user session automatically. It does this by generating a unique Session ID when a client sends its first request to your Web site. This Session ID is passed back to the client by means of a cookie or modified URL. For more information on sessions, check out the "The Session Object" section later in this chapter.

Creating a Web Application

As in Chapter 9, "Building .NET Windows Forms Applications", you will learn about creating ASP.NET Web applications by example. In this chapter you will recreate the Windows Forms application from chapter 9 as a Web Forms application.

To create a new Web Application:

1. From the Visual Studio .NET Start Page, click the New Project button.

2. In the New Project dialog's Project Types pane, select Visual C# to create a C# Web application or Visual Basic .NET to create a VB .NET Web application. In the Templates pane on the right, select ASP.NET Web Application.

3. Notice that the Name text box is disabled and contains the text "WebApplication1" and (if you're creating the Web Application on your local machine) the Location text box contains the text "http://localhost/WebApplication1". To change the name of the Web application, you must change the name of the directory in the Location text box. This is different from a Windows Forms application where you can change the name of the application and the directory independently. In this example, change the last part of the directory name from "WebApplication1" to "MyFirstWebApplication". As

you type this in, notice that it automatically changes the Name of the application to "MyFirstWebApplication" (**Figure 1**).

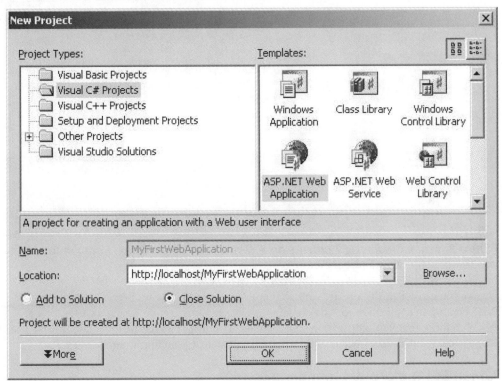

Figure 1. *The Location text box specifies the virtual root directory for your Web application.*

4. Click the OK button.

At this point, you may feel a bit like Al Gore when the "Creating the Web" dialog displays. While this dialog is displaying, VS .NET creates a new application for you using the ASP.NET Web Application template you selected. After a few moments, a new form named WebForm1.aspx is displayed in design mode in the Visual Studio .NET IDE (**Figure 2**).

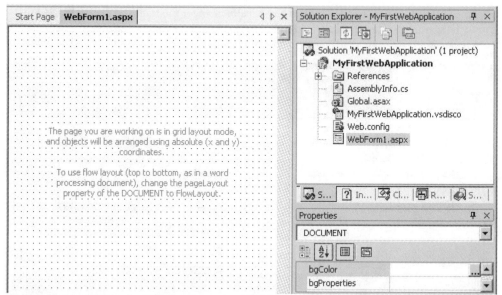

Figure 2. *Visual Studio .NET creates an ASP.NET Web Application from the template you select in the New Project dialog.*

As you can see this is already very similar to creating a Windows Forms application—VS .NET created an application for you containing a single form. Before taking a closer look at this Web form, first you'll do a little housekeeping and then learn a little more about what happens behind the scenes when using VS .NET to create a Web Forms application.

Renaming the project namespace

The housekeeping involves renaming the project's namespace. When you create a new Web application, VS .NET automatically sets your project's namespace to the same name as the project—which is most likely not what you want!

If you're using Visual Basic .NET, before you can change the project's namespace, you must first close the WebForm1.aspx. To do this, you can simply click the close button [X] to the right of the VS .NET IDE tabs.

To change the project's namespace, in the Solution Explorer, right-click on the project (the *second* node in the Solution Explorer) and select Properties from the shortcut menu, which launches the Property Pages dialog. In the left pane under the Common Properties folder, select General (if it's not already selected).

If you're using C#, in the right pane, change the Default Namespace from "MyFirstWebApplication" to "HW.NetBook.Samples". If you're using VB .NET, in the right pane, change the Root namespace to "HW.NetBook.Samples". When you're done, click the OK button to save changes.

Now you just need to change any existing references to the old name space. Select Edit | Find and Replace | Replace in Files from the main menu to launch the Replace in Files dialog. In the Find What box, enter "MyFirstWebApplication" and in the Replace with box enter "HW.NetBook.Samples" (make sure you type the case correctly if working with C#). Now click the Replace All button, which launches a Replace All warning dialog. Just click OK to ignore the warning. After clicking OK, a dialog appears telling you how many occurrences were replaced. If you're using C#, it should say, "4 occurrence(s) replaced". If you're using Visual Basic .NET it should say, "2 occurrence(s) replaced".

Understanding virtual directories

When you created the new Web application and specified the location of the application as "http://localhost/MyFirstWebApplication" (Figure 1), you were actually specifying a *virtual directory*. In the world of IIS, a virtual directory is a directory on the Web server that contains a Web application. It is virtual in the sense that it does not describe the exact physical location of a directory on the machine, but provides a higher-level virtual name that, behind the scenes, *is* associated with a real directory.

In the Location string, the "localhost" directory refers to the home directory of the Web Server. In IIS, this is set up by default to be c:\inetput\wwwroot, and therefore the MyFirstWebApplication virtual directory would be physically located in the c:\inetpub\wwwroot directory (**Figure 3**).

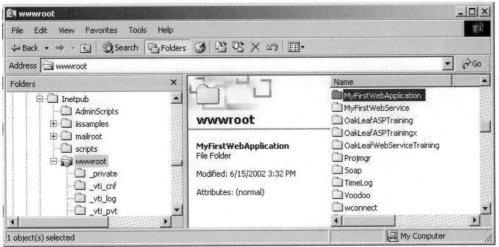

Figure 3. When you create a new Web application, VS .NET creates a virtual directory that, by default, is physically located in the c:\inetpub\wwwroot directory.

If you look in the new MyFirstWebApplication directory from within Windows Explorer, you'll see that VS .NET has created a variety of files and subfolders in your new virtual directory (**Figure 4**).

Name	S..	Type	Modified
📁 _vti_cnf		File Folder	6/15/2002 3:32 PM
📁 _vti_pvt		File Folder	6/15/2002 3:32 PM
📁 _vti_script		File Folder	6/15/2002 3:32 PM
📁 _vti_txt		File Folder	6/15/2002 3:32 PM
📁 bin		File Folder	6/15/2002 3:32 PM
Global.asax	1 KB	Active Server Application file	6/15/2002 3:32 PM
MyFirstWebApplication.csproj.webinfo	1 KB	WEBINFO File	6/15/2002 3:37 PM
MyFirstWebApplication.vsdisco	1 KB	VS.NET Web Service Dynamic Discovery File	6/15/2002 3:32 PM
WebForm1.aspx	1 KB	Web Form	6/15/2002 8:00 PM
WebForm1.aspx.cs	2 KB	C# Source file	6/15/2002 3:32 PM
Global.asax.cs	2 KB	C# Source file	6/15/2002 3:32 PM
Global.asax.resx	2 KB	.NET XML Resource Template	9/20/2001 7:25 AM
WebForm1.aspx.resx	2 KB	.NET XML Resource Template	9/20/2001 7:25 AM
AssemblyInfo.cs	3 KB	C# Source file	6/15/2002 3:32 PM
Web.config	4 KB	Web Configuration file	6/15/2002 3:32 PM
MyFirstWebApplication.csproj	6 KB	C# Project file	6/15/2002 3:32 PM

Figure 4. VS .NET places a variety of files in your Web application's virtual directory.

You'll be taking a closer look at some of these files in the next section, but for now, notice there is a project file in this directory (.csproj for C# or .vbproj forVB .NET), but no solution file (.sln). VS .NET puts the solution file in a subfolder of the "My Documents\Visual Studio Projects\" directory. In the example, it creates a subfolder named "MyFirstWebApplication" and places the MyFirstWebApplication.sln and associated .suo file in this folder. So, when you need to reopen your Web application after restarting Visual Studio .NET, you can find your solution in this folder.

However, this does not mean your Web application's source code is stored in two different places. Remember the solution is simply a container—similar to Visual FoxPro's project (PJX) file—with links to projects and files. For now, all your source code is stored in your Web application's virtual directory.

A closer look at the Web form

Now look a little closer at "WebForm1" in your new Web application. A Web form can be viewed in either Design mode (Figure 2) or in HTML mode. If WebForm1 is not currently opened in the IDE, double-click on the form in the Solution Explorer. To switch to HTML mode, either click on the HTML tab at the bottom left of the Web Forms designer or right-click the Web form and select View HTML Source from the shortcut menu. As you make changes to the Web form in design mode, VS .NET automatically changes the HTML source accordingly. On the other hand, if you know something about HTML, you can manually edit the HTML source and your changes will be reflected in Design mode.

If you view the HTML source of WebForm1, you will see the following HTML.
In C#:

```
<%@ Page language="c#" Codebehind="WebForm1.aspx.cs" AutoEventWireup="false"
Inherits="HW.NetBook.Samples.WebForm1 %>
<!DOCTYPE HTML PUBLIC "-//W3C//DTD HTML 4.0 Transitional//EN" >
```

```
<HTML>
  <HEAD>
    <title>WebForm1</title>
    <meta name="GENERATOR" Content="Microsoft Visual Studio 7.0">
    <meta name="vs_defaultClientScript" content="JavaScript">
    <meta name="vs_targetSchema"
content="http://schemas.microsoft.com/intellisense/ie5">
  </HEAD>
  <body MS_POSITIONING="GridLayout">
    <form id="Form1" method="post" runat="server" >
    </form>
  </body>
</HTML>
```

If you're using Visual Basic .NET, the only line that's different is the first line at the top of the page:

```
<%@ Page language="vb" Codebehind="WebForm1.aspx.vb" AutoEventWireup="false"
Inherits="HW.NetBook.Samples.WebForm1 %>
```

This first line of code is known as a *page directive*. The "Page Language" attribute tells the compiler the language used for the code contained in the Web page (typically "c#" or "vb"). The "CodeBehind" setting specifies a *code-behind* file associated with the .aspx file—in this case either WebForm1.aspx.cs (C#) or WebForm1.aspx.vb (VB .NET).

The code-behind file and code-behind class

An ASP.NET Web page consists of two main parts—the visible representation stored in the .aspx file and associated code stored in a .cs or .vb code-behind file (which gets its name from "the code file behind the form".) This structure lets you separate the user interface from the executable code. When you create a Web page in Visual Studio .NET, it automatically creates both an .aspx file and a code-behind file. It associates the two by placing the name of the code-behind file in the .aspx page directive as seen in the previous section.

If you look at the list of files in the Solution Explorer, by default, you won't see the code-behind file. To make this file visible, click on Solution Explorer's "Show All Files" icon button, the second button from the right at the top of the window. When you click this button, a plus sign appears next to the WebForm1.aspx file. If you expand the plus sign, you will see the associated code-behind file (**Figure 5**).

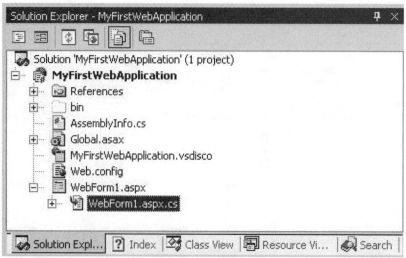

***Figure 5**. If you click on the "Show All Files" icon button in the Solution Explorer, you can see your Web form's code-behind file.*

To view the contents of the code-behind file, double-click the file in the Solution Explorer and VS .NET opens it in the IDE. The code-behind file contains the following code-behind class definition.

In C# (excluding the namespace directives):

```
public class WebForm1 : System.Web.UI.Page
{
  private void Page_Load(object sender, System.EventArgs e)
  {
      // Put user code to initialize the page here
  }

}
```

In Visual Basic .NET:

```
Public Class WebForm1
    Inherits System.Web.UI.Page

[Web Form Designer Generated Code]

  Private Sub Page_Load(ByVal sender As System.Object,ByVal e As _
    System.EventArgs) Handles MyBase.Load
        'Put user code to initialize the page here
  End Sub

End Class
```

As you can see, VS .NET automatically added code to this code-behind file that defines a class named WebForm1 derived from the System.Web.UI.Page class.

Now here's the interesting part—look back at the WebForm1.aspx page directive:

```
<%@ Page language="c#" Codebehind="WebForm1.aspx.cs" AutoEventWireup="false"
Inherits="HW.NetBook.Samples.WebForm1 %>
```

Notice the "Inherits" attribute specifies the .aspx page inherits from the WebForm1 class (belonging to the HW.NetBook.Samples namespace). When you compile your Web application under Visual Studio .NET, the .aspx file is compiled into a class derived from the code-behind class! This means you can add methods and other members to the WebForm1 code-behind class and they will be inherited by the class created from the .aspx file at runtime. You will see examples of how this works later in this chapter.

Hello .NET World!

Before diving further into the details of ASP.NET Web applications, you can get some immediate gratification by creating a simple "Hello .NET World!" Web page.

To start, select the WebForm1.aspx file in design mode. This involves clicking the WebForm1.aspx tab and making sure the Design tab at the bottom left of the IDE is selected. Notice the text in the middle of the Web form (**Figure 6**) states the Web form is set to work in "grid layout" mode, and objects dropped on the form are arranged using absolute coordinates. For this example, you will change the Web form to use "flow layout", which is more like a word processing document (you'll use grid layout mode later in this chapter). To switch to flow layout, go to the Properties Window and change the pageLayout property to "FlowLayout". When you do this, the dotted grid lines disappear and the text in the middle of the Web form changes accordingly.

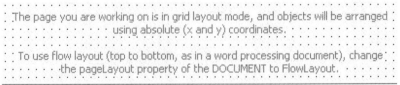

Figure 6. By default, Web forms are set to work in "grid layout" mode, but you can change their mode to "flow layout" to behave more like a word processing document.

Now, drag and drop a label from the VS .NET Toolbox onto the Web form (make sure the Web Forms tab of the Toolbox is selected). The label is automatically placed in the upper left-hand corner of the form. Next, go to the Properties Window, change the (ID) property from "Label1" to "lblHelloWorld", and then change the Text property to "Hello .NET World!". This changes the visible text of the label on the Web form accordingly.

Now change the font of the label. Click to the right of the label control on the Web form (click at the point where your mouse pointer is an "I-beam" rather than a quad-arrow) and you should see the Formatting toolbar (**Figure 7**).

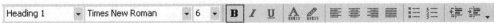

Figure 7. The Formatting toolbar allows you to change the appearance of visual elements on your Web form.

Open the combo box that is set to "Normal" by default and select "Heading 1" instead as shown in Figure 7. When you do this, it increases the font size and bolds the label text.

Now you're ready to compile and run your Web application. To do this, click the Start button or press F5. When the Web application runs, you should see the text "Hello .NET World!" in large, bold letters (**Figure 8**).

Figure 8. *The obligatory Hello World application provides immediate gratification for building your first Web application.*

Now that you've gotten your first, simple Web application under your belt, it's time for a quick overview of the different types of controls available to you when creating Web Forms applications.

Different types of controls

There are three basic types of Web controls in ASP.NET:

- HTML controls
- HTML server controls
- Web Forms controls

HTML controls

HTML controls are the "classic" controls such as <h1>, <input>, and <div>. These controls are not processed by the Web server, but are sent directly to the client browser for rendering. If you want the lightest-weight (but least capable) controls for your Web forms, use HTML controls.

HTML server controls

HTML server controls are one step above regular HTML controls regarding capability. Although the HTML for these controls looks very similar to classic HTML controls, they have the added ability to enable server-side processing, which includes data binding and responding to events (discussed later in this chapter). These controls are designed to be most like original HTML controls, so developers who are familiar with classic HTML controls should feel very comfortable using these new ASP.NET counterparts.

Web Forms controls

Web Forms controls are the most capable of all the ASP.NET controls. Rather than trying to imitate classic HTML controls, Web Forms controls more closely resemble Windows forms controls. They can also enable server-side processing, as do HTML server controls, but they are even more powerful. For example, they can automatically detect the level of HTML support provided by a browser and adjust their HTML output accordingly. In addition, they are useful in creating more complex controls such as the ad rotator and calendar controls. Based on their advanced capabilities, these are the controls used for the examples in this chapter.

 *To use Web Forms controls on your Web pages, make sure you have the Web Forms tab selected in Visual Studio .NET's Toolbox when you drag and drop controls on your forms.*

Now that you know about the different types of controls you can use in creating Web Forms, take a closer look at what's going on behind the scenes with ASP.NET.

The global.asax file

Take a look at another file shown in the Solution Explorer—the global.asax file. When you first create a new Web Application or Web Service through Visual Studio .NET, a global.asax file is automatically placed in the root directory of your application. At run time, the global.asax file is automatically parsed and compiled by the CLR into a dynamically-generated class derived from the .NET HttpApplication base class. As its name suggests, this class represents a Web application and it's used to process requests from users.

If you right-click the global.asax file and select Open With from the shortcut menu, it displays the Open With dialog. Select "Source Code (Text) Editor" and then click the Open button. When the file opens, you will see an *application directive* similar to the page directive found in the WebForm1.aspx file.

Here it is in C#:

```
<%@ Application Codebehind="Global.asax.cs"
        Inherits="HW.NetBook.Samples.Global"%>
```

And in Visual Basic .NET:

```
<%@ Application Codebehind="Global.asax.vb"
        Inherits="HW.NetBook.Samples.Global" %>
```

The "Codebehind" attribute specifies the name of the associated code-behind file, and the "Inherits" attribute specifies the class from which the global.asax file inherits—in this case HW.NetBook.Samples.Global.

Right-click on global.asax in the Solution Explorer and select View Code from the shortcut menu to open the code-behind file named global.asax.cs (C#) or global.asax.vb (VB .NET). If you look at the code contained in this code-behind file, you'll see it defines a class named Global derived from the System.Web.HttpApplication class.

In C#:

```
public class Global : System.Web.HttpApplication
{
  public Global()
  {
        InitializeComponent();
  }
  // The rest of the class not shown for space reasons
}
```

In Visual Basic .NET:

```
Public Class Global
    Inherits System.Web.HttpApplication

#Region " Component Designer Generated Code "

    Public Sub New()
        MyBase.New()

        'This call is required by the Component Designer.
        InitializeComponent()

        'Add any initialization after the InitializeComponent() call

    End Sub

  ' The rest of the class not shown for space reasons

#End Region
End Class
```

The first time a user requests any resource or URL within your Web application, your Web application starts and the global.asax file is parsed and compiled into a class derived from this Global class. The object instantiated from this class processes requests from the user.

If you look further down in the class definition, you'll see application and session event handlers for the following events:

- Application_Start
- Session_Start
- Application_BeginRequest
- Application_EndRequest
- Application_AuthenticateRequest
- Application_Error
- Session_End
- Application_End

You place code in any of these empty event handler methods to respond to the corresponding ASP.NET events. You can also add your own custom members (such as methods, properties, fields) to this class. For example, at Application Startup you may want to call Server.MapPath to determine the current server path and store it in a static variable. This saves you from making this call over and over again (and incurring a performance hit) throughout your application. Add the following code shown in grey to your global.asax file.

In C#:

```csharp
public class Global : System.Web.HttpApplication
{
    public static string ServerPath;

    public Global()
    {
        InitializeComponent();
    }

    protected void Application_Start(Object sender, EventArgs e)
    {
        Global.ServerPath = Global.ServerPath = Server.MapPath("");
    }

    // The rest of the class definition not shown here for space reasons
}
```

In Visual Basic .NET:

```vbnet
Public Class Global
    Inherits System.Web.HttpApplication

    Public Shared ServerPath As String

#Region " Component Designer Generated Code "

    Public Sub New()
        MyBase.New()

        'This call is required by the Component Designer.
        InitializeComponent()

        'Add any initialization after the InitializeComponent() call

    End Sub

    ' The rest of the class not shown for space reasons

#End Region

    Protected Sub Application_Start(sender As [Object], e As EventArgs)

        Global.ServerPath = Server.MapPath("")
```

```
   End Sub 'Application_Start


End Class
```

Now you can reference the static ServerPath property from anywhere within your Web application. For example, the following code derives a fully qualified path to a config.xml file by prepending the value stored in Global.ServerPath to the file name.

Here's the code in C#:

```
string ConfigFile = Global.ServerPath + "\\config.xml";
```

And here it is in Visual Basic .NET:

```
Dim ConfigFile As String = Global.ServerPath + "\config.xml"
```

Global objects

As a subclass of the HttpApplication base class, this Global class exposes some important objects globally accessible throughout your Web application. Some of these are:

- Server
- Application
- Session
- Response
- Request
- User
- Site

Each of these objects is detailed in the following sections.

The Server object

The Server object is an instance of the System.Web.HttpServerUtility class. This object has properties and methods allowing you to get and set information regarding the machine where the Web server is running as well as helper methods for processing Web requests.

Here is an example of accessing the MachineName property of the Server object.
In C#:

```
string ServerName = Server.MachineName;
```

In Visual Basic .NET:

```
Dim ServerName As String = Server.MachineName
```

Notice you simply need to type the name of the Server object followed by the property or method to access it from code. **Table 1** lists some other commonly used members of the Server object.

Table 1. *Commonly used members of the Server object*

Member name	Type	Description
MachineName	Property	Property that stores the server's computer name
ScriptTimeout	Method	Gets and sets the server's request time-out
ClearError	Method	Clears the last error
GetLastError	Method	Returns the last error
HtmlDecode	Method	Decodes a string that has been encoded to eliminate invalid HTML characters
HtmlEncode	Method	Encodes a string to be displayed in a browser
MapPath	Method	Returns the physical file path of the specified virtual directory
Transfer	Method	Transfers execution to the specified Web page
UrlDecode	Method	Decodes a string encoded for HTTP transmission and sent to the server in a URL
UrlEncode	Method	Encodes a string for HTTP transmission from the server to the client via the URL

The Application object

The Application object is an instance of the System.Web.HttpApplicationState class allowing you to share global data and objects across multiple sessions in an ASP.NET application. The Application object has a Contents dictionary collection property where you can add data and objects at runtime that can be accessed from any user session. Although you can specifically reference the Contents collection property to add or access items in the collection, because it has been defined as an indexer, you simply access the Contents collection by using the indexer syntax (For more information on Indexers, see Chapter 5, "Object Orientation in C# and Visual Basic. NET").

For example, add the following code shown in grey to the Application_Start method of the global.asax file. This code adds a new string object named "ConnectString" to the Contents collection.

In C#:

```
protected void Application_Start(Object sender, EventArgs e)
{
  Global.ServerPath = Global.ServerPath = Server.MapPath("");
  Application["ConnectString"] =
}
```

And in Visual Basic .NET:

```
Sub Application_Start(ByVal sender As Object, ByVal e As EventArgs)
    Global.ServerPath = Server.MapPath("")
    Application("ConnectString") =
End Sub
```

To access this string, you use a similar syntax, but you must cast the value to the appropriate type—this is because all objects stored in the collection are stored as the Object type. For example, the following code gets the value of the ConnectString item from the Application object.

In C#:

```
string Connect = (string)Application["ConnectString"];
```

In Visual Basic .NET:

```
Dim Connect As String = CStr(Application("ConnectString"))
```

In a nutshell, the Application object provides an easy way to store data and objects accessible from any user session.

Application object pitfalls

There are a few things to watch out for when using the Application object. First of all, if you have a Web farm (a single Web site that contains multiple Web servers) or a Web garden (a single Web server machine with multiple processors), be aware that the Application object is specific to a single process running on a single processor. This means sessions running on different processors or different physical machines do not have access to the same Application object. If you need truly global access to data from all sessions running in a Web farm or Web garden, you can store the information in a globally accessible database or data file, such as an XML file.

If you allow clients to modify global data stored in the Application object, you need to be aware of concurrency issues. Take for example the following code making use of a Counter value in the Application object.

In C#:

```
int Count = (int)Application["Counter"];
Count += 1;
Application["Counter"] = Count;
```

And in Visual Basic .NET:

```
Dim Count As Integer = CInt(Application("Counter"))
Count += 1
Application("Counter") = Count
```

What happens if another session increments the Application object's Counter value between the time this session gets the value, increments it, and stores it back to the Application object? The first session's increment of the Counter would be lost. To prevent this, you call the Application object's Lock and Unlock methods.

In C#:

```
Application.Lock();
int Count = (int)Application["Counter"];
Count += 1;
```

```
Application["Counter"] = Count;
Application.UnLock();
```

In Visual Basic .NET:

```
Application.Lock()
Dim Count As Integer = CInt(Application("Counter"))
Count += 1
Application("Counter") = Count
Application.UnLock()
```

The call to the Application object's Lock method causes the Application object to lock access to any items subsequently accessed in the Contents collection. For example, once the second line of code executes, the "Counter" variable is locked to any other sessions, until the call to Application.Unlock is made. Obviously, if you lock the Application object, you want to unlock it as quickly as possible! Also beware of any "deadly embrace" problems you may encounter when you allow a piece of code to lock more than one variable. If Process A has the first variable locked and Process B has the second variable locked, they could each be waiting indefinitely for the other process to unlock the variable.

Fortunately, if you don't unlock the Application logic after locking it, the Web server unlocks the Application object when it finishes processing the .aspx file.

The Session object

The Session object is an instance of the System.Web.SessionState.HttpSessionState class. In the same way the Application object stores information accessible from all sessions in an application, the Session object stores session state—information accessible from all Web forms in a single user session. The unique session ID keeps each session's data separate from all other session data.

The Session object also has a Contents dictionary collection property accessible with indexer syntax. For example, the following code adds a new string object named "ISBN" that contains an ISBN number to the Contents collection.

In C#:

```
Session["ISBN"] = "0-596-00171-1";
```

And in Visual Basic .NET:

```
Session("ISBN") = "0-596-00171-1"
```

Here's an example of accessing this item in C#:

```
string ISBN = Session["ISBN"];
```

And in Visual Basic .NET:

```
Dim ISBN As String = Session("ISBN")
```

The Session object is extremely useful for storing information that needs to be passed from one page to the next in a given session.

> 📝 *By default, Session state is stored in memory outside of the ASP.NET process. This means if the server is restarted or crashes (IIS—not the physical server), session state is not lost! For other Session state options see the "Caching data and objects" section later in this chapter.*

The Session object has a number of other useful properties and methods. Some of the most frequently used members are listed in **Table 2**.

Table 2. *Commonly used members of the Session object*

Member name	Type	Description
IsCookieless	Property	If True, specifies the session ID is embedded in the URL. If False, indicates the session ID is stored in an HTTP cookie.
IsNewSession	Property	Returns a boolean value indicating if the session was created with the current request.
Mode	Property	Specifies how session state is cached. The value of this setting is one of the four SessionStateMode enumerations: InProc (the default), Off, SqlServer, StateServer. For more information on session state caching, see the "Caching Data and Objects" section later in this chapter.
SessionID	Property	Gets the current unique session ID.
Abandon	Method	Cancels the current session.
Clear	Method	Clears all values from the session state.

The Response object

The Response object is an instance of the System.Web.HttpResponse class and is one of the most important objects in ASP.NET. This object sends information from the Web server to the client.

For example, the following code displays a simple "Hello .NET World" message to the client's browser.

In C#:

```
Response.Write("Hello .NET World");
```

And in Visual Basic .NET:

```
Response.Write("Hello .NET World")
```

The Response object can also redirect to another page. The following example redirects the client to the Hentzenwerke web site.

In C#:

```
Response.Redirect("http://www.hentzenwerke.com");
```

And in Visual Basic .NET:

```
Response.Redirect("http://www.hentzenwerke.com")
```

Table 3 lists some other commonly used properties and methods of the Response object.

Table 3. Commonly used members of the Response object

Member name	Type	Description
Buffer	Property	Specifies whether output should be buffered (wait until the entire Response is finished processing).
Expires	Property	Specifies the number of minutes before a page cached in a browser expires.
IsClientConnected	Property	Returns a boolean value indicating if the client is still connected.
Flush	Method	Sends all buffered output to the client.
Redirect	Method	Redirects a client to the specified URL.
Write	Method	Writes the specified information to the client.

The Request object

The Request object is an instance of the System.Web.HttpRequest class, and one of the most important ASP.NET objects. This object allows you to read HTTP values sent from the client to the Web server. You learn a lot about the client from the properties of the Request object.

For example, the following code uses the Browser property of the Request object to return an HttpBrowserCapabilities and display information about the client's browser (**Figure 9**).

In C#:

```
HttpBrowserCapabilities bc = Request.Browser;
Response.Write("<H1>Browser capabilities</H1>");
Response.Write("Type = " + bc.Type + "<br>");
Response.Write("Platform = " + bc.Platform + "<br>");
Response.Write("Supports Frames = " + bc.Frames + "<br>");
Response.Write("Supports Cookies = " + bc.Cookies + "<br>");
```

In Visual Basic .NET:

```
Dim bc As HttpBrowserCapabilities = Request.Browser
Response.Write("<H1>Browser capabilities</H1>")
Response.Write(("Type = " + bc.Type + "<br>"))
Response.Write(("Platform = " + bc.Platform + "<br>"))
Response.Write(("Supports Frames = " + bc.Frames + "<br>"))
Response.Write(("Supports Cookies = " + bc.Cookies + "<br>"))
```

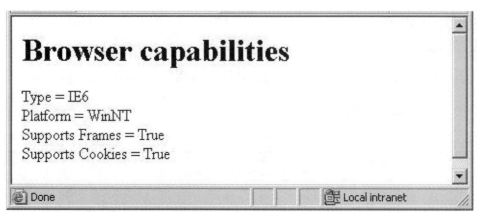

Figure 9._You can use the Request object to find out information about a client's browser._

The User object

The User object is an instance of the System.Security.Principal.WindowsPrincipal class. You can use this object to check the Windows group membership of the current user, if the user has been authenticated. For example, the following code uses the IsInRole method of the User object to see if the user is in the Windows Group "Guests".

In C#:

```
bool IsAdministrator = User.IsInRole("Guests");
```

In Visual Basic .NET:

```
Dim IsAdministrator As Boolean = User.IsInRole("Guests")
```

For more information on users and security, see Chapter 14, ".NET Security".

The Site object

The Site object is an instance of the System.Security.Policy.Site class. This object can be used to determine the Web site where an assembly originates.

For more information on security, see Chapter 14, ".NET Security".

Making changes to global.asax at run time

If you make changes to the global.asax file while the Web application is running, ASP.NET page framework detects the change. It completes all outstanding requests, sends the Application_OnEnd event to any listeners, and restarts the application.

ASP.NET configuration files

There are two main configuration files used by ASP.NET:

- Machine.config

- Web.config

In ASP.NET, configuration information is stored in XML configuration files. This makes remote administration a snap because you can edit these files using any standard XML parser or text editor. In addition, these files can be edited without stopping and restarting the server. Once the changes are made to the configuration files, the new settings apply to any new client requests.

Machine.config

The Machine.config file is the root configuration file that provides default settings for the entire Web server. This file is located beneath your Web server's Windows directory in the <Windows Directory>\Microsoft.NET\Framework\<version>\CONFIG folder.

Each Web application inherits default configuration settings from the Machine.config file.

Web.config

Each Web application can have one or more Web.config files that apply ASP.NET configuration settings to its own directory and all subdirectories. These files are used to override or extend the configuration settings inherited from the Machine.config file. For more information on how this inheritance works, check out the .NET Help topic "Configuration Inheritance".

Here are some examples of settings found in the Web.config file:

```
<compilation
    defaultLanguage="c#"
    debug="true"
/>
```

The compilation element contains a defaultLanguage setting indicating the default language of your Web application. The debug setting specifies whether you want the compiler to create debug information for your pages. This is obviously desirable when first creating and testing your Web application. However, when you're ready to deploy a completed, well-tested application, you should set debug to "false" to generate a more compact (and faster) version of your Web application devoid of debug information.

Here's another element in Web.config named "customErrors".

```
<customErrors
    mode="RemoteOnly"
/>
```

The mode setting in this element specifies how to display ASP.NET error messages to users. This setting has three possible values as you can see by reading the comments above the setting in the Web.config file:

- On – Always display custom (friendly) messages

- Off – Always display detailed ASP.NET error information

- RemoteOnly – (the default) Display custom (friendly) messages to users not running on the local Web server. This setting is recommended for security purposes, so you do not display application detail information to remote clients.

For more information on these and other settings, check out the .NET Help topic "ASP.NET Configuration".

Creating the Customer Orders Web form

Now you're ready to create a Customers Orders Web form similar to the Windows Form created in the previous chapter. Before creating this form, remove the "Hello .NET World!" label added earlier in this chapter. To do this, right-click on the label in design mode and select Delete from the shortcut menu. Also, set the style back from "Heading1" to "Normal" by clicking on the Web form in the location where the label was then select "Normal" from the Format toolbar.

Renaming the Web form code-behind file and class

Next, rename the Web form file to something more meaningful. In the Solution Explorer, right-click the WebForm1.aspx file and select Rename from the shortcut menu. Change the name of the file to CustomerOrders.aspx. Notice this also changes the name of the code-behind file (CustomerOrders.aspx.cs in C# or CustomerOrders.aspx.vb in VB .NET). Now that you've changed the name of the source code file, you need to change the name of the actual Web form class. To do this, double-click the code-behind file in the Solution Explorer, which opens the code file in the Visual Studio .NET IDE. Change the name of the class from "WebForm1" to "CustomerOrders".

In C#:

```
public class CustomerOrders : System.Web.UI.Page
```

In Visual Basic .NET:

```
Public Class CustomerOrders
    Inherits System.Web.UI.Page
```

Adding controls to the Web form

Now it's time to add some controls to the Web form. Make sure the CustomerOrders.aspx is open in design mode, then drag and drop a label from the VS .NET Toolbox onto the Web form. With the label control selected, go to the Properties Window and change the (ID) property to "lblCustomerID" and the Text property to "Customer ID:".

Next, drag and drop a TextBox control from the Toolbox to the Web form. The text box should be automatically placed to the right of the label. Go to the Properties Window and change the (ID) property to txtCustomerID.

Now add a Submit button to the Web form. Click to the right of the text box—this places the cursor to the immediate right of the text box. Press the space bar three times to add a bit of space between the text box and the button you're getting ready to add. Next, drag and drop a Button from the Toolbox to the right of the text box. With the button selected, go to the Properties Window and set the button's (ID) property to "btnSubmit" and its Text property to "Submit".

Before adding the next control, you need to create a new line in the Web form. To do this, click to the immediate right of the text box and press the Enter key. This should drop the cursor down beneath the Customer ID label. Drag and drop a DataGrid control from the Toolbox onto the Web form directly below the Customer ID label. In the Properties Window, change its (ID) property to grdOrders. At this point, your Web form should look the same as the form shown in **Figure 10**.

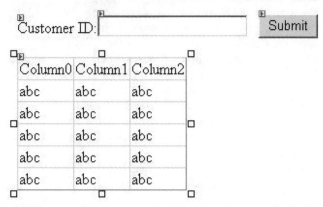

Figure 10. You drag and drop controls from the VS .NET toolbox onto a Web form the same way as you do with a Windows Form.

If you're not particularly fond of the default font for controls on this form, you can easily change the fonts of all controls. First, select all controls, go to the Properties Window, and expand the Font node. You can then select different font attributes. In the sample code, I've selected a Font Name of "Verdana" and a Font Size of "Smaller".

Next, you can improve the appearance of the DataGrid by applying an auto-format style to it. With the DataGrid selected in design mode, go to the Properties Window, and click the AutoFormat hyperlink label (**Figure 11**).

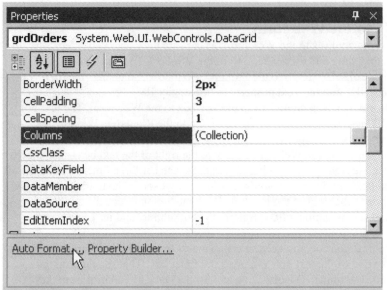

Figure 11. *Select the Auto Format hyperlink in the Properties Window to automatically apply a visual style to a DataGrid.*

In the Auto Format dialog, select any scheme you want, but for this example, I chose "Professional 2". After selecting the scheme, click OK to apply the scheme to the DataGrid.

Now it's time to specify columns for the DataGrid. Click on the DataGrid in design mode and go to the Properties Window. Select the Columns property and click the ellipses button (…) next to the Columns property. This launches the grdOrders Properties dialog allowing you to add one or more columns to the DataGrid. You are going to add four columns to the grid that hold Order ID, Order Date, Ship Name, and Ship Country.

First, uncheck the Create columns automatically at run time box at the top of the dialog. This prevents columns from being automatically generated from the data source at rum time. You don't need them dynamically generated because you are going to manually specify all columns at design time.

Notice this dialog has a mover box that lets you add items from the left side of the mover to the right side. In the left mover list box, there are four different column types to choose from:

- Bound column

- Button column

- Hyperlink column

- Template column

The Bound Column option creates a column bound to a data source. The Button Column option allows you to add buttons to the DataGrid that the user can click, usually to start off some process or to edit, update, or delete items in the DataGrid. The Hyperlink Column allows you to add a hyperlink label to a column that the user can click, which usually redirects them to another form where they can edit the selected item. A Template Column allows you to create a column containing any combination of HTML, text, and controls.

For the first column, add a hyperlink column containing the Order ID. This allows users to click on the column to select an order to be edited. It also launches an Order Edit page and passes the ID of the selected Order to that page. To add this column, select Hyperlink Column in the Available columns list, and then click the mover button (>) to add the column to the Selected columns list. When you do this, it displays HyperLinkColumn properties at the bottom of the dialog (**Figure 12**).

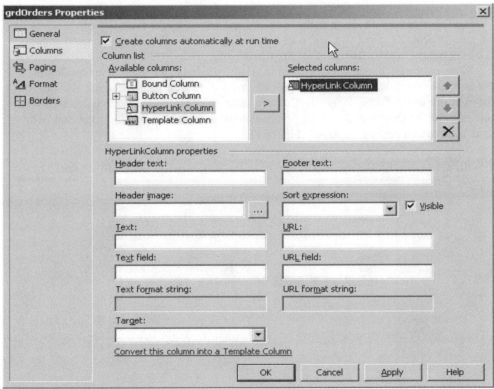

Figure 12. *The Web Forms DataGrid Properties dialog allows you to add a variety of columns to your DataGrid.*

In the Header text box and the Text field box, enter "Order ID". This sets the OrderID field as the data source for the hyperlink text displayed in this column. In the URL field box, enter "OrderID", and in the URL format string box enter "OrderEdit.aspx?orderID={0}". The URL field specifies the data source field containing the value to be passed to the target page—in this case, the OrderID field. The first part of the URL format string (OrderEdit.aspx) specifies the target Web page requested when a user clicks on an Order ID hyperlink. The second part of the URL format string (?orderID={0}) specifies a parameter named "orderID" is passed to the target page. The "{0}" is a substitution parameter. ASP.NET substitutes the value of the field specified in the URL field text box (in this case OrderID) when it creates the link at run time. For example, if the currently selected order ID is 10372, the link created is:

```
OrderEdit.aspx?orderID=10372
```

The value of the orderID parameter is easily retrieved from within the OrderEdit page you will soon create.

Now add a bound column to the DataGrid by selecting Bound Column in the Available columns list and clicking the mover button. When you do this, a different set of properties displays in the bottom half of the dialog. In the Header text box, enter "Order Date" and in the Data field box enter "OrderDate".

Add another bound column to the DataGrid and set its Header text to "Name" and its Data field to "ShipName". Next, add one more bound column to the DataGrid, settings its Header text to "Country" and its Data field to "ShipCountry".

Now, set the width of each column in the DataGrid. In the left pane of the grdOrders Properties dialog, select Format. When you do this, a TreeView named Objects is displayed in the right side of the dialog. Select the Columns node and you will see the four columns you just added to the DataGrid. Select the first column (Columns[0]) and a Width text box and associated combo box are displayed (**Figure 13**).

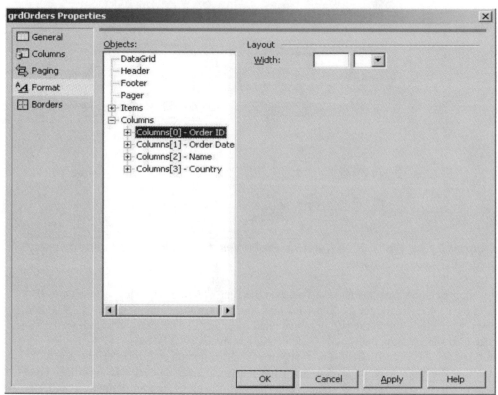

Figure 13. You can set the widths of DataGrid columns in the Properties dialog.

In the Width text box, enter 75 for the Order ID column. When you enter the width, a "px" (an abbreviation for "pixels") displays in the combo box—just accept the "px" setting. Next, set the width of the Order Date column to 100, the Name column to 200, and the Country column to 100. When you're done, click the OK button to close the dialog and apply the new column settings to your DataGrid. If you look at the CustomerOrders form in design mode, it should look like **Figure 14**.

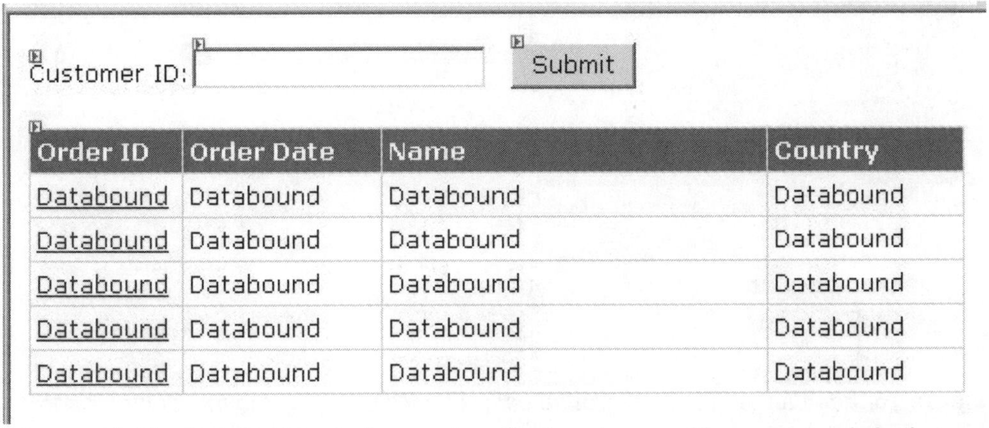

Figure 14. *The DataGrid in design mode reflects column settings you apply in the DataGrid's Properties dialog.*

Next, change the background color of the Web form to grey. Click on the Web form in design mode, go to the Properties Window, and select the bgColor property. Click the ellipses button (…) next to the property to launch the Color Picker dialog. You can pick any color you like, but for this example, I selected the Named Colors tab, and selected the "Gainsboro" grey color in the far right center of the color palette (**Figure 15**). Click the OK button to select the color.

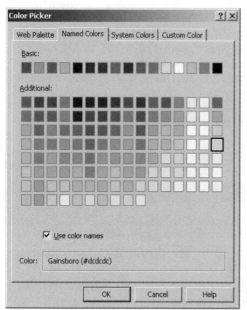

Figure 15. *You can set the background color of a Web form using the Color Picker*

Now you need to set up data access for the form by reusing business objects created for your Windows Forms application in the previous chapter.

Accessing data by means of business objects

In Chapter 9, "Building .NET Windows Forms Applications", you created three different business objects—Orders, OrderItem, and Shipper. You can use these same business objects in your Web Forms application. There are a few ways to accomplish this, but the easiest method right now is adding the source code files to your Web Forms application.

To add these source code files, right-click your Web Forms project in the Solution Explorer and select Add | Add Existing Item from the shortcut menu. In the Add Existing Item dialog, navigate to the "Simple Windows Application" directory you created in the previous chapter, and select the five business object source code files (**Figure 16**). These are Business.cs, Data.cs, OrderItemBusiness.cs, OrderBusiness.cs, and ShipperBusiness.cs. If you created a Visual Basic .NET Windows Forms application, these files will have a "vb" extension rather than a "cs" extension. After selecting all five files, click the Open button.

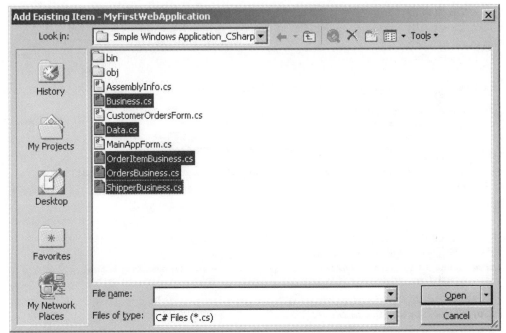

Figure 16. *You can add files belonging to one .NET project to any other .NET project*

After clicking the Open button, these five files should be listed in the Solution Explorer.

Typically, with business objects that are going to be used from multiple projects, you should create a separate Class Library project in Visual Studio .NET and add your business object source code files to this project. You can then compile a DLL containing just your business object classes. This DLL can then be referenced from multiple projects (such as a Windows Form application and a Web Forms application).

Now you need to add code to the Web form to retrieve data from the business object that is displayed in the Orders DataGrid. To do this, edit the CustomerOrders.aspx.cs (C#) or CustomerOrders.aspx.vb (VB .NET) code file. At the top of the code file, add the following namespace reference.

In C#:

```
using HW.NetBook.Samples.Business;
```

And in Visual Basic .NET:

```
Imports HW.NetBook.Samples.Business
```

Go back to the CustomerOrders form in design mode and double-click the Submit button. This automatically adds an event handler to the code-behind file. Add the following code to this event handler.

In C#:

```
private void btnSubmit_Click(object sender, System.EventArgs e)
{
  // Instantiate the Orders business object
  Orders OrderObj = new Orders();

  // Get all Orders for the user-specified customer and bind
  // the DataGrid to the resulting DataSet
  DataSet ds = OrderObj.GetOrdersByCustomerID(this.txtCustomerID.Text);
  this.grdOrders.DataSource = ds;
  this.grdOrders.DataBind();
}
```

In Visual Basic .NET:

```
Private Sub btnSubmit_Click(sender As Object, e As System.EventArgs) _
      Handles btnSubmit.Click

   ' Instantiate the Orders business object
   Dim OrderObj As New Orders()

   ' Get all Orders for the user-specified customer and bind
   ' the DataGrid to the resulting DataSet
   Dim ds As DataSet = OrderObj.GetOrdersByCustomerID(Me.txtCustomerID.Text)
   Me.grdOrders.DataSource = ds
   Me.grdOrders.DataBind()


End Sub 'btnSubmit_Click
```

This code instantiates the Orders business object, calls its GetOrdersByCustomerID method, and passes the value of the Customer ID text box. It then binds the DataGrid to the resulting DataSet.

Testing the Customer Orders Web form

Now you're ready to test the Customer Orders Web form to see if what you've done so far is working properly. To do this, select Build | Build Solution from the menu. If everything compiles correctly, run the Web Forms application by pressing F5 or click the Run button (if it doesn't compile correctly, fix the errors and compile again). When Internet Explorer opens, you should see the Customer ID label and text box as well as the Submit button (**Figure 17**).

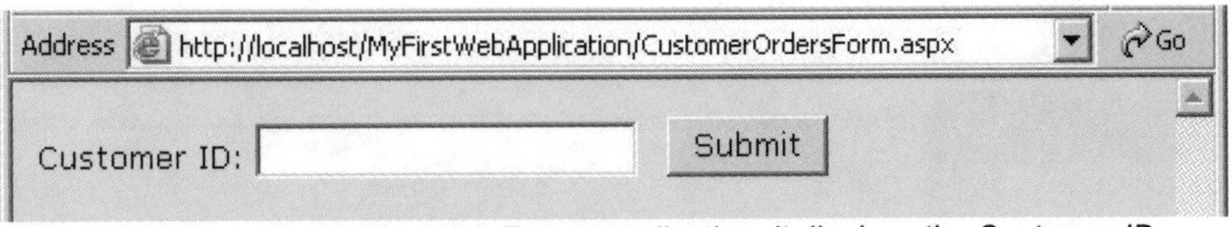

Figure 17*. When you run the Web Forms application, it displays the Customer ID label and text box as well as the Submit button.*

To test the application's data access abilities, enter the text "QUEEN" in the Customer ID text box and click the Submit button. After a few moments, you should see a list of orders displayed in the Orders DataGrid (**Figure 18**).

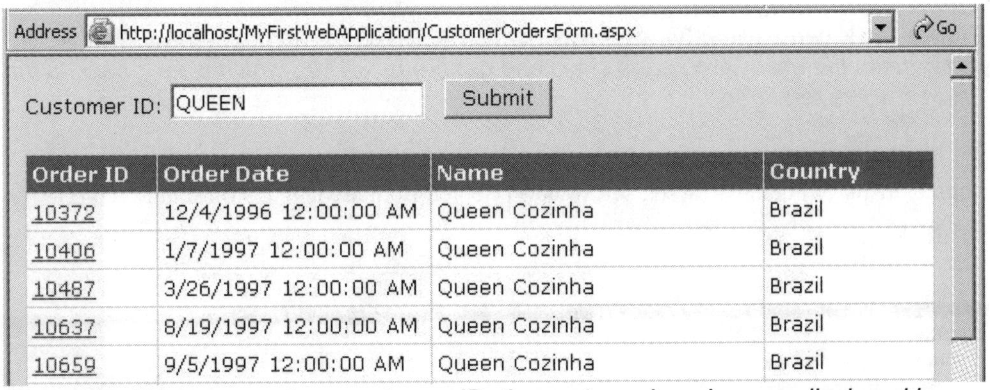

Figure 18*. When you enter a customer ID, the customer's orders are displayed in the DataGrid.*

At this point, if you try to click on any of the order ID hyperlink labels, you would get an error, because you haven't created the Order Edit Web form. You'll do this soon, but first take a closer look at what's happening behind the scenes.

A look at the flow of events

When you first run the Web Forms application the following occurs (see also **Figure 19**):

1. The browser sends a request to the Web server for the CustomerOrders.aspx page.

2. The Web server receives the request and instantiates the CustomerOrders Web page class.

3. The Web page's Page_Init event fires.

4. The Web page's Page_Load event fires.

5. The Web server processes the page and sends HTML output back to the browser.

6. The browser renders the HTML for display to the user.

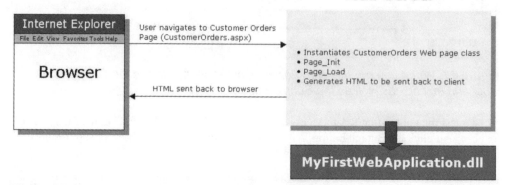

Figure 19. *When a client browser requests an ASP.NET Web page, the server instantiates the associated page class and generates HTML, which is sent back to the browser to be rendered.*

To see the HTML passed back to the browser, run the application, and when the page is initially displayed in the browser, select View | Source from the menu. You should see HTML that looks something like this:

```
<!DOCTYPE HTML PUBLIC "-//W3C//DTD HTML 4.0 Transitional//EN" >
<HTML>
  <HEAD>
    <title>WebForm1</title>
    <meta content="Microsoft Visual Studio 7.0" name="GENERATOR">
    <meta content="C#" name="CODE_LANGUAGE">
    <meta content="JavaScript" name="vs_defaultClientScript">
    <meta content="http://schemas.microsoft.com/intellisense/ie5"
name="vs_targetSchema">
  </HEAD>
  <body bgColor="gainsboro">
    <form name="Form1" method="post" action="CustomerOrders.aspx" id="Form1">
<input type="hidden" name="__VIEWSTATE"
value="dDwxMTU0MzQ2MTEzO3Q8O2w8aTwxPjs+O2w8dDw7bDxpPDc+Oz47bDx0PEAwPDs7O3s7Ozs7
Ozs+Ozs+Oz4+Oz4+Oz6oG5OBeOfpfCgjFYH5BiaCehjOwg==" />

    <P>
        <span id="lblCustomerID" style="font-family:Verdana;font-
size:Smaller;">Customer ID:</span>
        <input name="txtCustomerID" type="text" id="txtCustomerID" style="font-
family:Verdana;font-size:Smaller;" />  
        <input type="submit" name="btnSubmit" value="Submit" id="btnSubmit"
style="font-family:Verdana;font-size:Smaller;" /></P>
    <P>
    </P>
  </form>
  </body>
</HTML>
```

In addition to the normal HTML you would expect to see, notice there is also a hidden "input" element located in the middle of the HTML with the name "_VIEWSTATE" and a value string of seemingly incomprehensible characters. This hidden field is the mechanism used by ASP.NET to transfer page *state* information between the browser and the server. In the context of a Web page, "state" refers to the values of a Web page's variables and controls. Since the Web is a stateless environment, you need some mechanism to store and retrieve the state of a page as it gets passed back and forth between the browser and the server.

To understand more fully how this works, take a look at the sequence of events occurring when a user retrieves orders for a specified customer using your Web application.

When the user enters a customer ID and clicks the Submit button, the following occurs (see also **Figure 20**):

1. Clicking the Submit button raises the Click event on the browser.

2. The CustomerOrders page posts back to the Web server, including the value entered by the user in the Customer ID text box.

3. In response, the Web server instantiates the CustomerOrders Web page class.

4. The Web page's Page_Init event fires.

5. The Web page's Page_Load event fires.

6. The event handler for the Submit button's Click event (btnSubmit_Click) is executed to respond to the Click event raised on the browser.

7. The btnSubmit_Click event handler code instantiates the Orders business object, retrieves the Customer ID value from the text box, and passes it to the object's GetOrdersByCustomerID method.

8. The Orders DataGrid is bound to the DataSet returned from the Orders object.

9. The Web server processes the page again and sends HTML back to the browser.

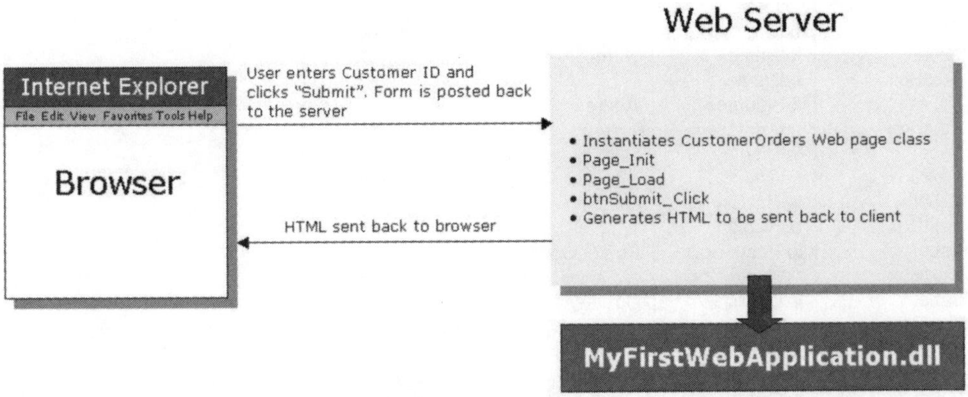

Figure 20. During a round-trip, a Web form is posted to the server, processed, and sent back to the browser again.

> The process of sending a Web form from the browser to the Web server then back again is known as a "round trip".

If you view the source code in your browser again, this time you'll see HTML for the DataGrid. In addition, you'll notice the state stored in the hidden field is considerably larger than before. This is because it now contains state information for the DataGrid that was passed back from the Web server.

Creating the Order Edit form

Now we need to create an Order Edit Web form that lets users edit a selected order. In the Solution Explorer, right-click on the project node and select Add | Add Web Form from the shortcut menu to launch the Add New Item dialog with the Web Form template pre-selected. In the Name text box, change the name of the Web form to OrderEdit.aspx, and then click the Open button. This opens the new OrderEdit form in design mode. For this form, leave the pageLayout property set to "GridLayout". This gives you a similar feel as creating Windows forms—you can position controls anywhere on the design surface.

Next, go to the Properties Window and select the bgColor property. Click the ellipses button (...) next to the property to launch the Color Picker dialog. Again, as you did for the CustomerOrders form, click the Named Colors tab and select the "Gainsboro" grey color on the far right center of the palette.

Now you're ready to drop some controls on the Web form. First select the Web form in design mode. For easier placement of controls, select Format | Snap to Grid from the main menu. Next, drag and drop the controls listed in **Table 4** on the form, setting their ID and Width properties as specified in the table. Note that the Size setting in Table 4 is only a suggestion—you can set the size to any value you wish. For an idea of where to locate the controls, see **Figure 21**.

Table 4. Class, ID, text, and size of controls on the Order Edit Web form

Class	Control ID	Text	Size
Label	lblOrderID	Order ID:	-
TextBox	txtOrderID		100
Label	lblName	Name:	-
TextBox	txtName		260
Label	lblAddress	Address:	-
TextBox	txtAddress		328
Label	lblCity	City:	-
TextBox	txtCity		175
Label	lblRegion	Region:	-
TextBox	txtRegion		185
Label	lblPostalCode	Postal Code:	-
TextBox	txtPostalCode		107
Label	lblCountry	Country:	-
TextBox	txtCountry		185
Label	lblShippers	Shippers:	-
DropDownList	cboShippers		175
Label	lblOrderItems	Order Items	-
DataGrid	grdOrderItems		355

Again, if you want to change the font of all controls on this form, drag a "lasso" around the controls to select them all, go to the Properties Window, and change the Font properties to whatever you like. In the sample code, I've changed the Font Name to "Verdana" and the Font Size to "Smaller".

Now select a color scheme for the Order Items DataGrid. Select the DataGrid in design mode and click the <u>AutoFormat</u> hyperlink label at the bottom right of the Properties Windows (Figure 11). In the Auto Format dialog choose a scheme from the list and click OK to close the dialog (in the sample code, I've selected the "Colorful 1" scheme).

Next, add columns to the Order Items DataGrid. Select the DataGrid in design mode, go to the Properties Window, and select the Columns property. Click on the ellipses (…) button next to the Columns property to launch the DataGrid Properties dialog. First, uncheck the Create columns automatically at run time checkbox, and then add four bound columns to the DataGrid as shown in **Table 5**.

Table 5. Properties for columns in the DataGrid on the Order Edit Web form

Column Type	Header Text	Data Field
Bound Column	Product	ProductID
Bound Column	Unit Price	UnitPrice
Bound Column	Qty	Quantity
Bound Column	Discount	Discount

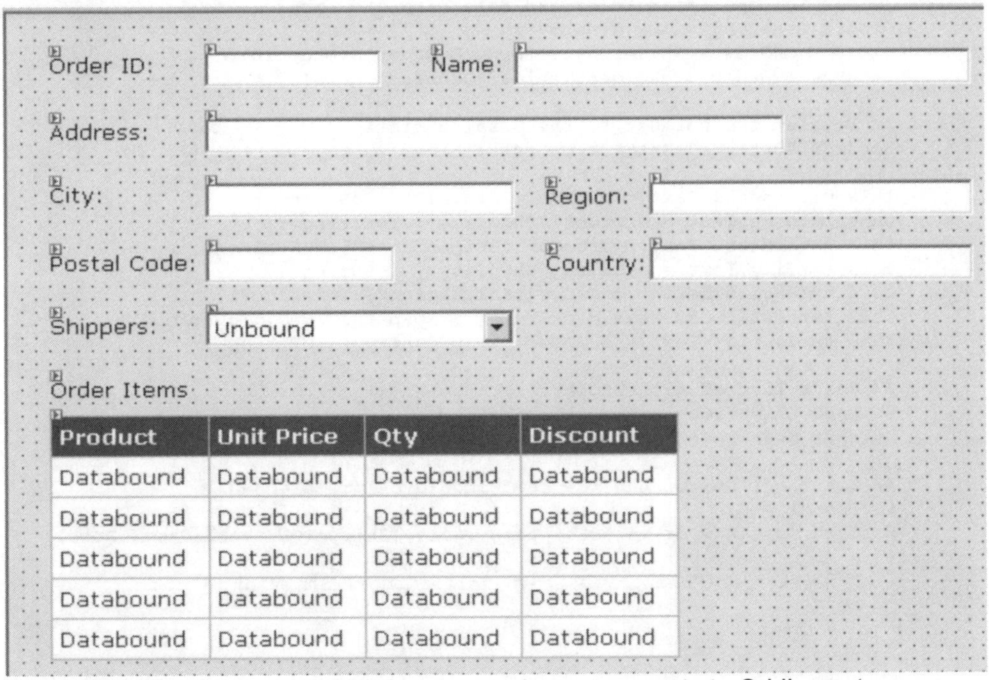

Figure 21. When you set a Web form's pageLayout property to GridLayout, you can place controls on the form wherever you like—similar to a Windows form.

Now it's time create data access and data binding code for the Shippers DropDownList and the Order Items DataGrid controls so they can display their corresponding data at run time. Double-click the OrderEdit form design surface, which places you in the Page_Load event handler method. Before adding code to this method, go to the top of the code file and add the following namespace reference.

In C#:

```
using HW.NetBook.Samples.Business;
```

And in Visual Basic .NET

```
Imports HW.NetBook.Samples.Business
```

Now go back down to the bottom of the code file and add the following code to the Page_Load Event.

In C#:

```csharp
private void Page_Load(object sender, System.EventArgs e)
{
  if (! IsPostBack)
  {
      // Get the Order ID passed to this page
      int OrderID = int.Parse(Request.QueryString["orderID"]);

      // Get the specified order and data bind the order controls
      Orders OrderObj = new Orders();
      DataSet dsOrder = OrderObj.GetOrderByOrderID(OrderID);
      DataRow drOrder = dsOrder.Tables["Orders"].Rows[0];

      // Persist the DataSet to the Session state
      Session["OrderDataSet"] = dsOrder;

      this.txtOrderID.Text = drOrder["OrderID"].ToString();
      this.txtName.Text = drOrder["ShipName"].ToString();
      this.txtAddress.Text = drOrder["ShipAddress"].ToString();
      this.txtCity.Text = drOrder["ShipCity"].ToString();
      this.txtRegion.Text = drOrder["ShipRegion"].ToString();
      this.txtPostalCode.Text = drOrder["ShipPostalCode"].ToString();
      this.txtCountry.Text = drOrder["ShipCountry"].ToString();

      // Get a list of all shippers
      Shipper ShipperObj = new Shipper();
      DataSet dsShippers = ShipperObj.GetShippers();

      // Get the index of the row that should be preselected
      int Index = 0;
      foreach (DataRow dr in dsShippers.Tables[ShipperObj.TableName].Rows)
      {
          if ((int)dr["ShipperID"] == (int)drOrder["ShipVia"])
          {
              break;
          }
          Index++;
      }
```

```
        // Data bind the combo box
        this.cboShippers.DataTextField = "CompanyName";
        this.cboShippers.DataValueField = "ShipperID";
        this.cboShippers.DataSource = dsShippers;
        this.cboShippers.SelectedIndex = Index;
        this.cboShippers.DataBind();

        // Get all order items for the specified order id
        OrderItem OrderItemObj = new OrderItem();
        DataSet dsOrderItems = OrderItemObj.GetOrderItems(OrderID);
        this.grdOrderItems.DataSource = dsOrderItems;
        this.grdOrderItems.DataBind();
    }
}
```

And in Visual Basic .NET

```
Private Sub Page_Load(ByVal sender As System.Object, _
  ByVal e As System.EventArgs) Handles MyBase.Load
    If Not IsPostBack Then
        ' Get the Order ID passed to this page
        Dim OrderID As Integer = Integer.Parse(Request.QueryString("orderID"))

        ' Get the specified order and data bind the order controls
        Dim OrderObj As New Orders()
        Dim dsOrder As DataSet = OrderObj.GetOrderByOrderID(OrderID)
        Dim drOrder As DataRow = dsOrder.Tables("Orders").Rows(0)

        ' Persist the DataSet to the Session state
        Session("OrderDataSet") = dsOrder

        Me.txtOrderID.Text = drOrder("OrderID").ToString()
        Me.txtName.Text = drOrder("ShipName").ToString()
        Me.txtAddress.Text = drOrder("ShipAddress").ToString()
        Me.txtCity.Text = drOrder("ShipCity").ToString()
        Me.txtRegion.Text = drOrder("ShipRegion").ToString()
        Me.txtPostalCode.Text = drOrder("ShipPostalCode").ToString()
        Me.txtCountry.Text = drOrder("ShipCountry").ToString()

        ' Get a list of all shippers
        Dim ShipperObj As New Shipper()
        Dim dsShippers As DataSet = ShipperObj.GetShippers()

        ' Get the index of the row that should be preselected
        Dim Index As Integer = 0
        Dim dr As DataRow
        For Each dr In dsShippers.Tables(ShipperObj.TableName).Rows
            If CInt(dr("ShipperID")) = CInt(drOrder("ShipVia")) Then
                Exit For
            End If
            Index += 1
        Next dr

        ' Data bind the combo box
        Me.cboShippers.DataTextField = "CompanyName"
        Me.cboShippers.DataValueField = "ShipperID"
        Me.cboShippers.DataSource = dsShippers
        Me.cboShippers.SelectedIndex = Index
        Me.cboShippers.DataBind()
```

```
        ' Get all order items for the specified order id
        Dim OrderItemObj As New OrderItem()
        Dim dsOrderItems As DataSet = OrderItemObj.GetOrderItems(OrderID)
        Me.grdOrderItems.DataSource = dsOrderItems
        Me.grdOrderItems.DataBind()
    End If
End Sub
```

First this code checks the form's IsPostBack property to determine if the page is being loaded for the first time or in response to a post back from the Web browser. If it's being loaded in response to a post back, all of the code in this method is bypassed. This is necessary because running this code on a post back would overwrite any changes the user makes to the order.

If IsPostBack is false, the code in this method retrieves the value of the orderID parameter passed to it from the CustomerOrders page. It does this by calling the ASP.NET Request object's QueryString method, passing the name of the parameter. The QueryString method returns a string value that is converted into an integer.

Next, the code instantiates the Orders object and calls its GetOrderByOrderID method, passing the order ID received from the Customer Orders page. Notice after retrieving the DataSet from the Orders object, it persists the DataSet to the Session object. This is done because later in this particular example you are going to update the selected order stored in the DataSet. Storing the DataSet in the Session state allows you to retrieve the DataSet from the Session object when the update is performed. If you didn't persist the DataSet, you would lose all of your changes when the form is posted back to the Web site.

After persisting the Orders DataSet, controls are bound to the DataSet. Next, DataSets are retrieved from the Shippers and OrderItems business objects and the controls are bound to data.

Here's a special note about binding to a DropDownList control. If you want to pre-select an item in the DropDownList control, the only way you can do this is by setting its SelectedIndex property. However, when you bind to a DataSet, there's no straightforward way to retrieve the index of the DataRow you want selected. That's why there's a "for each" loop in this method—it loops through the DataRows to find the index of the Shipper DataRow whose Shipper ID field contains the same value as the Order's ShipVia field. It would be *much* better if Microsoft came up with an easier way to do this—perhaps by means of a SelectedValue property.

Here's another important point—typically, in a Web forms application, if you need to retrieve data from the back end for read-only purposes, you can use a DataReader and Data Command object rather than a DataSet, since a DataReader provides faster (though read-only) access to data. This means any place in the application where I require read-only data (as in the case of Shippers) then I would use a DataReader rather than a DataSet. For more information on using a DataReader, see Chapter 7, "Data Access with ADO.NET".

Testing the Order Edit form
Now it's time to test your work on the Order Edit form so far. Compile and run the Web application by pressing the Start button or pressing F5. The Customer Orders Web form

appears first. Enter the word "QUICK" in the Customer ID text box and click Submit. This fills the Orders DataGrid with all orders for the specified customer.

Click on any hyperlink label in the Order ID column to display the Order Edit form (**Figure 22**).

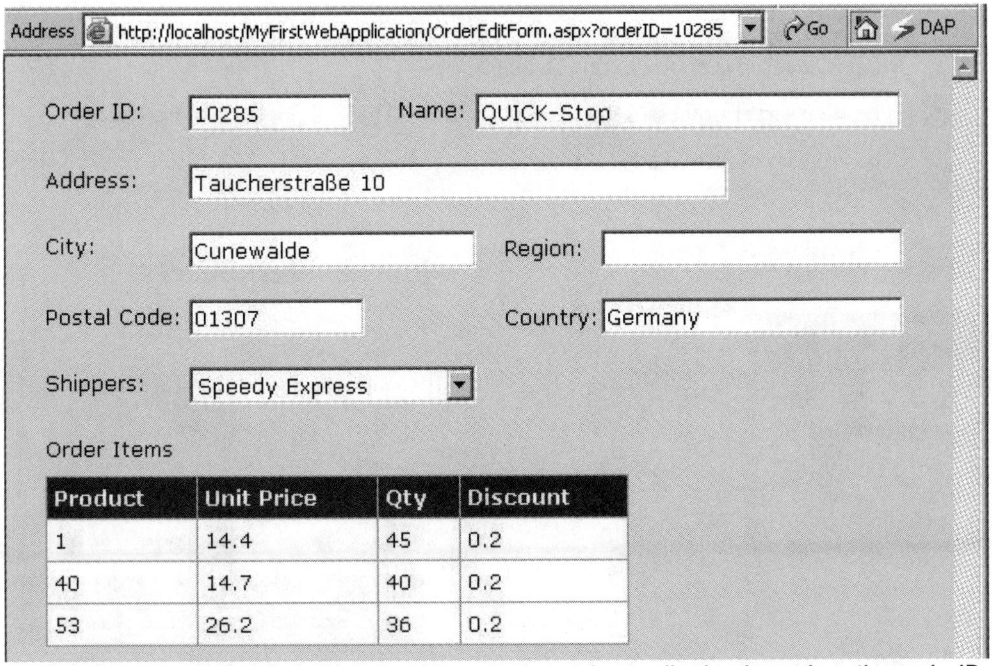

Figure 22. The Order Edit Web form knows the order to display based on the orderID parameter passed to it from the Customer Orders page.

If you take a close look at Internet Explorer's Address box at the top of Figure 22, you'll see a string "?orderID=10285" at the end of the URL. This is the order ID selected in the Customer Orders form. This parameter is passed to the Order Edit form when you click on the hyperlink label in the first column of the Order Items DataGrid. This value is also used in the Order Edit page to retrieve data from the Orders and OrderItem business objects.

A look at the flow of events

When the user clicks on an Order in the CustomerOrders form, the following occurs (see **Figure 23** also):

1. A request is sent to the Web Server for the OrderEdit Web page. In this request, an orderID parameter is passed containing the selected order ID.

2. The Web server receives the request and instantiates the OrderEdit Web page class.

3. The Web page's Page_Init event fires.

4. The Web page's Page_Load event fires. Within this event, a check is performed to determine if the page is being loaded for the first time or in response to a post back. In this case, it's the first time the page is loaded, so the Orders business object is instantiated, a DataSet containing the order returns from the Orders object, and the Web server controls are bound to the DataSet.

5. All order items are retrieved from the Order Items business object and the Order Items DataGrid is bound to this DataSet.

6. The Web server processes the page and sends HTML output back to the browser.

7. The browser renders the HTML for display to the user.

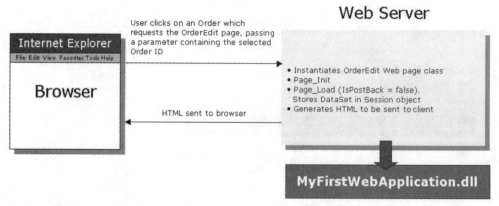

Figure 23. The diagram shows the flow of events when a user clicks on an Order in the CustomerOrders form.

Again, if you want to see what was sent back to the browser, select View | Source from the Internet Explorer menu.

Updating data

Now it's time to add updating capabilities to the Order Edit Web page. Start by adding a button to the form. In the sample code, I've added it directly below the Country text box. Set the button's (ID) property to "btnUpdate" and its Text to "Update".

Next, double-click the new Update button. This adds an event handler method named btnUpdate_Click to the Web form. Add the following code to this method.

In C#:

```
// Retrieve the original Orders DataSet from the Session object
DataSet dsOrders = (DataSet)Session["OrderDataSet"];

// Instantiate the orders business object and get the table name
Orders OrderObj = new Orders();
string OrderTable = OrderObj.TableName;
```

```
// Save the values in the Web server control to the Orders DataSet
dsOrders.Tables[OrderTable].Rows[0]["ShipName"] =
  this.txtName.Text;
dsOrders.Tables[OrderTable].Rows[0]["ShipAddress"] =
  this.txtAddress.Text;
dsOrders.Tables[OrderTable].Rows[0]["ShipCity"] =
  this.txtCity.Text;
dsOrders.Tables[OrderTable].Rows[0]["ShipRegion"] =
  this.txtRegion.Text;
dsOrders.Tables[OrderTable].Rows[0]["ShipPostalCode"] =
  this.txtPostalCode.Text;
dsOrders.Tables[OrderTable].Rows[0]["ShipCountry"] =
  this.txtCountry.Text;
dsOrders.Tables[OrderTable].Rows[0]["ShipVia"] =
  this.cboShippers.SelectedItem.Value;

// Tell the Orders business object to save the DataSet
OrderObj.SaveDataSet(dsOrders);

// Redirect back to the Customer Orders Web page
Response.Redirect("CustomerOrders.aspx");
```

And in Visual Basic .NET:

```
' Retrieve the original Orders DataSet from the Session object
Dim dsOrders As DataSet = CType(Session("OrderDataSet"), DataSet)

' Instantiate the orders business object and get the table name
Dim OrderObj As New Orders()
Dim OrderTable As String = OrderObj.TableName

' Save the values in the Web server control to the Orders DataSet
dsOrders.Tables(OrderTable).Rows(0)("ShipName") = _
    Me.txtName.Text '
dsOrders.Tables(OrderTable).Rows(0)("ShipAddress") = _
    Me.txtAddress.Text '
dsOrders.Tables(OrderTable).Rows(0)("ShipCity") = _
    Me.txtCity.Text '
dsOrders.Tables(OrderTable).Rows(0)("ShipRegion") = _
    Me.txtRegion.Text '
dsOrders.Tables(OrderTable).Rows(0)("ShipPostalCode") = _
    Me.txtPostalCode.Text '
dsOrders.Tables(OrderTable).Rows(0)("ShipCountry") = _
    Me.txtCountry.Text '
dsOrders.Tables(OrderTable).Rows(0)("ShipVia") = _
    Me.cboShippers.SelectedItem.Value '

' Tell the Orders business object to save the DataSet
OrderObj.SaveDataSet(dsOrders)

' Redirect back to the Customer Orders Web page
Response.Redirect("CustomerOrders.aspx")
```

This code retrieves the Order DataSet you persisted to the Session object earlier. Next, it retrieves values from the Web server controls and stores them in the Order DataSet. It then passes the DataSet to the Orders business object's SaveDataSet method. Afterwards, it passes control back to the Customer Orders form.

To test the Web application's new updating capabilities, compile and run the application by clicking the Run button or pressing F5. In the Customer Orders form, enter a Customer ID and click the Submit button to display all orders for the customer. Next, select an order from the Orders DataGrid, which takes you to the Order Edit page. In this page, change one or more of the values at the top of the form (i.e. the "Region"), and click the Update button. After the record is updated, control should be transferred back to the Customer Orders page.

A look at the flow of events

When the user clicks the update button on the OrderEdit form, the following occurs (see **Figure 24** also):

1. The user clicks on the Update button, raising the Click event on the browser.

2. The OrderEdit page is posted back to the Web server, including all values entered in any of the Web server controls.

3. In response, the Web server instantiates the OrderEdit Web page class.

4. The Web page's Page_Init event fires.

5. The Web page's Page_Load event fires.

6. The event handler for the Update button's Click event (btnUpdate_Click) is executed to respond to the Click event raised on the browser.

7. The btnUpdate_Click event handler code retrieves the Orders DataSet (that was stored earlier) from the Session object. It then updates the DataSet from the Web server controls and uses the Orders business object to save the DataSet.

8. The code in the btnUpdate_Click method redirects to the CustomerOrders page.

9. The Web server responds to the redirection and instantiates the CustomerOrders page class. It goes through the normal instantiation process, and then the Web server processes the page and generates HTML to send back to the client browser.

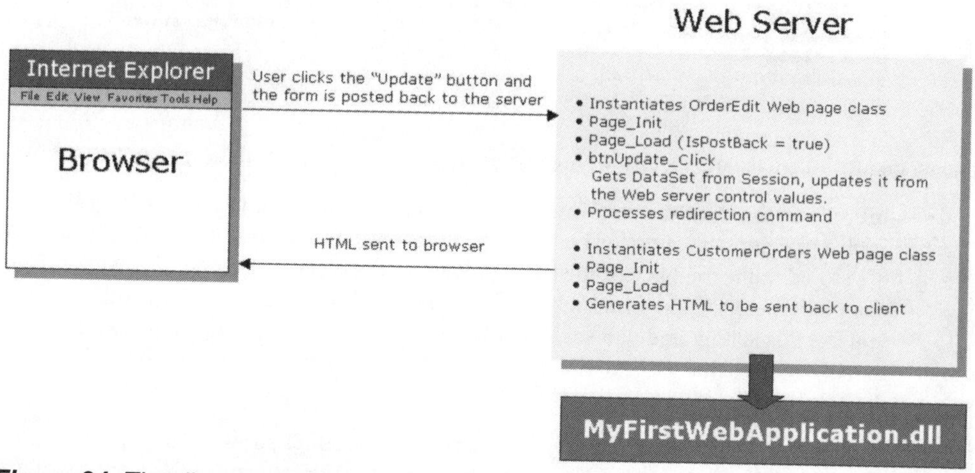

Figure 24. *The diagram shows the flow of events when the user clicks the update button on the OrderEdit form.*

Caching data and objects

In this example, you persisted the DataSet to the ASP.NET Session object. There are actually a variety of ways to cache data and objects in an ASP.NET application. The following sections describe some of these options.

The Session object

As you saw in the sample code for this chapter, the Session object gives you quick access to data and objects. However, session data is duplicated for every user connected to your Web application. This means you need to be wary of situations where you need to persist more than just a few records in a DataSet, because ASP.NET saves a unique copy of the DataSet for each user session. On the plus side, the Session object works well in Web farm and Web garden architectures.

> For more information on ASP.NET session state, see the .NET Help topic "Session State".

The web.config file

When you create a new Web Application or Web Service, VS .NET creates a web.config file for your project. Among other things, this file allows you to configure the way the Session works. The settings that control sessions are found in the <sessionState> element. Here is an example of what this element looks like:

```
<sessionState
        mode="InProc"
```

```
            stateConnectionString="tcpip=127.0.0.1:42424"
            sqlConnectionString="data source=127.0.0.1;user id=sa;password="
            cookieless="false"
            timeout="20"
/>
```

The mode attribute lets you specify where the Session object stores its data. The options are:

- InProc - In the local memory on the Web server (the default). Use this setting if your Web application has low traffic. Although this option performs the fastest because it's stored in the memory of the same process as the worker process, it consumes computer memory and with high traffic could bog down your server. In addition, if you use this setting and you scale to a Web farm, you'll need to do some extra work to make sure each user gets directed to the proper server within the farm that stores their Session data.

- StateServer - The memory of a remote server. This setting allows you to easily scale your application to a Web farm because it stores Session objects in the memory of a computer than can be accessed by all servers in the farm. However, since the session information is still stored in memory, you can again run into problems if you get high traffic on your Web site and the Session data consumes a large chunk of memory.

- SqlServer - In a SQL Server database. This is the best setting to ensure the highest scalability. This solution is scaleable because it doesn't consume memory—Session objects are stored in a SQL Server database. In addition, it's usable in a Web farm, because all servers in the farm have access to the SQL Server database.

- Off – Turns off session state

The stateConnectionString attribute specifies the server name and port where session state is stored when the mode attribute is set to "StateServer".

The sqlConnectionString attribute is used to specify the connection string for SQL Server when the mode attribute is set to "SqlServer".

The cookieless attribute lets you specify if cookies are used to maintain session state. If set to true, the session state is maintained by modifying URLs with an ID uniquely identifying the session rather than using cookies.

The timeout attribute specifies the number of minutes a session can be idle before it is abandoned.

The Application object

The Application object stores data and objects viewable from all user sessions. However, the Application Object does not work with Web farms. So, if creating the most scaleable Web application is high on your needs list, you should avoid storing state in the Application object to avoid reworking your application in the future.

The Cache object

The ASP.NET Cache object is visible across sessions (as is the Application object). It has the added ability of letting you associate duration, priority, and decay factors for any items you store in it. These settings allow the Cache object to limit the impact of cache data on the server's memory. When memory begins to fill up with cached data, the Cache object purges data based on its priority and how recently it was used. One drawback of the Cache object is it does not work with Web farms.

Using a Web Service for caching

Rather than using the Session object, you can create a custom Web Service for caching. This has an advantage over the Session object in being accessible outside the confines of IIS.

Using session-specific XML files

Another caching option allowing you to reduce the memory demands of your Web server is storing information on the server in session-specific XML files. You identify XML files with a particular session by using the Session ID. The Session ID is a unique, random string generated for each session. You retrieve this string from the Session object's SessionID property (Session.SessionID).

Protection against IIS crashes

When I was writing this chapter, I had the unfortunate experience of having my computer reboot while I was working with Visual Studio .NET on the sample Web application. This reboot caused IIS to cease functioning because it corrupted a key file—MetaBase.bin. The MetaBase.bin file stores a variety of configuration settings on versions of IIS prior to 6.0 (where it has been replaced by XML files).

If you're working with a version of IIS that uses the MetaBase.bin file, you can save yourself some headaches by making a backup of this file using the Internet Services Manager (In Windows XP, it's called Internet Information Services). You launch it from Control Panel's Administrative Tools or in Windows 2000, from the Start | Programs | Administrative Tools | Internet Services Manager menu.

If you're using Windows 2000, once the Internet Services Manager dialog appears, right-click on the server node and select Backup/Restore Configuration from the shortcut menu (**Figure 25**). If you're using Windows XP, you need to select the All Tasks option to see the Backup/Restore Configuration option.

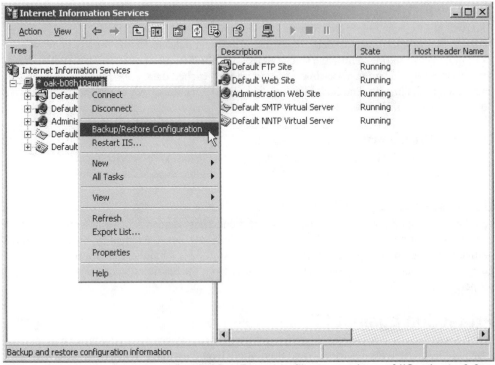

Figure 25. *Making a backup of your MetaBase.bin file on versions of IIS prior to 6.0 helps you recover from accidental reboots of your Web server machine.*

When you select this option, the Configuration Backup/Restore dialog appears (**Figure 26**). If you previously created any configuration backups, these appear in the Backups list. You can choose to Delete a backup, Restore a backup (you'd do this to recover from a fatal crash), or create a new backup.

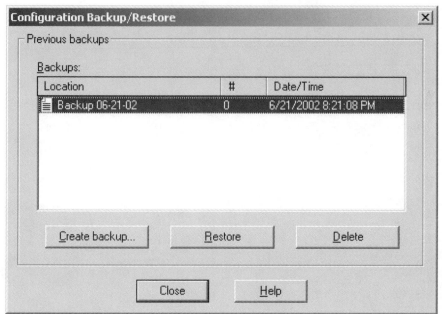

Figure 26. The Configuration Backup/Restore dialog allows you to create new backups, restore backups, or delete backups of your MetaBase.bin file.

If you click the Create backup... button, it prompts you for a Configuration backup name. Just enter a descriptive name, click the OK button, and it automatically creates a backup of your MetaBase.bin file.

Conclusion

Microsoft's .NET team has done a great job in bringing Web development to the masses, providing an environment that makes it easy to create event-driven Web Forms applications. If you create business objects for your .NET applications, you don't have to duplicate your application logic when building both a Windows Forms and Web Forms application—most of the work is done once in building business objects either type of application can use.

However, Web Forms is only half of ASP.NET—Chapter 12 introduces you to the other half—"XML Web Services".

Chapter 11
.NET XML

XML has taken the software world by storm. Everything from configuration files and databases (such as SQL Server) to Microsoft Office and Web Services have the ability to work with XML. In many ways, the .NET Framework was built with XML in mind. This chapter discusses incorporating XML into your .NET applications and also offers an overview of XML base classes for reading, writing, and manipulating XML.

Microsoft has done a good job making .NET and Visual Studio .NET great tools for working with XML. As already mentioned in Chapter 3, "Introduction to C#", you can create XML comments in your C# source code and build Comment Web pages from them. In addition to this, Visual Studio .NET has an extremely capable tool for working with XML—the XML Designer. This tool makes it easy to create XML files, schemas, and (from the schemas) ADO.NET DataSets.

In addition to design-time tools, the .NET Framework class library has an entire namespace (System.Xml) containing powerful base classes that allow you to read, write, and manipulate XML in just about every way imaginable. Before diving into these tools, I'll discuss some fundamentals of XML and direct you to some resources for learning more of the basics.

XML basics

Why should you care about XML? When you get down to it, XML is really just a new text-based data format. However, two things make XML a "big deal".

The first is every major "player" in the software and database worlds has agreed to conform to this standard. This in itself is huge because it breaks down the barriers between software systems written on diverse platforms. For example, you can pass data or other information in XML format from a Microsoft application such as Visual FoxPro or .NET to an application written in a non-Microsoft language such as Java, running on a non-Microsoft UNIX or Linux platform, and be confident that these platforms and languages have tools to easily read and manipulate your XML document.

The second reason is that XML is self-describing. Other text formats such as comma-delimited or tab-delimited files require you to create a separate word processing document describing each field. You then have to write a program to read the text file, translate the data to the proper data type, and store it in your database of choice. This can be a lot of work.

In contrast, an XML document can have a related XML schema (stored "in line" with the data or stored in a separate file) to programmatically determine the structure and content of an XML document at runtime. This means no more writing special programs to import text files into your applications.

This chapter assumes a basic, working knowledge of XML—for more information on the basic structure and syntax of XML, check out the .NET Help topics "Introduction to XML" and "XML Technology Backgrounder". Another great resource is the MSDN Online XML

Developer Center Web site (http://msdn.microsoft.com/xml/default.asp). A good book on the subject is "Inside XML" by Steven Holzner (ISBN 0735710201).

Visual FoxPro 8's new XML support

Visual FoxPro 8 has added support for XML in a hierarchical format by adding a new XMLAdapter class. This class improves Visual FoxPro's ability to interoperate with XML produced from .NET DataSets.

As mentioned in Chapter 7, "Data Access with ADO.NET", a DataSet can contain multiple DataTables and you can create relationships between these tables. VFP 8 has the ability to read hierarchical XML produced from this kind of DataSet and convert it into separate VFP cursors. In cases where the hierarchical XML does not represent a collection of related tables, but is simply a single table representing the result of a multi-table SQL Join command, then this XML is converted into a single Visual FoxPro cursor.

For details on the XMLAdapter class, check the Visual FoxPro 8 Help file.

Introducing the XML Designer

Visual Studio .NET has an XML Designer making it incredibly easy to work with XML documents and XML schemas—even if you're not an XML expert. Although you *can* create XML files and schemas using a plain text editor such as Notepad, the visual tools in the XML Designer make you far more productive. You'll also see later in this chapter how you can work with ADO.NET DataSets in the XML Designer.

The XML Designer has three different viewing modes—XML view, Schema view, and Data view. You'll see a sample of each of these views in the next section

Manually creating a new XML file and schema

The best way to fully understand how the XML Designer works is to use it. This section takes you through the steps of manually creating a new XML file and schema. In this example you will create an XML file (and an associated schema) containing a partial list of the works of Shakespeare—helping you feel superior in both the technology and literary fields. Here's an overview of the main steps:

1. Create a new, empty XML file.

2. Create a new, empty Schema file.

3. Use the designer to create the schema.

4. Associate the schema and the XML file.

5. Add data to the XML file.

6. Validate the XML data.

The following sections detail each of these steps.

Creating a new XML file

Add a new, empty XML file to your project as follows:

1. From the Project menu (located in the main menu), select Add New Item. This displays the Add New Item dialog

2. In the Templates pane, select XML File. Change the name of the XML file in the Name text box to "Shakespeare.xml", and then click the Open button.

This creates a new XML file and automatically opens it in the XML Designer. The new XML file contains only one line—the XML header:

```
<?xml version="1.0" encoding="utf-8" ?>
```

This is the XML view of the XML Designer. As you'll see later in this chapter, XML view gives you IntelliSense, word completion, member lists, and color-coding.

Creating a new schema file

Using the Visual Studio .NET XML Designer to create a schema is similar to using the Table Designer in Visual FoxPro to define the structure of a table. Follow these steps to add a new, empty XML schema file to the project:

1. From the VS .NET main menu, select Project | Add New Item. This launches the Add New Item dialog.

2. In the Templates pane, select XML Schema. Change the name of the schema file in the Name text box to "ShakespeareSchema.xsd", and then click the Open button.

This creates a new schema file and automatically opens it in the XML Designer in Schema view. The schema is blank except for the text, To start, drag objects from the Server Explorer or the Toolbox to the design surface, or right-click here. This is what you'll do in the next section.

Designing the schema

Adding elements to a schema is similar to adding fields in the Visual FoxPro Table Designer—you specify the element name and the type of data it holds. In this example, you will define three elements of a Shakespeare play—its name, category, and number of acts.

Make sure the XML schema you just created is the currently selected tab in the Visual Studio .NET IDE. Next, if your Toolbox is auto-hidden, hover your mouse pointer over the Toolbox button and select the XML Schema tab (**Figure 1**). If the Toolbox button is not visible, select View | Toolbox from the main menu or type the shortcut key sequence Ctrl+Alt+X.

Figure 1. *The XML Schema tab of the VS .NET Toolbox contains items you can drag and drop on the XML Designer to create an XML schema.*

Table 1 provides a description of each item found in the XML Schema tab.

Table 1. *This table describes all of the items in the XML Schema tab of the Toolbox.*

Item	Description
element	An XML element
attribute	An element attribute
attributeGroup	An element used to group together a set of attribute declarations to be included as a group into complex type definitions.
complexType	A complex type that can include other elements or attributes.
simpleType	A simple type that can only contain text—it can't contain other elements or have attributes.
group	An element group used to declare how elements appear in a group. A *sequence* group declares all elements appear in the specified order, a *choice* group specifies only one of the elements in the group occurs, and in an *all* group, all elements occur or none at all.
any	An element to extend the XML document with elements not specified in the schema.
anyAttribute	An attribute to extend the XML document with attributes not specified in the schema.
facet	A facet element to restrict values of XML elements and attributes. Some of the most common facets are: • enumeration – limits an element to a set of acceptable values. • length – restricts an element value to a specific length. • maxLength – restricts the maximum length of an element value. • minLength – restricts the minimum length of an element value. • pattern – restricts the contents of an XML element to the specified pattern (i.e. numbers and/or letters). • whiteSpace –specifies how whitespace characters should be treated. The options are: preserve, replace, and collapse.
key	Used to specify table columns as primary or unique keys. You need to specify keys to create relations and constraints
Relation	Allows you to specify relations between elements

Drag and drop an element from the Toolbox to the design surface. This displays a small grid on the design surface (**Figure 2**).

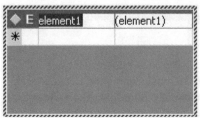

Figure 2. The element grid provides a visual tool for creating schema elements.

Change the default element name from "element1" to "ShakespearePlay", and then tab to the second column. The text "(ShakespearePlay)" automatically appears in the second column. Don't change the value of this column (the combo box in this column lists a variety of data types you can specify for elements). Press the TAB key twice to navigate from the first row to the center cell of the second row and Type "Name" in this column. Tab to the third column, open the combo box, and take a quick look at the list of available data types (**Figure 3**). Close the combo box, leaving "string" as the selected item.

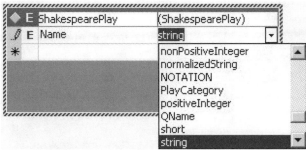

Figure 3. You can select the desired data type of a schema element from a combo box in the XML Designer.

Press the TAB key twice to go to the second column of the third row. Type "Category" in this cell and accept "string" as the default data type. Add one more element to the grid named "NumberOfActs" and set its type to "short".

To see the results of what you have created so far, click on the XML tab at the bottom left of the XML Designer. This changes the designer to XML view and displays the "behind-the-scenes" raw XML. Within the <xs:schema> element you can see the ShakespearePlay element with Name, Category, and NumberOfActs child elements:

```
<xs:element name="ShakespearePlay">
  <xs:complexType>
     <xs:sequence>
         <xs:element name="Name" type="xs:string" />
         <xs:element name="Category" type="xs:string" />
         <xs:element name="NumberOfActs" type="xs:short" />
```

```
      </xs:sequence>
   </xs:complexType>
</xs:element>
```

To save your changes so far, select File | Save ShakespeareSchema.xsd from the main menu or press Ctrl+S.

Next, create a parent element for ShakespearePlay called "WorksOfShakespeare". This element is the root node and allows you to have multiple ShakespearePlay records in your XML file belonging to the WorksOfShakespeare element. To create this new parent element, go back to Schema view by clicking the Schema tab at the bottom left of the XML Designer.

Drag another "element" from the Toolbox onto the design surface. Change the default name from "element1" to "WorksOfShakespeare". When you press TAB, "(WorksOfShakespeare)" is displayed in the data type column; accept this default.

To associate the ShakespearePlay element with the WorksOfShakespeare element, simply drag and drop the ShakespearePlay grid onto the WorksOfShakespeare grid (it's easiest to grab the design grid by clicking on the diamond in the upper left corner). The XML Designer displays a line between the two design grids representing the parent-child relationship of the data (**Figure 4**). If you later want to delete this relationship, you do so by manually editing the XML in the XML tab of the designer.

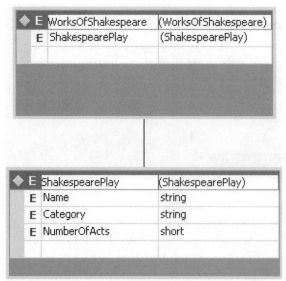

Figure 4. You can create hierarchical relationships between data by dragging and dropping the design grid containing the child data onto the parent grid.

> *You can create a relationship between two elements by right-clicking on one of the elements and selecting Add | New Relation… from the shortcut menu. This launches the Edit Relation dialog allowing you to set a variety of properties defining the relationship.*

Next, you need to specify how many ShakespearePlay elements can be added to the WorksOfShakespeare element. To do this, select the ShakespearePlay grid by clicking on the diamond in the upper left corner. Go to the Properties Window and set the maxOccurs property to "unbounded".

Creating a custom data type

In the previous section, you specified the data type of the Category element as "string". This indicates that when you create the actual XML data, you can set any string value for the play category. In reality, there are really only a few different categories of Shakespeare plays— Comedy, History, Tragedy, and Romance. To limit the categories to these values, you create a new custom data type called PlayCategory.

Drag and drop a simpleType from the Toolbox onto the XML Designer. This displays another grid on the design surface (**Figure 5**). Change the default name from "simpleType1" to "PlayCategory" and leave "string" as the data type.

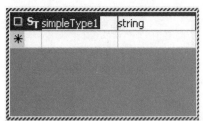

Figure 5. You can define your own custom data types in the XML Designer

Tab to the first column in the second row of the design grid. From the combo box in this cell select the only item available—facet (**Figure 6**). You can only use facets to build simple types, because simple types cannot include elements or attributes.

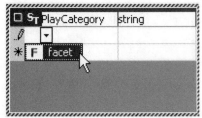

Figure 6. Facets are used to build simple type elements

Press the TAB key again to go to the second column in the second row. Open the combo box and take a quick look at the available properties, but leave the default "enumeration" selected.

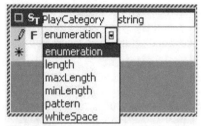

Figure 7*. You can specify facet properties such as enumeration, length, maxLength, and minLength.*

Next, Tab to the second column and enter "Comedy" as the first enumeration value. Add three more facet enumerations to the grid with the values "History", "Tragedy", and "Romance". When you're done, your design grid should look like the grid shown in **Figure 8**. You have now defined all of the possible Shakespearean play categories.

	S_T PlayCategory	string
F	enumeration	Comedy
F	enumeration	History
F	enumeration	Tragedy
F	enumeration	Romance

Figure 8*. You can create custom enumeration types to limit the data values that can be entered in a particular XML element.*

Now go back to the design grid containing the ShakespearePlay element and change the data type of Category from "string" to "PlayCategory" (which now appears in the data type combo box). At this point, save your changes by clicking the Save toolbar button or by typing Ctrl+S. To see what the XML for the schema looks like now, click the XML tab at the bottom left of the XML Designer and you should see the following:

```
<?xml version="1.0" encoding="utf-8" ?>
<xs:schema id="ShakespeareSchema"
targetNamespace="http://tempuri.org/ShakespeareSchema.xsd"
elementFormDefault="qualified" xmlns="http://tempuri.org/ShakespeareSchema.xsd"
xmlns:mstns="http://tempuri.org/ShakespeareSchema.xsd"
xmlns:xs="http://www.w3.org/2001/XMLSchema">
  <xs:simpleType name="PlayCategory">
    <xs:restriction base="xs:string">
      <xs:enumeration value="Comedy" />
      <xs:enumeration value="History" />
      <xs:enumeration value="Tragedy" />
      <xs:enumeration value="Romance" />
    </xs:restriction>
  </xs:simpleType>
  <xs:element name="WorksOfShakespeare">
    <xs:complexType>
      <xs:sequence>
        <xs:element name="ShakespearePlay" maxOccurs="unbounded">
```

```
            <xs:complexType>
                    <xs:sequence>
                            <xs:element name="Name" type="xs:string" />
                            <xs:element name="Category" type="PlayCategory"
/>
                            <xs:element name="NumberOfActs" type="xs:short"
/>
                    </xs:sequence>
            </xs:complexType>
      </xs:element>
   </xs:sequence>
 </xs:complexType>
 </xs:element>
</xs:schema>
```

Associating the schema with the XML file

Now it's time to associate the XML file you created earlier with this new XML schema. To do this, double-click the Shakespeare.xml file in the Solution Explorer (or select the Shakespeare.xml tab in the IDE). Next, go to the Properties Window and click the column to the right of the targetSchema property. Select "http://tempuri.org/ShakespeareSchema.xsd" from the combo box (**Figure 9**).

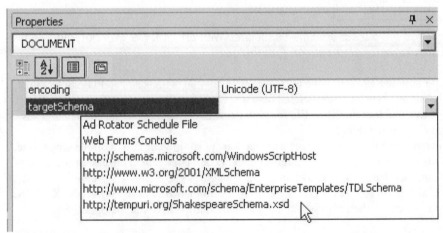

Figure 9. You associate an XML file with a schema by specifying a schema in the targetSchema property of the XML file.

This automatically adds the following WorksOfShakespeare element that references the ShakespeareSchema:

```
<WorksOfShakespeare xmlns="http://tempuri.org/ShakespeareSchema.xsd">

</WorksOfShakespeare>
```

As you can see in this XML element, when you create a new schema, Visual Studio .NET creates a default namespace "http://tempuri.org/" (read this as "temp URI"). You can replace this URI with your own URI that includes your company's web site URL. For example:

```
<WorksOfShakespeare xmlns="http://www.oakleafsd.com/ShakespeareSchema.xsd">
```

Adding data to the XML file

This section shows two different ways you can manually add data to the XML file.

The first way is adding data in XML view mode. Position your cursor between the opening and closing tags of the <WorksOfShakespeare> element in the Shakespeare.xml file. Next, press the TAB key for indentation and type the left angled bracket (<). This automatically displays a list of elements available in this context based on the ShakespeareSchema file (**Figure 10**).

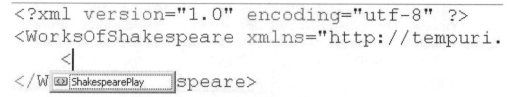

Figure 10. If you have a schema file associated with an XML file, you get IntelliSense in the XML Designer for elements and attributes

At this point in the XML file, the only element available is ShakespearePlay. Select this item from the list and type the right-angled bracket (>). The </ShakespearePlay> end tag is automatically inserted into the XML file for you. Press ENTER to move the end tag to a new line directly below the start tag.

Add an empty line between the start and end tags, position your cursor on the empty line, and press TAB to indent. Next, type the left-angled bracket (<) again. You should see a list of Category, Name, and NumberOfActs elements. Select the Name element from the list and type the right-angled bracket (>). The </Name> end tag is automatically inserted into the XML file for you. Type the text "Othello" (without the quotation marks) between the opening and closing Name tags.

Press the END key and then the ENTER key to go to the next line. Type the left-angled bracket again (<), but this time select the Category element and enter "Tragedy" as the category. Next add a NumberOfActs element and for the data between the tags, enter "5". When you're done, your XML file should look like this:

```
<?xml version="1.0" encoding="utf-8" ?>
<ShakespearePlay xmlns="http://tempuri.org/ShakespeareSchema.xsd">
  <Name>Othello</Name>
  <Category>Tragedy</Category>
  <NumberOfActs>5</NumberOfActs>
</ShakespearePlay>
```

To see this in Data view, click the Data tab at the bottom of the XML Designer. The Data view consists of two areas—the Data Tables pane on the left and the Data pane on the right (**Figure 11**).

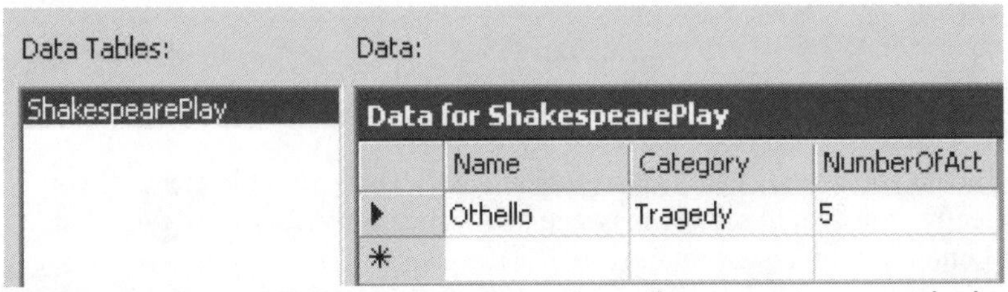

Data Tables:	Data:		
ShakespearePlay	**Data for ShakespearePlay**		
	Name	Category	NumberOfAct
	Othello	Tragedy	5

Figure 11. The XML Designer's Data view allows you to use a design grid to easily add data to an XML file.

The Data Tables pane displays all tables in the XML file. When you select a table, its associated data displays in the Data pane. What's even better is you can use this data grid for adding data to the XML file! This is the second way you can add data to an XML file from the XML Designer.

For example, add the following records to the grid (all of Shakespeare's plays have five acts—something you can casually mention to impress your friends at your next "tea and crumpets" party):

Name	Category	NumberOfActs
The Comedy of Errors	Comedy	5
Henry the Fifth	History	5
The Tempest	Romance	5

To see the XML generated by the records you added to the grid, select the XML tab at the bottom left of the XML Designer. Your XML file should look like this:

```
<?xml version="1.0" encoding="utf-8" ?>
<WorksOfShakespeare xmlns="http://tempuri.org/ShakespeareSchema.xsd">
  <ShakespearePlay>
      <Name>Othello</Name>
      <Category>Tragedy</Category>
      <NumberOfActs>5</NumberOfActs>
  </ShakespearePlay>
  <ShakespearePlay>
      <Name>The Comedy of Errors</Name>
      <Category>Comedy</Category>
      <NumberOfActs>5</NumberOfActs>
  </ShakespearePlay>
  <ShakespearePlay>
      <Name>Henry the Fifth</Name>
      <Category>History</Category>
      <NumberOfActs>5</NumberOfActs>
  </ShakespearePlay>
```

```
<ShakespearePlay>
    <Name>The Tempest</Name>
    <Category>Romance</Category>
    <NumberOfActs>5</NumberOfActs>
</ShakespearePlay>
</WorksOfShakespeare>
```

Validating XML data

To validate the XML data you added, select XML | Validate XML Data from the menu. If you entered the data correctly, you should see the message "No validation errors were found" in the status bar at the bottom left of Visual Studio .NET IDE.

To check if your enumeration limiting the values of the Category element is working properly, change the value of any category element to "Romantic Comedy", which is an invalid value. When you select XML | Validate XML Data again, you should get an error in the Task List complaining "The 'http://tempuri.org/ShakespeareSchema.xsd:Category' element has an invalid value according to its data type".

To get rid of this error, simply restore the original value of the category element, save changes, and then run the XML validation again.

Creating ADO.NET Typed DataSets from an XML schema

This section assumes you have read Chapter7, "Data Access with ADO.NET", which explains what DataSets are and how they are used in .NET applications.

There are two types of DataSets—typed and untyped. The difference is simple—a typed DataSet has an associated XML schema and an untyped DataSet does not. A typed DataSet is a subclass of the .NET DataSet base class. It supplies methods and properties to access data in a type-safe way rather than iterating through collections to get to the data you want, which is much more convenient. For more information on typed and untyped DataSets see the .NET Help topic "Introduction to DataSets".

Adding a new DataSet to the project

To add a new DataSet to your project, do the following:

1. Select Project | Add New Item from the main menu to display the Add New Item dialog.

2. In the Templates pane, select Data Set. Change the default name of the DataSet in the Name text box to "ClientProjects.xsd" and click the Open button.

This creates a new XML schema file named ClientProjects.xsd and automatically opens it in the XML Designer in Schema view. The schema is blank except for the text, To start, drag objects from the Server Explorer or the Toolbox to the design surface, or right-click here. This schema file is used to define the structure of the DataSet.

Another new code file named ClientProjects.cs (if you're working with C#) or ClientProjects.vb (if you're working with Visual Basic .NET) is also added to the project. To see this file, click the Show All Files icon button in the Solution Explorer and expand the ClientProjects.xsd node (**Figure 12**).

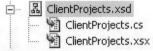

Figure 12. *When you add a DataSet to a project, VS .NET adds a schema file used to define the structure of the DataSet as well as a code file containing the class definition of the DataSet.*

This code file contains the actual class definition for the new ClientProjects DataSet, which can be instantiated when finished and used to access and manipulate the specified data. The ClientProjects.xsd file is the schema you will now use to define the structure of the DataSet (the .xsx file is a VS .NET designer layout file that you can ignore).

Adding tables to the DataSet

In this section you will add elements to the schema to represent tables and fields in a DataSet. First, make sure that you have the ClientProjects.xsd tab selected in the IDE, and then follow these steps:

1. Drag and drop an element from the Toolbox onto the schema design surface.

2. Change the default name from "element1" to "Client". This represents the Client table and next you will define elements to represent fields in the table.

3. Tab to the second column of the second row. Type the string "ClientID" in this column and press the Tab key. This displays the default data type "string" in the third column; accept this default.

4. Add the additional elements as shown in **Figure 13** for the Client table.

5. Drag and drop a second element from the Toolbox onto the schema design surface.

6. Change the default name from "element1" to "Project". This represents the Project table.

7. Add the additional elements as shown in Figure 13 for the Project table and save changes.

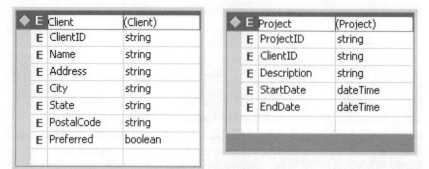

Figure 13. You can create DataSet tables in the XML Designer's Schema view.

Creating primary keys

To create a primary key in the Client table:

1. Select the ClientID row in the Client design grid by clicking to the left of the "E". Right-click on the column and select Add | New Key... from the shortcut menu. This launches the Edit Key dialog (**Figure 14**).

2. Change the name of the key to "ClientIDKey".

3. Make sure the Element combo box has the "Client" table selected and the Fields combo box has the "ClientID" field selected.

4. Select the Dataset primary key check box and click OK. After the dialog closes, a key icon displays next to the ClientID element indicating it has an associated key.

5. Create a primary key named "ProjectIDKey" for the ProjectID field in the Project table in the same way you created a key on the ClientID field in the Client table.

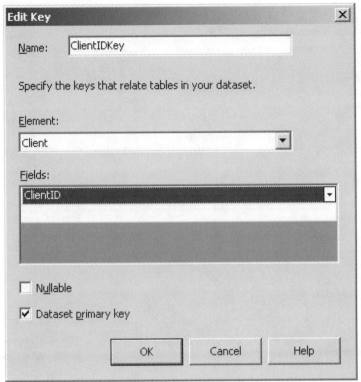

Figure 14. *The Edit Key dialog allows you to create keys on fields in tables.*

Creating a relationship between the tables

To create a relationship between the Project and Client tables:

1. Right-click anywhere on the Project table and select Add | New Relation... from the shortcut menu to launch the Edit Relation dialog (**Figure 15**).

2. The default settings shown in the dialog should all be correct. For example, the default relation Name should be "ClientProject". The Parent element should be set to "Client" and the Child element to "Project". Make sure your dialog has the same settings as that dialog shown in Figure 15.

3. Click OK to save the relation.

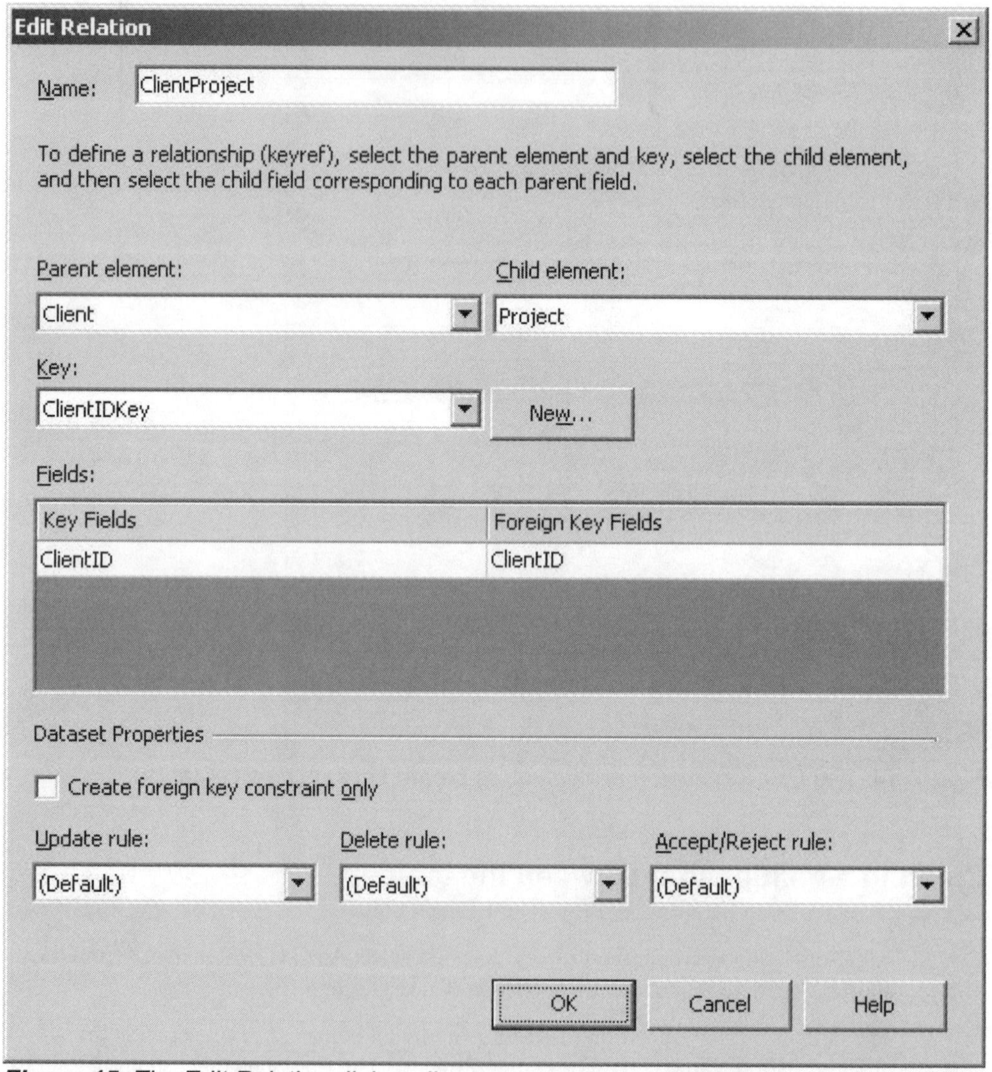

Figure 15. *The Edit Relation dialog allows you to create relationships between tables in a DataSet.*

When the Edit Relation dialog saves the relation, it displays a relationship link between the Client and Project tables (**Figure 16**).

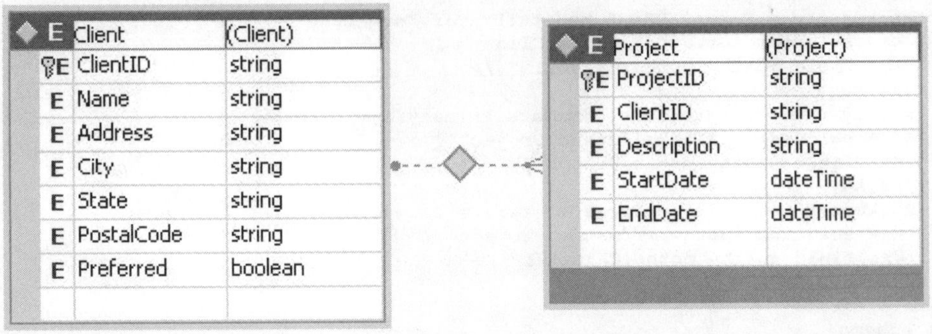

Figure 16. *The XML Designer shows key fields and relationships between tables in a DataSet.*

You can examine the behind-the-scenes XML schema by clicking the XML tab at the bottom of the Designer. Your XML schema should look as follows:

```
<?xml version="1.0" encoding="utf-8" ?>
<xs:schema id="ClientProjects"
targetNamespace="http://tempuri.org/ClientProjects.xsd"
elementFormDefault="qualified" attributeFormDefault="qualified"
xmlns="http://tempuri.org/ClientProjects.xsd"
xmlns:mstns="http://tempuri.org/ClientProjects.xsd"
xmlns:xs="http://www.w3.org/2001/XMLSchema" xmlns:msdata="urn:schemas-
microsoft-com:xml-msdata">
  <xs:element name="ClientProjects" msdata:IsDataSet="true">
    <xs:complexType>
      <xs:choice maxOccurs="unbounded">
        <xs:element name="Client">
          <xs:complexType>
            <xs:sequence>
              <xs:element name="ClientID" type="xs:string" minOccurs="0" />
              <xs:element name="Name" type="xs:string" minOccurs="0" />
              <xs:element name="Address" type="xs:string" minOccurs="0" />
              <xs:element name="City" type="xs:string" minOccurs="0" />
              <xs:element name="State" type="xs:string" minOccurs="0" />
              <xs:element name="PostalCode" type="xs:string" minOccurs="0" />
              <xs:element name="Preferred" type="xs:boolean" minOccurs="0" />
            </xs:sequence>
          </xs:complexType>
        </xs:element>
        <xs:element name="Project">
          <xs:complexType>
            <xs:sequence>
              <xs:element name="ProjectID" type="xs:string" minOccurs="0" />
              <xs:element name="ClientID" type="xs:string" minOccurs="0" />
              <xs:element name="Description" type="xs:string" minOccurs="0" />
              <xs:element name="StartDate" type="xs:dateTime" minOccurs="0" />
              <xs:element name="EndDate" type="xs:dateTime" minOccurs="0" />
            </xs:sequence>
          </xs:complexType>
        </xs:element>
      </xs:choice>
```

```
    </xs:complexType>
    <xs:key name="ClientIDKey" msdata:PrimaryKey="true">
      <xs:selector xpath=".//mstns:Client" />
      <xs:field xpath="mstns:ClientID" />
    </xs:key>
    <xs:key name="ProjectIDKey" msdata:PrimaryKey="true">
      <xs:selector xpath=".//mstns:Project" />
      <xs:field xpath="mstns:ProjectID" />
    </xs:key>
    <xs:keyref name="ClientProject" refer="ClientIDKey">
      <xs:selector xpath=".//mstns:Project" />
      <xs:field xpath="mstns:ClientID" />
    </xs:keyref>
  </xs:element>
</xs:schema>
```

Notice the Client and Project elements are peers and both are direct children of the ClientProject element, which represents the DataSet. This is because both the Client and Project elements represent a table in the DataSet. Also, notice the ClientIDKey and ProjectIDKey elements are direct children of the ClientProject DataSet allowing the key to control unique values throughout the DataSet.

Creating XML schemas and DataSets from existing data

In the previous sections you learned how to create XML schemas and DataSets from scratch. The following steps show you how to create them from existing data, using the SQL Server Northwind database Products table.

1. In the Solution Explorer, right-click on the project you want to add the XML schema to, and select Add | Add New Item from the shortcut menu. This displays the Add New Item dialog.

2. In the Add New Item dialog, select DataSet in the Templates pane. Change the Name of the DataSet schema to "Products.xsd".

3. Click the Open button. This adds a new schema file named Products.xsd to your project as well as a new DataSet class stored in the Products.cs (C#) or Products.vb (Visual Basic .NET) file.

4. In the Server Explorer, expand the Data Connections node, and then expand the node for the connection to the Northwind database. If the Server Explorer is not visible, select View | Server Explorer from the main menu.

5. Expand the Tables node (**Figure 17**). You can also expand the Views or Stored Procedure node if you want to create a DataSet from these instead.

6. Drag and drop the Products table onto the schema design surface. If you only want a subset of fields to appear in the schema, expand the Products node, select the desired fields, and drop them on the schema.

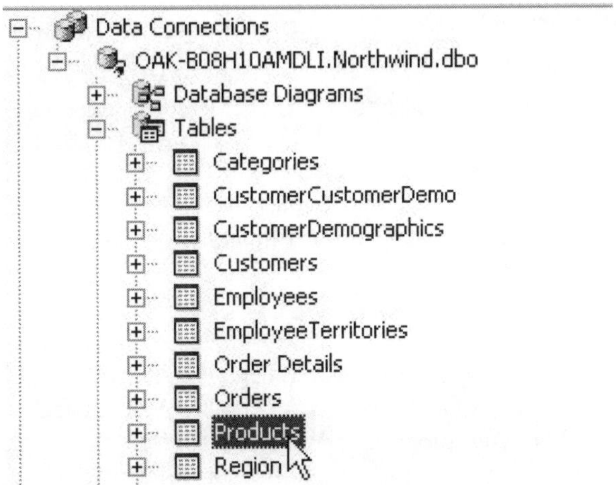

Figure 17. You can drag and drop tables, views, or stored procedures onto the XML Designer in Schema view to create a schema and DataSet from existing data.

After dropping the Products table on the Schema Designer, Visual Studio .NET creates a schema file and associated DataSet from the table.

File types in the XML Designer

The XML Designer allows you to edit a wide variety of XML-based files. **Table 2** lists the different viewing modes of the XML Designer and the types of files supported in each mode. Of particular interest to Visual FoxPro developers is the Data mode where you can view XML data in a data grid, much like VFP's Browse window.

Table 2. This table lists the three XML Designer viewing modes and the files supported in each mode.

Viewing mode	File Types
XML mode – Edit XML in a text-editing window with IntelliSense, word completion, member lists, and color coding	.xml – XML files .xsd – XML schema .xslt – Extensible Stylesheet Language (XSL) Transformations .wsdl – Web Services Description Language document .resx – Resource files .tdl – Template Description Language files .wsf – Windows Script Host .hta – HTML Application file .disco – XML Web Service static discovery file .vsdisco – XML Web Service dynamic discovery file .config – Application Configuration file
Schema mode – Create and edit XML schemas and ADO.NET DataSets	.xsd
Data mode – Modify XML data files in a structured data grid.	.xml

The next few sections provide an overview of the XML Designer's viewing modes. After that you will see practical examples demonstrating how to use the XML Designer in each of these modes.

XML in the .NET Framework

The System.Xml namespace contains dozens of classes that allow you to programmatically work with XML. This section gives you an overview of some of the primary classes to show you the functionality available to your .NET applications.

Reading XML with the XmlTextReader

The XmlTextReader class provides fast, forward-only access to XML data. It can read XML from a file, a stream, or TextReader. A stream is an object used to read data from an outside source into your program and to write data from your program to an outside source—that source can be as diverse as a file, a network connection, or an area of memory. A TextReader is an object that can read a sequential series of characters. The example below shows you how to read XML from a file.

The first step involves loading the XML file into the XmlTextReader object. This is easily done by instantiating an XmlTextReader object and passing the name of the XML document in the class constructor. For example:

In C#:

```
XmlTextReader ReadXml = new XmlTextReader("..\\..\\chapters.xml");
```

And in Visual Basic .NET:

```
Dim ReadXml As New XmlTextReader("..\..\chapters.xml")
```

There are a variety of methods available for traversing the XML document. **Table 3** lists a few of the more common methods.

Table 3. This table lists commonly used methods of the XmlTextReader class

XmlTextReader method	Description
Read	Reads the next node from the stream.
ReadStartElement	Checks that the current node is an element and advances to the next. Optionally, you can specify an element name to verify that the current node is an element with the specified name.
ReadEndElement	Checks that the current node is an end tag and advances to the next node.
ReadElementString	Returns the data of the current node and advances to the next node.

To show the context where these methods can be used, here is an example using an XmlTextReader to traverse the Chapters.xml file (one of the XML files you can find in the sample source code for this book) and display its contents in a message box.

In C#:

```
string ChapterList = "", ChapterID="", ChapterTitle="";

// Open the text file in the XML reader
XmlTextReader ReadXml = new XmlTextReader("..\\..\\chapters.xml");

// Read the root node of the file
ReadXml.ReadStartElement("Book");
while (true)
{
  // Read the next chapter starting element
  ReadXml.ReadStartElement("chapter");
  // Read the chapter's child id element
  ChapterID = ReadXml.ReadElementString();
  // Read the chapter's child title element
  ChapterTitle = ReadXml.ReadElementString();
  ChapterList += ChapterID + " - " + ChapterTitle + "\n";
  // Read the chapter ending element
  ReadXml.ReadEndElement();
  // Move to the next node. If it's not a chapter element, exit
  ReadXml.Read();
  if (ReadXml.Name != "chapter")
  {
      break;
  }
}
// Close the XML document
ReadXml.Close();
// Display the chapter list
MessageBox.Show(ChapterList,"XmlTextReader");
```

And in Visual Basic .NET:

```
Dim ChapterList As String = ""
Dim ChapterID As String = ""
Dim ChapterTitle As String = ""

' Open the text file in the XML reader
Dim ReadXml As New XmlTextReader("..\..\chapters.xml")

' Read the root node of the file
ReadXml.ReadStartElement("Book")

While True
    ' Read the next chapter starting element
    ReadXml.ReadStartElement("chapter")
    ' Read the chapter's child id element
    ChapterID = ReadXml.ReadElementString()
    ' Read the chapter's child title element
    ChapterTitle = ReadXml.ReadElementString()
    ChapterList += ChapterID + " - " + ChapterTitle + ControlChars.Lf
    ' Read the chapter ending element
    ReadXml.ReadEndElement()
    ' Move to the next node. If it's not a chapter element, exit
    ReadXml.Read()
    If ReadXml.Name <> "chapter" Then
      Exit While
```

```
    End If
End While

' Close the XML document
ReadXml.Close()
' Display the chapter list
MessageBox.Show(ChapterList, "XmlTextReader")
```

This code instantiates an XmlTextReader and calls its ReadStartElement method to read the "Book" root node and advance to the first "chapter" starting element. In the `while` loop, ReadStartElement is used to read the starting "chapter" element and advance to the next node. The ReadElementString method is used to read the chapter id and title, automatically advancing to the next node with each call. The call to ReadEndElement reads the ending "chapter" element and advances to the next node. The call to the Read method checks if the current node is *not* a "chapter" node, and if it's not, the `while` loop is exited.

For more information on the properties, methods and events of the XmlTextReader class, see the .NET Help topic "XmlTextReader Members".

Writing XML with the XmlTextWriter

The XmlTextWriter class is useful for programmatically creating an XML document. XmlTextWriter offers fast, forward-only generation of XML. This means, you can use this class to create a new XML document, but not to append XML to an existing document, because the XmlTextWriter overwrites the original contents of the document. For editing capabilities, you need to use the .NET XML DOM. For details, see the "The XML Document Object Model (DOM)" section later in this chapter.

This section will show you how to create a new XML file using the XmlTextWriter class. The first step is identifying the document where the XML is written. This can be done by instantiating an instance of the XmlTextWriter class and passing the name of the XML document in the constructor.

Here is the code in C#:

```
XmlTextWriter WriteXml = new XmlTextWriter("TestWrite.xml",null);
```

And in Visual Basic .NET:

```
Dim WriteXml As New XmlTextWriter("TestWrite.xml", Nothing)
```

There are a variety of methods available for writing XML. **Table 4** lists a few of the more common methods.

Table 4. This table lists commonly used methods of the XmlTextWriter class

XmlTextReader method	Description
WriteStartDocument	Writes the XML declaration.
WriteEndDocument	Closes any elements or attributes that have not been closed yet (no ending tags), and then puts the writer back in the Start state.
WriteComment	Writes out an XML comment containing the specified text.
WriteStartElement	Writes out the specified start tag.
WriteEndElement	Closes the last open element.
WriteAttributeString	Writes an attribute with the specified value to the last element start tag.
WriteElementString	Writes out the specified element and element data.
Close	Closes the stream.

To show the context where these methods can be used, here is an example that uses an XmlTextWriter to create an XML file named TestWrite.xml containing a small part of my family tree. My father is the parent node and my siblings are all child nodes (I couldn't resist the pun).

In C#:

```csharp
XmlTextWriter WriteXml = new XmlTextWriter("TestWrite.xml",null);

// Specify the XML formatting
WriteXml.Formatting = Formatting.Indented;
WriteXml.Indentation = 3;
WriteXml.IndentChar = ' ';

// Write the XML declaration
WriteXml.WriteStartDocument(false);

// Write an XML comment
WriteXml.WriteComment("Generated by the XmlTextWriterDemo class");

// Write the root node
WriteXml.WriteStartElement("McNeishSiblings");

// Write an attribute to the root node
WriteXml.WriteAttributeString("father","Phillip William McNeish, Sr.");

// Write sibling nodes
WriteXml.WriteElementString("sibling","Linda Lee");
WriteXml.WriteElementString("sibling","Phillip William, Jr.");
WriteXml.WriteElementString("sibling","Kevin James");
WriteXml.WriteElementString("sibling","Penny Ann");
WriteXml.WriteElementString("sibling","Terri Lynn");
WriteXml.WriteElementString("sibling","Wendy Gale");
WriteXml.WriteElementString("sibling","Matthew William");

// Write the root node ending
WriteXml.WriteEndElement();

// Close the XML document
WriteXml.Close();
```

And in Visual Basic .NET:

```
Dim WriteXml As New XmlTextWriter("TestWrite.xml", Nothing)

' Specify the XML formatting
WriteXml.Formatting = Formatting.Indented
WriteXml.Indentation = 3
WriteXml.IndentChar = " "

' Write the XML declaration
WriteXml.WriteStartDocument(False)

' Write an XML comment
WriteXml.WriteComment("Generated by the XmlTextWriterDemo class")

' Write the root node
WriteXml.WriteStartElement("McNeishSiblings")

' Write an attribute to the root node
WriteXml.WriteAttributeString("father", "Phillip William McNeish, Sr.")

' Write sibling nodes
WriteXml.WriteElementString("sibling", "Linda Lee")
WriteXml.WriteElementString("sibling", "Phillip William, Jr.")
WriteXml.WriteElementString("sibling", "Kevin James")
WriteXml.WriteElementString("sibling", "Penny Ann")
WriteXml.WriteElementString("sibling", "Terri Lynn")
WriteXml.WriteElementString("sibling", "Wendy Gale")
WriteXml.WriteElementString("sibling", "Matthew William")

' Write the root node ending
WriteXml.WriteEndElement()

' Close the XML document
WriteXml.Close()
```

In this code, you first instantiate the XmlTextWriter, passing the name of the XML file, TestWrite.xml. Next, set formatting properties on the writer, specifically to create XML with an indentation of 3 spaces. The WriteStartDocument method is used to write the XML declaration (i.e. <?xml version="1.0" standalone="no" ?>). Next, a comment is written to the XML file using the WriteComment method. The WriteStartElement method is used to create the opening tag of the root node, and WriteAttributeString is used to add an attribute to the root node. WriteElementString is called multiple times to add an element for each of my siblings. Finally, the WriteEndElement method is called to write the root node element ending and Close is called to close the stream.

Here is what the resulting XML file looks like:

```
<?xml version="1.0" standalone="no"?>
<!--Generated by the XmlTextWriterDemo class-->
<McNeishSiblings father="Phillip William McNeish, Sr.">
   <sibling>Linda Lee</sibling>
   <sibling>Phillip William, Jr.</sibling>
   <sibling>Kevin James</sibling>
   <sibling>Terri Lynn</sibling>
   <sibling>Wendy Gale</sibling>
   <sibling>Matthew William</sibling>
</McNeishSiblings>
```

For more information on the available properties, events and methods of the XmlTextWriter class, see the .NET Help topic "XmlTextWriter Members".

XSLT Transformation

XSLT (eXtensible Style Sheet Transforms) is a language that allows you to transform an XML document into another document with a different structure or format. For example, you can transform an XML document into an HTML document for display or into an XML document containing a subset of the original XML data. For more information on XSLT, see the .NET Help topic "XSLT Fundamentals".

An XSLT file contains transformations that are applied against a file. The XSLT file can be applied to an XML document by an XSLT processor. The .NET XslTransform class located in the System.Xml namespace is such a processor.

In this section, you will create an XSLT file that transforms the Shakespeare.xml file you created earlier in this chapter. The first step involves adding a new XSLT file to your project.

1. Right-click on the project and select Add | Add New Item... from the shortcut menu. This launches the Add New Item dialog

2. In the Templates pane, select XSLT File. Change the Name of the XSLT file to "Shakespeare.xslt" and click the Open button.

This adds a new XSLT file to your project and opens it in the XML Designer. This file contains the following XML, where the <stylesheet> tags mark the beginning and end of the style sheet in the XSLT file:

```
<?xml version="1.0" encoding="UTF-8" ?>
<stylesheet version="1.0" xmlns="http://www.w3.org/1999/XSL/Transform">
</stylesheet>
```

Using the XML Designer, manually enter the following into the Shakespeare.xslt file:

```
<?xml version="1.0" encoding="UTF-8" ?>
<xsl:stylesheet version="1.0" xmlns:xsl="http://www.w3.org/1999/XSL/Transform">
   <xsl:template match="/">
   <HTML>
      <TITLE>Partial List of Shakespeare's Works</TITLE>
      <BODY>
         <TABLE BORDER="1">
            <TR>
```

```
                <TD><B>Title</B></TD>
                <TD><B>Category</B></TD>
                <TD><B>Acts</B></TD>
            </TR>
            <xsl:for-each select="WorksOfShakespeare/ShakespearePlay">
                <TR>
                    <TD><xsl:value-of select="Name" /></TD>
                    <TD><xsl:value-of select="Category" /></TD>
                    <TD><xsl:value-of select="NumberOfActs" /></TD>
                </TR>
            </xsl:for-each>
        </TABLE>
    </BODY>
  </HTML>
 </xsl:template>
</xsl:stylesheet>
```

This file contains a mix of HTML (<TITLE>, <BODY>, <TABLE>) that creates a table with three columns (Title, Category, and Acts), as well as XSLT directives that extract data from the associated XML file and display it in the HTML page.

The text, <xsl: template match="/"> specifies the nodes where the template is applied. In this case, match="/" specifies it is applied to the root node. The <xsl:for-each select="WorksOfShakespeare/ShakespearePlay"> text specifies that a table row (<TR>) is created for each <ShakespearePlay> element found in the XML file that is a child element of the <WorksOfShakespeare> element.

The three xsl:value-of text statements select the values of the <Name>, <Category>, and <NumberOfActs> elements and place them in cells of the table.

Using the XslTransform class

Now that you have an XML file and an associated XSLT file, you can use the .NET XslTransform class to apply the transformation file to the XML file and display the result.

Here's the code in C#:

```
XslTransform XslTrans = new XslTransform();
string OutputFile = "TransformOutput.html";

// Load the XSLT file
XslTrans.Load("..\\..\\Shakespeare.xslt");

// Transform the XML file and output it to the specified HTML file
XslTrans.Transform("..\\..\\Shakespeare.xml", OutputFile);

// Display the HTML file in a browser
System.Diagnostics.Process.Start(OutputFile);
```

Here's the code in Visual Basic .NET:

```
Dim XslTrans As New XslTransform()
Dim OutputFile As String = "TransformOutput.html"

' Load the XSLT file
XslTrans.Load("..\..\Shakespeare.xslt")
```

```
' Transform the XML file and output it to the specified HTML file
XslTrans.Transform("..\..\Shakespeare.xml", OutputFile)

' Display the HTML file in a browser
System.Diagnostics.Process.Start(OutputFile)
```

In this code, the call to the Load method loads the Shakespeare.xslt file. Next, a call is made to the Transform method that takes the XML file, applies the XSLT file to it, and sends the output to the specified HTML file. The last line of code calls the .NET Process class's Start method, which launches the process associated with the extension of the specified file. In this case, the file has an HTML extension, so your default browser is launched, displaying the output file (**Figure 18**).

Title	Category	Acts
Othello	Tragedy	5
The Comedy of Errors	Comedy	5
Henry the Fifth	History	5
The Tempest	Romance	5

Figure 18.An XSLT file can be used to transform an XML file into HTML for display.

For more information on the XslTransform class, see the .NET Help topic "XSLT Transformations with the XslTransform Class".

The XML Document Object Model (DOM)

As described previously, the XmlReader and XmlWriter classes provide fast, forward-only access to XML data, however, they cannot edit XML. This is where the XML Document Object Model (DOM) comes into play. The DOM lets you read, manipulate, and modify an XML document. The DOM represents XML in memory as a hierarchy of nodes.

To show you some of the capabilities of the .NET XML DOM, the following code adds a new node to the Shakespeare.xml file. It appends a new Shakespearean play "Hamlet" to the list of plays found in Shakespeare.xml and writes out the XML to a new file named UpdatedPlays.xml.

Here's the code in C#:

```
// Load the document
XmlDocument XmlDoc = new XmlDocument();
XmlDoc.Load("..\\..\\Shakespeare.xml");

// Create a new <ShakespearePlay> element
XmlElement Play = XmlDoc.CreateElement("ShakespearePlay");

// Create a new <Name> element and add it to <ShakespearePlay>
XmlElement Name = XmlDoc.CreateElement("Name");
Name.InnerText = "Hamlet";
```

```
Play.AppendChild(Name);

// Create a new <Category> element and add it to <ShakespearePlay>
XmlElement Category = XmlDoc.CreateElement("Category");
Category.InnerText = "Tragedy";
Play.AppendChild(Category);

// Create a new <NumberOfActs> element and add it to <Shakespeare>
XmlElement Act = XmlDoc.CreateElement("NumberOfActs");
Act.InnerText = "5";
Play.AppendChild(Act);
XmlDoc.DocumentElement.AppendChild(Play);

// Write out the new XML file
XmlTextWriter TextWriter = new XmlTextWriter("..\\..\\UpdatedPlays.xml",null);
TextWriter.Formatting = Formatting.Indented;
XmlDoc.WriteContentTo(TextWriter);
TextWriter.Close();
```

Here's the code in Visual Basic .NET:

```
' Load the document
Dim XmlDoc As New XmlDocument()
XmlDoc.Load("..\..\Shakespeare.xml")

' Create a new <ShakespearePlay> element
Dim Play As XmlElement = XmlDoc.CreateElement("ShakespearePlay")

' Create a new <Name> element and add it to <ShakespearePlay>
Dim Name As XmlElement = XmlDoc.CreateElement("Name")
Name.InnerText = "Hamlet"
Play.AppendChild(Name)

' Create a new <Category> element and add it to <ShakespearePlay>
Dim Category As XmlElement = XmlDoc.CreateElement("Category")
Category.InnerText = "Tragedy"
Play.AppendChild(Category)

' Create a new <NumberOfActs> element and add it to <Shakespeare>
Dim Act As XmlElement = XmlDoc.CreateElement("NumberOfActs")
Act.InnerText = "5"
Play.AppendChild(Act)
XmlDoc.DocumentElement.AppendChild(Play)

' Write out the new XML file
Dim TextWriter As New XmlTextWriter("..\..\UpdatedPlays.xml", Nothing)
TextWriter.Formatting = Formatting.Indented
XmlDoc.WriteContentTo(TextWriter)
TextWriter.Close()
```

This code creates an instance of the XmlDocument class and loads the Shakespeare.xml file into it. Next, calling the XmlDocument's CreateElement method creates a new ShakespearePlay element. Afterwards, child elements (Name, Category, NumberOfActs) are created using the same technique. Each element's data is defined by setting the XmlElement's InnerText property. The Play object's AppendChild method is called to add each child element to the Play element. Finally, an XmlTextWriter is created, and a new XML file,

UpdatedPlays.xml, is specified as the file to be written. A reference to the XmlTextWriter object is passed to the XmlDocument's WriteContentTo method and the updated XML document is written out to the UpdatedPlays.xml file.

For more information on the .NET XML DOM, see the .NET Help topic "XML Document Object Model (DOM)".

Querying XML data with XPathNavigator

XPath (XML Path Language) is a query language specifically designed to select a subset of elements from an XML document. In the .NET Framework, the XPathNavigator class lets you perform XPath queries on any XML data store that implements the IXPathNavigable interface.

> *For more information on XPath, see the .NET Help topic "XPath".*

There are three classes in the .NET Framework that implement this interface: XPathDocument, XmlDocument, and XmlDataDocument. You use the XPathNavigator class to select elements from the XML data stores of these objects. XPathNavigator supplies both forward and backward navigation, but read only access. If you want the ability to edit an XML data store, you need to use the .NET XML DOM instead.

To demonstrate the capabilities of the XPathNavigator class, the following code selects all of the Shakespeare tragedies from the Shakespeare.xml file. If you haven't been running the sample code in this chapter up to this point, there may only be one tragedy in your XML file, (and hopefully you'll see the humor in this).

Here is the code in C#:

```csharp
string PlayList = "";

// Load the document
XPathDocument XmlDoc = new XPathDocument("..\\..\\Shakespeare.xml");
XPathNavigator XPathNav = XmlDoc.CreateNavigator();

// Select all Shakespeare Tragedies
XPathNodeIterator Iterator =
XPathNav.Select("descendant::ShakespearePlay[Category='Tragedy']");

// Iterate through all Tragedies
while (Iterator.MoveNext())
{
  // Create an iterator for the current <ShakespearePlay> element
  XPathNodeIterator PlayIterator =
      Iterator.Current.SelectDescendants(XPathNodeType.Element,false);

  // Iterate through all child elements of the current <ShakespearePlay>
  while (PlayIterator.MoveNext())
  {
      PlayList += PlayIterator.Current.Value + " ";
  }
}
MessageBox.Show(PlayList);
```

Here is the code in Visual Basic .NET:

```
Dim PlayList As String = ""

' Load the document
Dim XmlDoc As New XPathDocument("..\..\Shakespeare.xml")
Dim XPathNav As XPathNavigator = XmlDoc.CreateNavigator()

' Select all Shakespeare Tragedies
Dim Iterator As XPathNodeIterator = _
  XPathNav.Select("descendant::ShakespearePlay[Category='Tragedy']")

' Iterate through all Tragedies
While Iterator.MoveNext()
    ' Create an iterator for the current <ShakespearePlay> element
    Dim PlayIterator As XPathNodeIterator = _
        Iterator.Current.SelectDescendants(XPathNodeType.Element, False)

    ' Iterate through all child elements of the current <ShakespearePlay>
    While PlayIterator.MoveNext()
       PlayList += PlayIterator.Current.Value + " "
    End While
End While

MessageBox.Show(PlayList)
```

First in this code, you create an instance of the XPathDocument class, specifying in the constructor the XML file to load. Next, you create an XPathNavigator by calling the XPathDocument object's CreateNavigator method. A call is made to the Select method of the XPathNavigator object, specifying all ShakespearePlay elements with a Category set to "Tragedy" should be selected, and the selected elements are stored in an XPathNodeIterator object.

The first `while` loop iterates through all the selected ShakespearePlay elements by calling the XPathNodeIterator's MoveNext method. Within the `while` loop, a second iterator is created and used by an inner `while` loop to iterate through all of the elements in the current ShakespearePlay element, building a string to be displayed.

For more information on the XPathNavigator and related classes, see the .NET Help topic "XPathNavigator in the .NET Framework".

Conclusion

There are a wide variety of classes in the .NET Framework and powerful tools in Visual Studio .NET for working with XML. This chapter just skims the surface of these capabilities, providing an overview of the kinds of things you can do with XML and .NET. I highly recommend checking out the suggested links in this chapter to get a fuller picture of .NET XML so you can take advantage of its power and flexibility in your applications.

Chapter 12
XML Web Services

It's nearly impossible to pick up a software-related journal these days that doesn't contain some mention of XML Web Services. This makes it easy to think of Web Services as pure hype, but in reality they may shape the next generation of software applications. XML Web Services are the other half of ASP.NET (the first half is Web Forms). This chapter helps you understand what XML Web Services are, and how you can use them in your .NET applications.

According to Microsoft's initial marketing push for .NET, XML Web Services are the cornerstone of .NET and the reason for its very existence. In reality, you may use .NET to create both Windows Forms and Web Forms applications without ever creating an XML Web Service. However, there are good reasons why you should consider doing so.

There's been a lot of interest in the FoxPro community over the fact that Visual FoxPro can both create and consume XML Web Services. In fact, VFP's Web Service capabilities are what places it under the ".NET umbrella". Although it's not a .NET language, Visual FoxPro allows you to create XML Web Services that can be consumed by .NET and it can consume XML Web Services created in .NET.

What is a Web Service?

A Web Service is a code module containing one or more functions accessible via the Internet. Desktop applications, Web applications, or even another Web Service can access Web Services. When you access a Web Service, you are making a function or method call over the Internet.

Web Services are:

- Language independent – They can be written in virtually any computer language and accessed by code written in any language

- Platform independent – They can run on any operating system and be accessed by client code running on any platform.

- Self-describing – Each Web Service has associated files that describe the services it provides and allows clients to call its methods.

Although most of the software you run is physically located on your own computer, running code on a computer that resides somewhere across the Internet is actually a common occurrence—it happens all the time as you surf the Web, although surfing the Web is not the same as accessing a Web Service. So, first you'll look at what happens when you surf the Internet, and then see how Web Services takes this approach a step further.

As you navigate to different sites with your browser, you request Web pages located on Web servers across the Internet. Behind the scenes, especially when accessing Web pages with dynamic content, a Web server runs code in response to your request and sends HTML, script code, and so on, back to your computer. In this manner, you're indirectly running code that resides on a Web server.

When using technologies such as ASP or ASP.NET pages, the code that's being executed is often stored in methods of business components located on the Web server. For example, in Chapter 10, "Building Web Applications with ASP.NET", you created a Web Forms application that allowed users to view and edit orders for a specified customer. As shown in **Figure 1**, when the user enters a Customer ID and clicks the Submit button, the Web server instantiates the Orders business object and calls its GetOrdersByCustomerID method. The Web Server produces an HTML list of customer orders to send back to your browser.

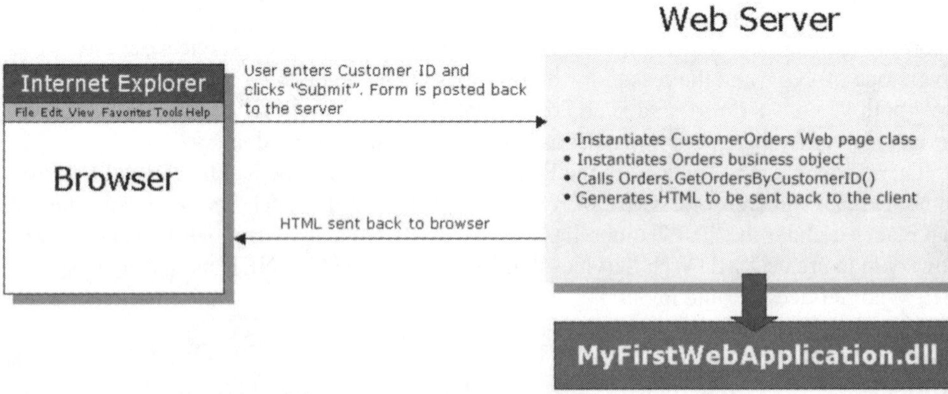

Figure 1. When you access ASP or ASP.NET pages, you are often indirectly causing code to be executed on a Web server.

For the most part, this approach works well. However, XML Web Services let you take this paradigm a step further, giving you greater control. They effectively allow you to call the GetOrdersByCustomerID method of the Orders business object directly. Just think about how useful this is. If you are able to call the method directly, you can retrieve a list of customer orders as an XML string and manipulate it in your own software applications, and even persist it to a local data store. Later in this chapter, you're going to build a Web Service allowing you to do just that.

This type of Web Service is private by nature, established between business partners. You may have certain clients that you allow to access the Web Service, but you certainly don't want to provide free access to the rest of the world. In contrast, there are other types of Web Services that are intended for public consumption. For example, Fed-Ex™ has a public Web Service letting you track packages. You simply pass your tracking number to the Web Service and it returns a string containing tracking information.

At this point, you will build an ASP.NET XML Web Service and explore the technologies behind Web Services along the way.

Creating a Customer Orders Web Service

To create a .NET XML Web Service:

1. Launch Visual Studio .NET, and click the New Project button on the Start Page.

2. In the left pane of the New Project dialog (**Figure 2**), select Visual C# Projects or Visual Basic Projects, depending on the language you want to use. In the Templates pane on the right, select ASP.NET Web Service.

3. Notice the Name text box is disabled and contains the text "WebService1", and if you're creating the Web Service on your local machine, the Location text box contains the text "http://localhost/WebService1". To change the name of the Web Service, you must change the name of the directory in the Location text box. Change the name "WebService1" to "Customer Orders Web Service, and then click the OK button.

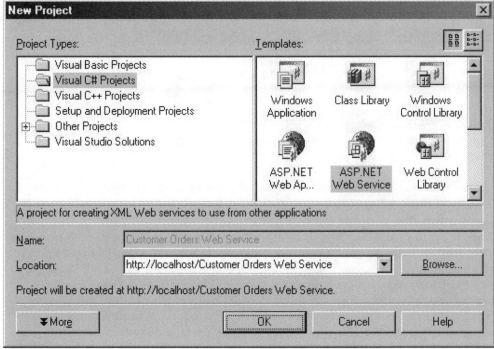

Figure 2. *You can choose to create a C# or Visual Basic ASP.NET Web Service in the New Project dialog.*

At this point, Visual Studio .NET briefly displays the Creating the Web dialog while it creates a new ASP.NET Web Service from the template you have selected. After a few moments, a new Web Service file is displayed in the IDE (**Figure 3**).

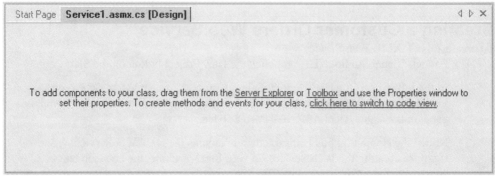

Figure 3. VS .NET automatically creates a Web Service file when you create a new ASP.NET Web Service.

Rename this Web Service file so it's a little more descriptive. To do this, with the Web Service file selected in design mode, go to the Properties Window and change the Name property from "Service1" to "CustomerOrders" (**Figure 4**).

Figure 4. You change the name of the Web Service in the Visual Studio .NET Properties Window.

You'll take a closer look at this file soon, but you need to do a little housekeeping first.

Renaming the project namespace

When you create a new Web Service, ASP.NET automatically sets your project's namespace to the same name as your project (as it also does when building Windows Forms and Web Forms applications). To change the default namespace in VB .NET, you must first close the CustomerOrders page (you don't need to do this in a C# project). Next, go to the Solution Explorer and right-click on the project (the second node from the top). From the shortcut menu, select Properties, which launches the Property Pages dialog. In the left pane of the dialog, under the Common Properties folder, select General if it's not already selected.

If you're using C#, in the right pane, change the Default Namespace from "Customer_Orders_Web_Service" to "HW.NetBook.Samples". If you're using Visual Basic .NET, in the right pane, change the Root namespace to "HW.NetBook.Samples". When you're done, click the OK button to save changes.

To change all existing references to the original namespace, from the main menu select Edit | Find and Replace | Replace in Files. In the Replace In Files dialog's Find what text box, enter "Customer_Orders_Web_Service". In the Replace with text box, enter

"HW.NetBook.Samples", (make sure you enter this with the exact case shown here). Click the Replace All button. This launches a warning dialog—simply press OK to ignore the warning. When the find and replace is finished, it displays a dialog indicating how many occurrences were replaced. If you're using C#, it should say "4 occurrence(s) replaced". If you're using Visual Basic .NET, it should say "2 occurrence(s) replaced". Click the OK button to close these dialogs.

Web Service virtual directories

When you use Visual Studio .NET to create a Web Service, it automatically creates a virtual directory for you.

> *For more information on virtual directories, see Chapter 10, "Building Web Applications with ASP.NET".*

This virtual directory contains your new Web Service project and related files (**Figure 5**). However, as with Web Forms applications, the actual Solution file is stored in a subfolder of the "My Documents\Visual Studio Projects\" directory. Again, this means when you reopen your Web Application after restarting Visual Studio, you will find your solution in this folder.

Name	Size	Type	Modified
bin		File Folder	7/12/2002 12:45 PM
AssemblyInfo.cs	3 KB	C# Source file	7/12/2002 12:46 PM
Customer Orders Web Service.csproj	6 KB	C# Project file	7/12/2002 12:46 PM
Customer Orders Web Service.csproj.webinfo	1 KB	WEBINFO File	7/12/2002 12:45 PM
Customer Orders Web Service.vsdisco	1 KB	VS.NET Web Service Dynamic Discovery File	7/12/2002 12:46 PM
Global.asax	1 KB	Active Server Application file	7/12/2002 1:14 PM
Global.asax.cs	2 KB	C# Source file	7/12/2002 12:46 PM
Global.asax.resx	2 KB	.NET XML Resource Template	9/20/2001 7:25 AM
Service1.asmx	1 KB	Web Service	7/12/2002 1:14 PM
Service1.asmx.cs	2 KB	C# Source file	7/12/2002 12:46 PM
Service1.asmx.resx	2 KB	.NET XML Resource Template	9/20/2001 7:25 AM
Web.config	4 KB	Web Configuration file	7/12/2002 12:46 PM

Figure 5. *Visual Studio .NET places a variety of files in your Web Service's virtual directory.*

Before taking a closer look at these files first take a behind-the-scenes look at the Web Service file.

A closer look at the Web Service file

You can view a Web Service file in either design view or code view. To switch to code view, you select the click here to switch to code view hyperlink on the page or right-click the file and select View Code from the shortcut menu. When you do this, you should see the following class definition in C#:

```
public class CustomerOrders: System.Web.Services.WebService
```

```
{
  public CustomerOrders ()
  {
      //CODEGEN: This call is required by the ASP.NET Web Services Designer
      InitializeComponent();
  }

  // WEB SERVICE EXAMPLE
  // The HelloWorld() example service returns the string Hello World
  // To build, uncomment the following lines then save and build the project
  // To test this web service, press F5

  //         [WebMethod]
  //         public string HelloWorld()
  //         {
  //             return "Hello World";
  //         }
}
```

And in Visual Basic .NET:

```
Public Class CustomerOrders
    Inherits System.Web.Services.WebService

    ' WEB SERVICE EXAMPLE
    ' The HelloWorld() example service returns the string Hello World.
    ' To build, uncomment the following lines then save and build the project.
    ' To test this web service, ensure that the .asmx file is the start page
    ' and press F5.
    '
    '<WebMethod()> Public Function HelloWorld() As String
    '   HelloWorld = "Hello World"
    ' End Function

End Class
```

As you can see, this code defines a class named CustomerOrders derived from the .NET Framework's System.Web.Services.WebService class. Also notice the method that is commented out at the bottom of the class definition. As described in the comments above it, you can uncomment this code and then build and run this sample Web Service, which you will do in the next section

Running the "Hello World" Web Service

To run the sample "Hello World" Web Service, select all of the commented code in the HelloWorld method (including the WebMethod attribute), and then click VS .NET's Uncomment icon button (**Figure 6**). Alternately, to uncomment code, you can select Edit | Advanced | Uncomment Selection from the main menu.

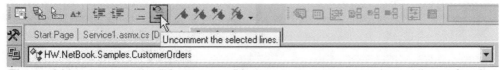

Figure 6. *You can use the "Uncomment" button to uncomment selected lines of code.*

To save, build, and run the Web Service in one step, just press the F5 button. After a few moments, a Web Service help page displays in your Web browser. This page lists all of your Web Service methods and gives you a link to Service method help pages that allow you to test your Web Service methods (*very* cool!).

What's nice about this is the page is generated and displayed for any user who tries to call your Web Service without the proper parameters. You can try this for yourself by typing the URL of your Web Service into your browser's Address box. For example:

```
http://localhost/Customer Orders Web Service/Service1.asmx
```

The upper portion of the Web Service help page (**Figure 7**) displays the name of your Web Service (CustomerOrders), and a single HelloWorld operation—this is the method that you just uncommented. It also displays a warning about changing the default namespace of your Web service—you'll do this a bit later.

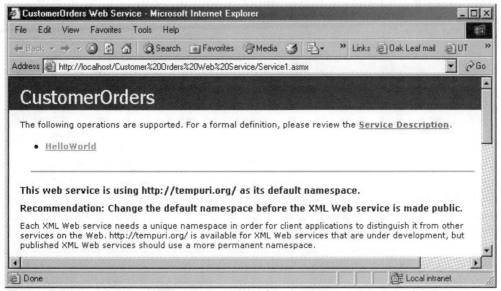

Figure 7. *Visual Studio .NET creates a Web Service help page customized to your Web Service.*

To test the Web Service, click the <u>HelloWorld</u> hyperlink. This displays the Service method help page (**Figure 8**), which includes a description of the operation and an Invoke button that allows you to test the Web Service.

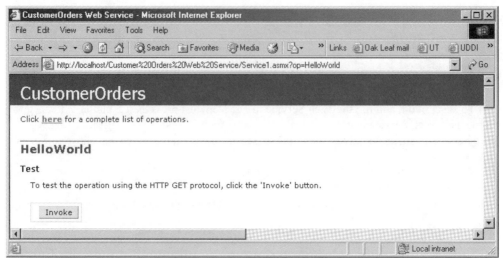

Figure 8. *The Service method help page displays a description of the operation and an Invoke button that allows you to call the Web Service method.*

At this point, click the Invoke button. Behind the scenes, the Service method help page calls the HelloWorld test method and displays the return value in a new browser window (**Figure 9**).

Figure 9. *The Service method help page launches another browser window that displays the return value passed back from the Web Service method.*

As you can see, although the code in the HelloWorld method returns a simple string, it is converted into XML when it returns to the Web Service caller. At this point, close the Browser window, so you can work further with the Web Service project.

Web Service project files

Now that you've created a simple .NET Web Service, take a quick look at the files within a Web Service project.

The global.asax file automatically added to your Web Service project by Visual Studio .NET is exactly the same as the global.asax file that it includes in new Web Forms projects. The same is also true of the Web.config file. If you create a new Web Service project and compare these files to a new Web Forms project, you'll find no differences. For more information on these files, see Chapter 10, "Building Web Applications with ASP.NET".

The vsdisco file

There is one file you'll find in Visual Studio .NET Web Service projects you won't find in a Web Forms application—the vsdisco file. This file is a Web Services discovery file used by Visual Studio .NET as it searches through folders on your development Web server looking for available XML Web Services.

If you look in the Solution Explorer, you will see a file named "Customer Orders Web Service.vsdisco". If you double-click this file, VS .NET opens it in the IDE. By default, it contains the following XML data:

```
<?xml versio_="1.0" encodi_g="utf-8" ?>
<dynamicDiscovery xmlns="urn:schemas-dynamicdiscovery:disco.2000-03-17">
<exclude pa_u104 ?="_vti_cnf" />
<exclude pa_h="_vti_pvt" />
<exclude pa_u104 ?="_vti_log" />
<exclude pa_u104 ?="_vti_Ucript" />
<exclude pa_h="_vti_txt" />
<exclude pa_u104 ?="Web References" />
</dynamicDiscovery>
```

As you can see, the file contains a <dynamicDiscovery> root node with several <exclude> child nodes. The <exclude> nodes contain a relative path to folders VS .NET should *not* search when it's going through the directories on your Web server looking for Web Services.

For more information, see the .NET Help topic "Deploying XML Web Services in Managed Code".

Using business objects

Now it's time to reference and use the business objects you created in Chapter 9, "Building .NET Windows Forms Applications". Again, there are a number of ways to accomplish this, but the easiest method is adding the business object source code files to the Web Service project.

To add these source code files, right-click on your Web Service project in the Solution Explorer and select Add | Add Existing Item from the shortcut menu. In the Add Existing Item dialog, navigate to the "Simple Windows Application" directory you created in the previous chapter, and select the three business object source code files (**Figure 10**). These are Business.cs, Data.cs, and OrdersBusiness.cs. If you created a Visual Basic .NET Windows Forms application, these files will have a "vb" extension rather than a "cs" extension. After selecting all three files, click the Open button.

Figure 10. *You can add files belonging to one .NET project to any other .NET project*

After clicking the Open button, the three files should be listed in the Solution Explorer.

> *Typically, with business objects that are going to be used from multiple projects, you should create a separate Class Library project in Visual Studio .NET and add your business object source code files to this project. You can then compile a DLL containing just your business object classes. This DLL can then be referenced from multiple projects*

Creating custom Web methods

Now, you're ready to add to the WebService file a custom Web method that instantiates and calls a method of the Orders business object. First, go back to the code-behind file (Service1.asmx.cs or Service1.asmx.vb), and comment out the HelloWorld method you previously uncommented. Make sure you also comment out the line containing "[WebMethod]". For more information on this attribute, see the section "The WebMethod attribute" later in this chapter.

Next, add the following namespace reference to the top of the code-behind file so you can access the Orders business object class.

In C#:

```
using HW.NetBook.Samples.Business;
```

In Visual Basic .NET:

```
Imports HW.NetBook.Samples.Business
```

Now, add the following method to the bottom of the CustomerOrders WebService class definition—make sure it's directly below the commented out Hello World Web Method.
In C#:

```
[WebMethod (Description="Returns orders for the specified customer")]
public DataSet GetOrdersByCustomerID(string custID)
{
  // Instantiate the Orders business object
  Orders OrderObj = new Orders();

  // Call its GetOrdersByCustomerID method
  return OrderObj.GetOrdersByCustomerID(custID);
}
```

In Visual Basic .NET:

```
<WebMethod(Description:="Returns orders for the specified customer")> _
Public Function GetOrdersByCustomerID(ByVal custID As String) As DataSet
    ' Instantiate the Orders business object
    Dim OrderObj As New Orders()

    ' Call its GetOrdersByCustomerID method
    Return OrderObj.GetOrdersByCustomerID(custID)
End Function 'GetOrdersByCustomerID
```

This Web method instantiates the Orders business object and calls its GetOrdersByCustomerID method, passing the custID value it receives from the client calling the Web Service. Notice the method specifies a DataSet as the return value. Even though the return value is specified to be a DataSet, if you call the Web Service, you actually get the DataSet returned in XML format.

Unfortunately, Visual FoxPro 7 cannot work with the XML returned from a Web Service in this fashion (this *should* be fixed in Visual FoxPro 8). If you want to create a Web Service that a Visual FoxPro 7 client can consume, you explicitly convert the DataSet to XML and return the XML string from the Web Service method as shown in the following code (for this example, I leave the GetOrdersByCustomerID method returning a DataSet as shown above).
In C#:

```
[WebMethod (Description="Returns orders for the specified customer")]
public string GetOrdersByCustomerID(string custID)
{
  // Instantiate the Orders business object
  Orders OrderObj = new Orders();

  // Call its GetOrdersByCustomerID method
  DataSet dsOrders = OrderObj.GetOrdersByCustomerID(custID);
  return dsOrders.GetXml();
}
```

And in Visual Basic .NET

```
<WebMethod(Description:="Returns orders for the specified customer")> _
Public Function GetOrdersByCustomerID(ByVal custID As String) As String

    ' Instantiate the Orders business object
    Dim OrderObj As New Orders()

    ' Call its GetOrdersByCustomerID method
    Dim dsOrders As DataSet = OrderObj.GetOrdersByCustomerID(custID)
    Return dsOrders.GetXml()

End Function
```

Before taking a closer look at what happens behind the scenes with the Web Service, first look at the WebMethod and WebService attributes.

The WebMethod attribute

If you place a WebMethod attribute directly above a method declaration, the method is exposed by Visual Studio .NET as a public method of the XML Web Service. A WebService class can have multiple methods, but only those that possess the WebMethod attribute are exposed as part of the Web Service.

As you can see in the new method you created, the WebMethod attribute also allows you to specify a method description. **Table 1** lists other properties of the WebMethod attribute that you can also set.

Table 1. WebMethod properties

Property	Description	Default
BufferResponse	Specifies if ASP.NET should buffer the entire response before sending it to the client.	true
CacheDuration	Specifies if the result set of each unique parameter set should be cached, and if so, for how many seconds.	0
Description	Gives a description for the Web Service method.	""
EnableSession	Specifies if session state is enabled for a Web Service method.	false
MessageName	Specifies an alias for an overloaded method name.	""
TransactionOption	Specifies transaction options for a Web Service method. Possible values are: • Disabled • Not Supported • Supported • Required • RequiresNew	Disabled

For more information on each of these properties, see the .NET Help topic "Using the WebMethod Attribute".

The WebService attribute

As shown in Figure 7 earlier in this chapter, when you run the HelloWorld Web Service, the Web Service test page displays a warning about changing the name of the Web Service's namespace from "http://tempuri.org/" to your own, unique namespace. To do this, you need the WebService attribute.

The WebService attribute is applied to a Web Service by placing it directly above the Web Service class definition. For example, place the following attribute definition above the CustomerOrders WebService class definition.

In C#:

```
[WebService(Namespace="http://servername/xmlwebservices/",
    Description="Customer Orders Web Service")]
```

In Visual Basic .NET:

```
<WebService(Namespace:="http://servername/xmlwebservices/", _
    Description:="Customer Orders Web Service")> _
```

The first part of the WebService attribute declaration specifies the Namespace property. Specifying this value replaces the Web Service's default "http://tempuri.org/" namespace. When creating a Web Service, you can specify your own unique URL by using the Namespace property. As shown in the second line of the declaration, you can also specify a Description property, which provides a description for the entire Web Service class.

Running the Customer Orders Web Service

Now you're ready to run the Customer Orders Web Service. To do this, press the F5 key to save all changes, compile the Web Service application, and run it. When your browser is launched, you should see the Web Service help Page shown in **Figure 11**.

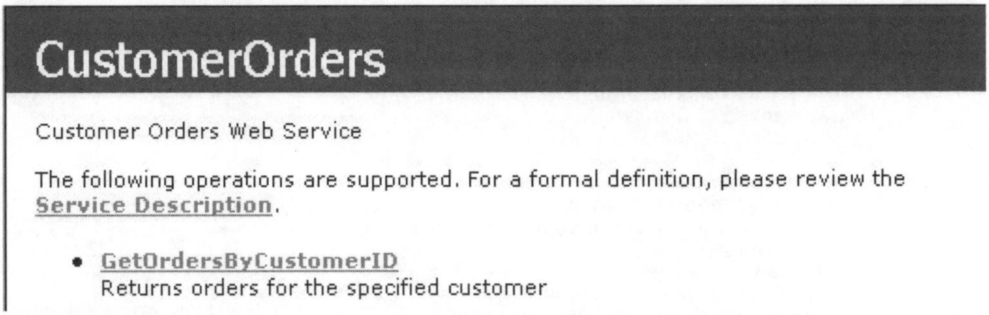

CustomerOrders

Customer Orders Web Service

The following operations are supported. For a formal definition, please review the Service Description.

*   GetOrdersByCustomerID
    Returns orders for the specified customer

Figure 11. The WebService and WebMethod attributes allow you to specify descriptions (and other properties) for your Web Service and its methods.

Notice the top of the page displays the name of the Web Service class, "CustomerOrders". Beneath the name is the description you supplied in the WebService attribute. At the bottom of the page is the GetOrdersByCustomerID along with the description you supplied in the WebMethod attribute.

If you click on the GetOrdersByCustomerID link, the Service method help page is displayed (**Figure 12**).

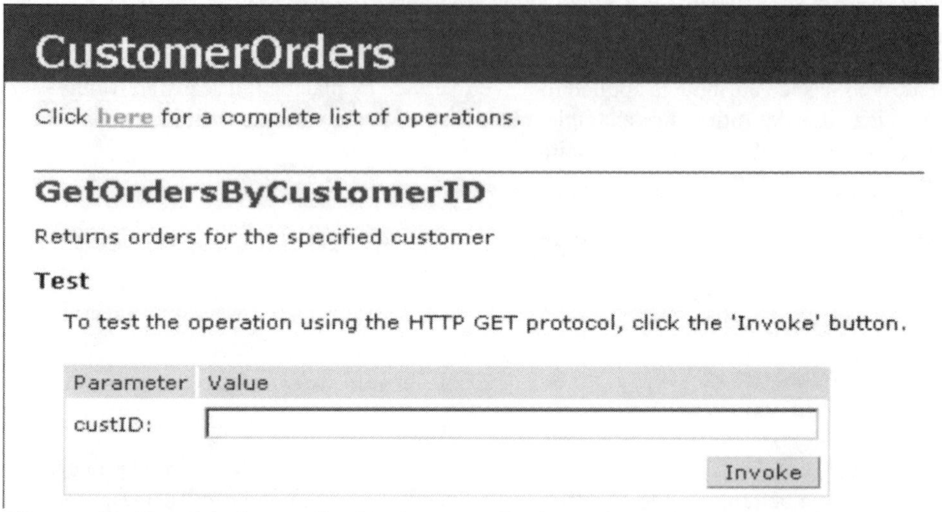

Figure 12. *The Service method help page displays a user input control for each parameter of your Web Service method.*

As you can see, the Service Method help page displays an input text box for each parameter of a Web Service method. In this case, you just have one—custID. Enter the value "QUICK" in the custID text box, and then click the Invoke button. A new browser window displays the XML returned from the method (**Figure 13**).

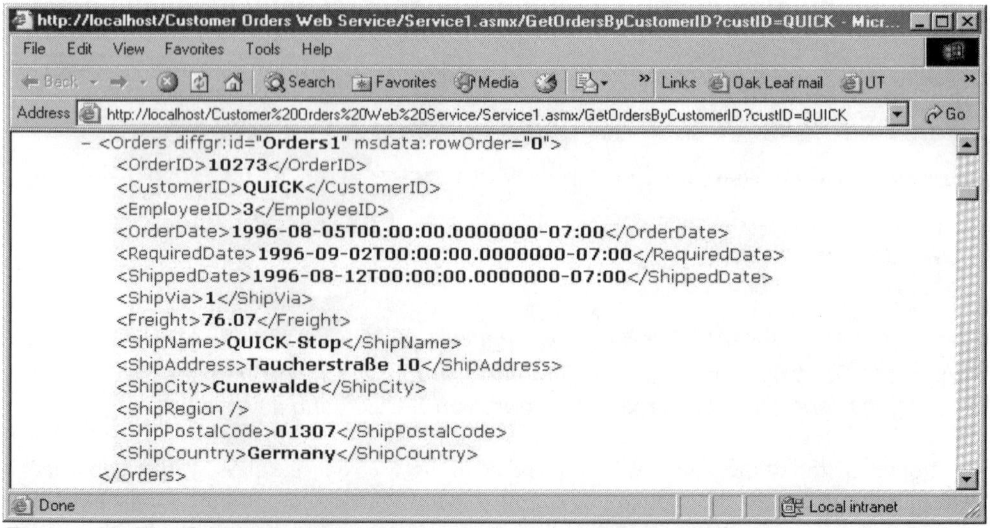

Figure 13. *The Service method help page launches a second browser window that contains the XML returned from the CustomerOrders Web Service.*

The Web Services Description Language (WSDL) file

Now that you've created and tested a Web Service, you can take a closer look behind the scenes at some of the standards that make XML Web Services possible. I'll start with the Web Services Description Language (WSDL) file.

A Web Service's WSDL file (pronounced "wis-dle") is roughly equivalent to a COM server's type library. Remember, a type library describes the classes and methods publicly available in a COM server. In the same way, a WSDL file (also known as a *service description document*) describes the public classes and methods available in a Web Service.

Type libraries work great for COM servers, but they are Microsoft-specific—and Web Services are not. So, when the W3C committee chose a format to describe Web Services, they chose XML—a widely accepted, platform-neutral, extensible standard. WSDL defines an XML grammar for describing Web Services.

If you want to view your Web Service's WSDL file, you do so from the Web Service help page (Figure 11). If you click the Service Description link, it launches a browser window that displays your Web Service's WSDL file (**Figure 14**).

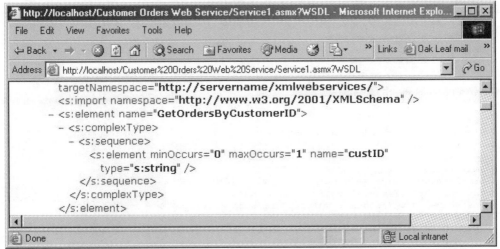

Figure 14. Visual Studio .NET automatically generates a WSDL file for your Web Services.

As shown in Figure 14, the WSDL file contains information on each public method, along with the method's parameters and return value (not shown in the figure). By default, when you create a Web Service in Visual Studio .NET, your WSDL file is dynamically generated. You can also create a WSDL file, place it on your Web server, and make its location known to your customers (or the general public) so they can download the file and determine how to access your Web Service.

A full explanation of the structure and contents of a WSDL file is beyond the scope of this book. For more information, see the .NET Help topic "XML Web Service Description", which also contains a link to the WSDL specification (http://www.w3.org/TR/wsdl).

SOAP

Another XML-based standard key to Web Services is Simple Object Access Protocol (SOAP). SOAP is a protocol for exchanging structured and type information on the Web.

You can actually view some of the SOAP formatting for your Web Service from the Service Method Help Page. For example, here is the SOAP request and response shown on the GetOrdersByCustomerID Service Method Help Page.

Here is the SOAP request:

```
POST /Customer%20Orders%20Web%20Service/Service1.asmx HTTP/1.1
Host: localhost
Content-Type: text/xml; charset=utf-8
Content-Length: length
SOAPAction: "http://servername/xmlwebservices/GetOrdersByCustomerID"

<?xml version="1.0" encoding="utf-8"?>
<soap:Envelope xmlns:xsi="http://www.w3.org/2001/XMLSchema-instance"
xmlns:xsd="http://www.w3.org/2001/XMLSchema"
xmlns:soap="http://schemas.xmlsoap.org/soap/envelope/">
  <soap:Body>
    <GetOrdersByCustomerID xmlns="http://servername/xmlwebservices/">
      <custID>string</custID>
    </GetOrdersByCustomerID>
  </soap:Body>
</soap:Envelope>
```

And here is the SOAP response:

```
HTTP/1.1 200 OK
Content-Type: text/xml; charset=utf-8
Content-Length: length

<?xml version="1.0" encoding="utf-8"?>
<soap:Envelope xmlns:xsi="http://www.w3.org/2001/XMLSchema-instance"
xmlns:xsd="http://www.w3.org/2001/XMLSchema"
xmlns:soap="http://schemas.xmlsoap.org/soap/envelope/">
  <soap:Body>
    <GetOrdersByCustomerIDResponse xmlns="http://servername/xmlwebservices/">
      <GetOrdersByCustomerIDResult>
        <xsd:schema>schema</xsd:schema>xml</GetOrdersByCustomerIDResult>
    </GetOrdersByCustomerIDResponse>
  </soap:Body>
</soap:Envelope>
```

For more information on the SOAP standard, check out the .NET Help topic "XML Web Service Wire Formats", which contains a link to the W3C Web site (http://www.w3.org/soap).

Consuming Web Services

As mentioned earlier in this chapter, desktop applications, Web applications, or other Web Services can consume Web Services. In this section, you will create a desktop application that accesses the Customer Orders Web Service.

The ability to access a Customer Orders Web Service from a desktop application can be extremely useful. For example, if you have placed orders with one of your suppliers, it would be great to call a Web Service on your supplier's Web site that allowed you to retrieve all of your orders and display them within one of your own desktop applications. This is good for your supplier, because they don't have to pay a humanoid to research the information and send it to you. It's also good for you, because not only can you display this information in your own custom application, you can now manipulate and store the information in your own database.

Before going any further, close your Web Service application. Next, to create a new Windows Application, from the Start Page of VS .NET, click the New Project button. In the left pane of the New Project dialog, select either Visual C# Projects or Visual Basic Projects. In the Templates pane on the right, select Windows Application. In the Name text box, enter "WinForms Web Service Consumer", and specify the desired location for your new project in the Location text box (**Figure 15**). When you're done, click the OK button to create your new Windows application.

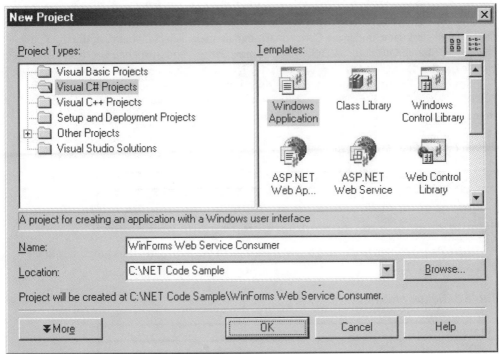

Figure 15. *You can consume a Web Service from a Windows application (shown here), a Web Forms application, or another Web Service.*

When Visual Studio .NET finishes creating your new project, you see a new form named "Form1" in the IDE. You will use this form to display the user interface controls and call the Web Service. This is different than what you did in Chapter 9, "Building .NET Windows Forms Applications", because in this case, you just need a bare bones application to call your Web Service. First, you need to make a few changes to the form. With the form selected in the IDE, go to the Properties Window, change the Name property to

"WebServiceConsumerForm", the Size property to 640, 260, and the Text property to "Web Service Consumer".

Now you need to perform one additional step, which is different depending on whether you're using C# or Visual Basic .NET. In C#, right-click on the form and select View Code from the shortcut menu. At the bottom of the code-behind file, find the line of code that calls Application.Run:

```
Application.Run(new Form1());
```

And change it to:

```
Application.Run(new WebServiceConsumerForm());
```

In Visual Basic .NET, go to the Solution Explorer, right-click the project node (second from the top), and select Properties from the shortcut menu. This launches the Property Pages dialog. In the left pane, under the Common Properties node, select General. In the right pane, change the Startup Object to "WebServiceConsumerForm", and then click OK to save the change.

Now select Form1 in design mode and drag and drop a DataGrid control from the VS .NET Toolbox onto the form. If the Toolbox is not visible in the IDE, select View | Toolbox from the main menu. Change the DataGrid properties to the values shown in **Table 2**.

Table 2. *DataGrid properties*

Property	Value
Name	grdOrders
Location	40, 30
Size	550, 140

Next, drag a Button from the VS .NET Toolbox to the form and set its properties to the values shown in **Table 3**.

Table 3. *Button properties*

Property	Value
Name	btnCallWS
Location	345, 195
Size	100, 23
Text	Call Web Service

Next, drag and drop a TextBox from the Toolbox onto the form and sets its properties to the values shown in **Table 4**.

Table 4. *Text Box properties*

Property	Value
Name	txtCustomerID
Location	185, 195
Size	135, 20
Text	(empty string)

When you're done, your form should look like the form shown in **Figure 16**.

Figure 16. *This Windows form is used to access the Customer Orders Web Service.*

Adding a reference to the Web Service

Now it's time to add a reference to the Customer Orders Web Service to your project. To do this, go to Solution Explorer, right-click the References node, and select Add Web Reference from the shortcut menu (**Figure 17**).

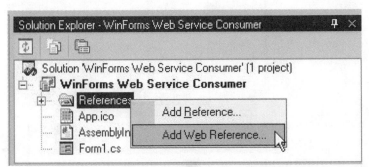

Figure 17. *You can add a reference to a Web Service to your project by right-clicking* References *in the Solution Explorer and selecting* Add Web Reference *from the shortcut menu.*

Selecting this option launches the Add Web Reference dialog. The left pane of the dialog displays information about the UDDI Directory. You'll look at this later, but for now, you just want to reference the local Customer Orders Web Service.

The Address combo box at the top of the dialog allows you to select a previously used Web Service or enter a URL and file name for the Web Service you want to reference. In this case, you want to enter a reference to your Web Service's .asmx file:

```
http://localhost/Customer Orders Web Service/Service1.asmx
```

When you enter this URL and press enter, it shows the familiar Web Service help page displaying a description of the Web Service and its operations (**Figure 18**). In the right pane, there are <u>View Contract</u> and <u>View Documentation</u> hyperlinks. If you click the <u>View Contract</u> link, it displays the WSDL file in the dialog's left pane. If you click the <u>View Documentation</u> link, it displays any extra documentation you created for your Web Service.

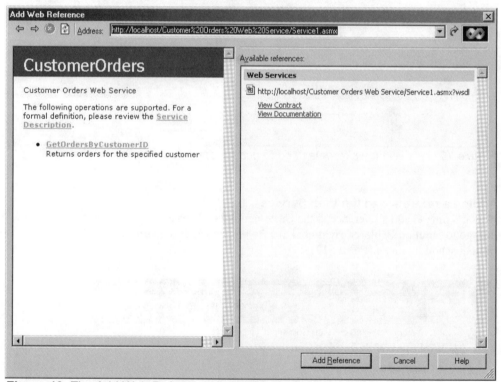

Figure 18. *The Add Web Reference dialog allows you to search for Web Services you can reference in your .NET projects.*

To add a reference to the Customer Orders Web Service to your project, click the Add Reference button. If you look in the Solution Explorer, you can see this adds a new localhost node containing three new files (**Figure 19**). Visual Studio.NET uses the name of this node as part of the namespace for the Web Service so, rename it to something more informative. To do this, right-click on the localhost node, select Rename from the shortcut menu, and then rename the node from "localhost" to "CustomerOrdersWebService".

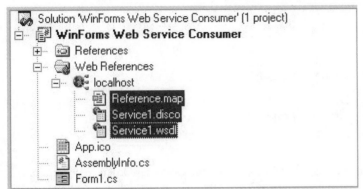

Figure 19. *Adding a Web Reference to your project adds three new files to your project.*

Now, take a closer look at the files added to the project. In order to see all of the file detail, click the Show All Files button at the top of the Solution Explorer (**Figure 20**).

Figure 20. *Click the Show All Files button to display all file detail in your project.*

Expand the CustomerOrdersWebService node, and you'll see three files. Reference.map is an XML file that maps URLs to local cached copies of the Service1.disco and Service1.wsdl files. Service1.disco is a Web Service discovery file. For more information on .disco files, see the "Web Services Discovery" section later in this chapter. Service1.wsdl is a local copy of the Customer Orders Web Service WSDL file.

If you expand the Reference.map node, you'll see a file named Reference.cs (or Reference.vb). Open this file by double-clicking it and you'll see the definition of a class named CustomerOrders based on the .NET Framework's SoapHttpClientProtocol class.

In C# (shown partially):

```
public class CustomerOrders :
    System.Web.Services.Protocols.SoapHttpClientProtocol
{
    . . .
}
```

And in Visual Basic .NET (shown partially):

```
Public Class CustomerOrders
    Inherits System.Web.Services.Protocols.SoapHttpClientProtocol
    . . .
End Class
```

This is a proxy class you can use to call methods on the Customer Orders Web Service. When you call a Web Service method, you don't actually call the method on a Web Service's object directly. Rather, you instantiate a local proxy class (based on the .NET Framework's SoapHttpClientProtocol class) that passes the call on to the Web Service (**Figure 21**).

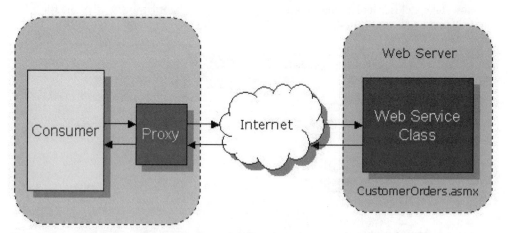

Figure 21. When you add a Web Service reference to your project, VS .NET automatically creates a local proxy class that you can use to indirectly call methods of the Web Service.

Calling the Web Service

Now you're ready to add code to the form to call the Web Service. To do this, select the Form1.cs [Design] tab (or Form1.vb), and double-click the Call Web Service button. This adds a new btnCallWS_Click event handler method to the form.

Before adding code to this method, go to the top of the form and add a reference to the CustomerOrders proxy class' namespace.

In C#:

```
using WinForms_Web_Service_Consumer.CustomerOrdersWebService;
```

And in Visual Basic .NET:

```
Imports WinForms_Web_Service_Consumer.CustomerOrdersWebService
```

Now, go back to the bottom of the code-behind file and add code to the btnCallWS_Click event handler method.
In C#:

```csharp
private void btnCallWS_Click(object sender, System.EventArgs e)
{
  // Instantiate the Web Service proxy class
  CustomerOrders CustomerOrdersWS = new CustomerOrders();

  // Call the Web Service and store the returned DataSet into dsOrders
  DataSet dsOrders =
    CustomerOrdersWS.GetOrdersByCustomerID(this.txtCustomerID.Text);

  // Bind the DataSet to the Orders DataGrid
  this.grdOrders.SetDataBinding(dsOrders, dsOrders.Tables[0].TableName);
}
```

And in Visual Basic .NET:

```vbnet
Private Sub btnCallWS_Click(ByVal sender As System.Object, _
    ByVal e As System.EventArgs) Handles btnCallWS.Click
    ' Instantiate the Web Service proxy class
    Dim CustomerOrdersWS As New CustomerOrders()

    ' Call the Web Service and store the returned DataSet into dsOrders
    Dim dsOrders As DataSet = _
        CustomerOrdersWS.GetOrdersByCustomerID(Me.txtCustomerID.Text)

    ' Bind the DataSet to the Orders DataGrid
    Me.grdOrders.SetDataBinding(dsOrders, dsOrders.Tables(0).TableName)
End Sub 'btnCallWS_Click
```

In this method, the first line of code instantiates the CustomerOrders Web Service proxy object. The next line calls the Web Service, passing the value stored in the Customer ID text box, and storing the return value in the dsOrders DataSet. The last line of code binds the DataSet to the DataGrid.

Running the Customer Orders Web Service consumer

Now it's time to run the Customer Orders Web Service consumer project. To do this, press F5, and Visual Studio .NET automatically saves all changes, compiles the project, and runs it. To test the Web Service, once the form displays, enter the text "QUICK" in the text box, and then click the Call Web Service button (**Figure 22**).

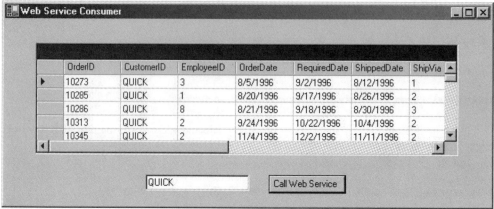

Figure 22. *The Web Service Consumer form calls the Customer Orders Web Service to retrieve the orders for the specified customer, and then displays them in the DataGrid.*

If this is the first time your Web server has started up, it will take several seconds before any records are displayed in the DataGrid. However, subsequent calls should respond far more quickly (you can try other customer IDs such as "QUEEN", "OCEAN", and "CHOPS").

Before continuing to the next section, close the Web Service Consumer form to avoid any conflicts.

Web Services Discovery

Do you want to be discovered or not? If your Web Service is of a private nature, you probably don't. You will only inform your business associates of its existence and not tell the rest of the world. However, you may want to create a Web Service intended for public consumption. How can others learn about your Web Service and the details of how to call its methods? This is accomplished by a process called *discovery*.

Discovery with UDDI

Universal Description, Discovery, and Integration (UDDI) is a registry that allows you to locate Web Services. If you have a Web Service you want to make public, you register information about your Web Service in the UDDI directory, and others can learn about your Web Service by searching the UDDI registry.

As you saw earlier in this chapter, when you add a Web Reference to your project, Visual Studio .NET provides an interface you can use to search the UDDI directory. Let's go back to this form and use it to search the UDDI directory.

Right-click the Add References node in the Solution Explorer and select Add Web Reference from the shortcut menu. This displays the Add Web Reference dialog (**Figure 23**).

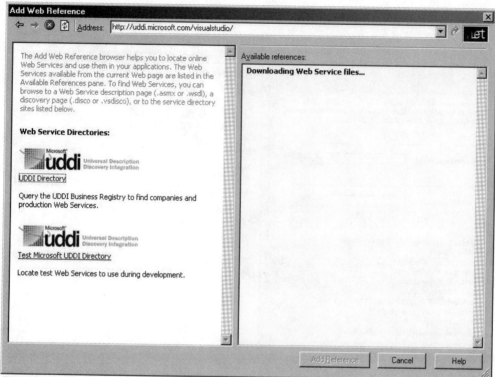

Figure 23. *The Add Web Reference dialog allows you to search the UDDI directory for Web Services exposed on the Internet.*

In the left pane there are two hyperlinks. The <u>UDDI Directory</u> link allows you to search for "real, live" Web Services, and the <u>Test Microsoft UDDI Directory</u> link allows you to search for "test" Web Services. Click the <u>UDDI Directory</u> link and the message "Downloading Web Service Files" appears in the right pane. After several seconds, the UDDI Search Tool is displayed in the left pane (**Figure 24**).

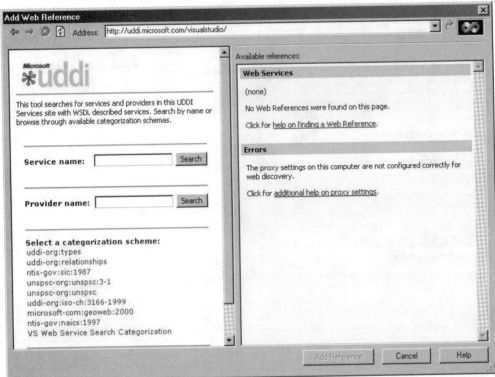

***Figure 24**. The UDDI search tool allows you to search for Web Services by name or by category.*

The UDDI search tool allows you to search for Web Services by Service name, Provider Name, or category. For example, type the word "weather" into the Service Name text box and click the Search button. As of the writing of this book, several weather Web Services registered with UDDI are displayed in the left pane of the Add Web Reference dialog (**Figure 25**).

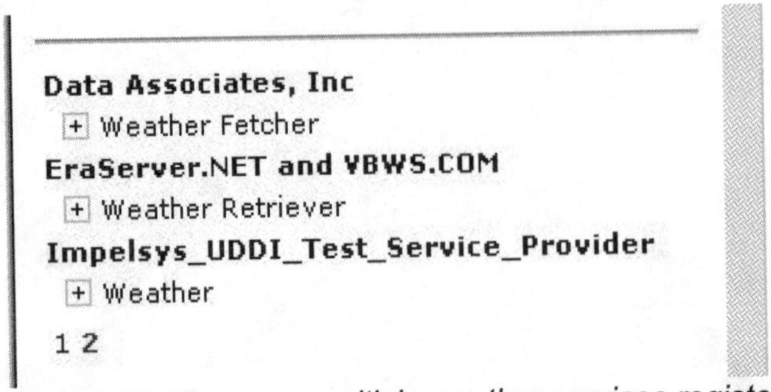

Data Associates, Inc
   [+] Weather Fetcher
EraServer.NET and VBWS.COM
   [+] Weather Retriever
Impelsys_UDDI_Test_Service_Provider
   [+] Weather

1 2

***Figure 25**. There are multiple weather services registered with UDDI.*

Pick the "Weather Retriever" Web Service from the list (if you don't see this specific Web Service, just choose another one). Expand the node of the "Weather Retriever" Web Service and you will see a more detailed description of the Web Service (**Figure 26**). The Service Description details that this Web Service retrieves Weather information based on a specific zip code. Also, notice the link displayed under "Interface definitions" references an .asmx file. It tells you that this is a .NET Web Service (although it doesn't have to be a .NET Web Service to work properly in this example!)

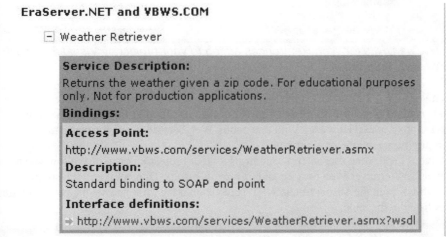

Figure 26. *Clicking the Interface definitions link enables the Add Reference button, allowing you to add a Web Service reference to your project.*

Adding a Web Service reference from UDDI

If you click the Interface definitions link, the message "Downloading Web Service files…" appears in the right pane. After several seconds, the Web Services WSDL file appears in the left pane, and the Add Reference dialog is enabled. Click the Add Reference button to add a reference to the Weather Fetcher Web Service to your project. When you do this, Visual Studio .NET adds three files to your project. Notice the URL for the Web Service is shown in reverse order (**Figure 27**).

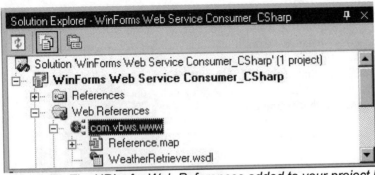

***Figure 27.** The URLs for Web References added to your project by Visual Studio.NET are shown in reverse order.*

When you added the local Customer Orders Web Service to the project, you renamed the "localhost" node to something more descriptive because it is used as the namespace of the Web Service proxy class. However, with this public Web Service, leave the name "as is" because it provides a unique namespace.

Next, you'll add some user interface controls to your project's Form1 that allow you to call the Weather Retriever Web Service and display its results. Drag and drop the controls listed in **Table 5** from the Visual Studio.NET Toolbox onto the form and set the corresponding properties listed in the table.

***Table 5.** Weather Web Service user interface controls*

Control	Property	Value
GroupBox		
	Name	grpWeather
	Location	40, 249
	Size	540, 165
	Text	Weather
Label		
	Name	lblZipCode
	AutoSize	True
	Location	80, 30
	Text	Zip Code:
TextBox		
	Name	txtZipCode
	Location	145, 28
	Size	135, 20
	Text	(empty string)
Button		
	Name	btnCallWS2
	Location	305, 28
	Size	100, 23
	Text	Call Web Service
TextBox		
	Name	txtWeather
	Location	25, 70
	MultiLine	True
	Size	490, 75

Calling the Web Service

Now you are ready to add code to the form that calls the Web Service and displays the result. Double-click the btnCallWS2 button to automatically add a new event handler method named btnCallWS2_Click to the form's code-behind file. Before adding code to this method, go to the top of the code-behind file and add a reference to the Web Service proxy object's namespace.

In C#:

```
using WinForms_Web_Service_Consumer.com.vbws.www;
```

And in Visual Basic .NET:

```
Imports WinForms_Web_Service_Consumer_Visual_Basic.com.vbws.www
```

Now add the following code to the btnCallWS2_Click method at the bottom of the code-behind file.

In C#:

```csharp
private void btnCallWS2_Click(object sender, System.EventArgs e)
{
  // Instantiate the WeatherRetriever Web Service proxy
  WeatherRetriever WeatherRetrieverWS = new WeatherRetriever();

  // Call the Web Service's GetWeather method
  CurrentWeather WeatherReport =
    WeatherRetrieverWS.GetWeather(this.txtZipCode.Text);

  // Display the results
  this.txtWeather.Text = WeatherReport.Conditions + "\r\n" +
    "Temperature: " + WeatherReport.CurrentTemp + "\r\n" +
    "Humidity: " + WeatherReport.Humidity + "\r\n" +
    "Barometer: " + WeatherReport.Barometer + "\r\n" +
    "Barometer Direction: " + WeatherReport.BarometerDirection;
}
```

And in Visual Basic .NET:

```vb
Private Sub btnCallWS2_Click(ByVal sender As System.Object, _
    ByVal e As System.EventArgs) Handles btnCallWS2.Click
    ' Instantiate the WeatherRetriever Web Service proxy
    Dim WeatherRetrieverWS As New WeatherRetriever()

    ' Call the Web Service's GetWeather method
    Dim WeatherReport As CurrentWeather = _
      WeatherRetrieverWS.GetWeather(Me.txtZipCode.Text)

    ' Display the results
    Me.txtWeather.Text = WeatherReport.Conditions & ControlChars.CrLf & _
        "Temperature: " & WeatherReport.CurrentTemp & ControlChars.CrLf & _
        "Humidity: " & WeatherReport.Humidity & ControlChars.CrLf & _
        "Barometer: " & WeatherReport.Barometer & ControlChars.CrLf & _
        "Barometer Direction: " & WeatherReport.BarometerDirection
End Sub
```

Running the Web Service consumer

Now you're ready to run the Web Service. To do this, just press F5 to save all changes, compile the project, and run the application. When the form is displayed, enter a zip code in the Zip Code text box (for example, "22903"), and then click the Call Web Service button. After several seconds, you should see the weather report for the specified zip code displayed in the text box at the bottom of the form (**Figure 28**).

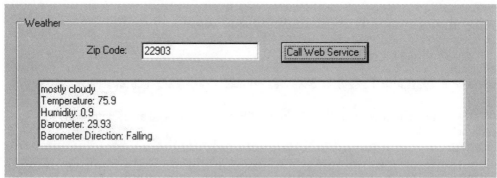

Figure 28. *This form demonstrates how to call a public Web Service discovered by means of UDDI.*

Conclusion

As you see from this chapter, Microsoft has made it very easy to both publish and consume Web Services in Visual Studio.NET. Although you may not initially find a use for Web Services in your application, as they become more and more mainstream, and as new, reliable Web Services become more prevalent, you may find they give your desktop and Web applications a level of interoperability they've never had before.

Chapter 13
Error Handling and Debugging
in .NET

Error handling in .NET is quite a bit different than error handling found in previous versions of VFP. However, both .NET and Visual FoxPro 8 have `try...catch...finally` **blocks that provide a far more powerful and flexible way to handle errors in your application. This chapter also discusses Visual Studio .NET's debugging tools. As you'll see, many are similar to Visual FoxPro's; some are better, and some are not!**

Errors are part and parcel of software applications. However, in weakly typed languages such as Visual FoxPro, you are more likely to create code containing bugs than in strongly typed languages that find far more errors at compile time. However, even the best of compilers can't find all of the logic errors you have in your code. In addition, problems can occur at runtime that have nothing to do with bugs in your code. At times resources are locked or unavailable, files become corrupt, and remote servers can go down. Your code needs to be able to handle all of these scenarios.

This is where error handling and debugging tools come to the rescue. This chapter discusses .NET error handling as well as Visual Studio .NET's debugging tools that help you identify errors in your .NET applications.

Common errors vs. exceptions

There are errors and there are exceptions. Errors are common problems that occur in an application from which the application can easily recover. For example, a user may enter an invalid value and your application can display a message warning them of this. A connection to a database may have been left open and the application can simply close it.

In contrast, exceptions, as suggested by their name, are uncommon or exceptional errors from which the application cannot recover. For example, you may not be able to connect to the application's database—this is exceptional, because the application is not be able to run properly without access to the data. A programmer may have passed an invalid value to a method—this is exceptional (hopefully!) and the method is not able to run.

In the case of common error handling, you should write defensive code that expects the expected and gracefully handles the problem. In the case of exceptions, you need to do something more. The following sections describe exception handling in .NET.

.NET Exceptions

In the .NET world, an exception is an object created when an error occurs in your application (this is also known as *throwing* an exception). The .NET Framework contains hundreds of different exception classes created when specific types of errors occur. With so many different exception classes, it's not practical that you become intimately familiar with each and every one. **Figure 1** shows just a few of the exception classes you commonly encounter and **Table 1** gives a brief description of each of these classes. As you get more experience writing .NET applications, you learn about the most common exceptions quickly enough!

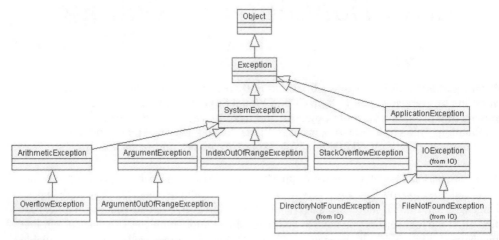

Figure 1*. Common .NET Exception classes.*

Table 1*. Common Exception class descriptions*

Property	Description
System.Exception	The base class for all other exception classes.
System.ApplicationException	The base class for all custom exception classes you create.
System.SystemException	The base class for all predefined exceptions in the System namespace.
System.ArithmeticException	The base class for arithmetic, casting, or conversion operation errors.
System.OverflowException	The exception thrown when there is an overflow in arithmetic, casting, or conversion operation.
System.ArgumentException	The exception thrown when an invalid argument is passed to a method.
System.IndexOutOfRangeException	The exception thrown when an attempt is made to access an array element that is out of the bounds of the array.
System.StackOverflowException	The exception thrown when the stack overflows with too many pending method calls. This can occur if you have a recursive, infinite loop in your code.
System.IO.IOException	The base class for all I/O exceptions.
System.IO.DirectoryNotFoundException	The exception thrown when a directory cannot be found.
System.IO.FileNotFoundException	The exception thrown when a file cannot be found.

Exceptions can be thrown by either the .NET Common Language Runtime or by an executing application. Some examples of CLR exceptions include ExecutionEngineException, StackOverflowException, and OutOfMemoryException. These exceptions are usually of such a critical nature that the application cannot recover from them. For more information, see the .NET Help topics for each of these classes.

Catching exceptions with `try...catch...finally`

.NET provides structured exception handling in the form of `try...catch...finally` blocks in both C# and Visual Basic .NET that allow you to catch and respond to exceptions thrown in your application. These blocks should be used to catch exceptions—not common errors. Here is a template showing how these `try...catch...finally` blocks are structured.

In C#:

```
try
{
  // Contains regular application code
}
catch
{
  // Contains error handling code
}
finally
{
  // Contains any cleanup code needed to close resources such
  // as files and connections that were opened in the try block
}
```

And in Visual Basic. NET:

```
Try
  ' Contains regular application code
Catch
  ' Contains error handling code
Finally
  ' Contains any cleanup code needed to close resources such
  ' as files and connections that were opened in the try block
End Try
```

The following sections explain what the `try`, `catch`, and `finally` blocks are and how they can be used in your applications.

The `try` block

You can surround any code that has the potential to cause an exception with a `try` block. A good example is trying to create a connection to a database. For any number of reasons, including the possibility that the database server is down, you may encounter an error when you attempt to connect to a database.

The `catch` block

As mentioned previously, when an error occurs in your application, a corresponding exception class representing that specific error is instantiated. The `catch` block allows you to get a reference to this exception object and respond accordingly. The `catch` block only executes if an exception occurs.

The `catch` block is optional. However, if you don't have a `catch` block, your `try` block must have an associated `finally` block, which is discussed in the next section. If you don't have a `catch` block associated with a `try` block, the runtime searches up the stack to find the next suitable `catch` block. See the "Nested `try` blocks" section later in this chapter for details.

The `finally` block

The `finally` block gives you a place to insert cleanup code that is executed whether or not an error is encountered in the `try` block. The `finally` block, although useful in many cases, is optional—if you don't have any specific cleanup code that needs to be run, you can leave it out. However, if you leave out the `finally` block, your `try` block must have an associated `catch` block.

A real-world example

Here's a real-world example showing how to use the `try...catch...finally` blocks when accessing data. This method connects to the SQL Server Northwind database and runs the "Ten Most Expensive Products" stored procedure. The result set is stored in a data reader that is iterated to build a string and displayed using the MessageBox class.

In C#:

```csharp
public void TryCatchDemo()
{
  SqlDataReader dr = null;

  // Create the connection string & configure the connection and command
objects
  string ConnectString = "server=(local);uid=sa;pwd=;database=NorthWind;";
  SqlConnection Conn = new SqlConnection(ConnectString);
  SqlCommand Cmd = new SqlCommand("Ten Most Expensive Products", Conn);
  Cmd.CommandType = CommandType.StoredProcedure;

  try
  {
      // Open the connection and execute the stored procedure
      Conn.Open();
      dr = Cmd.ExecuteReader();

      // Get all records in the result set
      string Products = "";
      while (dr.Read())
      {
          // Access the data in the current row
          Products += dr.GetString(0) + ", " + dr.GetDecimal(1) + "\n";
      }
      MessageBox.Show(Products, "try...catch...finally demo");
      }
  catch (Exception e)
  {
      // Log the Exception
      ExceptionLog.Log(e);
  }
```

```
finally
{
    // Close the data reader and connection
    if (dr != null)
    {
        dr.Close();
    }
    Conn.Close();
}
}
```

And in Visual Basic .NET:

```
Public Sub TryCatchDemo()
    Dim dr As SqlDataReader = Nothing

    ' Create the connection string and configure
    ' the connection and command objects
    Dim ConnectString As String = _
        "server=(local);uid=sa;pwd=;database=NorthWind;"
    Dim Conn As New SqlConnection(ConnectString)
    Dim Cmd As New SqlCommand("Ten Most Expensive Products", Conn)
    Cmd.CommandType = CommandType.StoredProcedure

    Try
        ' Open the connection and execute the stored procedure
        Conn.Open()
        dr = Cmd.ExecuteReader()

        ' Get all records in the result set
        Dim Products As String = ""
        While dr.Read()
            ' Access the data in the current row
            Products += dr.GetString(0) + ", " & _
                dr.GetDecimal(1).ToString() & ControlChars.Lf
        End While
        MessageBox.Show(Products, "try...catch...finally demo")

    Catch e As Exception
        ' Log the Exception
        ExceptionLog.LogError(e)
    Finally
        ' Close the data reader and connection
        If Not (dr Is Nothing) Then
            dr.Close()
        End If
        Conn.Close()
    End Try
End Sub 'TryCatchDemo
```

There are several lines of code at the top of the method outside of the try...catch...finally blocks. These lines of code are not trouble spots, so they can safely reside outside of the try block. Within the try block is code with the potential for error. This is where a connection to SQL Server is opened, the stored procedure is executed, and the result set is processed.

If everything goes smoothly

If no errors are encountered in the `try` block, the `finally` block is executed, which performs cleanup by closing the data reader and the connection object.

If an error occurs

What if an error occurs (for example, the specified stored procedure doesn't exist) on the line of code that executes the stored procedure?

In C#:

```
dr = Cmd.ExecuteReader();
```

In Visual Basic .NET:

```
dr = Cmd.ExecuteReader()
```

When the error occurs, control is immediately passed to the `catch` block. Remember the CLR instantiates an exception object when an error occurs—this is also known as "throwing an exception". The `catch` block is the mechanism the CLR uses to pass a reference to this object. If you look at the code, you'll see the `catch` block declares a parameter of the type "Exception" named "e".

In C#:

```
catch (Exception e)
```

In Visual Basic .NET:

```
Catch e As Exception
```

This is how the CLR passes the exception object to the `catch` block.

Within the `catch` block is a single line of code that passes the exception object reference to the static Log method of the ExceptionLog class (one of your custom sample classes). This method logs the error for future reference. Check out the "Logging Errors" section later in this chapter for information on extracting and logging error information from this exception object.

> *In reality, if a critical error occurred during an operation similar to the one in the sample, you probably wouldn't catch the error at this level. Depending on the context where the code is called, you may want to let the client code catch the error instead and respond accordingly.*

Remember, if an exception is thrown, the `finally` method is still executed. This means the cleanup code that closes the data reader and connection object is executed after the `catch` block is run. This ensures you don't leave a connection to the database open. Notice the code performs a check to see if the data reader object `dr` is null.

In C#:

```
finally
{
    // Close the data reader and connection
    if (dr != null)
    {
        dr.Close();
    }
    Conn.Close();
}
```

And in Visual Basic .NET:

```
Finally
    ' Close the data reader and connection
    If Not (dr Is Nothing) Then
        dr.Close()
    End If
    Conn.Close()
```

This check is necessary, because if an error occurs while executing the stored procedure, the data reader may not be returned and the variable may be null.

After the `finally` block is executed, control is passed to the end of the `finally` block. This is what you want, because if the stored procedure did not execute correctly, you don't want to continue processing. This is different from Visual FoxPro 7, where the Error event executes and control is passed back to the line immediately following the code that generated an error.

Visual FoxPro 8 introduces Try...Catch structured exception handling to the FoxPro language. For details, see the VFP 8 Help file.

Catching specific exceptions

The previous example shows how you can use the `catch` block to catch all exceptions. However, there may be times where you would like to catch specific exceptions and handle them differently. The following code sample shows how to do this.

In C#:

```
public void CatchOverFlow()
{
    long MyLong = 3000000000;
    int MyInteger;
```

```
try
{
    // Store the value of MyDouble into MyInteger
    checked
    {
        MyInteger = (int)MyLong;
    }
}
catch(OverflowException e)
{
    // Do additional processing…
    MessageBox.Show("Caught an arithmetic overflow exception.", "Catch demo");

    // Catch a specific exception
    ExceptionLog.LogError(e);
}
catch(Exception e)
{
    // Catch the generic exceptions
    ExceptionLog.LogError(e);
}
finally
{
    // Cleanup code
}
}
```

In Visual Basic .NET:

```
Public Sub CatchOverFlow()
    Dim MyLong As Long = 3000000000
    Dim MyInteger As Integer

    Try
        ' Store the value of MyDouble into MyInteger
        MyInteger = CInt(MyLong)

    Catch e As OverflowException
        ' Do additional processing
        MessageBox.Show("Caught an arithmetic overflow exception.", "Catch
demo")

        ' Catch a specific exception
        ExceptionLog.LogError(e)

    Catch e As Exception
        ' Catch the generic exceptions
        ExceptionLog.LogError(e)

    Finally
        ' Cleanup code

    End Try

End Sub 'CatchOverFlow
```

The code within the `try` block takes the value of MyLong and casts it to an integer. However, since the largest positive value an integer can hold is a 2,147,483,647, this code generates an exception.

Notice the C# code contains a `checked` block surrounding the code that stores the value of MyLong into MyInteger, but the Visual Basic .NET code does not:

```
checked
{
  MyInteger = (int)MyLong;
}
```

In C#, an arithmetic overflow condition does not automatically cause an exception to be thrown. If you want an exception to be thrown, you need to surround the code with a `checked` block. In Visual Basic .NET, you don't have a choice—an exception is always thrown when an overflow condition is encountered. Alternately, you can tell the C# compiler you want all code checked by using the "/checked" compiler option.

Notice there are two `catch` blocks in this code. The first `catch` block is specifically checking for an OverflowException error and the second block is checking for a generic Exception. If code in the `try` block generates an exception other than an OverflowException, it is caught by the second `catch` block.

The OverflowException `catch` block has a placeholder for "Do additional processing". In the real world, you could change the default exception message to something more informative. The technique for doing this is discussed later in this chapter under the "System.Exception" section.

Catching all exceptions

If an exception is not caught in a `catch` block, the Common Language Runtime catches it for you. If this happens, an *un*-user friendly message is displayed and your program terminates. The best way to avoid a situation where your code does not catch an error is to use nested `try` blocks.

Nested `try` blocks

Nested `try` blocks allow you to bracket one `try` block with another that sits at a higher level. Here is some sample code demonstrating how this works.

In C#:

```
public void NestedTry()
{
  try
  {
      try
      {
          int x;
          int y = 0;
          // Divide 100 by 0 (throws an exception)
          x = 100 / y;
      }
      catch (OverflowException e)
```

```
    {
        ExceptionLog.LogError(e);
    }
    finally
    {
        // cleanup
    }
  }
  catch (Exception e)
  {
        ExceptionLog.LogError(e);
  }
  finally
  {
        // cleanup
  }
}
```

And in Visual Basic .NET:

```
Public Sub NestedTry()
    Try
        Try
            Dim x As Integer
            Dim y As Integer = 0
            ' Divide 100 by 0 (throws an exception)
            x = CInt(100 / y)
        Catch e As OverflowException
            ExceptionLog.LogError(e)
        Finally
            ' cleanup
            MessageBox.Show("Running the inner finally block")
        End Try
    Catch e As Exception
        ExceptionLog.LogError(e)
    Finally
        ' cleanup
    End Try
End Sub 'NestedTry
```

The inner `try` block contains code that divides 100 by the variable `y`, which contains the value zero. Running this code throws a DivideByZeroException. Notice, however, the inner `catch` block only checks for an OverflowException. In this situation, the .NET runtime determines there is no `catch` block for the exception that was thrown and does the following:

1. Runs the inner `finally` block associated with the inner `catch`.

2. Searches for a suitable `catch` block further up the stack.

3. When it finds the outer `catch` block that checks for *any* exception, it executes the code within it.

4. Executes the outer `finally` block.

Although this sample code nests `try` blocks within a single method, you can nest them at any level in your application calling chain. In fact, it's a good idea to bracket your entire

application in a `try` block as a final check for any unhandled exceptions within
your application.

For example, in C#:

```
static void Main()
{
    try
    {
        Application.Run(new MainAppWindow());
    }
    catch (Exception e)
    {
        ExceptionLog.LogError(e);
    }
    finally
    {
        // Cleanup
    }
}
```

And in Visual Basic .NET:

```
Shared Sub Main()
    Try
        Application.Run(New MainAppWindow())
    Catch e As Exception
        ExceptionDisplay.ShowError(e)
        ExceptionLog.LogError(e)
    Finally
        ' cleanup
    End Try
End Sub
```

With your application bracketed this way, you can be sure that all uncaught exceptions
are intercepted and logged. However, if an exception is not caught until it gets to this point,
the application stops executing. In contrast, if you catch an exception at the point it occurs
(or some layer between the actual error and the topmost `try...catch...finally` block),
then application execution passes to the associated `finally` block and application
execution continues.

At times, you may not know how to handle an exception at the level where the error
occurs. For example, you may have a library of classes used by a variety of applications.
Because you don't know the context where a particular class is used, you often don't know
how to properly respond to exceptions. In cases like this, you should allow the calling code to
handle any exceptions that may occur. However, you may still want to catch generic
exceptions and throw your own custom exception objects to provide the calling code with
more specific information.

Throwing your own exceptions

Not all exceptions are automatically generated by the .NET runtime. Some are the result of perfectly valid .NET code that simply won't work. For example, the contents of a file may have become corrupt, a particular file may not exist, or it may be locked. If you detect error conditions within your application, you can manually throw exceptions from within your code.

For example, the following class contains a method called IsBirthMonth, which accepts an integer and determines if it is my birth month (October). The code checks to see if the value of the month parameter is between 1 and 12. If it's not, an exception is thrown—specifically an ArgumentOutOfRangeException, which is one of the .NET Framework's exception classes.

In C#:

```
public class ThrowExceptionDemo
{
  public bool IsBirthMonth(int month)
  {
    bool BirthMonth = false;

    if (! (month >= 1 && month <= 12))
    {
      throw new ArgumentOutOfRangeException();
    }

    if (month == 10)
    {
      BirthMonth = true;
    }

    return BirthMonth;
  }
}
```

In Visual Basic .NET:

```
Public Class ThrowExceptionDemo

    Public Function IsBirthMonth(month As Integer) As Boolean
        Dim BirthMonth As Boolean = False

        If Not(month >= 1 And month <= 12) Then
            Throw New ArgumentOutOfRangeException()
        End If

        If month = 10 Then
            BirthMonth = True
        End If

        Return BirthMonth
    End Function 'IsBirthMonth
End Class 'ThrowExceptionDemo
```

If you have an application-level try...catch...finally block in place, the block would catch this exception.

Displaying and Logging Errors

Up to this point I've glossed over how to respond to exceptions that are caught by simply calling ExceptionLog.LogError. In this section I'll show you how to retrieve error information from an Exception object and display or log the error. Before doing this, first take a closer look at the System.Exception class.

System.Exception

As mentioned previously, all exception classes—both the .NET Framework classes and your own custom exceptions—are derived from the System.Exception class. **Table 2** contains a list of the Exception class's public properties with a brief description of each.

Table 2. System.Exception properties

Property	Description
HelpLink	Specifies a Uniform Resource Name (URN) or Uniform Resource Locater (URL) link to the Help file associated with the exception. **Example:** "file:///C:/Applications/MyHelp.html#MyError1"
Message	The text of the error message.
Source	Specifies the name of the object that caused the error.
TargetSite	Specifies the method that threw the exception.
StackTrace	Contains a string detailing the call stack at the time the exception occurred.
InnerException	Specifies a previous exception that caused the current exception. If there is no previous exception, this property is null.

One of the most important properties of the Exception object is Message. This property contains the text of the error message. The .NET runtime supplies a default message that is stored in this property. For example, the default message displayed when the IsBirthMonth method throws its exception is:

```
"Specified argument was out of the range of valid values."
```

You can override this default message by specifying a different message in the constructor of the exception class. The ArgumentOutOfRangeException class has four different constructors you can choose. The constructor signature I've selected in this example expects three parameters:

- Parameter Name

- Actual Value

- Message

Here's the modified code in C#:

```
throw new ArgumentOutOfRangeException("month",
  month,"Values for month must be between 1-12");
```

And in Visual Basic .NET:

```
Throw New ArgumentOutOfRangeException("month", _
    month, "Values for month must be between 1-12")
```

Now when this exception is thrown, the default message is:

```
" Values for month must be between 1-12."
```

This is much more descriptive than the generic "argument out of range" message.

Displaying exception information

To see the value of an exception object's message property (and other properties), the following sample code uses a class with a static method named "ShowError".
   In C#:

```
public class ExceptionDisplay
{
  public static void ShowError(Exception e)
  {
      MessageBox.Show("Error information\n\n" +
          "Message: " + e.Message + "\n" +
          "Source: " + e.Source + "\n" +
          "TargetSite: " + e.TargetSite + "\n" +
          "Stack trace: " + e.StackTrace,
          "Exception demo");
  }
}
```

And in Visual Basic .NET:

```
Public Class ExceptionDisplay

    Public Shared Sub ShowError(ByVal e As Exception)
        MessageBox.Show("Message: " & e.Message & ControlChars.Lf & _
            ControlChars.Lf & "Source: " & e.Source & ControlChars.Lf & _
            ControlChars.Lf & "TargetSite: " & e.TargetSite.ToString() & _
            ControlChars.Lf & ControlChars.Lf & "Stack trace: " & _
            ControlChars.Lf & e.StackTrace, "Exception demo")
    End Sub 'ShowError

End Class 'ExceptionDisplay
```

Here is a modified version of the IsBirthMonth method containing a catch block that calls this new static method.

In C#:

```csharp
public bool IsBirthMonth(int month)
{
  bool BirthMonth = false;

  try
  {
    if (! (month >= 1 && month <= 12))
    {
       throw new ArgumentOutOfRangeException("month",
           month,"Values for month must be between 1-12");
    }
  }

  catch (ArgumentOutOfRangeException e)
  {
    ExceptionDisplay.ShowError(e);
  }

  finally
  {
    if (month == 10)
    {
       BirthMonth = true;
    }
  }
  return BirthMonth;
}
```

And in Visual Basic .NET:

```vbnet
Public Function IsBirthMonth(ByVal month As Integer) As Boolean
    Dim BirthMonth As Boolean = False

    Try
        If Not (month >= 1 And month <= 12) Then
            Throw New ArgumentOutOfRangeException("month", _
                month, "Values for month must be between 1-12")
        End If

    Catch e As ArgumentOutOfRangeException
        ExceptionDisplay.ShowError(e)
        ExceptionLog.LogError(e)

    Finally
        If month = 10 Then
            BirthMonth = True
        End If
    End Try
    Return BirthMonth
End Function 'IsBirthMonth
```

If you run this code from the book's sample application, you'll see the message box shown in **Figure 2**.

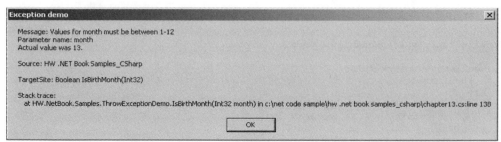

Figure 2. *Important information can be gleaned from the properties of an exception object.*

As you can see, the Message property contains a three-part string that includes the error message, the parameter name, and the actual value, each shown on their own line.

If you do not set the Source property, it defaults to the name of the assembly where the error occurred—in this case, "HW .Net Book Samples_CSharp", or if you're using Visual Basic .NET, "HW .Net Book Samples_Visual Basic".

The TargetSite property contains a string specifying the method that threw the exception, in this case "IsBirthMonth". As shown, it also includes the type of the parameter and the type of the return value.

The StackTrace property provides information regarding the methods in execution at the time the exception is thrown. As seen in Figure 2, the example only lists a single class and method—the ThrowExceptionDemo class and the IsBirthMonth method. It also lists the source code file and line number where the error was thrown.

Logging exception information
Typically, you should create a way to save exception information to some type of log file. In this section, you'll see a few easy ways to do this.

Figure 3 contains a UML class diagram of an ExceptionLog class. This is a custom class found in this chapter's sample code that allows you to save exception information to an XML log file. Saving exceptions as XML gives you the ability to easily read and manipulate the exception data using either .NET run time or design time tools.

ExceptionLog
+ LogFile + ApplicationName
+ CreateLogFile() + LogError(e : System.Exception) : void

Figure 3. *The ExceptionLog class found in this chapter's sample code provides a means to save errors to a log file.*

The ExceptionLog's LogFile property specifies the name of the XML log file. The ApplicationName property identifies the name of the application that generated the exception. Specifying the name of the application lets you save exception data from multiple applications into a single exception log.

The ExceptionLog's CreateLogFile method creates a new log file with the name given in the LogFile property.

Here is the code for this method in C#:

```csharp
public static void CreateLogFile()
{
  // Create an XmlTextWriter, specifying the name of the new XML log file
  XmlTextWriter xtw = new XmlTextWriter(LogFile, null);

  // Write the XML declaration at the top of the file
  xtw.WriteStartDocument();

  // Add a comment to the file indicating the date/time created
  xtw.WriteComment("Log file created: " + DateTime.Now);

  // Add an empty <EventLog> element
  xtw.WriteStartElement("EventLog");
  xtw.WriteEndElement();

  // Close the stream
  xtw.Close();
}
```

And in Visual Basic .NET:

```vb
Public Shared Sub CreateLogFile()
    ' Create an XmlTextWriter, specifying the name of the new XML log file
    Dim xtw As New XmlTextWriter(LogFile, Nothing)

    ' Write the XML declaration at the top of the file
    xtw.WriteStartDocument()

    ' Add a comment to the file indicating the date/time created
    xtw.WriteComment(("Log file created: " + DateTime.Now.ToString()))

    ' Add an empty <EventLog> element
    xtw.WriteStartElement("EventLog")
    xtw.WriteEndElement()

    ' Close the stream
    xtw.Close()

End Sub 'CreateLogFile
```

This method uses an XmlTextWriter to create the new XML log file, and then writes:

- The XML declaration at the top of the file.

- A comment indicating the date and time the file was created.

- An empty <EventLog> element.

> *For more information about using the XmlTextWriter class and other XML classes referenced in this chapter, see Chapter 11, ".NET XML".*

Now take a look at the code in the ExceptionLog's LogError method.
In C#:

```csharp
public static void LogError(Exception e)
{
    // If the log file doesn't exist, create it
    if (!File.Exists(LogFile))
    {
        CreateLogFile();
    }

    // Open the log file
    XmlDocument XmlDoc = new XmlDocument();
    XmlDoc.Load(LogFile);

    // Create a new Exception element
    XmlElement ExceptionEntry = XmlDoc.CreateElement("Exception");

    // Create a new DateTime element
    XmlElement DateTimeChild = XmlDoc.CreateElement("DateTime");
    DateTimeChild.InnerText = DateTime.Now.ToString();
    ExceptionEntry.AppendChild(DateTimeChild);

    // Create an Application element
    XmlElement ApplicationChild = XmlDoc.CreateElement("Application");
    ApplicationChild.InnerText = ApplicationName;
    ExceptionEntry.AppendChild(ApplicationChild);

    // Create a new Message child element
    XmlElement MessageChild = XmlDoc.CreateElement("Message");
    MessageChild.InnerText = e.Message;
    ExceptionEntry.AppendChild(MessageChild);

    // Create a new Source child element
    XmlElement SourceChild = XmlDoc.CreateElement("Source");
    SourceChild.InnerText = e.Source;
    ExceptionEntry.AppendChild(SourceChild);

    // Create a new TargetSite child element
    XmlElement TargetSiteChild = XmlDoc.CreateElement("TargetSite");
    TargetSiteChild.InnerText = e.TargetSite.ToString();
    ExceptionEntry.AppendChild(TargetSiteChild);

    // Create a new Stacktrace child element
    XmlElement StackTraceChild = XmlDoc.CreateElement("StackTrace");
    StackTraceChild.InnerText = e.StackTrace;
    ExceptionEntry.AppendChild(StackTraceChild);

    // Add the entire ExceptionEntry to the XML document
    XmlDoc.DocumentElement.AppendChild(ExceptionEntry);
```

```
    // Write out the updated XML file
    XmlTextWriter xtw = new XmlTextWriter(LogFile, null);
    xtw.Formatting = Formatting.Indented;
    XmlDoc.WriteContentTo(xtw);
    xtw.Close();
}
```

And in Visual Basic .NET:

```
Public Shared Sub LogError(ByVal e As Exception)
    ' If the log file doesn't exist, create it
    If Not File.Exists(LogFile) Then
        CreateLogFile()
    End If

    ' Open the log file
    Dim XmlDoc As New XmlDocument()
    XmlDoc.Load(LogFile)

    ' Create a new Exception element
    Dim ExceptionEntry As XmlElement = XmlDoc.CreateElement("Exception")

    ' Create a new DateTime element
    Dim DateTimeChild As XmlElement = XmlDoc.CreateElement("DateTime")
    DateTimeChild.InnerText = DateTime.Now.ToString()
    ExceptionEntry.AppendChild(DateTimeChild)

    ' Create an Application element
    Dim ApplicationChild As XmlElement = XmlDoc.CreateElement("Application")
    ApplicationChild.InnerText = ApplicationName
    ExceptionEntry.AppendChild(ApplicationChild)

    ' Create a new Message child element
    Dim MessageChild As XmlElement = XmlDoc.CreateElement("Message")
    MessageChild.InnerText = e.Message
    ExceptionEntry.AppendChild(MessageChild)

    ' Create a new Source child element
    Dim SourceChild As XmlElement = XmlDoc.CreateElement("Source")
    SourceChild.InnerText = e.Source
    ExceptionEntry.AppendChild(SourceChild)

    ' Create a new TargetSite child element
    Dim TargetSiteChild As XmlElement = XmlDoc.CreateElement("TargetSite")
    TargetSiteChild.InnerText = e.TargetSite.ToString()
    ExceptionEntry.AppendChild(TargetSiteChild)

    ' Create a new Stacktrace child element
    Dim StackTraceChild As XmlElement = XmlDoc.CreateElement("StackTrace")
    StackTraceChild.InnerText = e.StackTrace
    ExceptionEntry.AppendChild(StackTraceChild)

    ' Add the entire ExceptionEntry to the XML document
    XmlDoc.DocumentElement.AppendChild(ExceptionEntry)
```

```
' Write out the updated XML file
Dim xtw As New XmlTextWriter(LogFile, Nothing)
xtw.Formatting = Formatting.Indented
XmlDoc.WriteContentTo(xtw)
xtw.Close()

End Sub 'LogError
```

This method first checks to see if the exception log file exists. If the file doesn't exist, it makes a call to the CreateLogFile method, which creates a new file. Next, it opens the log file in an instance of the XmlDocument class and creates a new <Exception> element. Afterwards, it adds DateTime, Application, Message, Source, TargetSite, and StackTrace child elements. Finally, it writes out the log file using an XmlTextWriter object in conjunction with the XmlDocument.WriteContentTo method.

Here's an example of a single entry in the XML Exception log file:

```
<?xml version="1.0"?>
<!--Log file created: 6/30/2002 9:59:50 AM-->
  <Exception>
    <DateTime>6/30/2002 11:22:03 AM</DateTime>
    <Application>HW .NET Sample app</Application>
    <Message>Values for month must be between 1-12
Parameter name: month
Actual value was 13.</Message>
    <Source>HW .NET Book Samples_CSharp</Source>
    <TargetSite>Boolean IsBirthMonth(Int32)</TargetSite>
    <StackTrace>    at HW.NetBook.Samples.ThrowExceptionDemo.IsBirthMonth(Int32
month) in c:\net code sample\hw .net book samples_csharp\chapter13.cs:line
139</StackTrace>
  </Exception>
</EventLog>
```

In a real-world application, you may prefer to write your errors to a Windows 2000 event log on a local or remote computer rather than to an XML log file. One advantage of doing this is being able to use the Windows Event Viewer to view, search, archive, export, and maintain event logs. Check out the .NET Help topic "Logging Application, Server, and Security Events" for information on how to do this.

Creating your own custom exception classes

If there is an existing .NET Framework exception class that fits your needs, Microsoft recommends you use that class when throwing your own exceptions. For example, in the ThrowException demo class earlier in this chapter, the IsBirthMonth method used the .NET Framework's ArgumentOutOfRangeException class to indicate if an invalid month was passed to the method. This class was used because it perfectly suited the situation. However, if you run into a situation where there isn't an existing class that suits your needs, the .NET Framework provides the System.ApplicationException class specifically designed for the purpose of allowing you to create your own custom exception classes.

Deriving exceptions from the .NET System.ApplicationException class gives you a way to distinguish between exceptions defined in the .NET Framework and custom exceptions you define. ApplicationException has four different overloaded constructor methods as shown in **Table 3**.

Table 3. *ApplicationException constructor methods*

Method	Description

public ApplicationException()
public ApplicationException(string);
public ApplicationException(string, Exception)
 	
public ApplicationException(SerializationIfnfo, StreamingContext);
	Simple constructor
	Constructor with error message
	Constructor with an error message and a reference to the inner exception that caused the original exception
	Deserialization constructor

The .NET Help topic, "Best Practices for handling exceptions", states that when you create your own exception classes you should implement at least the first three constructors shown in Table 3. The fourth constructor is a *deserialization* constructor and is optional. Implementing this constructor allows your custom exceptions to be passed from one machine to another. In this chapter, you will only implement the first three. For information on implementing the serialization constructor, see the on-line article by Eric Gunnerson of Microsoft at the following URL:

```
http://msdn.microsoft.com/library/default.asp?url=/library/en-
us/dncscol/html/csharp08162001.asp
```

The following sample code demonstrates defining a custom exception class derived from ApplicationException.

> *Microsoft recommends you always end exception class names with the word "Exception" as they have done in the .NET Framework. This provides consistency and makes it easy for others to identify your exception classes.*

In C#:

```
public class ConfigurationFileNotFoundException : ApplicationException
{
  public ConfigurationFileNotFoundException()
  {
  }

  public ConfigurationFileNotFoundException(string message)
      : base(message)
  {
  }

  public ConfigurationFileNotFoundException(string message, Exception inner)
      : base(message, inner)
  {
  }
}
```

In Visual Basic .NET:

```
Public Class ConfigurationFileNotFoundException
    Inherits ApplicationException

    Public Sub New()
    End Sub 'New


    Public Sub New(ByVal message As String)
        MyBase.New(message)
    End Sub 'New


    Public Sub New(ByVal message As String, ByVal inner As Exception)
        MyBase.New(message, inner)
    End Sub 'New
End Class 'ConfigurationFileNotFoundException
```

Here is an example of code that throws this custom exception. It checks if a particular configuration file exists and if it doesn't, the ConfigurationFileNotFoundException is thrown.
In C#:

```
public class CustomExceptionDemo
{
  public void OpenDbcConfigFile()
  {
     if (!File.Exists("mmconfigx.xml"))
     {
       throw new ConfigurationFileNotFoundException("Application configuration
file not found.");
     }
  }
}
```

And in Visual Basic .NET:

```
Public Class CustomExceptionDemo

    Public Sub OpenAppConfigFile()
        If Not File.Exists("mmconfigx.xml") Then
            Throw New ConfigurationFileNotFoundException( _
                "Application configuration file not found.")
        End If
    End Sub 'OpenAppConfigFile

End Class 'CustomExceptionDemo
```

Again, if you can find an existing .NET exception class that suits your needs use it. Otherwise, feel free to create your own custom exceptions based on the ApplicationException class.

> *Throughout this chapter, there are several tips for exception handling "best practices". In addition to these suggestions, I highly recommend the .NET Help topic "Best Practices for Handling Exceptions".*

Debugging your application

The rest of this chapter is devoted to the variety of tools available in Visual Studio .NET for debugging your applications. I'll take a look at each of these tools and show you the basics of how to use each.

Setting and clearing breakpoints

One of the most important debugging tools is the ability to set breakpoints in your application. Visual Studio .NET makes it easy to set breakpoints and step through the code in your application. You'll find .NET's approach to breakpoints is similar to Visual FoxPro's, but with some additional features.

The easiest way to set a breakpoint is clicking in the left column of the code-editing window next to the line where you want to break (**Figure 4**). You can easily clear the breakpoint by clicking again in the left column at the same location.

```
// If the log file doesn't exist, create it
if (!File.Exists(LogFile))
{
    CreateLogFile();
}
```

Figure 4. Clicking in the left column of the code-editing window allows you to easily set and clear breakpoints.

Another easy way to set a breakpoint is to right-click on a line of code and select Insert Breakpoint or New Breakpoint from the shortcut menu.

Using the Breakpoints window

The Breakpoints window contains a list of all breakpoints currently set in your application (**Figure 5**). To launch the Breakpoints window, select Debug | Windows | Breakpoints from the main menu or type Ctrl+Alt+B.

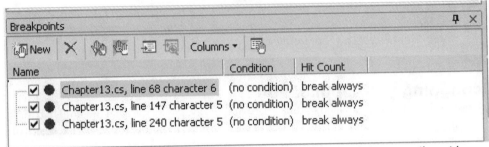

Figure 5. The Breakpoints window shows you all the breakpoints currently set in your application.

By default, there are three columns displayed in the Breakpoints window—Name, Condition, and Hit Count. You can specify additional or different columns by clicking the Columns button at the top of the Breakpoints window and selecting or deselecting columns from the list. Notice the name column includes the source code file name, the line number and the *character position*. Although you don't normally care about the character position, you *do* care if you have multiple commands on a single line and want to know which command the breakpoint refers to.

You can enable or disable a breakpoint by checking or clearing the check box in the Name column. To view the source code line associated with a breakpoint, double-click on the breakpoint or right-click on the breakpoint and select Go To Source Code from the shortcut menu. You can also clear all breakpoints or disable all breakpoints by clicking the corresponding buttons at the top of the Breakpoints window.

Creating new breakpoints

To add a new breakpoint using the Breakpoints window, click the New button at the top of the window to launch the New Breakpoint dialog (**Figure 6**).

The New Breakpoint dialog allows you to set breakpoints:

- When program execution reaches a specified location in a function.

- When program execution reaches a specified line number in a file.

- When program execution reaches the instruction at the specified address.

- When the value of a variable changes.

For additional information on each of these options, click the Help button on the corresponding page of the New Breakpoint dialog.

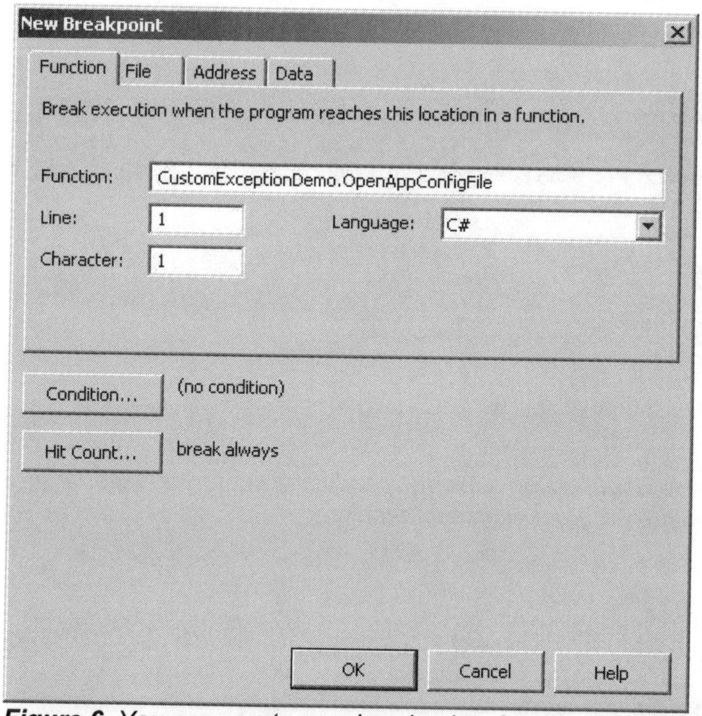

Figure 6. *You can create new breakpoints for a function, file, address, or data (variables) using the New Breakpoint dialog.*

If you click the Condition button, it launches a Breakpoint Condition dialog (**Figure 7**) allowing you to specify a break that occurs when a condition is true or has changed.

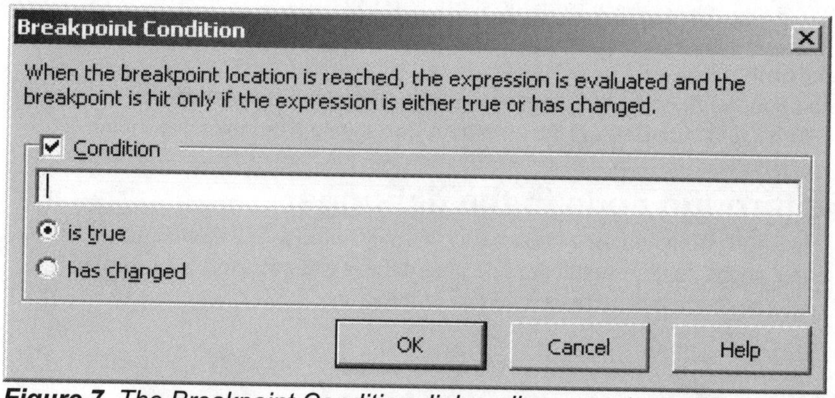

Figure 7. *The Breakpoint Condition dialog allows you to specify a condition that is true or has changed before a breakpoint is hit.*

If you click the Hit Count... button, it launches the Breakpoint Hit Count dialog (**Figure 8**). This dialog lets you specify how many times a breakpoint is hit before program execution breaks. You can set a specific count, a multiple of a count, or a hit count greater than or equal to a specified value.

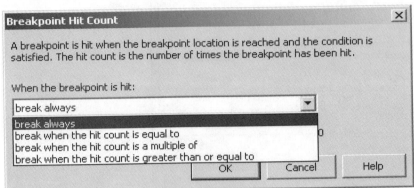

Figure 8. The Breakpoint Hit Count dialog lets you specify a count for the number of times a breakpoint is hit before program execution breaks.

Editing existing breakpoints
To edit an existing breakpoint, select the breakpoint you want to edit, and click the Properties button (the button to the far right) at the top of the Breakpoints window. This launches the same dialog described when creating a new breakpoint. You can also right-click a breakpoint and select Properties from the shortcut menu.

Deleting existing breakpoints
To delete an existing breakpoint, select the breakpoint you want to delete, and click the Delete button (the second from the left) at the top of the Breakpoints window. You can also right-click on a breakpoint and select Delete from the shortcut menu.

Ignoring breakpoints
If you want to start your application but ignore all existing breakpoints, you can do so by pressing Ctrl+F5 or by selecting Debug | Start Without Debugging from the main menu.

Navigating through code in the debugger
When you run your application and hit a breakpoint, Visual Studio .NET automatically opens the associated source code file, highlights the line where the break occurred, and displays an arrow in the left column of the code editing window (**Figure 9**).

```
// If the log file doesn't exist, create it
if (!File.Exists(LogFile))
{
    CreateLogFile();
}
```

Figure 9. VS .NET shows you the line of code where a break occurs.

At this point, you can choose Step Into, Step Over, or Step Out from the Debug menu to navigate through your code. You can also use the shortcut keys, which are F11 (Step Into), F10 (Step Over), and Shift+F10 (Step Out). These have the same meaning as in the Visual FoxPro debugger.

To navigate to a different line, possibly even a line earlier in the stack, right-click on the line and select Set Next Statement. This feature is invaluable when you're debugging your application and want to rerun or completely skip over code.

If you page up or down in the source code so you can't see the stack pointer arrow in the left column, or if you're editing another source code file and want to go back to the next line to be executed, simply right-click in the code-editing window and select Show Next Statement from the shortcut menu.

Another option that's extremely handy is the ability to continue program execution up to a given line and then break—but without setting an actual breakpoint. To do this, right-click on the line of code you want to stop at, and select Run to Cursor from the shortcut menu. This causes application execution to continue until it hits the selected line, at which point it breaks again.

To resume normal program execution after stopping for a breakpoint, you can simply press F5 or click the Continue button (**Figure 10**) at the top of the Visual Studio .NET IDE.

Figure 10. *Click Continue to resume program execution after hitting a breakpoint.*

Examining values in the Watch window

When your program is running, you can use the Watch window to view the values of variables and expressions, as well as edit the value of a variable. The Watch window in VS .NET is similar to Visual FoxPro's, but with some additional features.

To launch the Watch window, you must first run your application and be in break mode. Once your application is running, from the Debug menu choose Windows | Watch, and select Watch1, Watch2, Watch3, or Watch4. If you've ever filled up your Watch window in Visual FoxPro, you'll be glad to see four different Watch windows in VS .NET you can use to avoid the clutter of too many watch values in a single window.

As with Visual FoxPro, the VS .NET Watch windows persist their values from one VS .NET session to another. This means if you specify a Watch value, close Visual Studio .NET, and restart, your values still show up in the Watch window.

Although you can manually type variables or expressions into a Watch window, you can also easily add watch values by dragging and dropping selected text in the code-editing window into a Watch window. For example, if you set a breakpoint in this chapter's sample code (Chapter13.cs or Chapter13.vb) in the ThrowExceptionDemo.IsBirthMonth method at the line of code that calls ExceptionLog.LogError, you can drag the variable "e" from the source code, and drop it into a Watch window. If you do this, the variable "e" is displayed in the Watch window (**Figure 11**) along with its associated value and type. If you want to change the value of the variable "e", simply click on the text in the Value column and enter a new value.

Figure 11. You can examine the values of variables and expressions and change the values of variables in one of VS .NET's four Watch windows.

Notice there is a plus sign in the Name column next to the variable "e". Whenever you enter the name of an object variable or array into the Watch window, a tree control appears next to the variable name. You expand and contract this tree control to show or hide additional values (such as properties) of the object.

In Visual FoxPro, you can double-click in the column to the left of a Watch value to specify program execution to break when the value of the variable or expression changes. In VS .NET, you do this through the Breakpoints window (see the "Using the Breakpoints window" section earlier in this chapter for details).

The QuickWatch window

Visual Studio .NET also has a QuickWatch window (**Figure 12**) you can use as an alternate to the Watch windows if you want to view or edit a variable or expression quickly. QuickWatch is a modal dialog, so if you want to look at a value and step through code to see how the value changes, you need to use the Watch window instead.

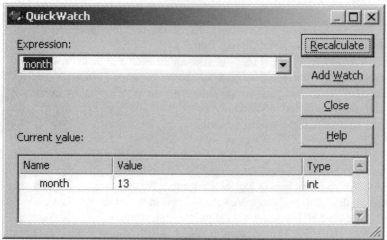

Figure 12. The QuickWatch window allows you to easily view variables and expressions and edit variable values.

To launch the QuickWatch window, the debugger must be in break mode, and then select Debug | QuickWatch from the menu or press Ctrl+Alt+Q.

When you click the Recalculate button, it evaluates the variable or expression you have entered in the Expression text box and displays it in the Current value. If you click the Add Watch button, the expression or variable is automatically added to the Watch window.

The Command window

Expecting Visual Studio .NET Command Window to be similar to Visual FoxPro's Command Window, is like renting a Bruce Willis action-adventure DVD and finding out they've accidentally put "Pee-Wee's Big Adventure" in the box instead! Unfortunately, the VS .NET Command Window is *nothing* in comparison to Visual FoxPro's Command window. Take a closer look at its functionality (or lack thereof) and you'll see what I mean.

The Command Window (**Figure 13**) is used to issue commands or to debug and evaluate expressions. To launch the Command Window, select View | Other Windows | Command Window from the main menu or simply press Ctrl+Alt+A.

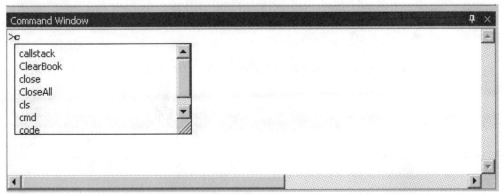

Figure 13. The Visual Studio .NET Command Window has a long way to go to be as capable as the Visual FoxPro Command Window.

There are two different Command Window modes—Command mode and Immediate mode. You know you're in Command mode if the greater than symbol appears as a command prompt. You know you're in Immediate mode if the title of the window is Command Window – Immediate. If you're in Command mode, you switch to Immediate mode by typing "immed" and pressing Enter. If you're in Immediate mode you go to Command mode by entering ">cmd" in the Command Window.

Command mode

When working in Command mode, you can enter IDE commands directly into the Command Window, bypassing the VS .NET menu system. If you're expecting to instantiate objects from the Command Window you'll be sadly disappointed—this capability is non-existent.

There are a number of predefined command aliases you can enter in the Command Window to save time. For example, if you enter "nav" in Command mode, it automatically brings up the VS .NET browser in the IDE. If you enter the letter "k" in Command mode, it displays the call stack. If you want to evaluate expressions while in Command mode, you use the eval command. For example, entering the following command displays a string containing the current date and time:

```
eval DateTime.Today.ToString()
```

For a list of all pre-defined VS .NET command aliases, see the .NET Help topic "Pre-defined Visual Studio Command Aliases". You can also type "alias" in the Command Window and it shows you all of the aliased commands. For more information on Visual Studio commands and instructions on creating your own aliases, see the .NET Help topic "Visual Studio Commands".

Immediate mode

The Immediate mode of the Command Window allows you to issue commands, debug, and evaluate expressions, as well as view and change the values of variables while debugging.

For example, while debugging a program, you can enter the following command in Immediate mode to determine if the mmconfig.xml file exists in the current directory:

```
File.Exists("mmconfig.xml")
```

If the file exists, it displays "true" in the Command Window (**Figure 14**). Otherwise, it displays "false".

Figure 14. You can enter commands to be executed in the Immediate mode of the Command window.

The Call Stack window

The Call Stack window (**Figure 15**) allows you to see functions on the call stack as well as any parameters and their values. For example, if you set a breakpoint in the sample code's ThrowExceptionDemo.IsBirthMonth method on the line that calls ExceptionLog.LogError, the Call Stack window shows you the fully qualified class name, the method name, the type and value of the parameter (int month = 13), and the line number.

To see the Call Stack window, when your application is in Break mode, select Debug | Windows | Call Stack from the main menu or press Ctrl+Alt+C.

Figure 15. The Call Stack *window allows you to see functions on the call stack as well as parameters and their values.*

If you double-click on another function in the call stack, it highlights the associated source code in the code-editing window of the IDE (**Figure 16**).

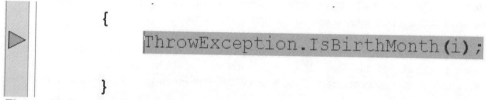

Figure 16. Double-clicking on another function other than the next statement to be executed opens the associated source code in the IDE.

If you want to hide some of the information displayed, right-click on the Call Stack window and clear the checkbox next to the information you want to hide. For example, if you don't want to see line numbers in the Call Stack window, clear the Show Line Numbers option.

The Autos window

In C#, the Autos window (**Figure 17**) displays variables used in the current statement or in the previous statement. The name "Autos" is derived from the fact that the debugger identifies these variables for you automatically. In Visual Basic .NET, the Autos window displays variables used in the current statement, as well as three statements before and after the current statement.

To launch the Autos window when your application is in Break mode, select Debug | Windows | Autos from the main menu or type Ctrl+Alt+V, A (press Ctrl+Alt+V, release, and press the letter "A").

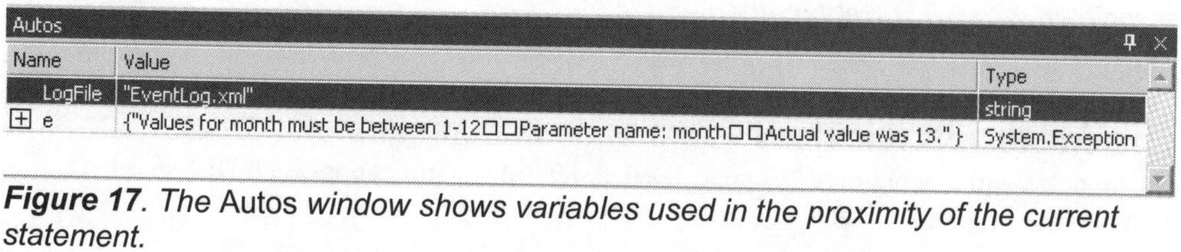

Name	Value	Type
LogFile	"EventLog.xml"	string
⊞ e	{"Values for month must be between 1-12□□Parameter name: month□□Actual value was 13."}	System.Exception

Figure 17. The Autos *window shows variables used in the proximity of the current statement.*

Note the variables in the Autos window change accordingly if you select a different function in the Call Stack window. You change the value of variables in the Autos window by double-clicking the Value column and entering the new value.

The Locals window

The Locals window (**Figure 18**) displays variables local to the current execution location. To launch the Locals window, when your application is running, select Debug | Windows | Locals from the main menu or type Ctrl+Alt+V, L (press Ctrl+Alt+V, release, and press the letter "L").

Name	Value	Type
⊞ this	{HW.NetBook.Samples.ThrowExceptionDemo}	HW.NetBook.Samples.ThrowExceptionDemo
month	11	int
BirthMonth	false	bool

Figure 18. The Locals *window displays all local variables visible in the current execution context and allows you to change their associated values.*

As with other Debug windows, you change the value of variables in the Locals window by double-clicking the Value column and entering a new value. The variables displayed in the Locals window change accordingly if you select a different function in the Call Stack window.

The This/Me windows

The This/Me (**Figure 19**) windows allow you to view the members of the object associated with the current method. It's called the This window in C# (and C++) and the Me window in VB .NET. To launch the window, when your application is running, select Debug | Windows | This (or Me) from the main menu or by typing Ctrl+Alt+V, T (press Ctrl+Alt+V, release, and press the letter "T").

Name	Value	Type
⊟ this	{HW.NetBook.WindowsUI.SampleCodeForm}	HW.NetBook.WindowsUI.SampleCodeForm
⊞ System.Windows.Forms.Form	{HW.NetBook.WindowsUI.SampleCodeForm}	System.Windows.Forms.Form
⊞ cboChapters	{System.Windows.Forms.ComboBox}	System.Windows.Forms.ComboBox
⊞ lblChapters	{System.Windows.Forms.Label}	System.Windows.Forms.Label
⊞ lstSamples	{SelectedItem="Throw an exception	System.Windows.Forms.ListBox
⊞ lblSamples	{System.Windows.Forms.Label}	System.Windows.Forms.Label
⊞ cmdRunSample	{Text="&Run Sample"}	System.Windows.Forms.Button
⊞ cmdClose	{Text="&Close"}	System.Windows.Forms.Button
components	null	System.ComponentModel.Container

Figure 19. The This/Me windows allow you to view the members of the object associated with the current method.

The Modules window

The Modules window (**Figure 20**) provides detailed information about each DLL and EXE used by your program.

Figure 20. *The* Modules *window provides a list of all DLLs and EXEs used by your program.*

To view the Modules window, select Debug | Windows | Modules from the main menu, or type Ctrl+Alt+U. You click on any column to sort the items in the list.

Miscellaneous debug windows

There are a variety of other debug windows listed in **Table 4** that are also available to you. For more information on each of these windows, check the .NET Help file.

Table 4. *Miscellaneous debug windows*

Method	Description
Memory window	Allows you to view large buffers, strings, and other data that do not display well in Watch or Variable windows.
Disassembly window	Allows you to view your source code in assembly language.
Registers window	Allows you to view the values stored in CPU registers.
Exceptions window	Allows you to change the way the debugger handles specific exceptions or categories of exceptions.
Threading window	Allows you to view and control threads in a multi-thread program.

Tracing and Instrumenting your applications

You can add tracing and debugging information to a .NET application that lets you monitor its execution while you're developing the application and also after you've deployed it. The .NET Framework provides Trace and Debug classes with methods allowing you to get information about code coverage, performance profiling, and also allow you to create Assert statements, similar to ASSERTs in Visual FoxPro. These classes can be used in both .NET Windows applications as well as ASP.NET applications.

The Trace and Debug classes are the same except the procedures and functions of the Trace class are compiled into release builds of your application and those of the Debug class are not.

Code tracing and debugging

The Debug and Trace classes can be used during development to display messages in the Output window of Visual Studio .NET. For example, the following code uses the WriteLine method of the Debug and Trace classes.

In C#:

```
using system.diagnostics;

public class DebugDemo
{
  public void MyMethod()
  {
      Debug.WriteLine("Debug.WriteLine output");
      Trace.WriteLine("Trace.WriteLine output");
  }
}
```

And in Visual Basic .NET:

```
Import System.Diagnostics

Public Class DebugDemo

    Public Sub MyMethod()
        Debug.WriteLine("Debug.WriteLine output")
        Trace.WriteLine("Trace.WriteLine output")
    End Sub 'MyMethod
End Class 'DebugDemo
```

This code displays the messages "Debug.WriteLine output" and "Trace.WriteLine output" in the Output window (**Figure 21**).

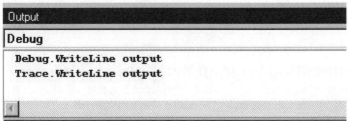

Figure 21. *The Debug and Trace WriteLine methods allow you to display messages in the VS .NET Output window.*

When you compile a release build of your application, you can specify that you do not want to include debug information in your final executable. For more information, see the .NET Help topic "Compiling Conditionally with Trace and Debug".

Trace listeners

When you are developing your application, all Debug and Trace information is written to the VS .NET Output window. However, in a deployed application, you need to specify an output target for this information called a *trace listener*.

Trace listeners come in the following flavors:

- TextWriterTraceListener – Sends output to a TextWriter or other Stream class.

- EventLogTraceListener – Sends output to an event log.

- DefaultTraceListener (the default) – Sends output to Visual Studio .NET's Output window.

The following code demonstrates how to implement a TextWriterTraceListener. In C#:

```csharp
// Creates the Trace Log text file (or open it if it already exists)
FileStream TraceLog = new FileStream("TraceLog.txt",
  FileMode.OpenOrCreate);

// Creates the Trace Listener
TextWriterTraceListener TextListener = new
  TextWriterTraceListener(TraceLog);

// Add the Listener to the Listeners collection
Trace.Listeners.Add(TextListener);

Debug.WriteLine("Debug.WriteLine TextWriterListener test: " +
  DateTime.Now);
Trace.WriteLine("Trace.WriteLine TextWriterListener test: " +
  DateTime.Now);

// Flush the output of the TextListener
TextListener.Flush();

// Remove the Listener from the Listeners collection
Trace.Listeners.Remove(TextListener);
```

In Visual Basic .NET:

```vbnet
' Creates the Trace Log text file (or open it if it already exists)
Dim TraceLog As New FileStream("TraceLog.txt", FileMode.OpenOrCreate)

' Creates the Trace Listener
Dim TextListener As New TextWriterTraceListener(TraceLog)

' Add the Listener to the Listeners collection
Trace.Listeners.Add(TextListener)

Debug.WriteLine(("Debug.WriteLine TextWriterListener test: " & _
    DateTime.Now.ToString()))
Trace.WriteLine(("Trace.WriteLine TextWriterListener test: " & _
    DateTime.Now.ToString()))

' Flush the output of the TextListener
TextListener.Flush()

' Remove the Listener from the Listeners collection
Trace.Listeners.Remove(TextListener)
```

The first line of code creates a new FileStream for a text file named TraceLog.txt. The second parameter in the FileStream constructor uses the FileMode enumeration to indicate the TraceLog.txt file should be opened if it already exists or created if it does not. The second line of code creates a new TextWriterTraceListener object, passing a reference to the TraceLog FileStream. The third line adds the listener to the Trace object's Listeners collection. Typically this initialization code occurs someplace in your application startup.

The next two lines of code write out Debug and Trace messages. In a real application, you can have any number of these calls to Debug or Trace throughout your application. These messages are written out to the TraceLog.txt file (**Figure 22**). In addition, they are still written to the VS .NET Output window. This is because VS .NET automatically adds a DefaultTraceListener to the Trace object's Listener collection behind the scenes.

Figure 22. A TextWriterListener can output your Debug and Trace information to a text file.

The last two lines of code flush the TextListener and remove it from the Trace object's Listener collection. You can do this at any point in the application when you want to stop writing messages to the trace log file.

Additional Debug and Trace methods

The Debug and Trace classes have additional methods you can use for writing output to listeners. **Table 5** lists these different methods and how they are used.

Table 5. Miscellaneous debug windows

Method	Description
Assert	Checks for a condition and displays a message (or the call stack) if the condition is false.
Fail	Emits an error message.
Write	Writes information to the trace listeners in the Listener collection.
WriteIf	Writes information to the trace listeners in the Listener collection if a condition is true.
WriteLine	Writes information to the trace listeners in the Listener collection. Similar to the Write method, but writes out the message on a new line.
WriteLineIf	Writes information to the trace listeners in the Listener collection if a condition is true. Similar to WriteIf, but writes out the message on a new line.

For more information on using these methods, see the .NET Help topic "Adding Trace Statements to Application Code".

Error handling in ASP.NET applications

When it comes to handling errors in ASP.NET applications, there are a few additional settings you should know about found in your application's web.config file.

Debug mode

By default, when you create a new ASP.NET application, the web.config file Visual Studio .NET generates specifies that your application runs in debug mode. Here's the debug setting contained within the compilation tag:

```
<compilation
    defaultLanguage="c#"
    debug="true"
/>
```

When debug mode is set to true, you get additional debugging information when your ASP.NET application encounters errors. Although setting this to true is useful for debugging, you also incur a huge performance penalty. So when you actually deploy your application, you should set debug to "false".

Custom error messages

The web.config file also contains a setting that specifies the users who should see user-friendly messages and the users who should see error details that include a stack trace. This setting is found in the customErrors element:

```
<customErrors
mode="RemoteOnly"
/>
```

The three possible values for this setting are:

- On – Always display user-friendly error messages.

- Off – Always display detailed error messages.

- RemoteOnly – Display user-friendly error messages to users not running on the local Web server, otherwise, display detailed error messages.

The default value for this setting is "RemoteOnly".

ASP.NET tracing

In order to see trace output in an ASP.NET application, you need to turn on tracing, which is typically done at the application-level in the web.config file. The trace setting can be found within the trace element:

```
<trace
    enabled="false"
    requestLimit="10"
    pageOutput="false"
    traceMode="SortByTime"
    localOnly="true"
/>
```

To turn on tracing, set the enabled property to "true". If the pageOutput property is set to "true", the trace output is displayed at the bottom of each ASP.NET page. If it's set to "false", trace output is saved in a file named "trace.axd" found in your Web application's root directory.

Conclusion

There are a number of advancements in .NET's error handling and debugging capabilities making it easier to detect and fix bugs in your software. With the exception (no pun intended) of the Command Window, you'll find Visual Studio .NET's debugging tools more advanced and capable than those of Visual FoxPro. In the final analysis, it's up to you as the developer to learn how to use these tools well to provide your end-users with solid, well-debugged code.

Chapter 14
.NET Security

As sophisticated hackers continue to spawn new generations of malicious computer viruses, security has become an increasingly important issue for both software developers and end users. Microsoft has taken security to new levels in the .NET Framework. Not only does it help you avoid running potentially destructive code, it also gives you the ability to implement user security for denying and granting user access.

Just about every software application needs some type of security. In Visual FoxPro applications, security usually takes the form of preventing users from accessing secure areas of the application or from viewing and editing sensitive data. In VFP, you have to design and write your own security code or purchase a third-party application framework that provides this functionality for you. In contrast, there are two main types of security built right into the .NET Framework—*role-based security* and *code access security*.

Role-based security allows you to control what end users can do in your .NET applications. This is similar to the security you are probably already using in your Visual FoxPro applications. There may be functionality in your application you don't want certain groups of users to access. You may have other areas of your application where you allow some users to have read-write privileges and others to have read-only privileges. The .NET Framework contains classes that provide this ability.

Code access security is not available in Visual FoxPro applications. It is enforced by the .NET runtime and helps you avoid running "evil" code that can do bad things to your computer. Code access security has become particularly important with the advent of .NET's new deployment model allowing you to easily install .NET assemblies downloaded from the Internet on your computer. The downside of this model is assemblies may contain code that intentionally (or unintentionally) wreaks havoc on your computer. Because Microsoft is moving to this sort of Internet-downloadable software distribution model, they spent resources incorporating security into the .NET Framework.

The first part of this chapter focuses on code access security introducing the tools and classes provided by the .NET Framework and the Windows operating system you can use to define and enforce security for your desktop and Internet applications. The second part of the chapter shows you how to define and enforce role-based security. Fortunately, Microsoft has created a consistent model so once you learn one type of security you can easily learn the other.

Code Access Permissions

I'm not a big fan of running code from unknown sources on my computer. Although I'm religious about backing up my laptop—which is my main development machine—it would be a real pain to get it back in working order after being demolished by malicious code.

.NET helps you breathe a little easier in this regard if you're careful and follow the rules. .NET allows you to grant or deny code the permission to perform a particular type of operation or access a specific resource. For example, you may want to deny an assembly the permission to perform read or write operations to files and directories on your local computer or network drives. You may also want to deny permission to access resources such as your local hard drive, your database, or your Windows Registry. This is where .NET *permissions* come in.

The .NET Framework has a variety of permission classes that enforce restrictions on managed code. **Table 1** lists the different permission classes found in the framework. I'll take a closer look at these classes later in this chapter and show you how to implement them in your .NET applications.

Table 1. .NET code access permissions

Permission	Description	Namespace
DirectoryServicesPermission	Access to the System.DirectoryServices classes.	System.DirectoryServices
DNSPermission	Access to the Domain Name System (DNS).	System.Net
EnvironmentPermission	Read or write environment variables.	System.Security.Permissions
EventLogPermission	Read or write access to event log services.	System.Diagnostics
FileDialogPermission	Access files selected by the user in an Open dialog box.	System.Security.Permissions
FileIOPermission	Read, append, or write files or directories.	System.Security.Permissions
IsolatedStorageFilePermission	Access private virtual file systems.	System.Security.Permissions
IsolatedStoragePermission	Access isolated storage, which is storage associated with a specific user and some aspect of the code's identity, such as its Web site, publisher, or signature (abstract base class).	System.Security.Permissions
MessageQueuePermission	Access message queues through the managed Microsoft Message Queue (MSMQ) interfaces.	System.Messaging
OleDbPermission	Access to databases using OLE DB.	System.Data.OleDb
PerformanceCounterPermission	Access performance counters.	System.Diagnostics
PrintingPermission	Access printers.	System.Drawing.Printing
ReflectionPermission	Discover information about a type at run time.	System.Security.Permissions
RegistryPermission	Read, write, create, or delete registry keys and values.	System.Security.Permissions
SecurityPermission	Execute, assert permissions, call into unmanaged code, skip verification, and other rights.	System.Security.Permissions
ServiceControllerPermission	Access running or stopped services.	System.ServiceProcess
SocketPermission	Make or accept connections on a transport address.	System.ServiceProcess
SqlClientPermission	Access to SQL Databases.	System.Data.SqlClient
UIPermission	Access user interface functionality.	System.Security.Permissions
WebPermission	Make or accept connections on a Web address.	System.Net

As you peruse Table 1, you will see some permission classes that make a lot of sense, such as FileIOPermission, OleDbPermission, and SqlClientPermission. However, other classes such as UIPermission may seem unnecessary—why would you prevent code from displaying a message to the user?

Here's a good example—a few times a year I get e-mails from well-meaning friends and relatives warning me of a virus that's sweeping the globe. I'm told I can easily fix the problem by deleting a particular virus-laden file from my hard drive. In reality, the file I am told to delete has *nothing* to do with a virus, but is actually a file necessary to the Windows operating system. The moral of this story is that I may not want code from unknown sources popping up dialogs telling users to perform actions that can debilitate their computers.

Figure 1 displays all of the classes from Table 1 in a UML class diagram, to give you a clearer picture of the code access permission class hierarchy.

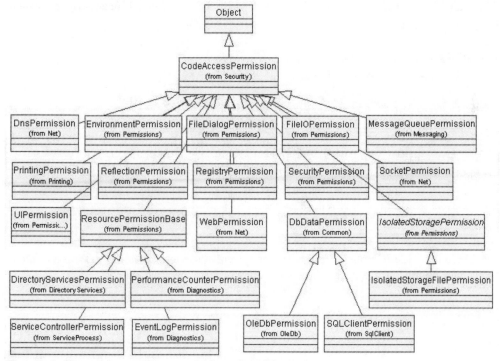

Figure 1. The code access permission class hierarchy.

Creating custom code access permissions

Although the built-in permission classes cover many of the permissions you need to administer in your application, there are times when you need to create your own custom permission classes. For examples of when and how you should create your own custom permissions, see the .NET Help topic "Creating Your Own Code Access Permissions".

It's a matter of trust

How much do you trust the code you're getting ready to run? If you've written it yourself, and it resides on your local machine, the level of trust should be pretty high! However, if you've just downloaded an assembly from the Internet and a company you are not familiar with publishes it, your level of trust should be very low. So how do you specify which permissions apply to a particular assembly? This is done by means of a *security policy*.

Security policy

A security policy is a set of rules telling the .NET runtime what permissions to grant to assemblies from different sources. When the runtime gets ready to run an assembly, it determines the identity of the assembly (such as where the code came from and who published it) and then checks the security policy to determine the rights it should be given.

Security policy levels

There are four different security policy levels as shown in **Table 2**.

Table 2. Security policy levels

Policy level	Description	Specified by
Enterprise	Applies to all managed code for every computer and user on the network.	Administrator
Machine	Applies to all managed code on a computer.	Administrator
User	Applies to code in all the processes associated with the current operating system user.	Administrator or user
Application domain	Applies to managed code in the host's application domain.	Set programmatically

These four security policies form a hierarchy, with the enterprise policy at the top of the food chain (**Figure 2**), and each subsequent policy beneath the previous.

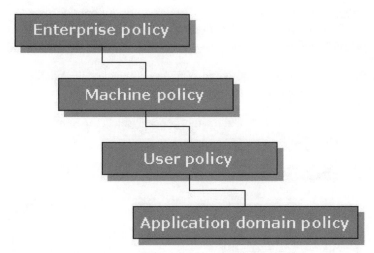

Figure 2. *Security policy hierarchy.*

You set permissions at the enterprise level that apply to all computers and users on the network. Permissions set at the machine level apply to all users on a given machine and the user policy specifies permissions for the current operating system user. The application domain security policy level lets you specify security for a particular application domain.

> *.NET's application "domain" replaces the "process" as the smallest unit of application isolation on a Windows system. You can have multiple domains within a single process that isolate applications from each other. For more information, see the .NET Help topic "Application Domains Overview".*

At run time, when determining the permissions for an assembly, all security policy levels are evaluated, and the code is granted the minimum permissions granted by any of the levels.

In this chapter, I discuss security policies at the machine level. For information on setting security policy for all other levels, see the .NET Help topic "Security Policy Best Practices".

Viewing and configuring code access security policies

There are two .NET tools you can use to configure code access security policies. The first is the Code Access Security Policy Tool (Caspol.exe) command-line utility. The other tool is the .NET Framework Configuration tool (Mscorcfg.msc) that provides a graphical user interface for configuring security policies. Although Caspol provides more capabilities, I will show you the .NET Framework Configuration tool in the sections that follow because its graphical interface helps you better understand the .NET Framework's security concepts. For more information on Caspol, see the .NET Help topic "Code Access Security Policy Tool (Caspol.exe)".

The enterprise, machine, and user-level security policies can be configured using one of these .NET configuration tools, but the application domain policy can only be set programmatically.

To launch the .NET Framework Configuration tool in Windows 2000, click the Windows Start button and select Programs | Administrative Tools | Microsoft .NET Framework Configuration. In Windows XP go to the Control Panel, select Administrative Tools, and then select Microsoft .NET Framework Configuration. When the tool appears, select the Runtime Security Policy node in the left pane (**Figure 3**).

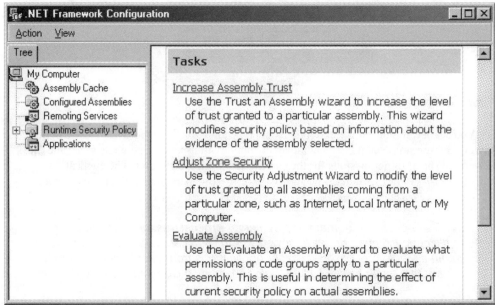

Figure 3. _The .NET Framework Configuration tool can be used to configure code access security policies._

The .NET Framework Configuration tool allows you to configure settings by using either wizards or configuration dialogs. The right pane contains a list of tasks with wizards. You will run one of these wizards later in the chapter, but first look at the tree view in the left pane.

If you expand the Runtime Security Policy node, you see the three configurable policy levels—Enterprise, Machine, and User (**Figure 4**).

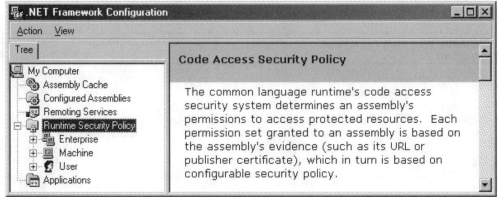

Figure 4. *Security policy can be configured at the Enterprise, Machine, and User levels.*

If you expand the Machine node, you see three additional nodes—Code Groups, Permission Sets, and Policy Assemblies (**Figure 5**).

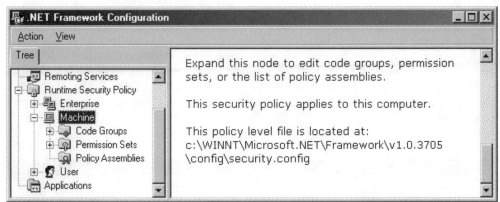

Figure 5. *Each policy level contains Code Groups, Permission Sets, and Policy Assemblies nodes.*

The Enterprise and User policy levels also contain these nodes, but again, I am concentrating on the machine-level security policy in this chapter. The following sections describe what each of these nodes represents.

Code groups

Each security policy contains a hierarchy of *code groups*. A code group is a logical grouping of code with similar characteristics, such as where the code came from (for example, Local machine, Internet, Intranet).

For code to be included in a particular group, it must meet a specific membership condition. Each code group has only one code membership condition. The .NET Framework has eight default membership conditions represented by the classes listed in **Table 3**.

Table 3. *Code group membership conditions*

Membership condition	.NET class	Membership requirement
All code	AllMembershipCondition	A membership condition for all code.
Application Directory	ApplicationDirectoryMembership Condition	Assemblies located in the same directory or in a child directory of the running application.
Hash	HashMembershipCondition	The hash value of the assembly.
Publisher	PublisherMembershipCondition	Assemblies digitally signed with a specified certificate.
Site	SiteMembershipCondition	The HTTP, HTTPS, or FTP Web site where the code originated
Strong Name	StrongNameMembershipConditio n	Assemblies that have the specified strong name public key (and optionally name and version)
URL	UrlMembershipCondition	The URL where the code originated. An asterisk can be used as a wildcard character at the end of the URL. Examples: http://www.MySite.com/MyAssembly.dll ftp://ftp.MySite.com/pub/*
Zone	ZoneMembershipCondition	The zone, or region, where the code originated.

The .NET runtime uses the criteria listed in Table 3 (also known as *evidence*) to determine the placement of code into a code group.

Expand the Code Group node in the .NET Framework Configuration tool (**Figure 6**) and you see the All_Code node. This node forms the root of the code group tree and the top of the code group hierarchy. This is the first code group listed in Table 3. All .NET assemblies belong to this code group—no membership condition is necessary!

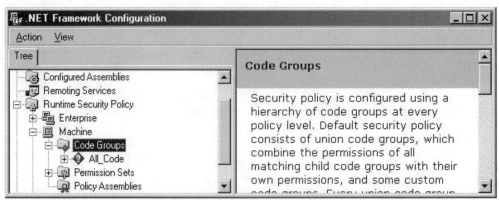

Figure 6. *All .NET assemblies belong to the All Code group by default—no membership condition is necessary.*

If you expand the All_Code node, you see a list of child code group nodes (**Figure 7**).

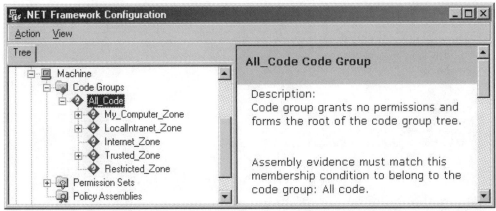

Figure 7. *The All_Code node sits at the top of a hierarchy of code group nodes that define membership conditions for assemblies.*

"Zone" is also one of the code groups listed in Table 3. Because zones are one of the most commonly used code group membership conditions, the following section details each type of zone used by .NET security policies.

Zones

The Zone code groups provide a way to specify membership conditions based on an assembly's origin. If you have toyed with Internet Explorer's security settings, you may be familiar with the concept of zones. **Table 4** lists the different zones used by .NET security policies.

Table 4. *Security policy zones*

Zone	Description
My Computer	Applies to code that exists on the local computer.
Local Intranet	Used for code located on a company's intranet.
Internet	This is a "catch all" zone used for code located on Web sites not specified as belonging to any other zone.
Trusted Sites	Used for code located on Web sites you trust. The URL of one or more Web sites can be added to the Trusted zone.
Untrusted Sites	Used for code located on Web sites you do NOT trust. The URL of one or more Web sites can be added to the Untrusted zone

Now, I'll show you how to use the .NET Framework Configuration tool's Security Adjustment Wizard to view the security policy zone settings on your local computer. Afterwards, I'll come back to the tree view and look at the settings in greater detail. To launch the wizard, select the Runtime Security Policy node in the left pane and click the Adjust Zone Security link in the right pane. This displays the Security Adjustment Wizard (**Figure 8**).

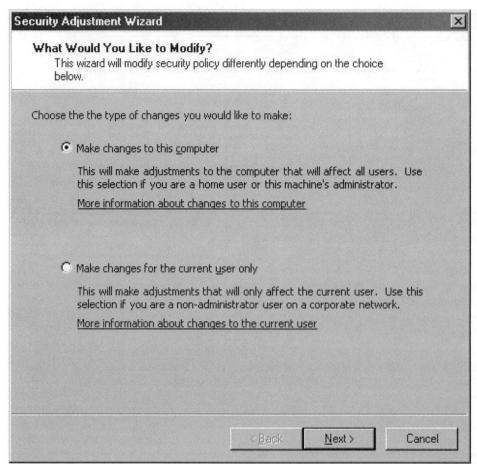

Figure 8. *The Security Adjustment Wizard allows you to modify security policy for the local computer or for the current user.*

The wizard allows you to modify the security policy for the local computer or the current user. Accept the default setting Make changes to this computer, click the Next button, and the Security Adjustment Wizard displays (**Figure 9**).

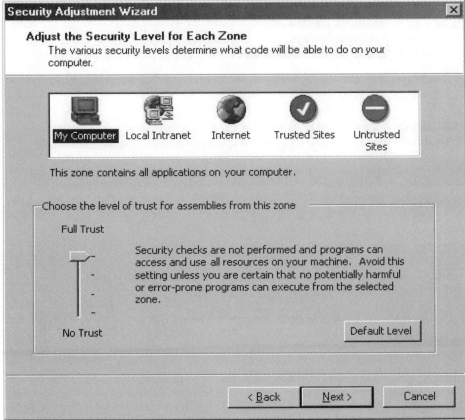

Figure 9. *The Security Adjustment Wizard allows you to configure security settings for assemblies coming from a particular zone.*

The top of the dialog displays a pane containing the different .NET security zones. Each of these corresponds to a zone code group node shown in Figure 7. To change the security level for a particular zone, select the zone at the top of the dialog and use the track bar at the bottom of the dialog to select the desired level of trust. To set the default level for a particular zone, click the Default Level button. Here are the different "level of trust" choices as described by their associated text:

- **Full Trust** – Security checks are not performed and programs can access and use all resources on your machine. Avoid this setting unless you are certain no potentially harmful or error-prone programs can execute from the selected zone. This is the default setting for the My Computer zone.

- **Medium Trust** – Programs might not be able to access most protected resources such as the registry or security policy settings, or access your local file system without user interaction. Programs can connect back to their site of origin, resolve domain names, and use all windowing resources. This is the default setting for the Local Intranet zone.

- **Low Trust** – Programs might not be able to access protected resources such as the registry, environment variables, domain names, or security policy settings. Programs have limited ability to use windowing resources and your local file system. This is the default setting for the Trusted Sites zone.

- **No Trust** – Programs might not be allowed to execute. This is the default setting for the Internet zone and the Untrusted Sites zone.

If you click the wizard's Next button, it displays a list of zones and their associated security levels (**Figure 10**). If you click Finish, it saves any changes you have made.

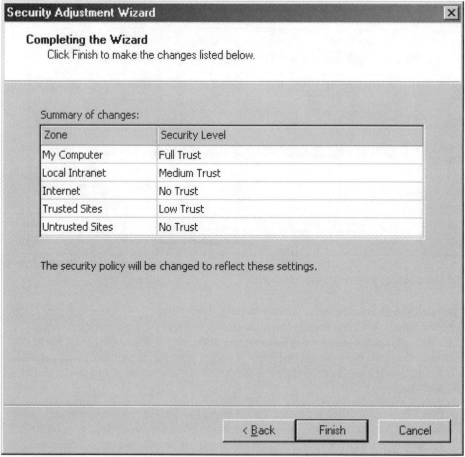

Figure 10. The last page of the Security Adjustment Wizard shows a list of all zones and their associated security level.

Specifying zone web sites

You can use Internet Explorer to specify the Web sites that belong to the Local intranet, Trusted sites, and Restricted sites zones.

From within Internet Explorer, select Tools | Internet Options from the main menu to launch the Internet Options dialog (**Figure 11**).

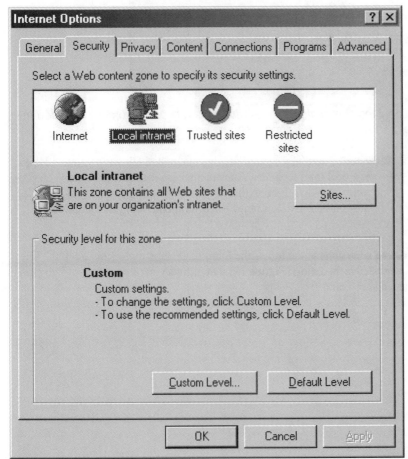

Figure 11. You can use the Internet Options dialog in Internet Explorer to specify the Web sites that belong to the Local intranet, Trusted sites, and Restricted sites zones.

Local Intranet zone

If you select the Local Intranet zone at the top of the Internet Options dialog, and then click the Sites button, it displays a Local intranet dialog (**Figure 12**) for specifying the Web sites included in the Local Intranet zone. All Web sites included in the Local Intranet zone use the security settings specified for this zone.

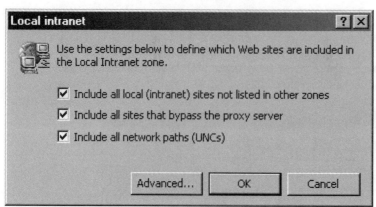

Figure 12. *The Local intranet dialog allows you to specify the Web sites included in the Local Intranet zone.*

If you click the Advanced... button, a second dialog is launched allowing you to add or remove Web sites from the Local intranet zone. You can also use this dialog to add Web sites that are *not* in your local intranet. You might do this if you want to give an external Web site the same permissions as sites on your local intranet—I recommend doing this judiciously!

Trusted sites

If you select the Trusted sites zone at the top of the Internet Options dialog and click the Sites button, it displays a Trusted sites dialog (**Figure 13**) that allows you to specify the Web sites included in the Trusted sites zone.

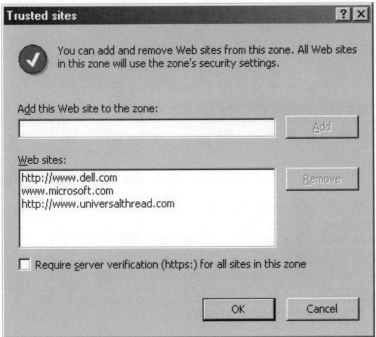

Figure 13. *The Trusted sites dialog allows you to add and remove Web sites from the Trusted sites zone.*

As you can see in Figure 13, I've added three Web sites to my Trusted sites zone, which grants additional "trusted" permissions to these Web sites.

Restricted sites

If you select the Restricted sites zone at the top of the Internet Options dialog and click the Sites... button, it displays the Restricted sites dialog (which is similar to the dialog shown in Figure 13) that allows you to add and remove Web sites from the Restricted sites zone.

Why would you want to restrict all software from a particular site? At times, you may determine that a site is known to contain unstable or malicious code. You can use this dialog to add that site to the list of restricted sites causing them to run in an extremely restricted environment or not allowing them to run at all!

Viewing code group detail

Now that you've seen a higher-level view of zone code groups, it's time to take a more detailed look at them. To do this, launch the .NET Framework Configuration tool again, and in the left pane, expand the Runtime Security Policy | Machine | Code Groups | All_Code node as shown in Figure 7.

If you select the My_Computer_Zone, a description of the code group is shown in the right pane. This description informs you this code group allows full access to all resources and the current policy level is "FullTrust".

At the bottom of the right pane is a list of Tasks that can be performed on the My_Computer_Zone code group—in this case, "Edit Code Group Properties" and "Add a Child Code Group". You can also choose to perform these tasks (and more) by clicking the Action menu pad or right-clicking the node and selecting New or Properties from the menu (**Figure 14**).

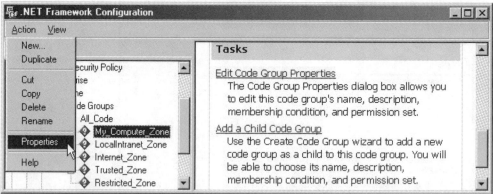

Figure 14. The .NET Framework Configuration tool allows you to add, duplicate, copy, delete, rename, and edit security code groups.

If you select New from the menu, it launches the code group Properties dialog, allowing you to create a new code group. If you select Properties from the menu, it also launches the code group Properties dialog (**Figure 15**).

This section describes the basics of the code group Properties dialog. For more information on creating your own custom code groups, see the .NET Help topic "Configuring Code Groups Using the .NET Framework Configuration tool".

The General tab of the dialog allows you to specify the name and description of the code group. At the bottom of the tab are two check boxes in the If the membership condition is met group box. As described by their associated text, these check boxes let you change how the .NET runtime evaluates permissions for the code group.

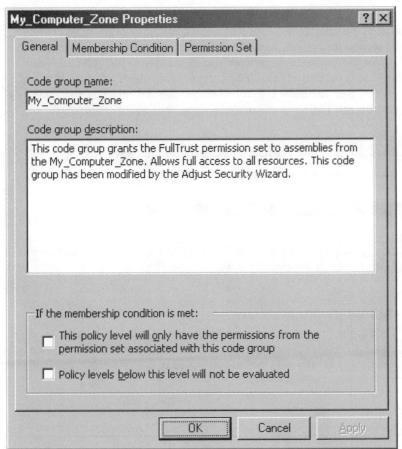

Figure 15. The code group Properties dialog lets you specify a code group's name, description, membership conditions, and permission set.

If you click the Membership Condition tab, you see two combo boxes. The first combo box allows you to select the condition type for the code group (**Figure 16**).

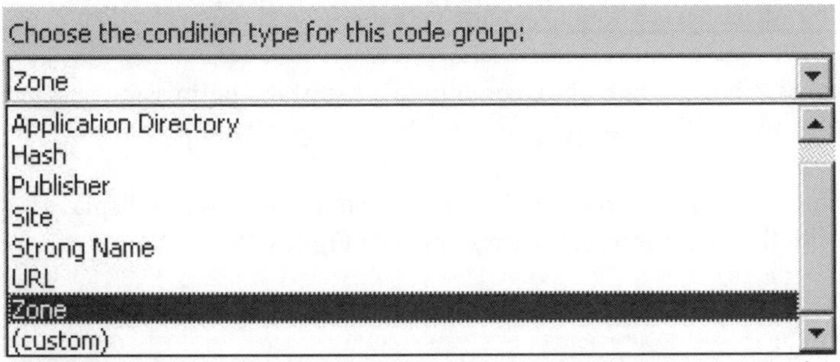

Figure 16.The Membership Condition tab allows you to select a membership condition type for the code group.

The options listed in this combo box are the same code group membership conditions listed in Table 3 earlier in this chapter. You can also select a custom code group you define yourself (see the next section for details). Based on the option you select in the upper combo box, additional input controls are displayed beneath it or, in the case of the "All Code" and "Application Directory" selection, no additional input controls are displayed at all. If "Zone" is selected in the condition type combo box, a second combo box is displayed allowing you to select the desired zone (**Figure 17**).

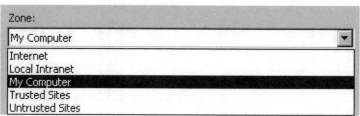

Figure 17. *When configuring a zone membership condition, a second combo box is displayed allowing you to select the desired zone.*

Permission sets

The third tab of the code group Properties dialog introduces a new concept—named permission sets. A named permission set is a grouping of one or more permissions given a friendly name and description. **Table 5** lists the built-in named permission sets found in the .NET Framework.

Table 5. *Built-in permission sets*

Permission set	Description
Full Trust	Full access to all resources.
Skip Verification	Skip verification of code in the assembly. This is a powerful permission that should only be applied to highly trusted code.
Execution	Permission to run, but no permission to use protected resources.
Nothing	No permissions. Code cannot run.
Local Intranet	The default policy permission set within an enterprise.
Internet	The default policy permission set suitable for code from an unknown origin.
Everything	All standard, built-in permissions, except the permission to skip verification.

At the top of the Permission tab is a combo box containing a list of the permission sets shown in Table 5. I'll discuss a few of these so you can get a better understanding of how permission sets work.

If you select the "LocalIntranet" option from the Permission set combo box, it displays the permissions associated with the Local Intranet permission set (**Figure 18**).

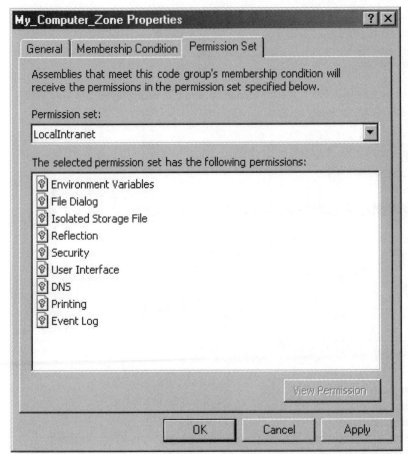

Figure 18. *The Permission Set tab of the code group Properties dialog allows you to view the permissions that belong to a given permission set.*

You can select any of the permissions in the list box and click the View Permission button to view details for the permission. For example, if you view details for the "File Dialog" permission, the Permissions Viewer dialog is displayed and informs you "The File Dialog Permission is unrestricted".

If you double-click the "Security" permission (which is the same as clicking the View Permission button), the Permissions Viewer dialog displays a list of security permissions that are granted and denied (**Figure 19**).

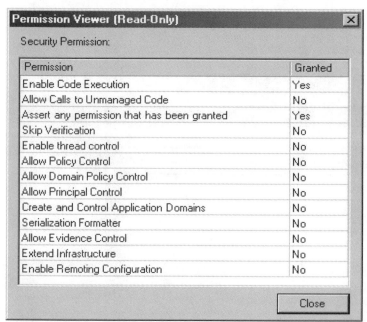

Figure 19. When you view a security permission in the Permission Viewer, it displays a list of permissions that have been granted or denied.

Creating custom permission sets

Notice when you edit one of the built-in permission sets, the title bar of the Permissions Viewer indicates the permission is (Read-Only). This is because all the built-in permission sets are read only. Although you can't edit built-in permission sets, you can create your own.

If you expand the Permission Sets node in the .NET Framework Configuration tool, you see a list of the built-in permission sets (**Figure 20**).

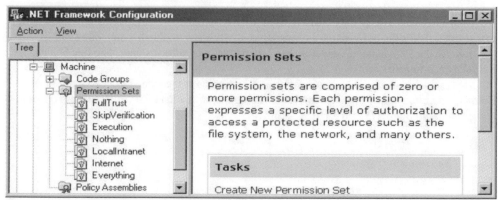

Figure 20. You can view the built-in permission sets and create your own custom permissions sets via the .NET Framework Configuration tool.

To create your own custom permission set, right-click on the Permission Sets node and select New from the shortcut menu. This launches the Create Permission Set wizard (**Figure 21**). This wizard is pretty intuitive, so I won't provide a detailed explanation of how to use it. If you need additional information, see the .NET Help topic "Configuring Permission Sets Using the .NET Framework Configuration Tool".

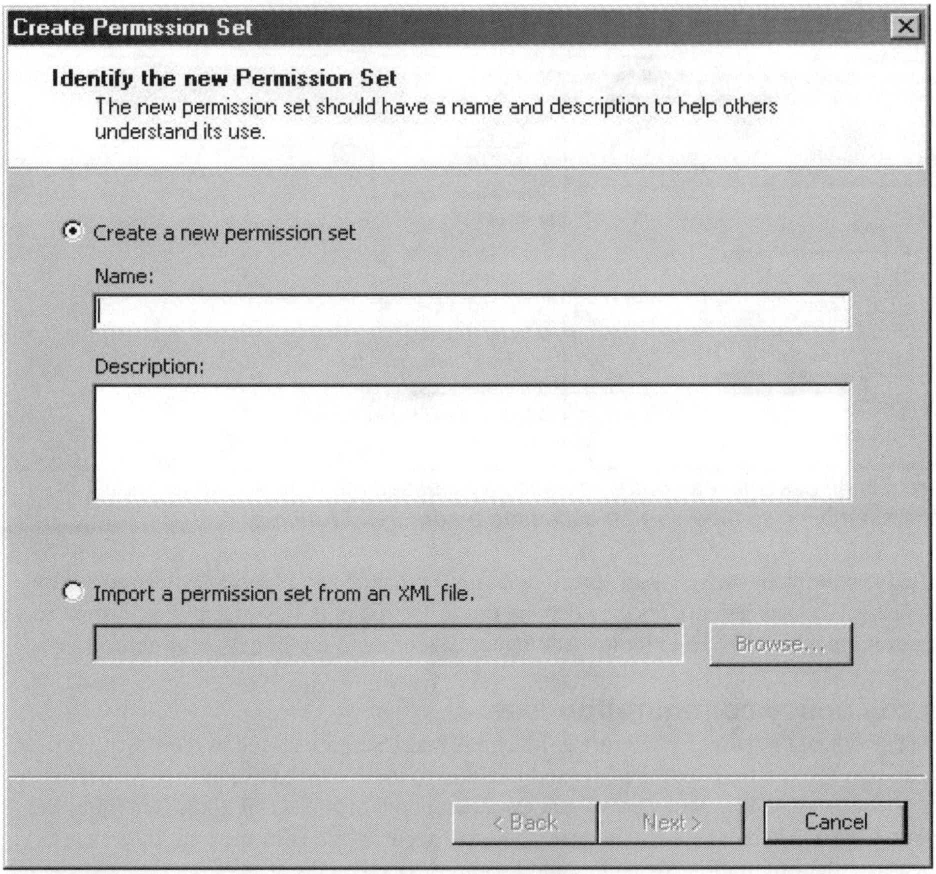

Figure 21. The Create Permission Set wizard allows you to create your own custom permission sets.

Any custom permission sets you create belong to the policy level in which they are created. For example, if you create a new permission set under the Machine node, the permission set belongs to the machine-level security policy. Any custom permission sets you create automatically display in the .NET Framework Configuration tool.

Policy assemblies

As mentioned earlier in the chapter, the .NET Framework implements permissions and membership conditions as classes. For the .NET runtime to evaluate security policies, the runtime must have full trust access to all assemblies containing permission and membership condition classes.

Now look at the .NET Framework assemblies that fall into this category. In the .NET Framework Configuration tool expand the Runtime Security Policy node, expand the Machine node (you could also choose the Enterprise or User nodes), and select the Policy Assemblies node. If you select the <u>View Policy Assemblies</u> link from the pane on the right, a list of all assemblies used during the Machine level's policy evaluation is displayed (**Figure 22**).

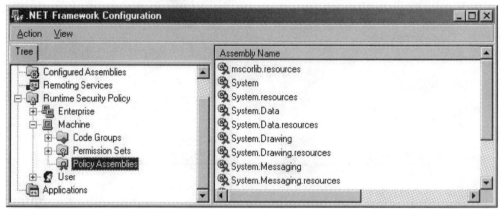

Figure 22. *All assemblies containing security classes must be added to the list of policy assemblies so they can be accessed by the .NET runtime.*

If you create your own custom security classes, you need to add the assembly containing these classes (and any assemblies they depend on) to the list of policy assemblies. For more information, see the .NET Help topic "Adding an Assembly to the Policy Assemblies List".

Security policy configuration files

Each security level's settings (Enterprise, Machine, and User) are stored in their own XML configuration file. To find out the name and location of these configuration files, select a security-level node in the .NET Framework Configuration tool and scroll to the bottom of the left pane. **Figure 23** shows where the machine-level security file is located on my computer. To see a list of configuration file names and locations based on the type of operating system you're using, see the .NET Help topic "Security Configuration Files".

Figure 23. *Each security level's settings are stored in its own configuration file.*

If you're the curious sort, you can open these configuration files in Visual Studio .NET (or your text editor of choice) to view their contents.

Evaluating assemblies

After you've set up your security policies, how can you determine which permissions or code groups will be applied to a particular assembly at runtime? The .NET Framework Configuration tool has an Evaluate Assembly wizard that allows you to do this!

To launch this wizard, right-click on the Runtime Security Policy node and select Evaluate Assembly from the shortcut menu. Follow the steps in the wizard to select an assembly and view the permissions granted to the assembly at runtime or the code groups that give permissions to the assembly.

Play well with others—request permissions

When the .NET runtime loads your assembly, how does it know the kind of things your code will do so it can determine up front whether your code has the proper permissions to perform these functions? The answer is that it doesn't—unless your assembly requests permissions!

You can place attributes in your assembly that indicate the permissions your assembly requires in order to function properly. When your code requests permissions, it gives the runtime an opportunity to refuse to run the assembly if one or more of the permissions your code requires is denied. This is better for the end user because they find out up front they cannot run your code, rather than finding out part way through using your software. Requesting permissions also makes it easier for administrators to set up security policy for your assembly and grant permissions accordingly.

Here is another incentive for requesting permissions—if you *don't* explicitly request permissions, you must write code that gracefully handles all situations where a required permission may not be granted at runtime (the .NET runtime raises an exception when a permission is denied).

You can also specify that your code receive a minimum set of permissions and no more. This makes for safer code, because bugs in your software cannot be exploited by evil minds to damage protected resources.

Requesting permissions

To demonstrate how to request permissions, you will build a console (command-line) application in Visual Studio .NET. On the Visual Studio .NET Start Page, click the New Project button to launch the New Project dialog (**Figure 24**).

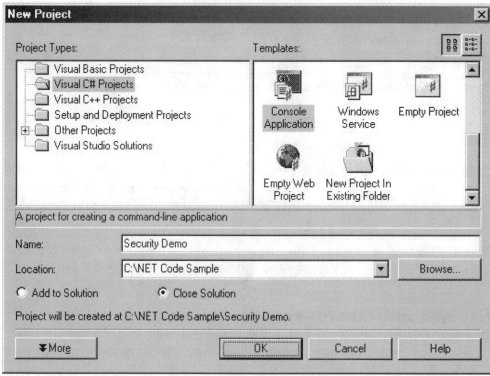

Figure 24. *This dialog shows the settings in the New Project dialog for creating a console application named "Request Permissions Demo".*

In the left pane of the dialog, select either Visual C# Projects or Visual Basic Projects. In the right pane, select Console Application. In the Name text box, enter "Security Demo". Also, make sure the Location text box contains the directory where you want to create the new project. When you're ready, click the OK button.

When VS .NET finishes creating your new console application, you should see a new file named Class1.cs (or Module1.vb) open in the IDE containing the following code.

In C#:

```
using System;

namespace Security_Demo
{
  /// <summary>
  /// Summary description for Class1.
  /// </summary>
```

```
class Class1
{
    /// <summary>
    /// The main entry point for the application.
    /// </summary>
    [STAThread]
    static void Main(string[] args)
    {
        //
        // TODO: Add code to start application here
        //
    }
}
}
```

And in Visual Basic .NET:

```
Module Module1

End Module
```

Notice when you create a Console Application in Visual Studio .NET, it creates a class file for C# and a module file for VB .NET. In this example, you really do want a class file, so if you created a VB .NET Console Application, you need to perform the following additional steps:

1. In the Solution Explorer, right-click on Module1.vb and select Delete from the shortcut menu. Click OK when the delete confirmation dialog displays.

2. Right-click the project node (the second node from the top) and select Add | Add Class... from the shortcut menu.

3. In the Add New Item dialog, accept the default class name "Class1.vb", and click the Open button. This adds a new file named "Class1.vb" to your project.

4. In the Solution Explorer, right-click on the project, and select Properties from the shortcut menu.

5. In the left pane of the Property Pages dialog, select General under the Common Properties node.

6. In the Startup Object combo box on the right, select "Sub Main". This tells VS .NET to use the class containing the Main method (which you'll add in a moment) as the startup object.

7. Click OK to save changes.

Now the Visual Basic .NET project is up to speed with the C# project.

The code in the C# file defines a single class named "Class1" with a single method named Main. If you're using C#, add the following code shown in grey to the Main method. This code displays the text "Security demo" to the console, and then waits for user input (you can also remove the "TO DO" comment).

In C#:

```
static void Main(string[] args)
{
  Console.WriteLine("Security Demo");
  Console.ReadLine();
}
```

In the Visual Basic .NET project there is a definition for a class named "Class1", but it does not have a Main method by default. Add the following code shown in grey to Class1, which includes a Main method declaration and the code that interacts with the console.

```
    <STAThread()> _
    Shared Sub Main(ByVal args() As String)
        Console.WriteLine("Security Demo")
        Console.ReadLine()
    End Sub 'Main

Public Class Class1
End Class
```

Now you're ready to get down to the business of requesting permissions. There are three different ways you can request permissions for assemblies:

- RequestMinimum – Tells the .NET runtime the specified permission must be granted in order for the assembly to run.

- RequestOptional – Tells the .NET runtime the specified permission would be nice to have granted, but the assembly will still run even if the permission is denied. If you request optional permissions, you must write code to gracefully handle situations where the permission is denied.

- RequestRefuse – Tells the .NET runtime the specified permission should *not* be granted to the assembly. This ensures your assembly only gets the permissions it needs and helps prevent others from misusing your assembly for malicious purposes.

In addition to permissions you can request at the assembly level, you can also request permissions at the class and method level. These permissions allow you to do things such as access resources not available to the caller and require all callers higher in the stack to be granted a particular permission. For more information, see the .NET Help topic "SecurityAction Enumeration".

Now you will add three assembly-level permission requests to the console application to demonstrate requesting "minimum", "optional", and "refuse" requests. Add the following code to the top of your Class1 source code file. In the C# source code file, place it directly beneath the **using System;** statement. In VB .NET, place it at the very top of the file.

In C#:

```
using System.Security.Permissions;

 [assembly:UIPermissionAttribute(SecurityAction.RequestMinimum,
  Unrestricted = true)]
[assembly:SecurityPermissionAttribute(SecurityAction.RequestOptional,
  Flags = SecurityPermissionFlag.UnmanagedCode)]
[assembly:FileIOPermissionAttribute(SecurityAction.RequestRefuse, "C:\\")]
```

In Visual Basic .NET:

```
Imports System.Security.Permissions

<Assembly: UIPermissionAttribute(SecurityAction.RequestMinimum, _
    Unrestricted:=True)>
<Assembly: SecurityPermissionAttribute(SecurityAction.RequestOptional, _
    Flags:=SecurityPermissionFlag.UnmanagedCode)>
<Assembly: FileIOPermissionAttribute(SecurityAction.RequestRefuse, _
    Read:="C:\")>
```

The first statement requests unrestricted access to the user interface and the clipboard. Because the specified SecurityAction is "RequestMinimum", the .NET runtime will not run the assembly unless this permission is granted.

The second statement requests access to unmanaged code. With the specified security action "RequestOptional", the .NET runtime still runs the assembly even if the permission is not granted.

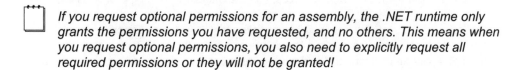

If you request optional permissions for an assembly, the .NET runtime only grants the permissions you have requested, and no others. This means when you request optional permissions, you also need to explicitly request all required permissions or they will not be granted!

The third statement requests access to files and folders on the C: drive be denied for this assembly. This helps guarantee the assembly cannot be used maliciously to read or write to the file system.

Requesting Permission Sets

Rather than requesting individual permissions, you can request the built-in permission sets "Nothing", "Execution", "Full Trust", "Internet", "LocalIntranet", and "SkipVerification". For example, the following code requests the "Internet" named permission set.

In C#:

```
[assembly:PermissionSetAttribute(SecurityAction.RequestMinimum,
Name="Internet")]
```

And in Visual Basic .NET:

```
<Assembly: PermissionSetAttribute(SecurityAction.RequestMinimum, _
    Name:="Internet")>
```

This is much more convenient than requesting individual permissions.

Role-based security

Now it's time to take a closer look at the other half of the .NET security picture—role-based security. As mentioned at the beginning of the chapter, this is the kind of security you may already have in your Visual FoxPro applications. You grant and deny permissions based on the identity of the current user.

.NET's role-based security can interoperate with COM+ Services or you can create your own custom authentication mechanism.

Users and roles

Like it or not, your software is going to have users! Users can either be people who are physically interacting with your software or they can be other programs accessing the functionality of your software.

A role is a category of users who have the same security privileges. For example, in a point-of-sale software application, you might have roles such as Administrator, Sales Rep, Accountant, and Stock Clerk. You may have several different real-world users who belong to each role—and for that matter, an individual user may be assigned multiple roles.

Identity objects

In the .NET Framework, *identity* objects represent application users. Identity objects contain a name, such as a user name or Windows account, and an authentication type, such as Kerberos V or NTLM.

The .NET Framework has a GenericIdentity class that represents a generic user, a WindowsIdentity class that represents a Windows user, and a PassportIdentity class for Microsoft Passport authentication. I'll take a closer look at the WindowsIdentity class in the upcoming sections of this chapter.

Principal objects

In the .NET Framework, a principal object represents both the identity *and* roles of an application user.

The .NET Framework class library has an IPrincipal interface defining the basic functionality of a principal object. It's a very simple interface that includes a single property and a single method. The Identity property lets you get the identity of the current principal. The IsInRole method allows you to determine if the current principal belongs to a specified role.

There are two classes in .NET that implement this interface—a GenericPrincipal class representing a generic principal, and a WindowsPrincipal class that allows you to check the Windows group membership of a Windows user (**Figure 25**). You can also build your own custom principal objects by creating a class that implements the IPrincipal interface. For more information on implementing interfaces, see Chapter 5, "Object-Orientation in C# and Visual Basic .NET".

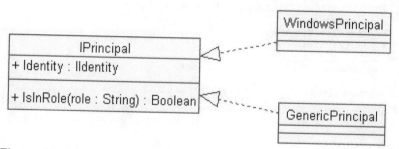

Figure 25. *As shown in this UML class diagram, the WindowsPrincipal and GenericPrincipal .NET classes implement the IPrincipal interface.*

Accessing the principal object

The .NET Framework makes information about the principal available to the current thread. For this example, I'll use the WindowsPrincipal class to show you how to access the principal object.

The first step in accessing the principal object is to indicate you want to use a WindowsPrincipal object. Go back to the console application you created earlier in the chapter and add the following namespace references at the top of the Class1 source code file.

In C#:

```
using System.Security.Principal;
using System.Threading;
```

And in Visual Basic .NET:

```
Imports System.Security.Principal
Imports System.Threading
```

Now change all of the code in the Main method to the following. First in C#:

```
static void Main(string[] args)
{
  /// Set the principal policy
  AppDomain.CurrentDomain.SetPrincipalPolicy(PrincipalPolicy.WindowsPrincipal);

  /// Get the current principal object
  WindowsPrincipal principal = (WindowsPrincipal)Thread.CurrentPrincipal;
```

```
/// Get the identity object
WindowsIdentity identity = (WindowsIdentity)principal.Identity;
string UserID = "Name: " + identity.Name + "\n" +
        "Anonymous: " + identity.IsAnonymous + "\n" +
        "Authenticated: " + identity.IsAuthenticated + "\n" +
        "Guest: " + identity.IsGuest + "\n" +
        "System: " + identity.IsSystem + "\n" +
        "Token: " + identity.Token + "\n" +
        "Administrator: " +
principal.IsInRole(WindowsBuiltInRole.Administrator);

    Console.WriteLine("User identity--" + "\n\n" + UserID);
    Console.ReadLine();
}
```

And in Visual Basic .NET:

```
<STAThread()> _
Shared Sub Main(ByVal args() As String)
    '/ Set the principal policy
    AppDomain.CurrentDomain.SetPrincipalPolicy( _
        PrincipalPolicy.WindowsPrincipal)

    '/ Get the current principal object
    Dim principal As WindowsPrincipal = CType(Thread.CurrentPrincipal, _
        WindowsPrincipal)

    '/ Get the identity object
    Dim identity As WindowsIdentity = CType(principal.Identity, _
        WindowsIdentity)
    Dim UserID As String = "Name: " & identity.Name & ControlChars.Lf & _
        "Anonymous: " & identity.IsAnonymous.ToString() & ControlChars.Lf & _
        "Authenticated: " & identity.IsAuthenticated.ToString() & _
        ControlChars.Lf & "Guest: " & identity.IsGuest.ToString() & _
        ControlChars.Lf & "System: " & identity.IsSystem.ToString() & _
        ControlChars.Lf & "Token: " & identity.Token.ToString() & _
        ControlChars.Lf & "Administrator: " & _
        principal.IsInRole(WindowsBuiltInRole.Administrator).ToString()

    Console.WriteLine(("User identity--" & ControlChars.Lf & _
        ControlChars.Lf & UserID))

    Console.ReadLine()

End Sub 'Main
```

As mentioned previously, this code first tells .NET to use a WindowsPrincipal object. Next, it retrieves the current principal object from the current thread using the static CurrentPrincipal property of the Thread class. Next, it gets the identity object from the principal object, building a string from the values of the identity object's properties. Finally, this string is displayed to the console. Notice the principal object's IsInRole method is used to determine if the user is in the role of Administrator.

Before this code can execute, there is one more step you need to take—request a code-access permission that allows you to manipulate the principal object. Add the following statement to the list of attribute declarations.

In C#:

```
[assembly:SecurityPermissionAttribute(SecurityAction.RequestOptional,
Flags = SecurityPermissionFlag.ControlPrincipal)]
```

In Visual Basic .NET:

```
<Assembly: SecurityPermissionAttribute(SecurityAction.RequestMinimum, _
    Flags:=SecurityPermissionFlag.ControlPrincipal)>
```

This is necessary because, as mentioned earlier, when you request an optional permission, .NET does not grant any other permissions unless they are specifically requested.

Now you're ready to run this sample console application. To do this, just press F5 to compile and run the application. This displays a DOS window containing your user identity information (**Figure 26**).

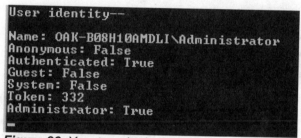

Figure 26. *You can obtain the current user's identity information from the principal object's Identity property.*

Performing security checks using the Principal object

There are several ways you can use the principal and identity objects to perform security checks. First of all, you can call the principal object's IsInRole method in your code to determine if the current user is in a particular role and grant or deny permissions accordingly.

Alternately, you can use PrincipalPermissionAttributes to declare role-based permission requirements similar to what you've already seen with code access security. The PrincipalPermissionAttribute class represents the identity or role the principal must match in order to be granted a particular permission.

For an example of how this can be done, first add the following namespace reference to the top of the Class1 source code file.

In C#:

```
using System.Security;
```

And in Visual Basic .NET:

```
Imports System.Security
```

Next, add the following method to the sample console application's Class1 class. In C#:

```
[PrincipalPermissionAttribute(SecurityAction.Demand,
   Role = "BUILTIN\\Administrators")]
public static void CreateUserAccount()
{
  //
  // Place code here to create user account
  //
  Console.WriteLine("Created user account!");
}
```

And in Visual Basic .NET:

```
<PrincipalPermissionAttribute(SecurityAction.Demand, _
    Role:="BUILTIN\Administrators")> _
  Public Shared Sub CreateUserAccount()
    '
    ' Place code here to create user account
    '
    Console.WriteLine("Created user account!")
End Sub 'CreateUserAccount
```

This code declares a method named "CreateUserAccount" that doesn't actually do much except display a message to the console. Conceptually, this method contains code that creates a new user account. Typically, only a system administrator should perform this sort of task. The attribute declaration preceding the method allows you to specify only users in the role of Administrator can run this method.

Now, add some code that calls this new method. Add the code shown in grey to the Main method, before the call to Console.ReadLine.
In C#:

```
Console.WriteLine("User identity--" + "\n\n" + UserID);

try
{
  CreateUserAccount();
}

catch (SecurityException e)
{
  Console.WriteLine("Error: " + e.Message + "\n" +
      "You must be an Administrator to create a user account");
}

Console.ReadLine();
```

In Visual Basic .NET:

```
Console.WriteLine(("User identity--" & ControlChars.Lf & _
    ControlChars.Lf & UserID))

Try
    CreateUserAccount()

Catch e As SecurityException
    Console.WriteLine(("Error: " & e.Message & ControlChars.Lf & _
        "You must be an Administrator to create a user account")) ¯

End Try

Console.ReadLine()
```

Now press F5 to compile and run the application. This code makes a call to the new CreateUserAccount method within a `try` block. If you are not an Administrator, the `catch` block runs, informing you of the need to be an Administrator to create a user account. If you *are* an administrator, you see the message "Created user account".

Web Application Security

Security for your Web applications is extremely important. Stories of hackers breaking into "secure" sites makes the news just about every week, and companies like Microsoft continually release updates to Web browser and Web server software to plug any holes that are found.

Fortunately, Microsoft had security well in mind when designing ASP.NET (which includes both Web Forms applications and Web Services). This section touches on a few of the key features of ASP.NET security and provides links where you can learn more.

Security in ASP.NET has two layers. The first layer is Internet Information Server (IIS), which has its own security model completely independent of ASP.NET. If a request is granted by IIS, it is passed on to the second layer, ASP.NET, which has its own security model and criteria that can be configured to accept or reject requests.

Restricting access to a Web site

There are three ways ASP.NET restricts users from accessing your Web site:

- Authentication – Verifying the identity of a user.

- Authorization – Determining if a user has permission to access a resource.

- Impersonation – Executing code under the context of an authenticated and authorized user.

The following sections discuss these in greater detail.

Authentication

IIS and ASP.NET examine a user's credentials (usually an ID and password) to determine their identity. These credentials are validated against an *authority*. If an authority identifies a user, they are considered "authenticated", and can continue on to authorization (discussed in the next section). Authentication is not a requirement for an ASP.NET application. If you do not authenticate clients, the user is considered *anonymous*.

> *Although authorization is not a requirement for an ASP.NET application, if there is any part of your ASP.NET application you must secure, you need to authenticate your users.*

Several types of authorities can validate a user's credentials:

- **Windows** – Windows authentication uses IIS to authenticate users. When a user is authenticated, IIS passes a security token to ASP.NET, which ASP.NET uses to create a WindowsPrincipal object as discussed earlier in this chapter.

- **Forms** – Forms authentication uses an HTML form to prompt users for an ID and password. These credentials are passed directly to code in your ASP.NET application, which usually authenticates the credentials against records in a SQL Server database or entries in an XML file. If a user is authenticated, a cookie is issued to the client that it must present on subsequent requests.

- **Passport** – Passport authentication uses Microsoft's centralized authentication service that provides a single logon and profile services for member sites.

- **None** – You can specify an authentication provider of "None" if your site does not authenticate users or if you have implemented your own custom authentication mechanism.

You specify the authentication provider you want to implement in a web.config or machine.config file (for a discussion of these files, see Chapter 10, "Building Web Applications with ASP.NET"). Here is an example of a configuration setting that enables Forms authentication:

```
<system.web>
   <authentication mode="Forms" />
</system.web>
```

For more information on authentication providers and the pros and cons of each, see the .NET Help topic "ASP.NET Authentication".

Authorization

Once a user has been authenticated, you can perform authorization to determine if they have the rights to access the resource they are requesting. There are two main types of authorization, *File Authorization*, and *URL Authorization*.

File Authorization

If you use Windows authentication, you can use File authorization to determine if a user can access a requested resource. File authorization ties into the Access Control List (ACL) security system in Windows NT, Windows 2000, and Windows XP. File authorization requires all valid users of a Web application to have a Windows user account. You can add users to groups and assign permissions to groups with the Windows Computer Management Console.

URL Authorization

You can use URL authorization in conjunction with any type of authentication. User, role, and permission information is placed in `<authorization>` elements stored in web.config and machine.config files.

Here is an example of URL authorization. This authorization section grants access to Jordan, Timothy, and Alexander, but denies access to Bob, and anonymous users (`"?"`):

```
<authorization>
  <allow users="Jordan", "Timothy", "Alexander", roles="Administrators" />
  <deny users="Bob" />
  <deny users="?" />
</authorization>
```

You can also grant or deny permission to the GET, HEAD, or POST HTTP verbs. For example, the following authorization section allows all users (`"*"`) to make GET requests, but denies all users except Greg to make POST requests.

```
<authorization>
  <allow verb="GET", users="*" />
  <allow verb="POST" users="Greg" />
  <deny verb="POST" users="*" />
</authorization>
```

By default, the machine.config file (which specifies default settings for all Web applications on your server) contains an authorization section that allows access to all users:

```
<allow users="*" />
```

With this default setting, if you don't specify differently in any of your web.config files, all users have access to your Web application.

For more information on File and URL authorization as well as the pros and cons of each, see the .NET Help topic "ASP.NET Authorization".

Impersonation

All code that runs on the Windows platform is associated with a user. By default, ASP.NET applications run using the "ASPNET" user account, which has reduced privileges by default. The ASPNET user account is automatically created when you install the .NET Framework on a machine with IIS installed. ASP.NET impersonation allows an ASP.NET application to execute with a different identity, usually that of the client making the request.

Impersonation is disabled by default. You enable impersonation by adding an `<identity>` section in a web.config or machine.config file. This is the default setting in the machine.config file:

```
<identity impersonate="false" >
```

If you want to enable impersonation for all Web applications on a machine, set the value of the "impersonate" attribute to "true" in the machine.config file. If you want to turn it on for a single ASP.NET application, add this setting to a web.config file located in the virtual directory of the Web application.

If impersonation is set to "true", when a request is processed from an authenticated user, ASP.NET assumes the identity of that user. If the user is not authenticated (anonymous), then ASP.NET runs as the IUSR_*MachineName* account.

You can also specify that ASP.NET always impersonate a specific user. To do this, add an `<identity>` section to a configuration file, specifying the user name and password. For example, the following code tells ASP.NET to impersonate the user "Markus" with the password "guacamole".

```
<identity impersonate="true" name="Markus" password="guacamole">
```

For more information on ASP.NET impersonation, see the .NET Help topic "ASP.NET Impersonation".

Conclusion

This chapter just scratches the surface of security in the .NET Framework. It would really take several hundred pages to give a comprehensive overview of .NET's security features. Microsoft continues to make a push for more comprehensive and advanced security features, so I recommend staying tuned to Microsoft's MSDN Web site for the latest information on security innovations for .NET.

Chapter 15
Interoperability with
Visual FoxPro

Microsoft has provided a two-way street for interoperability between .NET and "other" software such as Visual FoxPro. They have made it *extremely* easy to access your Visual FoxPro code from .NET and also access the functionality of .NET from Visual FoxPro. This chapter shows you how easy it is to bridge the divide between .NET and Visual FoxPro.

Most likely you have thousands of lines of Visual FoxPro code you've spent countless hours creating, debugging, tweaking, and enhancing until it suits your needs and those of your end users. Now with the arrival of .NET do you have to throw all this code away? Definitely not!

Fortunately, Microsoft is in the same boat as you. Think of all the software applications Microsoft produced without using .NET. Although Microsoft will rewrite some applications, rewriting all their applications in .NET would be a colossal undertaking without enough benefits to make it worthwhile.

Based on this, Microsoft made it very easy to interoperate with (I hate to use the word) "legacy" software so you can protect your code investment. Here are some examples of situations where you may need to interop with Visual FoxPro code from .NET:

- .NET Web Forms applications accessing Visual FoxPro business objects stored in a component library.

- .NET Windows Forms applications accessing middle-tier business objects stored in a component library.

- .NET XML Web Services accessing Visual FoxPro business objects stored in a component library.

- .NET Windows Forms applications accessing a Visual FoxPro Windows desktop application as an automation server (similar to how you access Microsoft Office applications from VFP).

Two technologies make this possible, COM (Component Object Model) and XML.

Interoperability via COM

Once upon a time there was COM. Microsoft created COM to provide interoperability between software applications and components written in diverse languages such as C++, Visual FoxPro, and Visual Basic. Even non-Microsoft languages such as Delphi jumped on the COM bandwagon.

COM lets you instantiate objects written in other languages, call their methods, access their properties, and respond to their events without knowing the language used to create the component.

COM moves into the 21st century by creating a bridge between .NET and the rest of the world. If you need to access your Visual FoxPro applications from .NET, you *must* compile your FoxPro code into a COM server.

Types of COM servers

There are two main types of COM servers—in-process servers (DLLs) and out-of-process servers (EXEs). Important differences exist between these two types of servers dictating which you should use in different situations.

In-Process servers

An in-process server is a DLL loaded and run within the same Windows process as the client. This provides fast access to objects contained in the server because there is no cross-process communication necessary. One limitation of in-process servers is they cannot interact with the user interface (you can't show forms, display messages, and so on).

Typically, in-process servers contain multiple business objects instantiated by clients that call their methods to perform a variety of functions. This model covers the first three scenarios discussed earlier in this chapter and is the most common way to access VFP code.

Out-Of-Process servers

An out-of-process server is an EXE running in its own Windows Process apart from the client. This model incurs a slight performance hit because of the extra work the operating system performs to pass calls from one process to another. However, out-of-process servers *do* have the ability to interact with the user interface.

This means you can start an out-of-process server, such as a Visual FoxPro desktop application, from within a .NET application and access its functionality programmatically— much the same way you access Microsoft Office applications from within Visual FoxPro.

Visual FoxPro's COM capabilities

Fortunately, the Microsoft Fox team continued to enhance Visual FoxPro's COM capabilities with each new version. These enhancements are critical in using newer technologies such as COM+ and .NET.

> *For more information on Visual FoxPro and COM, check out the book "What's New in Visual FoxPro 7" from Hentzenwerke Publishing.*

Interoperability via XML

Although COM gives you the ability to instantiate a Visual FoxPro object from .NET, you still need a mechanism for passing data between .NET and Visual FoxPro. The mechanism is XML.

Again, the Fox team comes to the rescue by providing built-in XML functionality starting with version 7.0 of VFP. The CursorToXml, XmlToCursor, and XmlUpdateGram functions convert between Visual FoxPro's native cursor format and XML, a key .NET data format.

You'll be looking closer at these functions in the next section as you build a Visual FoxPro component accessible from .NET.

Creating a Visual FoxPro COM server

In this section you'll create an in-process Visual FoxPro COM server to demonstrate how easy it is to access your VFP code from .NET.

The first step in building a COM server is creating a new Visual FoxPro project. Create a new, empty VFP project named comdemo.pjx in the bin\debug directory of this book's sample code. (Below the HW .NET Book Samples_CSharp directory if you're working with C#, or the HW .NET Book Samples_Visual Basic directory if you're working with VB .NET). After creating the new project, add a PRG file to the project and place the following class definition code in the PRG:

```
DEFINE CLASS Employee AS Session OLEPUBLIC

  cStartPath = ""

  PROCEDURE INIT
        *--- Issue SET commands appropriate for COM servers
        SET RESOURCE OFF
        SET EXCLUSIVE OFF
        SET REPROCESS TO 2 SECONDS
        SET CPDIALOG OFF
        SET DELETED ON
        SET EXACT OFF
        SET SAFETY OFF

        *--- Save the server startup path
        This.cStartPath = ADDBS(JUSTPATH(Application.ServerName))
        SET PATH TO (This.cStartPath)
  ENDPROC

*--- Get all Employees
PROCEDURE GetAllEmployees() AS String ;
      HELPSTRING "Returns an XML string containing all employees"

      LOCAL lcXML
      SELECT * FROM Employees INTO CURSOR Employee
      CURSORTOXML("Employee", "lcXML", 0, 0, 0, "1")
      USE IN Employee

      RETURN lcXML

ENDPROC

*--- Get the specified employee
PROCEDURE GetEmployeeByID(empID AS Integer) AS String ;
      HELPSTRING "Returns an XML string containing the specified employee"

      LOCAL lcXML
      SELECT * FROM Employees WHERE ;
        EmployeeID = empID INTO CURSOR Employee
      CURSORTOXML("Employee", "lcXML", 0, 0, 0, "1")
      USE IN Employee
```

```
          RETURN lcXML

     ENDPROC

ENDDEFINE
```

This code defines a class named Employee subclassed from Visual FoxPro's Session class. The Session class is used because it ensures all business objects have their own private data session. The OLEPUBLIC keyword tells the Visual FoxPro compiler to make the class public to users of the COM server. Only classes marked as OLEPUBLIC are visible and accessible to the outside world.

The Employee class contains three methods—Init, GetAllEmployees, and GetEmployeeByID. The Init method issues SET commands appropriate for COM servers. It also saves the DLL startup path and issues a SET PATH to this directory. This allows the other COM server methods to find the data they need.

The other two methods make use of the strong-typing AS clause introduced in Visual FoxPro 7.0. This clause specifies the type of method parameters and their return values. Both methods declare a String return value, which in this case is an XML string. The GetEmployeeByID method also uses the AS clause to declare a single integer parameter. The HELPSTRING keyword specifies the method description stored to the type library.

> Visual FoxPro's strong-typing features are only used for IntelliSense and to create type libraries for COM servers. The compiler does not enforce them!

Testing the Employee class

Before compiling the comdemo project into a COM server, it's best to test the business object classes within Visual FoxPro first. This is important because it's very difficult to debug VFP COM servers!

To test the Employee class, enter the following code in the VFP Command Window:

```
SET PROCEDURE TO business.prg
EmployeeObj = CREATEOBJECT("Employee")
?EmployeeObj.GetAllEmployees()
```

When you run the GetAllEmployees method, the resulting XML string containing all employees is displayed in the Visual FoxPro desktop.

You can test the GetEmployeeByID method by entering the following command in the Visual FoxPro Command Window. This time you'll use the STRTOFILE command to write the resulting XML string to a file, and then examine the file contents:

```
STRTOFILE(EmployeeObj.GetEmployeebyID(1), "Employee.xml")
MODIFY FILE Employee.xml
```

When you run the MODIFY FILE command, it displays the contents of the Employee.xml file that looks like this (I've left the schema information out for the sake of space):

```
<?xml version = "1.0" encoding="Windows-1252" standalone="yes"?>
<VFPData>
  <xsd:schema id="VFPData" xmlns:xsd="http://www.w3.org/2001/XMLSchema"
xmlns:msdata="urn:schemas-microsoft-com:xml-msdata">
  <!-- Left out the schema information to save space-->
  </xsd:schema>
  <employee>
    <employeeid>1</employeeid>
    <lastname>Davolio</lastname>
    <firstname>Nancy</firstname>
    <title>Sales Representative</title>
    <titleofcourtesy>Ms.</titleofcourtesy>
    <birthdate>1948-12-08T00:00:00</birthdate>
    <hiredate>1992-05-01T00:00:00</hiredate>
    <address>507 - 20th Ave. E.</address>
    <city>Seattle</city>
    <region>WA</region>
    <postalcode>98122</postalcode>
    <country>USA</country>
    <homephone>(206) 555-9857</homephone>
    <extension>5467</extension>
    <notes>Education includes a BA in psychology from Colorado State University
in 1970.  She also completed "The Art of the Cold Call."  Nancy is a member of
Toastmasters International.</notes>
    <reportsto>2</reportsto>
    <photopath/>
  </employee>
</VFPData>
```

As you can see, Visual FoxPro does all of the heavy lifting for you by converting the cursor into an XML string and automatically generating a schema to go with it!

Compiling the COM server

Now it's time to compile the COM server. To do this, click the Project Manager's Build button to launch the Build Options dialog (**Figure 1**). Select Multi-threaded COM server (dll) under Build Action, select Recompile All Files, and Display Errors under Options. When you're done, click the OK button to build the COM server.

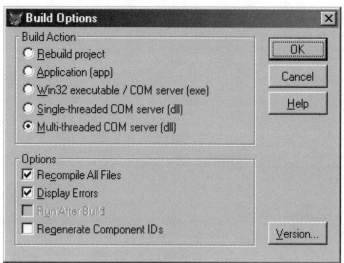

Figure 1. Visual FoxPro allows you to build both EXE and DLL COM Servers.

The build process creates three output files:

- comdemo.dll –COM server

- comdemo.tlb –Type Library

- comdemo.vbr –Registry file

The comdemo COM Server

The comdemo.dll file is the COM server and is the main output file. This file contains the compiled code for the Employee business object class, although in most cases COM servers contain multiple business object classes.

When you compile a COM server, all OLEPUBLIC classes in the server are automatically registered in the build machine's Windows Registry. You view these entries in the Registry using the Windows Registry Editor tool. To launch the Registry Editor, click the Windows Start button and select Run. In the Run dialog, enter "RegEdit" in the Open box, and then click OK.

When the Registry Editor dialog appears (**Figure 2**), in the left pane select the HKEY_CLASSES_ROOT node of the tree view. This is the node where your COM server's classes are registered.

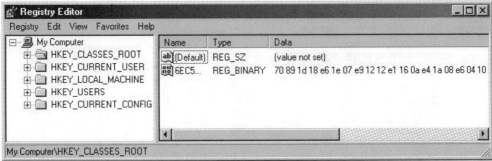

Figure 2. *The HKEY_CLASSES_ROOT node of the Windows Registry contains entries for your COM server classes.*

From the Registry Editor's Edit menu, select Find to launch the Find dialog (**Figure 3**). In the Find what box, enter "comdemo" and click the Find Next button.

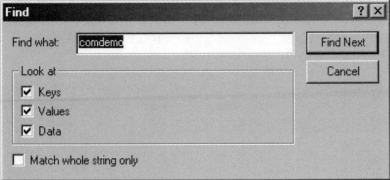

Figure 3. *The Registry Editor's Find dialog allows you to search for your COM server classes in the Windows Registry.*

After several seconds, the Registry Editor should find your comdemo.Employee class. This is indicated by the appearance of an expanded node in the tree view located in the left pane, and the string "comdemo.Employee" in the right pane under the Data column.

The node text in the left pane contains a series of alpha-numeric characters (**Figure 4**). This is the Employee object's Globally Unique Identifier (GUID). This GUID is an identifier generated during the compile process guaranteed to uniquely identify your COM object.

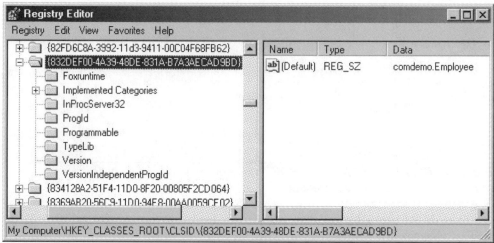

Figure 4. The Globally Unique Identifier (GUID) generated at compile time uniquely identifies your COM Server objects.

If you expand this node, you see sub-nodes containing additional information about your COM object.

The comdemo type library

Another by-product of the COM server build process is the comdemo.tlb file. This is your COM server's type library. A type library is a binary file describing the public classes in your COM server.

To view the contents of your server's type library, launch Visual FoxPro's Object Browser by selecting Tools | Object Browser from the main Visual FoxPro menu. Next, click the Open Type Library button (the button farthest left at the top of the Object Browser window). This launches the Open dialog (**Figure 5**).

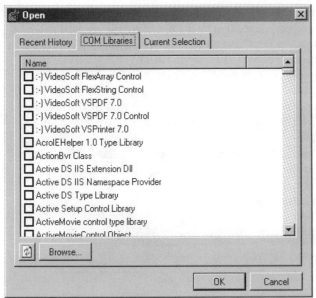

***Figure 5**. The Visual FoxPro Object Browser's Open dialog lets you select a type library to view in the Object Browser.*

Select the COM Libraries tab. It may take a few seconds before the tab gets focus as the Windows Registry searches for all COM libraries. Click the Browse button to launch the Open dialog (**Figure 6**). Navigate to the folder containing your comdemo type library.

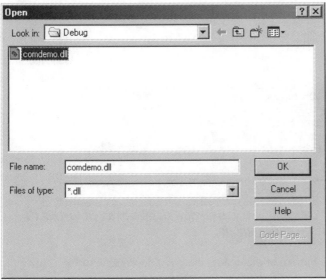

***Figure 6**. You can open either DLLs or TLBs in Visual FoxPro's Object Browser depending on the platform on which the COM server was created.*

Notice in Figure 6 the default file type is "*.dll". Isn't the type library stored in a TLB file? The answer is it can be stored in both, depending on the operating system used to create the COM server. If you build a Visual FoxPro COM server on a Windows NT, 2000, or XP machine, the type library is placed in the external TLB file *and* is also embedded within the DLL. If you build a VFP COM server on a Windows 98 machine, the type library is only found in the TLB file, not in the DLL.

If you've created the COM Server on Windows 98, in the Files of type combo box, select "*.tlb", select comdemo.tlb, and click OK. If you've created the server on a newer platform, just select comdemo.dll and click OK.

When you click OK, focus returns to the Object Browser (**Figure 7**) dialog. Expand the comdemo type library node shown in the left pane of the Object Browser, then expand the Classes node and select the Employee class beneath it. Next, in the right pane expand the Methods node and select the GetEmployeeByID method.

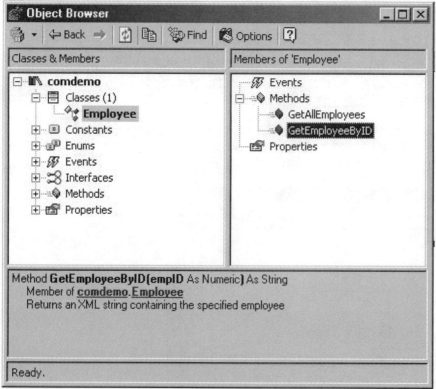

Figure 7. *The Object Browser dialog allows you to view details of all OLEPUBLIC classes and their public properties and methods.*

In the description pane at the bottom of the dialog, there is a description of the GetEmployeeByID method as shown in Figure 7. The description says the GetEmployeeByID method accepts a single numeric parameter and returns a string value. It also displays the method description you specified in the HELPSTRING attribute.

The comdemo Windows Registry file

The last of the three files generated by building your COM server is the comdemo.vbr
Windows Registry file. This file contains the GUIDs for the classes in your COM server. If
you open the comdemo.vbr file with a text editor you'll see something like this:

```
VB5SERVERINFO
VERSION=1.0.0

HKEY_CLASSES_ROOT\comdemo.Employee = comdemo.Employee
HKEY_CLASSES_ROOT\comdemo.Employee\NotInsertable
HKEY_CLASSES_ROOT\comdemo.Employee\CLSID = {832DEF00-4A39-48DE-831A-
B7A3AECAD9BD}
HKEY_CLASSES_ROOT\CLSID\{832DEF00-4A39-48DE-831A-B7A3AECAD9BD} =
comdemo.Employee
HKEY_CLASSES_ROOT\CLSID\{832DEF00-4A39-48DE-831A-B7A3AECAD9BD}\ProgId =
comdemo.Employee
HKEY_CLASSES_ROOT\CLSID\{832DEF00-4A39-48DE-831A-
B7A3AECAD9BD}\VersionIndependentProgId = comdemo.Employee
HKEY_CLASSES_ROOT\CLSID\{832DEF00-4A39-48DE-831A-B7A3AECAD9BD}\InProcServer32 =
comdemo.dll
HKEY_CLASSES_ROOT\CLSID\{832DEF00-4A39-48DE-831A-
B7A3AECAD9BD}\InProcServer32\"ThreadingModel" = Apartment
HKEY_CLASSES_ROOT\CLSID\{832DEF00-4A39-48DE-831A-B7A3AECAD9BD}\TypeLib =
{97FD3B3E-2115-4DEE-B50B-B8761A45C358}
HKEY_CLASSES_ROOT\CLSID\{832DEF00-4A39-48DE-831A-B7A3AECAD9BD}\Version = 1.0
HKEY_CLASSES_ROOT\CLSID\{832DEF00-4A39-48DE-831A-B7A3AECAD9BD}\Foxruntime =
VFP7T.DLL
HKEY_CLASSES_ROOT\INTERFACE\{17BE97B1-AAD2-4604-9253-DAB268C1E2F4} = Employee
HKEY_CLASSES_ROOT\INTERFACE\{17BE97B1-AAD2-4604-9253-
DAB268C1E2F4}\ProxyStubClsid = {00020424-0000-0000-C000-000000000046}
HKEY_CLASSES_ROOT\INTERFACE\{17BE97B1-AAD2-4604-9253-
DAB268C1E2F4}\ProxyStubClsid32 = {00020424-0000-0000-C000-000000000046}
HKEY_CLASSES_ROOT\INTERFACE\{17BE97B1-AAD2-4604-9253-DAB268C1E2F4}\TypeLib =
{97FD3B3E-2115-4DEE-B50B-B8761A45C358}
HKEY_CLASSES_ROOT\INTERFACE\{17BE97B1-AAD2-4604-9253-
DAB268C1E2F4}\TypeLib\"Version" = 1.0


; TypeLibrary registration
HKEY_CLASSES_ROOT\TypeLib\{97FD3B3E-2115-4DEE-B50B-B8761A45C358}
HKEY_CLASSES_ROOT\TypeLib\{97FD3B3E-2115-4DEE-B50B-B8761A45C358}\1.0 = comdemo
Type Library
HKEY_CLASSES_ROOT\TypeLib\{97FD3B3E-2115-4DEE-B50B-B8761A45C358}\1.0\0\win32 =
comdemo.dll
HKEY_CLASSES_ROOT\TypeLib\{97FD3B3E-2115-4DEE-B50B-B8761A45C358}\1.0\FLAGS = 0
```

As already mentioned, when you build a COM server, Visual FoxPro automatically
registers the COM server in the Windows Registry of the build machine. If you want to move
your COM server to a different machine, the VBR file allows you to register the class
definitions in the Windows Registry of the target machine.

For details on using the VBR file to register a Visual FoxPro COM server, see the VFP
Help topics "CliReg32.exe Remote Automation Utility" and "Using Remote Automation".

Testing the COM server from Visual FoxPro

Before accessing the comdemo server from .NET, it's a "best practice" to test it from Visual FoxPro first. To do this, enter the following commands in the VFP Command Window:

```
EmployeeObj = CREATEOBJECT("comdemo.Employee")
?EmployeeObj.GetAllEmployees()
```

This time you didn't have to issue a SET PROCEDURE command. Instead, you specified the name of the COM server ("comdemo") and the name of the business object ("Employee") in the CREATEOBJECT command. Visual FoxPro searches the Windows Registry for this COM object and instantiates it for you.

You test the GetEmployeeByID method by issuing the same command as you did earlier:

```
STRTOFILE(EmployeeObj.GetEmployeebyID(1), "Employee.xml")
MODIFY FILE Employee.xml
```

Now, knowing your COM server is working properly, it's time to access it from .NET.

Creating a .NET test project

Now you will make a very simple .NET Windows Application with a single form containing a DataGrid for testing the VFP COM server.

From the Visual Studio .NET Start Page, click the New Project button. In the left pane of the New Project dialog (**Figure 8**), select Visual C# Projects or Visual Basic Projects depending on the language you want to use for this project.

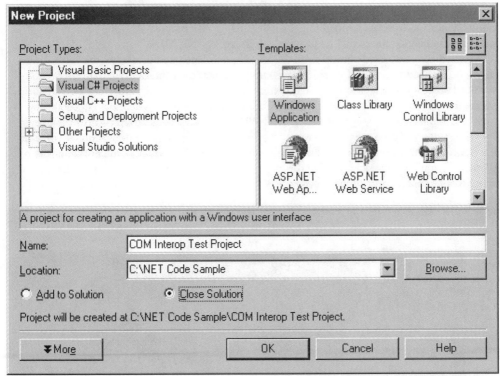

***Figure 8**. You can create a simple Windows Application to test a VFP COM server.*

In the Templates pane on the right, select Windows Application. In the Name box, change the name of the application to "COM Interop Test Project" and click OK. When VS .NET finishes creating your new project, it displays a form named "Form1" in the IDE. Normally, you would use this form to be your main application desktop window, but for this simple example you'll use it to host a DataGrid instead.

First, make the form big enough to hold a DataGrid with several columns. To do this, you simply resize the form by dragging its bottom right corner or you can select the Properties Window and change the form's Size property to something around 640,340. Also change the form's Text property to "COM Interop Test" and its Name property to "InteropTestForm".

If you're using C#, there is one additional step. In the Solution Explorer, right-click on Form1.cs and select View Code from the shortcut menu. Next, in the Main method of the form change the "Form1" reference to "InteropTestForm":

```
static void Main()
{
  Application.Run(new InteropTestForm());
}
```

If you're using Visual Basic .NET, there's also an additional step you need to take. In the Solution Explorer, right-click on the project and select Properties from the shortcut menu. In the left pane of the Property Pages dialog, beneath the Common Properties node, select

General. In the right side of the dialog, in the Startup object combo box, select "InteropTest Form". Click OK to save changes and close the dialog. Afterwards, view the form in design mode by clicking on the Form1.cs [Design] tab in the VS .NET IDE.

Now drag a DataGrid control from the VS .NET Toolbox and drop it on the form. You make the Toolbox visible by hovering your mouse pointer over the Toolbox tab. If you don't see the Toolbox tab, select View | Toolbox from the main menu. After dropping the DataGrid on the form, resize it to fill up most of the form. For example, you can set its Location property to 40,30, and its Size property to 550,220. Also change its Name property to grdEmployees.

Now drag and drop a Button control from the Toolbox onto the bottom of the form under the DataGrid. For example, set its Location property to 280,270. Change the button's Name property to btnGetData and its Text property to "Get Data". When you're done, your form should look like the form shown in **Figure 9**.

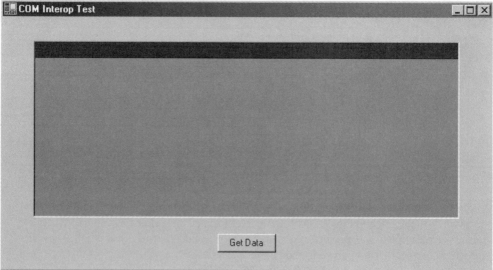

Figure 9. A simple form to test a Visual FoxPro COM server.

Click the Save All button at the top of the Visual Studio .NET IDE to save all changes you have made so far.

Referencing the Visual FoxPro COM server

Now you're ready to add a reference to the Visual FoxPro COM server to your new project. To do this, go in the Solution Explorer, right-click the Reference node beneath your project, and select Add Reference from the shortcut menu (**Figure 10**).

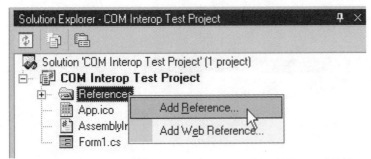

Figure 10. *You use the Solution Explorer for adding a COM server reference to a .NET project.*

This launches the Add Reference dialog. Select the COM tab (**Figure 11**), click the Browse button, and navigate to your comdemo project's directory.

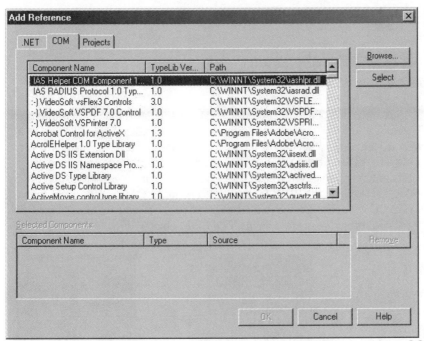

Figure 11. *The Add Reference dialog lets you add .NET assembly or COM component references to your .NET project.*

If you generated the COM server on a Windows 98 machine, select the comdemo.tlb file. If you generated the COM server on a newer operating system, select the comdemo.dll file and click the Open button. This takes you back to the Add Reference dialog, with the comdemo file shown in the Selected Components list at the bottom of the dialog. Click OK to add a reference to the COM server to your .NET project.

You should now see a comdemo node in the Solution Explorer beneath the References node (**Figure 12**).

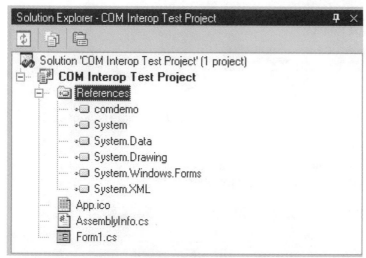

Figure 12. *COM Servers and .NET assemblies referenced from your .NET projects are listed under the References tab of your project*

If you select the comdemo node in the Solution Explorer and look at the Path property in the Properties Window, you will see it does not reference comdemo.dll. Rather, it refers to a .NET assembly named "Interop.comdemo.dll". This is a *Runtime Callable Wrapper* (RCW) automatically created by Visual Studio .NET when you added a reference to comdemo.dll. This RCW acts as an intermediary between .NET and the Visual FoxPro comdemo.dll (**Figure 13**). A wrapper class is created in the RCW for each class in your COM server. Rather than calling methods on a COM object directly, .NET calls methods on a wrapper class in the RCW that in turn calls the corresponding method on the VFP COM object.

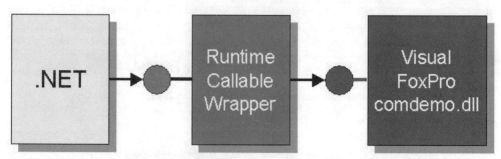

Figure 13. *Visual Studio .NET automatically creates a Runtime Callable Wrapper (RCW) that is an intermediary between .NET and your COM components.*

Take a closer look at this Runtime Callable Wrapper. Open the VS .NET Object Browser by selecting View | Other Windows | Object Browser from the shortcut menu. In the Object

Browser, you should see a node named "interop.comdemo" (**Figure 14**). Expand the comdemo node, and if you're using C#, you will see three items listed: Employee, EmployeeClass, and IEmployee (I'll look at VB .NET in a moment).

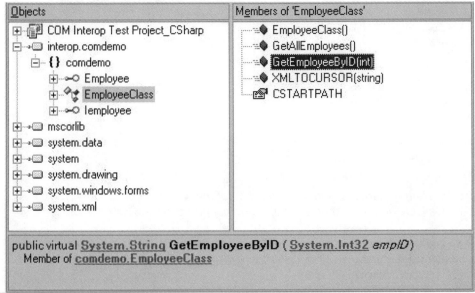

Figure 14. *You can view a Runtime Callable Wrapper from .NET's Object Browser.*

Both Employee and IEmployee are interfaces and EmployeeClass is the concrete class you need to instantiate from within .NET. As you can see, VS .NET takes the original class name and appends the suffix "Class". If you select the EmployeeClass node, three methods appear in the right pane—your two original methods, GetAllEmployees and GetEmployeeByID, and a new method called EmployeeClass, which is the .NET constructor method.

If you select the GetEmployeeByID method, details of the method display at the bottom of the Object Browser (Figure 14). As you can see, the GetEmployeeByID method returns a string value (System.String) and accepts a single integer parameter (System.Int32).

If you're using Visual Basic .NET, you should see a node named Interop.comdemo in the Object Browser (**Figure 15**). If you expand the comdemo node, you only see one class named Employee and no interfaces. This is a bit different than what you saw in C#, where there was one class named "EmployeeClass" and two interfaces. If you click on the Employee class, in the right pane you see all the same methods as in C#, except for the constructor method.

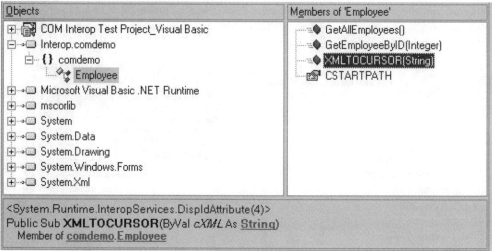

Figure 15. *Rather than showing you the name of the wrapper class, the VB .NET Runtime Callable Wrapper shows you the original name of the COM class.*

If you right-click on either pane of the Object Browser and select Show Hidden Members from the shortcut menu, the Iemployee interface is displayed (**Figure 16**), although the Employee interface shown in C# is not.

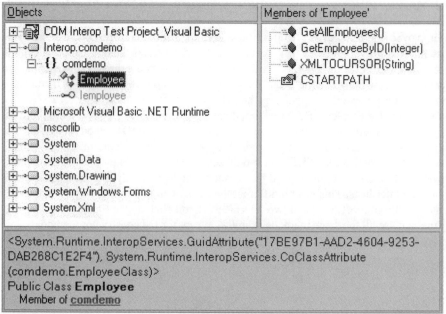

Figure 16. *If you select the Employee class in the VB .NET RCW, it displays the name of the wrapper class in the description pane at the bottom of the browser.*

Regarding the difference in the class name, if you select the Employee class in the Object Browser, the description pane at the bottom of the browser shows the class refers to comdemo.EmployeeClass. Because you need to instantiate the EmployeeClass in .NET (not the "Employee" class) I think the Runtime Callable Wrapper created by C# is more informative.

Using the COM server Employee object

Now it's time to add code to the Windows Form to instantiate the Employee business object and call its methods.

Select Form1 in design mode and double-click the Get Data button. This automatically adds a new btnGetData_Click event handler method to the form. Before adding code to this method, add a reference to the interop.comdemo namespace at the top of the code file (VS .NET assigns classes in your COM server to a namespace with the same name as your DLL). You should also add a reference to the System.IO namespace, which you'll need soon.

In C#:

```
using comdemo;
using System.IO;
```

In Visual Basic .NET:

```
Imports comdemo
Imports System.IO
```

Now, in the btnGetData_Click event handler method at the bottom of the code window, add the following code.

In C#:

```
private void btnGetData_Click(object sender, System.EventArgs e)
{
  // Instantiate the Employee class
  EmployeeClass Employee = new EmployeeClass();

  // Get an XML string containing all Employees
  string EmployeesXml = Employee.GetAllEmployees();

  // Create a new DataSet and fill it from the XML string
  DataSet dsEmployees = new DataSet();
  dsEmployees.ReadXml( new StringReader(EmployeesXml));

  // Clear and then set the DataBindings of the grid
  this.grdEmployees.DataBindings.Clear();
  this.grdEmployees.SetDataBinding(dsEmployees,
    dsEmployees.Tables[0].TableName);
}
```

In Visual Basic .NET:

```
Private Sub btnGetData_Click(ByVal sender As System.Object, _
    ByVal e As System.EventArgs) Handles btnGetData.Click
    ' Instantiate the Employee class
```

```
    Dim Employee As New EmployeeClass()

    ' Get an XML string containing all Employees
    Dim EmployeesXml As String = Employee.GetAllEmployees()

    ' Create a new DataSet and fill it from the XML string
    Dim dsEmployees As New DataSet()
    dsEmployees.ReadXml(New StringReader(EmployeesXml))

    ' Clear and then set the DataBindings of the grid
    Me.grdEmployees.DataBindings.Clear()
    Me.grdEmployees.SetDataBinding(dsEmployees, _
        dsEmployees.Tables(0).TableName)
End Sub
```

This code instantiates the EmployeeClass Runtime Callable Wrapper and calls its GetAllEmployees method. Behind the scenes, the RCW in turn calls the GetAllEmployees method on the Visual FoxPro Employees COM object, which returns an XML string containing all employees. The RCW takes the return value and returns it as a .NET string type.

Another feature worth noting is you get IntelliSense on methods of the RCW (**Figure 17**) because it is consuming the interface of your COM object and re-exposing it as a .NET interface.

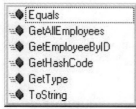

**Figure 17**. You get IntelliSense for your COM objects in Visual Studio .NET thanks to the Runtime Callable Wrapper.

Running the Interop sample

Now it's time to compile and run the Interop sample application. To do this, you can simply press F5. When the form is first displayed, the grid is empty. If you click the Get Data button, it runs code retrieving XML data from the Visual FoxPro Employee COM object and binding the DataGrid to the data. The data is then displayed in the DataGrid (**Figure 18**).

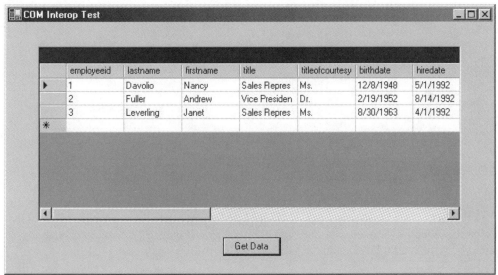

Figure 18. *XML data returned from a Visual FoxPro COM object is easily read into a .NET DataSet and displayed in a DataGrid.*

To close the sample form, click the close button [X] in the upper right corner of the form.

Using Visual FoxPro COM objects from ASP.NET

Although using Visual FoxPro COM objects from ASP.NET is similar to using them from a .NET Windows application, there are enough nuances to warrant creating a simple ASP.NET Web Forms application to demonstrate the differences.

Creating a Web Forms test application

From the Visual Studio .NET Start Page, click the New Project button. In the left pane of the New Project dialog, select Visual C# Projects or Visual Basic Projects depending on the language you want to use for this project.

In the Templates pane on the right, select ASP.NET Web Application. In the Location box, change the name of the application to "Web COM Interop Test Project", and then click the OK button. When VS .NET finishes creating your new Web project, it displays a form named WebForm1 in the IDE. You'll use this form to host a DataGrid containing records retrieved from the Visual FoxPro Employees COM object.

To do this, drag and drop a DataGrid from the Visual Studio Toolbox onto the upper left corner of the Web form. Next, change the appearance of the DataGrid similar to what you did on the Windows form. Go to the Properties Window, change the ID property to "grdEmployees", and the Width to 600px. When you're done, your grid should look like **Figure 19**.

Column0	Column1	Column2
abc	abc	abc
abc	abc	abc
abc	abc	abc
abc	abc	abc
abc	abc	abc

Figure 19. A Web Forms DataGrid can display data retrieved from a Visual FoxPro COM object.

Now go one step further with the DataGrid to make it look just a bit more attractive. With the DataGrid selected in design mode, click the <u>Auto Format</u> hyperlink at the bottom left of the Properties Window. This launches the Auto Format dialog (**Figure 20**). You can choose any style you wish, but for this example, I've chosen "Colorful 1".

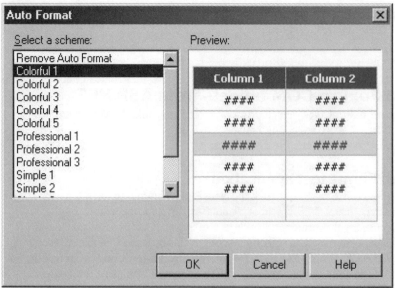

Figure 20. The Auto Format dialog allows you to easily change the appearance of your DataGrids.

Next, you need to specify the columns for the DataGrid. Unlike the Windows Forms DataGrid, which looks passable without specifying any column information, the Web Forms DataGrid needs a little more coaxing. To specify columns for the DataGrid, select the DataGrid on the Web Form, and then click the <u>Property Builder</u> hyperlink at the bottom left corner of the Properties Window. This launches the DataGrid Properties dialog (**Figure 21**).

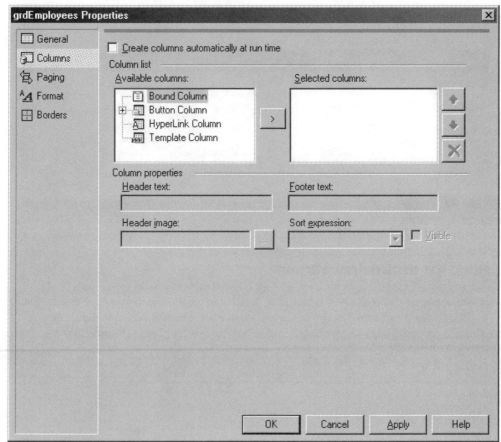

Figure 21. The DataGrid's Properties dialog lets you specify the columns to display in a Web Forms DataGrid.

Select the Columns item in the left pane and a columns mover control is displayed as shown in Figure 21. Next, clear the Create columns automatically at run time check box. Afterwards, select Bound Column in the Available Columns list and click the mover button (>) to add the bound column to the Selected columns list. In the Header Text box, enter "Last Name" and in the Data Field box enter "LastName".

Add three more bound columns to the DataGrid with Header Text and Data Field properties shown in **Table 1**. When you have added all of the columns to the DataGrid, click the OK button to close the dialog.

Table 1. Web Forms DataGrid columns

Header Text	Data Field
First Name	First Name
Title	TitleOfCourtesy
Home Phone	HomePhone

When you're done, your DataGrid should look like the one shown in **Figure 22**.

Last Name	First Name	Title	Home Phone
Databound	Databound	Databound	Databound
Databound	Databound	Databound	Databound
Databound	Databound	Databound	Databound
Databound	Databound	Databound	Databound
Databound	Databound	Databound	Databound

Figure 22. You should specify columns for your Web Forms DataGrids so they look more presentable.

Setting the aspCompat attribute

When you use a COM component from an ASP.NET page, you should set the page's aspCompat property to true. Do this now, and then I'll explain the importance of this setting.

Click on the Web Form design surface and go to the Properties Window. Select the aspCompat property, open its associated combo box, and select "True" (**Figure 23**).

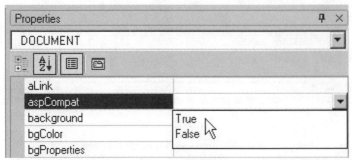

Figure 23. If you are accessing a COM component from an ASP.NET page, you should set the page's aspCompat property to True.

Normally, ASP.NET runs in multi-threaded apartment (MTA) mode. However, Visual FoxPro COM components are single-threaded apartment (STA) objects. The aspCompat property tells ASP.NET to execute in STA mode. Although you won't get an error if you don't change this setting, your application runs slowly and may experience deadlocks. For more information, see the .NET Help topic "COM Component Compatibility".

Referencing the Visual FoxPro COM server

Before going further, you need to add a reference to the Visual FoxPro COM server in your Web Forms project. To do this, in the Solution Explorer, right-click the References node and select Add Reference from the shortcut menu to launch the Add Reference dialog. Select the dialog's COM tab and click the Browse button. In the Select Component dialog, navigate to the folder containing comdemo.dll, select the file, and then click the Open button (If you're on a Windows 98 machine, select comdemo.tlb). This brings you back to the Add Reference dialog with "comdemo.dll" displayed in the Selected Components list. Click the OK button and VS .NET adds a Runtime Callable Wrapper assembly named "comdemo" under the References node of your project (**Figure 24**).

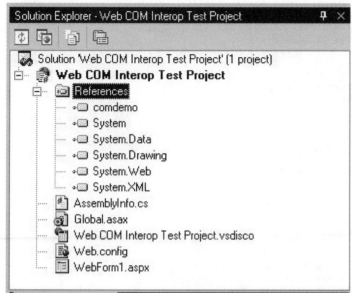

Figure 24. You can add a reference to a VFP COM server in your ASP.NET Web Forms application the same as in a .NET Windows Forms application.

Using the COM Server Employee object

Now it's time to add code to retrieve XML data from the Visual FoxPro Employees COM object and display it in the DataGrid. To do this, double-click the form's design surface. VS .NET displays the Web Form's code-behind file, adding a new event handler method called Page_Load. Before placing code in this method, add the following namespace references at the top of the code-behind file.

In C#:

```
using comdemo;
using System.IO;
```

And in Visual Basic .NET:

```
Imports comdemo
Imports System.IO
```

Next, add the following code to the Page_Load method.

In C#:

```csharp
private void Page_Load(object sender, System.EventArgs e)
{
  // Instantiate the Employee class
  EmployeeClass Employee = new EmployeeClass();

  // Get an XML string containing all employees
  string EmployeesXml = Employee.GetAllEmployees();

  // Create a new DataSet and fill it from the XML string
  DataSet dsEmployees = new DataSet();
  dsEmployees.ReadXml( new StringReader(EmployeesXml));

  // Data bind the grid to the DataSet
  this.grdEmployees.DataSource = dsEmployees;
  this.grdEmployees.DataBind();
}
```

And in Visual Basic .NET:

```vbnet
Private Sub Page_Load(ByVal sender As System.Object, _
    ByVal e As System.EventArgs) Handles MyBase.Load
    ' Instantiate the Employee class
    Dim Employee As New EmployeeClass()

    ' Get an XML string containing all employees
    Dim EmployeesXml As String = Employee.GetAllEmployees()

    ' Create a new DataSet and fill it from the XML string
    Dim dsEmployees As New DataSet()
    dsEmployees.ReadXml(New StringReader(EmployeesXml))

    ' Data bind the grid to the DataSet
    Me.grdEmployees.DataSource = dsEmployees
    Me.grdEmployees.DataBind()
End Sub
```

This code instantiates the EmployeeClass Runtime Callable Wrapper and calls the object's GetAllEmployees method, which returns an XML string containing all employees. It then fills a DataSet from the XML string and binds the grid to the DataSet.

Running the Web Interop sample

Now you're ready to run the Web Interop sample. To do this, press the F5 key to compile and run the project. When your Web browser appears, you should see a DataGrid containing data as shown in **Figure 25**.

Last Name	First Name	Title	Home Phone
Davolio	Nancy	Ms.	(206) 555-9857
Fuller	Andrew	Dr.	(206) 555-9482
Leverling	Janet	Ms.	(206) 555-3412

Figure 25*. The DataGrid displays XML data retrieved from the Visual FoxPro Employee COM object.*

Other resources

There are some great on-line articles available regarding COM Interop with Visual FoxPro. The first is Rick Strahl's on-line article ".NET Interop for Visual FoxPro Applications" found at the following URL:

`http://www.west-wind.com/presentations/VfpDotNetInterop/vfpDotNetInterop.htm`

Rick's article covers information not discussed in this chapter, such as returning Visual FoxPro objects from COM server methods for use in .NET. It also includes some interesting speed comparisons using classic ASP vs. ASP.NET to access Visual FoxPro COM objects.

Another great resource is Cathi Gero's on-line article "Using ASP.NET in Visual Studio .NET with Visual FoxPro 7.0". You can view this article at the following URL:

`http://msdn.microsoft.com/library/?url=/library/en-us/dnfoxgen7/html/usingaspnetwithvfp7.asp`

Cathi's article demonstrates the following four scenarios:

- Accessing Visual FoxPro Data Using OLE DB

- Accessing a Visual FoxPro COM component

- Accessing a Visual FoxPro 7.0 XML Web Service

- Accessing Visual FoxPro Data from an ASP.NET Web Service

You can also periodically check the Visual FoxPro "Got-Dot-Net" Web site for new information on this topic: http://www.gotdotnet.com/team/vfp/.

Conclusion

Microsoft has done a great job making it very easy to access "legacy" code from .NET and allowing you to save your investment in your existing Visual FoxPro applications. However, if you've placed most of your application logic within methods and events of your Visual FoxPro user interface, you need to migrate this code into business objects that can be instantiated and accessed from .NET Windows Forms applications, Web Forms applications, and Web Services.

Appendix A
Language Comparison Tables

The tables in this appendix provide a side-by-side comparison of Visual FoxPro, C#, and VB.NET's features.

Operator Comparison

Table 1 is an adaptation of the table found in the .NET Help topic "Operators compared in different languages".

Table 1. A comparison of Visual FoxPro, C#, and VB.NET operators

	Visual FoxPro	C#	VB.NET
Math			
Addition	+	+	+
Subtraction	-	-	-
Multiplication	*	*	*
Division	/	/	/
Modulus	%; MOD	%	Mod
Exponentiation	^, **	n/a	^
Assignment			
Assignment	=	=	=
Addition	+	+=	+=
Subtraction	-	-=	-=
Multiplication	*	*=	*=
Division	/	/=	/=
Integer Division	n/a	/=	\=
Concatenate	+, -, $	+=	&=
Modulus	%	%=	n/a
Left Shift	BITLSHIFT()	<<=	n/a
Right Shift	BITRSHIFT()	>>=	n/a
Bitwise-AND	BITAND()	&=	n/a
Bitwise-exclusive-OR	BITXOR()	^=	n/a
Bitwise-inclusive-OR	BITOR()	|=	n/a
Relational and equality			
Less than	<	<	<
Less than or equal to	<=	<=	<=
Greater than	>	>	>
Greater than or equal to	>=	>=	>=
Equal	=	==	=
Not Equal	<>, #, !=	!=	<>
Compare two object reference variables	COMPOBJ()	==	Is
Compare object reference type	n/a	x **is** Class1 (see also **as** and **typeof**)	**TypeOf** x Is Class1

Table 1, *continued*

	Visual FoxPro	C#	VB.NET
Relational and equality (continued)			
Compare strings	=	== -or- String.Equals()	=
Concatenate strings	+	+	&
Shortcircuited Boolean AND	n/a	&&	AndAlso
Shortcircuited Boolean OR	n/a	||	OrElse
Shift			
Left Shift	n/a	<<	n/a
Right Shift	n/a	>>	n/a
Scope Resolution			
Scope resolution	::	. and **base**	.
Postfix			
Array Element	( ), [ ]	[ ]	( )
Function call	( )	( )	( )
Type cast	n/a	(type)	CInt, CDbl, …, CType
Member selection	.	.	.
Postfix increment	n/a	++	n/a
Postfix decrement	n/a	--	n/a
Unary			
Indirection	n/a	* (unsafe mode only)	n/a
Address of	n/a	& (unsafe mode only; also see **fixed**)	AddressOf
Logical-not	!	!	Not
One's complement	BITNOT()	~	Not
Prefix increment	n/a	++	n/a
Prefix decrement	n/a	--	n/a
Size of type	n/a	sizeof	n/a
Bitwise			
Bitwise-AND	BITAND()	&	And
Bitwise-exclusive-OR	BITXOR	^	Xor
Bitwise-inclusive-OR	n/a	|	Or
Logical			
Logical-AND	AND	&&	And
Logical-OR	OR	||	Or
Conditional			
Conditional	IIF	?:	IIf Function ()
Pointer to member			
Pointer to member	n/a	. (Unsafe mode only)	n/a
Reference			
Reference	n/a	n/a (use reference types)	@

Keyword Comparison

Table 2 is an adaptation of the table found in the .NET Help topic "Keywords compared in different languages".

Table 2. *A comparison of Visual FoxPro, C#, and VB.NET keywords*

Purpose	Visual FoxPro	C#	VB.NET
Declare a variable	[implicit declaration]; also **PUBLIC, LOCAL, PRIVATE**	declarators (keywords include user-defined types and built-in types)	Private, Public, Friend, Protected, Static, Shared, Dim
Declare a named constant	#DEFINE	const readonly	Const
Create a new object	CREATEOBJECT, NEWOBJECT	new	New
Assign a variable to an object	=, also STORE	=	=
Function/method does not return a value	Void (COM Servers only)	void	Sub
Overload a function or method (Visual Basic: overload a procedure or method)	(No language keyword required for this purpose)	(No language keyword required for this purpose)	Overloads
Refer to the current object	This, ThisForm	this	Me
Make a nonvirtual call to a virtual method of the current object	n/a		MyClass
Retrieve character from a string	SUBSTR()	[ ]	GetChar
Declare a compound data type (Visual Basic: Structure)	n/a	struct, class, interface	Structure <members> End Structure
Initialize an object (constructors)	**Init** event	Constructors, or system default type constructors	Sub New()
Terminate an object directly	**Destroy** event	n/a	n/a
Method called by the system just before garbage collection reclaims an object	**Destroy** event	destructor	Finalize
Initialize a variable where it is declared	n/a	// initialize to a value int x = 23 // or use default constructor: int x = new int();	Dim x As Long = 5 Dim c As New Car(FuelTypeEnum.Gas)
Take the address of a function	n/a	delegate	AddressOf (For class members, this operator returns a reference to a function in the form of a delegate instance)
Declare that an object can be modified asynchronously	n/a	volatile	n/a

Table 2, continued

Purpose	Visual FoxPro	C#	VB.NET
Force explicit declaration of variables	_VFP.LanguageOptions	n/a. (All variables must be declared prior to use)	Option Explicit
Test for an object variable that does not refer to an object	**EMPTY(); ISNULL()**	**obj == null**	**obj = Nothing**
Value of an object variable that does not refer to an object	n/a	null	Nothing
Test for a database null expression	**ISNULL()**	n/a	IsDbNull
Test whether a Variant variable has been initialized	**EMPTY()**	n/a	n/a
Define a default property	n/a	by using indexers	Default

Appendix B
Data Type Comparison Table

The following table provides a side-by-side comparison of Visual FoxPro, C#, and Visual Basic.NET data types.

Data Type Comparison

Table 1 is an adaptation of the table found in the .NET Help topic "Data Types Compared in Different Languages".

Table 1. *A comparison of Visual FoxPro, C#, and VB.NET data types*

Storage size	Visual FoxPro	C#	VB.NET
16 bytes	Variant	n/a	n/a
Decimals	n/a	decimal	Decimal
Date	Date, DateTime	DateTime	Date, DateTime
(varies)	n/a	string	String
1 byte	Logical	byte	Byte
2 bytes	n/a	bool	Boolean
2 bytes	n/a	short, char (Unicode character)	Short, Char (Unicode character)
1 byte	Character	n/a	n/a
4 bytes	Integer	int	Integer
8 bytes	Float	long	Long
4 bytes	n/a	float	Single
8 bytes	Double	double	Double
4 bytes in table	General	n/a	n/a

Table 2. *A list of C# and VB.NET data types*

Type	C# Alias	VB .NET Alias	Range	Size
System.Byte	byte	Byte	0-255	Unsigned 8-bit integer
System.SByte	sbyte	Sbyte	-128 to 127	Signed 8-bit integer
System.Int16	short	Short	-32,768 to 32,767	Signed 16-bit integer
System.Int32	int	Integer	-2,147,483,648 to 2,147,483,647	Signed 32-bit integer
System.Int64	long	Long	-9,223,372,036,854,775,808 to 9,223,372,036,854,775,807	Signed 64-bit integer
System.UInt16	ushort	UInt16	0 to 65,535	Unsigned 16-bit integer
System.UInt32	uint	UInt32	0 to 4,294,967,295	Unsigned 32-bit integer
System.UInt64	ulong	UInt64	0 to 184,467,440,737,095,551,615	Unsigned 64-bit integer
System.Single	float	Single	$\pm 1.4 \times 10^{-45}$ to $\pm 3.4 \times 10^{38}$	7 digits (precision)
System.Double	double	Double	$\pm 5.0 \times 10^{-324}$ to $\pm 1.7 \times 10^{308}$	15-16 digits (precision)
System.Decimal	decimal	Decimal	1.0×10^{-28} to 7.9×10^{28}	28-29 significant digits
System.Boolean	bool	Boolean	True or False	
System.Char	char	Char	U+0000 to U+ffff	Unicode 16-bit character

Appendix C
The Visual FoxPro Toolkit
for .NET

This appendix discusses the Visual FoxPro Toolkit for .NET, which gives VFP developers a great boost up the .NET learning curve.

If you're proficient at Visual FoxPro, it can be frustrating when first learning .NET. You know how to do something in VFP, but you don't know the equivalent .NET base class or language feature to use. This is where the Visual FoxPro Toolkit for .NET comes to the rescue.

This toolkit was created by Kamal Patel and is in the public domain for the benefit of Visual FoxPro developers. You can download this toolkit from the Visual FoxPro "GotDotNet" site: http://www.gotdotnet.com/team/vfp/.

The toolkit is a class library with methods that correspond to Visual FoxPro functions. It allows you to enter familiar Visual FoxPro commands in your C# or Visual Basic .NET source code.,You can set up the toolkit in Visual Basic .NET so you can just type the Visual FoxPro command—without prefixing a class name—and a method is called on a corresponding class in the toolkit. In C#, you need to enter both a class and method name.

To use the toolkit, you must first install it, and then add a reference to it in your project. Source code is provided for both C# and Visual Basic .NET.

To give you an idea of how the toolkit works, you can use the Visual FoxPro StrToFile() command as an example. If you look up the StrToFile() command in the Visual FoxPro Toolkit for .NET Help file, the top of the Help file describes two different ways to call this function in the toolkit:

1. Receives a string and a file name as parameters and writes the contents of the string to that file.

2. Receives a string and a file name as parameters and writes the contents of the string to that file. Receives an additional parameter specifying whether the contents should be appended at the end of the file.

These two items translate into two overloaded methods in the toolkit. The Help file displays the signatures for each overload, as well as examples showing how to call these methods. Here is one of the examples in C#:

```
string lcString = "This is the line we want to insert in our file.";
VFPToolkit.strings.StrToFile(lcString, "c:\\My Folders\\MyFile.txt");
```

And in Visual Basic .NET:

```
Dim lcString As String = "This is the line we want to insert in our file."
StrToFile(lcString, "c:\My Folders\MyFile.txt")
```

This is great, but what's even better is the Help topic also shows you the code that is executed behind the scenes when you call the StrToFile method.

In C#:

```
public static void StrToFile(string cExpression, string cFileName)
{
  //Check if the sepcified file exists
  if (System.IO.File.Exists(cFileName) == true)
  {
      //If so then Erase the file first as in this case we are overwriting

      System.IO.File.Delete(cFileName);      }
  //Create the file if it does not exist and open it
  FileStream oFs = new
      FileStream(cFileName,FileMode.CreateNew,FileAccess.ReadWrite);
  //Create a writer for the file
  StreamWriter oWriter = new StreamWriter(oFs);
  //Write the contents
  oWriter.Write(cExpression);
  oWriter.Flush();
  oWriter.Close();
  oFs.Close();
}
```

And in Visual Basic .NET:

```
Public Shared Sub StrToFile(ByVal cExpression As String, _
  ByVal cFileName As String)
    'Check if the sepcified file exists
    If System.IO.File.Exists(cFileName) = True Then
        'If so then Erase the file first as in this case we are overwriting
        System.IO.File.Delete(cFileName)
    End If
    'Create the file if it does not exist and open it
    Dim oFs As FileStream = New _
        FileStream(cFileName, FileMode.CreateNew, FileAccess.ReadWrite)
    'Create a writer for the file
    Dim oWriter As StreamWriter = New StreamWriter(oFs)
    'Write the contents      oWriter.Write(cExpression)
    oWriter.Flush()
    oWriter.Close()
    oFs.Close()
End Sub
```

This code provides an education in using C# and Visual Basic .NET to access the functionality of the .NET Framework.

I've seen Visual FoxPro developers use this toolkit in a variety of ways. Some like to use the Visual FoxPro commands directly in their .NET code, providing familiar programming syntax. Others just keep the Help file on their desktop as "training wheels". Whenever they want to figure out how to do something in .NET, they look up the corresponding Visual FoxPro command in the Help file.

For more information on installing the toolkit, check out the Visual FoxPro Toolkit for .NET Help file.

Index

Note that you can download the PDF file for this book from www.hentzenwerke.com (see the section "How to download files" at the beginning of this book). The PDF is completely searchable and will provide additional keyword lookup capabilities not practical in an index.